American Evangelicals in Egypt

JEWS, CHRISTIANS, AND MUSLIMS
FROM THE ANCIENT TO THE MODERN WORLD

EDITED BY MICHAEL COOK, WILLIAM CHESTER JORDAN, AND PETER SCHÄFER

American Evangelicals in Egypt

MISSIONARY ENCOUNTERS IN AN AGE OF EMPIRE

Heather J. Sharkey

PRINCETON UNIVERSITY PRESS

PRINCETON AND OXFORD

Copyright © 2008 by Princeton University Press

Published by Princeton University Press, 41 William Street, Princeton,
New Jersey 08540

In the United Kingdom: Princeton University Press, 6 Oxford Street, Woodstock,
Oxfordshire OX20 1TW

Cloth ISBN: 978-0-691-12261-8
Paper ISBN: 978-0-691-16810-4

Library of Congress Cataloging-in-Publication Data

Sharkey, Heather J. (Heather Jane), 1967–
    American evangelicals in Egypt : missionary encounters in an age of empire /
Heather J. Sharkey.
        p. cm. — (Jews, Christians, and Muslims from the ancient to the modern world)
    Includes bibliographical references and index.
    ISBN 978-0-691-12261-8 (hardcover : alk. paper)
    1. Presbyterian Church—Missions—Egypt. 2. Americans—Egypt—History. I. Title.
    BV3570.S43 2008
    266'.02373062—dc22   2008004540

British Library Cataloging-in-Publication Data is available

This book has been composed in Palatino
Printed on acid-free paper. ∞
press.princeton.edu
Printed in the United States of America

For Ravi and Aruna

Contents

Illustrations

Acknowledgments

I OWE THANKS TO SO MANY.

This publication was made possible in part by a grant from the Carnegie Corporation of New York (Carnegie Scholars 2006), although the statements made and views expressed in this work are my responsibility alone. The American Philosophical Society and University Research Foundation of the University of Pennsylvania gave funds that enabled me to visit archives in the United States and abroad.

Ann Lesch offered boundless hospitality in Cairo, and I can never thank her enough.

Several colleagues read the manuscript and offered valuable feedback. Special thanks go to Robert L. Tignor and Robert Vitalis for detailed comments and suggestions. I am also grateful to Beth Baron, L. Carl Brown, Ellen Fleischmann, Heleen Murre-van den Berg, Dana L. Robert, and Israel Gershoni. Special thanks also go to John O. Voll, who has been a mentor to me in my Sudanese and now Egyptian endeavors.

John G. Lorimer and Stanley Skreslet, former Presbyterian missionaries to Egypt, as well as Donald Black, former secretary of the United Presbyterian Church's foreign mission board, offered unstinting help along the way by reading draft chapters, alerting me to errors, and pointing me to sources. I am grateful to several other former missionaries, too: Mary Louise Lorimer, Kenneth Nolin, Willis McGill, Marjorie Dye, and Martha Roy. John L. McClenahan, son of the late missionary R.S. McClenahan, also supplied valuable information. David Grafton, formerly of the Evangelical Seminary in Cairo and now of the Lutheran Theological Seminary of Philadelphia, graciously read much of the penultimate draft. Leaders of the Egyptian Evangelical community in Cairo were very generous in meeting me and answering questions. I am particularly grateful to Menes Abdel Noor, Emile Zaki, Nabil Abadir and the staff of CEOSS, and Tharwat Wahba. *Alf shukr.*

Betty S. Anderson, Eleanor Abdella Doumato, Firoozeh Kashani-Sabet, Ussama Makdisi, Charlotte van der Leest, Michael Marten, Inger Marie Okkenhaug, Eve Troutt Powell, Barbara Reeves-Ellington, Thomas Ricks, Umar Ryad, Paul Sedra, Shobana Shankar, Kathy Spillman, and Nancy Stockdale shared ideas, articles, and suggestions. Several graduate students were also gracious colleagues: Kaley Middlebrooks Carpenter, James De Lorenzi, Mehmet Ali Dogan,

Aleksandra Majstorac-Kobiljski, Karine Walther, Andrew Witmer, and Devrim Umit. Two colleagues who gave feedback on an early portion of this research—Arthur Goldschmidt Jr. and Shamil Jeppie—also offered valuable suggestions on my first book, *Living with Colonialism: Nationalism and Culture in the Anglo-Egyptian Sudan.* However, I neglected to thank Arthur and Shamil the first time, so my thanks to them are now twofold.

Several people invited me to present my research or to publish the results, and thereby helped me make progress. This list includes Jonathan Bonk and Dwight Baker at the Overseas Mission Studies Center in New Haven; May Davie at *Chronos* and the University of Balamand; Dick Douwes, formerly at the International Institute for the Study of Islam in the Modern World (ISIM) in Leiden; John Hunwick and R. S. O'Fahey at the Institute for the Study of Islamic Thought in Africa (ISITA) at Northwestern University; Haggai Erlich, Yehudit Ronen, Israel Gershoni, and other organizers of the Narrating the Nile conference at Tel Aviv University and the Open University of Israel; Rosalind I. J. Hackett of the International Association of the History of Religions (IAHR); Akram Khater of North Carolina State University; Reeva Simon and Eleanor Tejirian at Columbia University; and Benjamin L. Soares at the African Studies Centre in Leiden. During my first semester at the University of Pennsylvania in 2002, Lee Cassanelli invited me to give an African studies seminar, which inspired me to think about Middle Eastern missions comparatively. Nubar Hovsepian and Maggie Nassif also shared ideas during that early stage of research. The Department of Near Eastern Studies at Princeton also invited me to present preliminary research in 2002.

Brian Stanley at Cambridge University suggested that I join the mission history e-mail list, organized by Martha Smalley at Yale Divinity School, and his advice was excellent. I am especially grateful to list members Ryan Dunch, Kathleen Lodwick, and Rosemary Seton, who helped me "find" Ahmed Fahmy (an Egyptian Muslim who converted to Christianity in 1877) in the South China papers of the former London Missionary Society. This list also put me in touch with the vibrant Yale-Edinburgh Group on the History of the Missionary Movement and Non-Western Christianity.

I have never met Hanako Birks, but I owe her a debt. As a former commissioning editor at I. B. Tauris Publishers in London, she encouraged me to think about developing a short article (which appeared in the *ISIM Newsletter* published in Leiden) into a book. Her suggestions prompted me to broaden the scope of this research.

Colleagues at the University of Pennsylvania, and in my academic home, the Department of Near Eastern Languages and Civilizations

(NELC), have offered steadfast support. I am especially grateful to Roger Allen, Joseph Lowry, and Nili Gold, as well as to Margaret Guinan, Diane Moderski, and Linda Greene. I have had wonderful students, and I extend special thanks to the three groups of undergraduates and graduate students who took my seminar on the history of Muslim, Christian, and Jewish relations in the Middle East and North Africa. Their ideas helped me sharpen my own.

Many librarians and archivists helped me along the way. Thanks to William Kopycki, Arthur Kiron, and Debra Bucher at the University of Pennsylvania Libraries, and to their colleagues who make Penn such a rich and rewarding place to do research. Steve Urgola at the American University in Cairo welcomed me to the Manuscripts and Special Collections library and enabled me to see the Charles R. Watson papers in their uncatalogued state. Several staff members at the Presbyterian Historical Society in Philadelphia helped generously and made the research experience very congenial: Beth Bensman, Margery Sly, Bridget Arthur Clancy, Eileen Meyer Sklar, Kenneth Ross, Frederick Heuser, Art Baxter, Sharrie Bobrow, Nancy Taylor, and Leah Gass. Thanks also go to Dagmar Getz and Lara Friedman-Shedlov at the Kautz Family YMCA Archives of the University of Minnesota; Rosemary Mathew, Kathleen Cann, and Peter Meadows in the Bible Society Library within Cambridge University Library; Joanne Ichimura and other librarians in the archives of the School of Oriental and African Studies (SOAS), University of London; Kathy Wilkinson at the Council for World Mission; Martha Smalley and Joan Duffy at the Day Missions Library of Yale Divinity School; Rita Wesley in the library of the United Theological College in Bangalore; and the staff in the periodicals section of Dar al-Kutub, the Egyptian national library in Cairo. Glenn Ratcliffe took the digital photograph of the group portrait of Ahmed Fahmy's retirement party, from the London Missionary Society/Council for World Mission collection at SOAS.

Fred Appel at Princeton University Press has made this book a pleasure to write and publish. He gave helpful feedback on drafts and left me feeling eager to start my next book. Kathleen Cioffi, the production editor for this book, guided the manuscript smoothly through the publishing process, while Jennifer Backer copyedited the manuscript with meticulous care.

My biggest debts are to my family—to my mother and father, Jane and Richard Sharkey; my sisters, Donna, Diana, Jill, Joanne, and Jennifer; my brother, Brian; my mother- and father-in-law, Jaya and T. R. Balasubramanian; my husband; and my children—who have sustained me on a day-to-day basis. Sidekick, best friend, proofreader, font of ideas, and critic extraordinaire, Vijay Balasubramanian entertained our children on innumerable occasions around the world while I visited archives and conferences. He made this book possible, and made its production an adventure for all of us. Our children, Ravi and Aruna, have infused every day of my life with joy and meaning. I dedicate this book to them, and give thanks.

Abbreviations

ABS	American Bible Society
ACG	American College for Girls, Cairo
ACLSM	American Christian Literature Society for Moslems
AUC	American University in Cairo
BFBS	British and Foreign Bible Society
BSA	Bible Society Archives
CEOSS	Coptic Evangelical Organization for Social Services
CMS	Church Missionary Society
COEMAR	Commission on Ecumenical Mission and Relations
CUL	Cambridge University Library
CWM	Council for World Mission (the successor of the LMS and other societies)
EC-Synod	Egyptian Evangelical Church, Synod of the Nile
EGM	Egypt General Mission
IMC	International Missionary Council
LMS	London Missionary Society
MECC	Middle East Council of Churches
NAM	North Africa Mission
NECC	Near East Christian Council (later the Near East Council of Churches)
NMP	Nile Mission Press
PCUS	Presbyterian Church in the United States (southern-stream)
PCUSA	Presbyterian Church in the United States of America (pre-1958)
PC(USA)	Presbyterian Church (U.S.A.) (post-1983)
PHS	Presbyterian Historical Society
PMI	Pressly Memorial Institute, Assiut
SOAS	School of Oriental and African Studies, University of London
SOS	School of Oriental Studies, American University in Cairo
SVM	Student Volunteer Movement
UDHR	Universal Declaration of Human Rights
UPCNA	United Presbyterian Church of North America (1858–1958)
UPCUSA	United Presbyterian Church in the U.S.A. (1958–83)

WCC	World Council of Churches
WGMS	Women's General Missionary Society
WSSA	World's Sunday School Association
YDS	Yale Divinity School
YMCA	Young Men's Christian Association
YMMA	Young Men's Muslim Association

Note on Transliteration, Translation, and Spelling

In transliterating from Arabic, this book follows the system used in the *International Journal of Middle East Studies*. Exceptions include some personal names in cases where individuals had a preferred mode for writing their names in English texts. Thus, for example, the book refers to the Egyptian military officer Ahmad 'Urabi but to the Egyptian convert Ahmed Fahmy (with the latter rendition reflecting his own usage). Exceptions also include Egyptian place-names, which follow English conventions or the spellings used by missionaries. Unless otherwise indicated, translations from Arabic and French into English are the author's own.

1.1. Assiut College students in oval, c. 1921–23. UPCNA Board of Foreign Missions Photographs, Presbyterian Historical Society, Presbyterian Church (U.S.A.), Philadelphia.

CHAPTER 1

The American Missionary Encounter in Egypt

THE MISSIONARY ENCOUNTER

In 1854 American Presbyterian missionaries arrived in Egypt as part of a larger Anglo-American Protestant movement that aimed for universal evangelization. Protected by the armor of British imperial power and later by mounting American global influence, their enterprise flourished during the late nineteenth and early twentieth centuries and enabled them to establish the largest Protestant mission in the country. This book describes the massive, mutual, and ongoing transformations that their activities in Egypt set off.

In the century that stretched from 1854 until decolonization in the mid-1950s, American missionaries opened dozens of schools, medical facilities, and public libraries; initiated rural development programs to improve livestock and reduce the spread of endemic diseases; and vigorously promoted literacy campaigns, especially for the sake of Bible reading. They thought of themselves not only as Christian evangelizers but also as ambassadors for the United States and as promoters of American culture and modernity. However, despite a century of work among Egypt's Muslim majority and indigenous Coptic Christian minority, they gained few converts. By the mid-1950s they claimed some 200 living converts from Islam within a small Evangelical Presbyterian community of just under 27,000 members, most of whom had come from Coptic Orthodoxy.[1]

American missionaries nevertheless exerted a significant social impact on Egypt and influenced many Muslims and Coptic Christians who resisted or rejected evangelical appeals. Missionaries dramatically expanded educational opportunities for Egyptian females, both Muslim and Christian, and contributed to a reconfiguration of gender roles and relations.[2] They inadvertently mobilized anti-colonial nationalists and Islamists against a perceived cultural onslaught, galvanizing men like Hasan al-Banna, founder of the Muslim Brotherhood. By associating themselves with British colonial and American consular powers while working closely with local Christians, they planted doubts among many Muslims about the likely pro-Western sympathies of Egyptian Christians—doubts that continue to strain

Egyptian intercommunal relations today. Missionaries established a new Egyptian Protestant church, called the Evangelical Church, and spurred the indigenous Coptic Orthodox Church to revise its modes of worship. They started social service projects such as youth clubs that were so popular that Egyptian Muslim and Coptic Orthodox leaders rushed to develop homegrown alternatives.[3]

Missionary experiences in Egypt also had repercussions for American society, confirming the notion that "nations lie enmeshed in each others' history."[4] With counterparts in other Middle Eastern countries, missionaries in Egypt set a "founding relationship between America and the Arab world."[5] They transmitted information and opinions that influenced U.S. foreign policy toward the Middle East.[6] However, they also challenged U.S. policies, particularly after 1948 vis-à-vis Israeli and Palestinian affairs, when American Presbyterians in Egypt voiced loud support for the Arab peoples.[7] Discouraged by social obstacles in Egypt that hindered Muslim conversion to Christianity, missionaries led debates about religious liberty and human rights that continue to resonate in the halls of the U.S. Congress and Department of State.[8] Missionaries shaped many of the underpinnings of American Orientalism—American modes of imagining, speaking about, portraying, and behaving toward the Islamic world—whether these emanated from scholars, military planners, filmmakers, or tourists. Within American universities, they helped define the field that has been variously called Oriental, Near Eastern, and Middle Eastern studies.[9] (Indeed, it was a close ally of the Protestant evangelical cause, the American naval historian Alfred Thayer Mahan, who coined the term "Middle East" in 1902.)[10] Missionaries also provided new models for American public philanthropy in the "developing world."[11] Finally, missionaries helped stimulate far-reaching changes in American Christianity. They forced reassessments of Christian mission that still roil American Protestantism and mobilized women within churches to an unprecedented degree, paving the way for women's entry into the clergy.[12]

American missionary encounters bridged the United States to Egypt and were intensely local, global, and transnational at once. In Egypt and the United States, these encounters involved men, women, and children living in places that ranged from small farming communities to large cities. Egyptian participants in these encounters included those who attended missionary schools, sought treatment from missionary hospitals, and read missionary literature in Arabic or English; they even included those who railed against missionaries from the distance of a mosque pulpit or newspaper column. The American base of participation went beyond missionaries, too, to include above all the churchgoers who looked to a popular literature of Christian journals, travelogues, and storybooks for news and views of the Middle East. Individually, or as congregations, these rank-and-file churchgoers gave the money that kept missions afloat. The most dedicated and financially able gave funds to sponsor specific missionaries, institutions, or scholarships. In this manner, for example, financial bonds and special projects linked Presbyterians in Keokuk, Iowa, and Lyndhurst, New Jersey, to Assiut and Zagazig in Egypt.[13] Donations to missions could also be incidental and small-scale—as simple as putting coins in one of the envelopes that churches distributed during worship services, and then checking off a box to mark the money for "home" or "foreign" missions.[14] If nineteenth- and early twentieth-century Britain was a country of "absent-minded imperialists,"[15] then the United States in this same period was a country of "absent-minded evangelists." Americans could stay seated in their pews and send pennies to Egypt, or support work among Indians, whether of the Punjabi ("foreign mission") or Navajo ("home mission") variety.

As part of a Western colonial "visitation," missionary activity prompted reciprocal migrations. That is, Americans in Egypt helped issue the call—the cultural, political, and economic beckoning—that prompted Egyptian visits to the United States in the form of emigration and settlement.[16] The first members of the mission-sponsored Evangelical Church to make this move appear to have been a woman named Warda Barakat and her husband, Girgis Malaik, who left Egypt in 1882 and settled in Monmouth, Illinois, where there was a large United Presbyterian community.[17] In the twentieth century, Egyptian Evangelicals in the United States helped plant hybrid Arabic-speaking Presbyterian congregations in Pasadena, California, and elsewhere.[18] Many other immigrants were Egyptian Muslims and Copts who came to the United States to study after honing their English in schools that missionaries founded.

The American Presbyterians in Egypt also belonged to a global Protestant missionary order. They exchanged letters and information with missionaries in northern India, the Sudan, and Ethiopia who shared the same sponsor in the United Presbyterian Church, and communicated across denominational boundaries to missionaries arrayed throughout the Muslim world from Algiers to Jakarta. Leaders of the American mission in Egypt participated in conferences with missionaries from British, Dutch, German, Scandinavian, and other American organizations—and met in places like New York and Edinburgh, Jerusalem and Lucknow. In this way they helped foster a movement of Christian ecumenism or solidarity among Protestants. In the Middle East, this Protestant ecumenical movement took shape in the interwar era in the form of the Near East Christian Council (NECC), an organization that evolved in the early 1960s to become the Near East Council of Churches (also NECC), led by the indigenous Middle East churches. This organization evolved further in 1974 to become the Middle East Council of Churches (MECC) and included, by 1980, Protestant, Orthodox, and Catholic members. The inclusion of Middle Eastern Catholic churches in what had originally been a Protestant organization reflected improvements in Protestant-Catholic relations that followed the Suez Crisis of 1956 and the Second Vatican Council of 1962–65, when the Roman Catholic Church opened windows to intersectarian and interfaith dialogue.[19]

During their first century in Egypt, American missionaries helped Egyptian church members travel to places like Brazil and India for church conferences and study, and, more rarely, for employment. In this way Egyptian Protestants participated in the burgeoning ecumenical and missionary movements and in the global diffusion of Christian cultures. For example, in 1897, the chronicler of the American mission in Egypt proudly noted that one of its converts from Islam, a man named Ahmed Fahmy, was serving with the London Missionary Society (LMS) as a medical missionary in "Chang Chew" (Zhangzhou), southern China.[20] In another case, in 1911, the Americans sought employment for an Egyptian convert from Islam by placing him with a Danish mission in Aden.[21]

The British Empire and Britons were important to the American Presbyterians in Egypt. The Americans looked to British authorities in Egypt for protection and advice but, more important, developed close ties to British missionaries that led them to strategize and, increasingly by the 1930s, to commiserate together. The American missionaries' connections to the British in Egypt, and to American and global networks of Protestant evangelism, make their experiences a case study in the ambiguity of power. The American Presbyterians enjoyed power because they could marshal financial and political resources—above all, donations from the church at home, and protection from British and American consular authorities on the ground. After the British Occupation of 1882, the American missionaries also qualified for protection under the Capitulations—the set of legal and fiscal perquisites, enshrined in treaties, that Western powers had extracted from Ottoman authorities. Endowed with these advantages, missionaries were able to buy property, build schools, travel along the Nile, and distribute Christian tracts for free or at subsidized prices. For many years they even qualified for reduced-fare tickets on Egyptian railways.[22] Missionaries, in short, had the wherewithal to make their message heard up and down the country. Yet in the century after

1854 they often felt, by their own account, vulnerable—when budgets were cut, when converts recanted, or—increasingly in the twentieth century—when the Egyptian government, supported by Muslim nationalists, worked to curtail their activities. Indeed, the power of the American missionaries fluctuated and eventually waned with British influence in Egypt, and this in itself suggests the intricate relationship of missionary activity to imperial power.

Americans had launched their mission in Egypt in 1854 with the expectation or hope that universal evangelization would be possible. They did not expect everyone to convert, but they did presume that Egyptian men and women would be able to exercise individual free choice. They thought that missionaries would be free to deliver a Christian message and that Egyptians would then be free to accept it or not. But in his chronicle of the mission published in 1897, Andrew Watson claimed that when the Americans began work in Egypt, "They found Islam utterly opposed to the idea of religious liberty."[23] He meant that Islamic courts and government authorities favored Muslims over non-Muslims, and that Islamic law, reinforced by Egyptian Muslim social convention, maintained strong deterrents against leaving Islam. (Deterrents included disinheritance, loss of child custody, unilateral divorce for a man, marriage by proxy for a woman, and possibly death.)[24] Yet Andrew Watson believed that Egypt might be changing such that deep-rooted laws and practices might give way to what he expected would be Christianity's advantage. As the twentieth century opened, Andrew Watson's son, the educator Charles R. Watson, was even more sanguine in thinking that modern conditions, reinforced by international diplomacy, might lead to a form of religious liberty that would enable Egyptian Muslims to embrace Christianity and profess it in public.[25] However, the conditions for which Andrew and Charles Watson hoped did not materialize. This was partly because Egyptian Muslims felt beleaguered in the face of Western imperial encroachment and therefore mistrusted the motives of Christian missionaries who clamored for a form of religious liberty that served evangelical interests.[26]

In the history of the American mission in Egypt, the most acute disappointment that the Presbyterians faced was that the Egyptian government (confirming Egyptian Muslim social sentiments at large) never accepted the principle that the exercise of religious liberty and freedom might legitimately allow individuals to renounce Islam. By the mid-twentieth century, some American mission leaders were acknowledging that to be a Christian in Egypt was to live with a social debility, that attempting to evangelize among Muslims was dangerous for Egyptian Christians to do (as Egyptian Evangelical pastors had been claiming since the nineteenth century), and that conversion out of Islam—the religion of state, the religion of power—would be an unlikely choice for a Muslim.[27]

For missionaries, working in an age of empire had its disadvantages. One unintended impact that American missionaries had on Egypt was to trigger a backlash among Muslim nationalists and activists, who detected in the rare cases of Muslim conversion to Christianity, and in the broad influence of missionary schools, orphanages, and medical clinics, a threat to an Egyptian Muslim public order. By the early 1930s, Christian missionary activities had spurred Egyptian Muslim nationalists to press the government to promote and protect Islam as Egypt's religion of state, particularly by regulating mission schools; their activities also prompted Muslim activists to organize social services as a way of steering Muslims away from Christian missionaries. Anti-missionary agitation ultimately sharpened the lines dividing Muslim and Christian communities in Egypt and pushed missionaries toward a model of evangelism that either focused on the well-being of Christian communities or emphasized Christian faith as the *reason*, but not the goal, of missionary work.

By the late 1930s, it was becoming more difficult for the mission even to attract Copts into the Evangelical Church. Having risen to the challenge of Protestant and Catholic missionaries, the Coptic Orthodox Church was increasingly vibrant in its modes of worship and social outreach such that, as missionaries acknowledged, Copts had fewer reasons to leave it.[28] At the same time the number of Muslim "inquirers" was dwindling, so that Kamil Mansur, a lay preacher who had converted from Islam to Christianity in his youth and whom the mission had hired in 1918 as a special worker to Muslims, was addressing largely Christian audiences in Cairo and Alexandria.[29]

In the 1940s, when the Egyptian government tried to apply laws that forbade mission schools from teaching Christianity to Muslims, missionaries feared that one of their last lines of evangelical contact with Muslims was closing. In 1957, the government of Gamal Abdel Nasser went further: it notified the missionaries that, to continue operating their schools, they would have to continue admitting Muslim students without discrimination and hire government-approved Muslim teachers to instruct Muslim pupils about Islam on the grounds of mission schools. Policies like this encouraged missionaries to focus more of their efforts on social service activities within Christian communities. A retired missionary who had worked in Egypt during this period recalled that he and his colleagues were "of the strong opinion that the future of Christian work in Egypt lay more with the national church itself than with the institutions" like schools and hospitals.[30]

Thus in the late 1950s, missionaries developed a series of new grass-roots literacy projects among Christian villagers of Upper Egypt. These projects devolved leadership onto Egyptian clergy and were self-consciously ecumenical, insofar as they required Orthodox and Protestant clergy in each village to work together as a term of receiving financial support.[31] Meanwhile, following the Suez Crisis of 1956 (and therefore even before the start of the Second Vatican Council), the American Presbyterians began to cultivate warmer relations with Coptic Catholic leaders as well. This thaw reflected the growing sense that collegiality was in the interests of all Christians in Egypt.[32] Finally, by the late 1950s, American missionaries in Egypt were beginning to endorse a philosophy of interaction with Muslims that emphasized "respectful witness"—a notion of dialogue built on the premise that a worthy exchange with fellow believers in God need not aim for a change of faith. This approach harmonized with what became known as the interfaith dialogue movement.[33]

By the time the association of American Presbyterian missionaries voted to disband in 1966, a year before the Arab-Israeli war of 1967, Egypt had become a less cosmopolitan and more homogeneous society. In the aftermath of the Suez Crisis eleven years earlier, longstanding minority communities of Greeks, Italians, Armenians, and others had dispersed, French and British expatriates had left, while most of Egypt's tiny Jewish population was also gone, its members having opted or been pressured to leave.[34] In this context, Egypt's indigenous Christians, the Copts, were increasingly isolated in a Muslim milieu.[35] Meanwhile, several important changes were occurring in the United States. In contrast to Egypt, the American religious landscape was growing increasingly heterogeneous. For example, the American Presbyterians in Egypt noted that more of their former Muslim students were going the United States for advanced study, work, or settlement, thus contributing to the growth of an American Muslim minority.[36] Church attendance among Presbyterians was declining as new varieties of evangelical Protestantism attracted followers.[37] Women were claiming places within the Presbyterian clergy, contributing to what one of the first ordained female ministers later called an "epic social change."[38] Finally, some Presbyterian missionaries and mission executives, reappraising the church's history of complicity in the culture of racism vis-à-vis African Americans, were becoming active in the American civil rights movement.[39] Thus while anti-colonial nationalism may have been forcing overseas Presbyterian missions into retraction, church leaders in the United States had plenty to do in this period of social ferment. Weathering all these developments was the small but flourishing Coptic Evangelical Church, which testified to the century-long influence in Egypt of an

American evangelical movement that was waning in the United States among Presbyterians themselves.

The American mission in Egypt reflected the grassroots Presbyterian evangelical culture of its day. Hence it is worth looking at what missionaries in Egypt called the "home front"—the American social field from which the missionaries emerged.

From the eighteenth century to the present, there has never been a single American Presbyterian church, and this has had implications for Presbyterian missionaries in the Middle East and the wider world. To illustrate this point, staff members at the Presbyterian Historical Society in Philadelphia distribute a chart to visiting researchers to explain the church structures under which records are organized. Titled "The Presbyterian Family Connections," this chart sets out the lineages of Presbyterian churches in the United States from 1706 to the present.[40] Two points become clear at once because of the chart's bewildering arrangement of cross-cutting lines and bi-directional arrows. First, American Presbyterianism has been a plurality from the start, with today's churches descending from lines that arrived independently in the American colonies. Second, the "family" of American Presbyterianism can be graphed as a history of "unions" and "separations." A closer look at Presbyterian history shows that most separations occurred over political or social ideology—for example, over attitudes toward slavery in the mid-nineteenth century or the ordination of women in the late twentieth century. By contrast, most unions occurred when Presbyterians realized that the things they shared in common were more significant than the social issues that had once kept them apart. Presbyterians have shared, above all, an attitude toward church government emphasizing the laity's role in serving as elders (or presbyters) at local and regional levels of church administration. They have also shared a creed rooted in the heritage of the Protestant Reformation and Calvinism, a theological system associated with the French-Swiss thinker John Calvin (1509–1564) that rejected papal authority and elaborated ideas about God's omnipotence and grace vis-à-vis human salvation.[41]

The Presbyterian missionaries who founded the mission in Egypt in 1854 came from a church known as the Associate Reformed Church that was in the midst of negotiating a union with another branch of the Presbyterian tree in America, namely, the Associate Church. (The use of confusingly similar names for what were actually different organizations seems to have been a common feature of American Presbyterianism; this pattern prevails even today.) The two negotiating churches traced their lineage to dissenters in Scotland who had refused to recognize the authority of the English crown, and of government in general, over Scottish church affairs. However, by the time the Associate and Associate Reformed churches merged in 1858, thereby producing the United Presbyterian Church of North America (UPCNA), Scottish dissent and antiroyalism had long receded as issues of concern among the American descendants of Scottish immigrants and had been replaced by a strong antislavery platform.[42] Given this history, it is no accident that the church that sent missionaries to Egypt was also committed, in the United States, to work among African Americans and to what became known after the U.S. Civil War as "freedmen's missions."[43] In the long run, the UPCNA's outreach to African Americans helped diversify what had been until then, in the United States, a Presbyterian community of predominantly Scotch-Irish extraction.

In *The Arabists* (1993), a journalistic account of American missionaries and U.S. foreign-service experts in the Middle East, Robert Kaplan caricatures American Presbyterian missionaries in the Arab world and particularly in Beirut. He portrays them as members of an East Coast, Princeton-educated elite that was firmly connected to nodes of wealth and power. Kaplan's portrayal bears little resemblance to the American missionaries in Egypt, who in any case belonged to a different church from the American Presbyterian missionaries of Greater Syria. The Presbyterian missionaries who struck out in western Asia, as well as in Iran, belonged to the New York City–based Presbyterian Church U.S.A., which drew much of its membership from the mid-Atlantic region. The UPCNA missionaries in Egypt, by contrast, came from a church that had headquarters in Pittsburgh and Philadelphia and a membership base in Pennsylvania and midwestern states such as Ohio and Illinois.[44]

Nevertheless, in 1958, the distinction between the UPCNA and PCUSA lapsed when the two churches merged to produce a new entity, the United Presbyterian Church in the U.S.A. (UPCUSA). In 1983, the latter church merged again, this time with the southern-stream Presbyterian Church in the United States (PCUS), to produce what is today the Presbyterian Church (U.S.A.) (PC[USA]). Based in Louisville, Kentucky, the PC(USA) claimed in 2008 approximately 2.3 million members belonging to more than ten thousand congregations throughout the United States.[45]

To a large degree the UPCNA missionaries in Egypt reflected the demographic of their church in the late nineteenth and early twentieth centuries, though like most American Protestant missionaries in this period, they were better educated than the general population.[46] Most UPCNA missionaries were graduates of small midwestern Presbyterian liberal arts colleges (such as Muskingum College in Ohio, Monmouth College in Illinois, and Westminster College in Pennsylvania) that served as feeder schools for the mission.[47]

Marilynne Robinson's novel *Gilead* (2004), named after an Iowa community, offers an evocation of the home culture to which American missionaries in Egypt had links. Robinson's Gilead—a sleepy town in the 1950s that was once torn by the local history of opposition to slavery—is centered around its Protestant churches, simple structures reflecting the modest means of the people as well as their preference for spending on needs and causes, not architectural adornments. Many of the residents of Gilead never ventured very far beyond Iowa, the novel's narrator, John Ames, recalls, but some did go to college to learn more of the Bible and to study Hebrew and Greek, and a segment of those graduates, "and especially the young women, would go by themselves to the other side of the earth as teachers and missionaries and come back decades later to tell us about Turkey and Korea."[48] Intensely local and yet harnessed to the great world beyond, Gilead, Iowa, seems like the fictional embodiment of the small-town UPCNA communities in places like Oil City, Pennsylvania, that organized late nineteenth- and early twentieth-century "mission circles"—groups within congregations that provided grassroots financial and moral support for the American mission in Egypt.[49]

During its century of existence as a distinct church, from 1858 until 1958 when it merged with the larger Presbyterian Church U.S.A., the UPCNA never had more than about 250,000 members in the United States.[50] Its small size notwithstanding, the UPCNA supported and ran the enterprise in Egypt even as it pursued mission work in Sudan, Ethiopia, and northern India (in a region now mainly in Pakistan), and within the United States among African Americans, Native Americans, Mormons, and urban immigrants, including Chicago Jews, Pittsburgh Roman Catholic Italians, and San Francisco Chinese. Central to the missions of the UPCNA and other American Protestant churches were women, "the hard core of the missionary movement," who raised thousands of dollars annually "through coffee pouring, cookie sales, pennies collected, and the occasional generosity of a rich and pious widow."[51] In a period when the pastorate was restricted to men, UPCNA women also found church careers as missionaries, and by 1901 they outnumbered men in the Egyptian field—a rate of female participation that was in keeping with other American and British Protestant missions in this period.[52]

In a commemorative volume published in 1958 as the UPCNA celebrated its centennial and approached dissolution as a separate entity, a church historian declared that the UPCNA had witnessed two important developments during its century of existence. The first, he enthused, was "the climax of the greatest missionary effort since the first century A.D."[53] He was referring to the Anglo-American Protestant missionary enterprise that had gained momentum in the nineteenth century through the growth of voluntary Christian societies in Britain and North America. During its heyday in the late nineteenth and early twentieth centuries, this movement had become associated with a slogan—"the evangelization of the world in this generation"—that conveyed its universal aspirations, global ambitions, and cultural confidence.[54] The second development was the "birth of the Protestant ecumenical movement." Energized by cross-denominational encounters in mission fields overseas, this movement of Protestant cooperation gained a boost in 1910 at the World Missionary Conference in Edinburgh, took institutional shape in 1921 with the formation of the International Missionary Council, and gained a wider platform in 1948 with the debut in Geneva of the World Council of Churches (WCC), an organization that Protestant leaders sometimes conceptualized as a "Christian United Nations."[55] The UPCNA also participated in a third important development that this historian overlooked or could not yet detect: the dramatic impact on global Christian culture resulting from the propagation of Protestantism beyond Europe and North America. By the late twentieth century this process had led to the "de-Westernization" of Protestantism, as the demographic world center of Christianity shifted toward the African continent.[56]

The UPCNA was an integral part of the Anglo-American Protestant missionary movement and evinced the strong evangelical commitment that was the movement's paramount feature. In the nineteenth and twentieth centuries, Protestant evangelicals (among them American missionaries in Egypt) explained their impulse to evangelize in terms of what they called the "Great Commission," defined as an obligation to give witness to their faith including belief in Jesus as a savior. Evangelicals, in the past and still today, have traced this imperative to the Christian Bible, and specifically to verses that close the Book of Matthew (28:18–20). According to these verses, Jesus appeared to faithful supporters in the Galilee after his crucifixion and resurrection, and told them, "All authority in heaven and on earth has been given to me. Go therefore and make disciples of all nations, baptizing them in the name of the Father and of the Son and of the Holy Spirit, and teaching them to obey everything that I have commanded to you. And remember I am with you always, to the end of the age." However, making disciples of all nations was not the only force behind the evangelical impulse; equally strong was the desire to promote a Christian practice that emphasized the individual worshiper's connection to, and importance in the eyes of, God.

The mission enterprises of the UPCNA shared three broad features that distinguished the mainline American Protestant missions of the nineteenth and early twentieth centuries. First, they gained momentum from westward frontier expansion within what became the United States so that overseas and "home" missions developed in tandem. Second, unlike Britons and continental Europeans, American missionaries "had no *inhibitions* about money"; they took a businesslike approach to fund-raising, collecting pennies but also seeking big grants from industrial giants. (In this manner, the American Presbyterians in Egypt sought and received grants from the Rockefellers.)[57] Third, they were purveyors of American culture, and their Christianity—whether they realized it or not—was infused with American customs and attitudes.[58] Among these was arguably an American-style privileging of individuals over families and communities, and of individual religious faith and conviction over collective traditional practice.

The experiences of the UPCNA missions also fit the narrative of *Errand to the World: American Protestant Thought and Foreign Missions* (1987), a magisterial work of American intellectual history by William R. Hutchison, who was the son of a Presbyterian missionary to Iran and the son-in-law of a Presbyterian missionary to Egypt.[59] Hutchison acknowledges the import of the American foreign missionary movement as a grassroots local and grand-scale global affair. "The foreign mission enterprise in its heyday (about 1880 to 1930) was a massive affair," he notes, "involving tens of thousands of Americans abroad and millions at home. . . . It sent abroad, through most of its history, not only the largest contingents of Americans—dwarfing all other categories except that of short-term travelers—but also the most highly educated."[60] Missionaries mitigated American isolationism in the nineteenth and early twentieth centuries, and in the long run anticipated, substituted for, and perhaps accelerated the far-flung global engagement of the U.S. government and of American peoples.[61]

MISSIONS AND POSTCOLONIAL HISTORY

In the early twentieth century, leading American research universities had professors who published works on the history or practice of Christian missions.[62] But circumstances changed in the mid-twentieth century along with four developments that pertain to the contraction of interest in and pursuit of missions among the large established Protestant churches.

First, Ivy League institutions and other leading universities became increasingly secular or nonsectarian as they moved away from their Anglo-Protestant cultural roots—a trend that reflected, in part, the increasing ethnic and religious diversity of their students. Thus universities became less amenable to Christian missionary agendas. Second, mainline Protestant churches, Presbyterians among them, were compelled to pare down their overseas missions in the face of nationalist opposition. The newly independent governments of the Middle East and South Asia were especially keen to restrict Christian missionary work since many Muslim and Hindu nationalists viewed any spread of Christianity as a threat to religion-based cultural cohesion.[63] Third, the contraction of membership within the long-established American Protestant churches meant that these organizations became less culturally influential in the late twentieth century. The Presbyterians began to see a steep drop in membership in the 1960s as church attendance lapsed in their core northeastern and midwestern constituencies; by the early 1980s, surveys showed that 45 percent of Americans who had been raised as Presbyterians had switched to other churches or had stopped attending church entirely.[64] Fourth, a new generation of American and British historians emerged from the political left, often identifying with a Marxist intellectual tradition. These historians, who produced much of the cutting-edge scholarship in the 1960s and 1970s, were not interested in missionaries or religion per se but drew inspiration from popular resistance, political economy, and peasant or working-class history. Some of these new historians viewed missionaries as colonial collaborators who were as passé as the British Empire itself.[65] A leader of this leftist history was the British labor historian E. P. Thompson, author of *The Making of the English Working Class* (1963), who was the India-born son of Methodist missionaries.[66]

Ultimately, the convergence of these trends meant that in the 1960s mission history was falling out of fashion within leading research universities and was becoming the preserve of Christian theological seminaries and church-affiliated colleges. Meanwhile, a rift widened between what one could perhaps call secular academia and Christian academia—a rift that many scholars on both sides may have unconsciously welcomed.

The history of Christian missions came back into vogue in the 1990s as historians of South Asia, Africa, the Middle East, and the British Empire took a fresh look at histories of colonialism. In this milieu, scholars recognized missionaries as important agents of social change during the nineteenth and twentieth centuries. Kindling this interest was the emergence of postcolonial studies as a scholarly field,[67] coupled with a growing awareness of, and access to, colonial-era missionary archives.

Today, many of the postcolonial historians who are based in major research universities regard missionaries as agents or tools of imperialism. But there are also scholars who study mission history while sympathizing with or supporting the propagation of Christianity. Generally working within Christian seminaries and theology programs, these scholars are called missiologists. According to a textbook aimed at an audience of "missionaries, mission administrators and planners, and all Christians interested in the worldwide mission of the church," missiology is a branch of theology that "studies the movement of Christianity in the world, [and] the ways in which Christian faith becomes attached to different contexts."[68] This field is now thriving as non-Western Christianity becomes an increasingly visible and assertive cultural force within Christian transnational forums, challenging North American and British practices in the process. Just as cutting-edge sociologists have recognized the power of globalization to produce new forms of cultural heterogeneity[69]—and not homogeneity, as observers often assume—leading missiologists have been recognizing the power of Christianization to produce locally distinct Christian cultural formations even within unitary or affiliated denominations.

Missiologists tend to use the term "secular historian" to refer to a scholar who writes about the history of missions from a position of non-advocacy, and this term warrants scrutiny here, since this book neither advocates Christian missions nor endorses evangelization. The *Oxford English Dictionary* defines secularism as "the doctrine that morality should be based solely on regard to the well-being of mankind in the present life, to the exclusion of all considerations drawn from belief in God or in a future state." It also associates secularism with "the view that . . . the education provided at the public cost should be purely secular" in the sense that it should not profess, advocate, or privilege a particular religion or religious practice, such as prayer.[70]

Writing a secular history of Christian missions means that one does not write as an advocate for a particular religious worldview, in the sense that the dictionary definition conveys. But it does *not* mean that one ignores or minimizes the roles of religion in society, or the potential for religious beliefs to shape individual and collective behaviors.[71] Thus this book acknowledges the capacity of traditional religious structures, such as churches or mosques, to serve as vehicles for innovative social movements and activities, and the ability of religious communities to reconfigure and mobilize for broader social and political causes. It recognizes the power of faith and ideas, not merely money, power, and passions (as Marxists, Freudian psychologists, and others would have it), to serve as driving forces in history. While contending that missionary activities exerted far-reaching and unexpected social influences on Egyptians, it avoids reckoning missionary "success" or "failure" in terms of the numbers of formal conversions, since social realities were more complex than a win-or-lose, all-or-nothing rhetoric can describe.[72] It contends, in short, that people involved in missionary encounters changed significantly—and changed each other—without necessarily "converting" in the sense of either registering or announcing a shift of religious identity or spiritual life.

Regardless of the local reception of their efforts, missionaries were aware of themselves as participants in a global movement in which the mere fact of giving witness to their faith was potentially as important as how the message was received. Christian mission advocates described evangelization as an obligation, and it was undoubtedly a "self-constitutive" act.[73] Moreover, many of the American Presbyterians in Egypt did not regard formal declaration of Protestant faith as the only litmus test for successful evangelism. In the nineteenth century as in the twentieth, many saw social and religious reform as a worthy goal. In Egypt, some of the American Presbyterians argued that evangelization could take individuals unaware, so that some people who encountered missionaries but continued to regard themselves as Muslims or Coptic Orthodox might adopt new social values or attitudes toward God that reflected the core of a Reformed (i.e., Protestant) Christian message.[74] In a related vein, a few even suggested that the Christian message, inspired by the example of Jesus, was merely a route to something much larger—the apprehension of God—so that the formality of Christianization need not be the missionary's singular goal.

Writing in 1987 about the foreign mission movement in the history of American Protestantism, William R. Hutchison offered an explanation for why missionaries, despite their cultural importance, had until then "remained shadowy figures in narrations of religious and general history." He wrote, "The reason for such neglect is plain enough: these overseas Americans and their best-known objectives have seemed more than a little embarrassing" with their arrogance, cultural condescension, and zeal. Missionaries appeared in their own historical writings as self-satisfied do-gooders, and by the Vietnam era, "mainline academic[s]" simply avoided them. As the son and son-in-law of missionaries, Hutchison had known many missionaries personally but did not recollect "Bible-thumping soul-savers" among them; instead, he likened the ones he knew to Peace Corps types: ide-alistic, socially engaged, and progressive. Hutchison attributed part of the blame for stereotypes about overzealous missionaries to the missionaries themselves, who, when "telling the home folks what they wanted to hear, had regularly exaggerated both the centrality and the success of evangelism."[75]

Missionary stereotypes have arisen from many sources, including works of secular history and missiology, portrayals in popular culture, and even missionaries' own audience-driven hyperbole. This book tries to overcome these limitations by immersing itself in a vast body of works by and about missionaries and their activities, drawing on published books, archival records stored in the United States, Egypt, and Britain, and newspapers.[76] It draws insights, too, from conversa-tions with American missionaries, Egyptian pastors, and other church leaders and participants. Finally, this book benefits from a range of new works about Christian missionaries in the Middle East, the Mus-lim world, and the British Empire.[77] The goal here is to produce a his-tory of the American missionary encounter in Egypt that illuminates both the Egyptian and American dimensions of this historical ex-change while attending to the changing landscapes of social attitudes and religious beliefs. It aims to show that missionary history is not only "about" Christianity and its transmission but rather covers the social, cultural, and political lives of individuals and communities.[78]

Five chapters and a conclusion follow. Chapter 2 considers the his-tory of the American mission in Egypt from its founding in 1854 until the British Occupation of 1882. It discusses the nature and roots of the mission's evangelical impulse, and the impact that the mission had on the Christian culture of the Copts. Chapter 3 focuses on the years from 1882 to 1918, when American missionaries pursued more aggressive efforts to evangelize among Muslims, and when women assumed numerical preponderance within the mission, thereby en-abling the American Presbyterians to expand their activities among Egyptian females. Chapter 4 examines the rise of Egyptian Muslim nationalist opposition to missions, particularly in the late 1920s and early 1930s, and the ways in which missionaries responded by articu-lating a philosophy of individual religious liberty. It also considers the "rethinking" of foreign missions that representatives of several American Protestant churches, including the United Presbyterian Church, were beginning to promote, with consequences for the Americans in Egypt. Chapter 5 concentrates on the mission of the American University in Cairo, which opened its doors in 1920, and traces the evolving thought of its founder, Charles R. Watson, who spent a long career mulling over what an American Christian mission to Egyptians should mean. Chapter 6 surveys the period from 1945 to 1967, when political forces, arising out of Egyptian decolonization and the Arab-Israeli conflict, buffeted the American mission and contributed to the dissolution of the American Missionary Association in Egypt. In this period, the American Presbyterians also began to cultivate relations with Coptic Orthodox and Catholic clerics that were unprecedented for their warmth. The book concludes by evaluating the long-term impact of this missionary encounter as it occurred through the convergence of American history, Egyptian history, and the history of modern"world Christianities," and considers the mutual"conversions"and transformations that this encounter entailed.[79]

The American Mission, Coptic Reform, and the Making of an Egyptian Evangelical Community, 1854–82

> My business is with modern—not ancient—Egypt; with its
> moral ruins, and not its pictured tombs and stately temples.
> —Gulian Lansing, *Egypt's Princes* (1864)

IN 1852, FOUR YEARS after the U.S. government installed its first American-born consul in Egypt,[1] Dr. J. G. Paulding of the Associate Reformed Presbyterian Church mission in Damascus, Syria, visited Egypt to recover his health. Writing to leaders of his church in Pennsylvania, Paulding praised Egypt as an open field for Christian mission. Church leaders seized upon his idea, and in 1853, at a meeting in the western Pennsylvania town of Allegheny, entered the following decision in their register: "Resolved, That our missionaries be instructed to occupy Cairo at their earliest convenience."[2] This language of deployment and occupation anticipated the militant rhetoric that the British government used after its invasion of Egypt in 1882.

The Rev. Thomas and Henrietta McCague, husband and wife, left Philadelphia late in 1854. Their arrival in Egypt on November 15 of that year marked the debut of the American Presbyterian mission, which soon evolved into the largest Christian missionary enterprise in the country. By 1897, when the Rev. Andrew Watson published a chronicle of the mission's achievements over forty-three years ("not for the praise of men," he assured his readers, "but for the glory of God"), the mission had an American staff of almost fifty and had established an autonomous "Evangelical Church" (al-Kanisa al-Injiliyya), named in the hope that its members would spread *al-injil* (the gospel) universally in Egypt. In 1897, Watson noted that this Egyptian Presbyterian church claimed 5,355 members, called "Evangelicals" or Injiliyyun, who had formed dozens of autonomous congregations ranging from Alexandria to Luxor. Many thousands more, the vast majority of them Copts, attended Sunday worship.[3]

In the second half of the nineteenth century, the American missionaries tried to bring Copts into the Evangelical community as a way of prompting a reformation within the Coptic Orthodox Church. The latter church claimed a history stretching back to the arrival of Saint Mark the Evangelist in the Roman province of Egypt, but traced its independence to the Council of Chalcedon in 451, when leaders broke ranks with the prevailing Orthodoxy (and therefore with Byzantine authorities in Constantinople) over a theological question about the nature of Christ.[4] After 1854, American missionaries in Egypt repeatedly stated that the Coptic Orthodox Church was a dead church— sometimes also calling it a "mummified" or "embalmed" church.[5] "Christian in name, Christian in form," Andrew Watson wrote, "[the Coptic church] was well typified by the mummified human body taken out of the tombs."[6] As evidence of its lifelessness they pointed to what they claimed had been its failure to withstand the rise of Islam beginning in the seventh century, its hemorrhaging of Christian believers to the Muslim fold, and its subjection to Muslim tyranny in centuries that followed.

Islam had indeed spread so successfully in Egypt that by the time American missionaries arrived, Christians accounted for only a small fraction—perhaps 7 percent[7]—of an overwhelmingly Muslim population. Thus the American Presbyterians directed part of their mission toward what they regarded as the regeneration of Egyptian Christian life—a process that they hoped would lead in the long run to the country's re-Christianization. Not surprisingly, Coptic Orthodox leaders soon came to resent and resist American missionary challenges to their authority. Further complicating the social landscape were Roman Catholic and British Anglican missionaries, who pressed rival claims on the Copts as well.

Although the vast majority of Evangelicals eventually came from Coptic backgrounds,[8] American missionaries in Egypt had conceived of their mission as universal. (Their original sponsoring church, the Associate Reformed Presbyterian Church, claimed the distinction of having been the first American church to send a mission to the Middle East expressly for converting Jews.[9] That had been the original aim of the work started in Damascus in 1844, though in 1878 the Americans abandoned their work in Syria to Scottish and Irish Presbyterians.)[10] Reflecting on the situation in Egypt where he had served since 1861, Andrew Watson elaborated in 1906,

> The purpose of the mission was not as has been reported in some places, to labour among the various Christian sects especially, but to preach and teach the pure gospel of our Lord Jesus Christ to Jews, Moslems and nominal Christians where and when opportunity offered. It so happened that God in His providence opened

the door to the Copts, who, it would be easy to prove, were at the time in great ignorance of the Word of God. Instead of beating at the bolted and barred doors of Islam, at a time when there was no religious liberty, the missionaries entered at the open doors of "the lost sheep of Israel."[11]

The Americans' contest for Coptic allegiances ended with the emergence of an Egyptian Evangelical community whose members came primarily from Coptic Orthodox backgrounds but who implemented new ideas about Christian authority, church life, and worship.

MISSIONARY POLITICS: A NILE NARRATIVE FROM THE 1860S

The American Presbyterians had a knack for sensing opportunity in Egypt. When they began their mission in 1854, digging had just begun in the isthmus of Suez, railway and steamship lines were tying Egypt more tightly into the global economy, and the Egyptian tourist industry (catering to Europeans and Americans on expeditions to the Holy Land) was taking off. They arrived, too, as the British Anglican mission of the Church Missionary Society (CMS), starved of funds and staff, was waning after thirty years in the country. The CMS shut down in 1865 with the death of the Rev. John Lieder, who had started work in Egypt in 1825, although it later resumed operation in Egypt in 1882, following Britain's invasion.[12]

In 1854 the Americans numbered among a handful of Protestant missionaries in Lower Egypt, a region that included the cities of Cairo and Alexandria as well as the Delta in between, where the population was almost completely Muslim and rural. Sensing that they would find a warmer reception to their message among Copts, the Americans looked to Upper Egypt and to communities dotting the Nile from Fayoum to Luxor where most Copts lived. The Americans decided not to focus on urban, educated Coptic men (many of whom were accountants and tax collectors in government employ) but rather on Coptic *fellahin*, reasoning that, among "poor and simple-minded peasants," "the gospel has the freest course."[13] Thus in 1860 the Americans bought a riverboat, the *Ibis*, for sailing up-country to Coptic villagers. The American Presbyterians became so closely associated with this vehicle that some Egyptians remembered them years later not as Presbyterians but as "American Riverboat Missionaries."[14]

In 1861, as letters from the United States delivered news of civil war, the Rev. Gulian Lansing (1826–1892) set out on the *Ibis* for the riverboat's second missionary voyage.[15] Lansing kept a diary during his travels and later drew upon it to publish an account. Titled *Egypt's Princes* (in a reference to Psalm 68:31, "Princes shall come out of Egypt; Ethiopia shall haste to stretch out her hands unto God"),[16] Lansing's book offers fascinating glimpses into mid-nineteenth-century Christian politics as they played out on Egyptian terrain.

At first glance *Egypt's Princes* looks like a standard work of the missionary adventure genre that was so important to rousing American Protestant interest in missions.[17] However, Lansing tried to distance his book from the "stirring and romantic," noting that missionaries in Egypt, unlike their counterparts in Central Africa, found no wild beasts to slay. On the contrary, Lansing suggested that the big battle and "hard toil" facing missionaries in Egypt was learning Arabic: "I would rather traverse Africa from Alexandria to the Cape of Good Hope, than undertake a second time to master the Arabic language."[18]

As a mission survey-cum-travel account, *Egypt's Princes* aimed to generate domestic support while offering readers vicarious tourism. Lansing recounts stories about his visits to pharaonic temples, Coptic monasteries, and pashas' estates; mentions meetings with rich and in some cases titled European tourists and merchants, as well as with "black" Sudanese; and describes what he regarded as Egyptian laziness and despotism as well as the Coptic church's intrinsic corruption. He added evangelical heft to his account by recounting his dazzling sermons and polemical performances with Coptic and Muslim skeptics. With its smug, imperious tone, Lansing's account built the case for American missionary intervention in Egyptian and Coptic affairs.

Lansing's case against Coptic Orthodox practice was typical of American missionary accounts of the period. Coptic Orthodox worship, he claimed, consisted of monotonous rituals in which priests chanted masses and prayers in a "dead" language (liturgical Coptic) that no ordinary Copt understood. The penchant for ritual extended to what he regarded as incessant fasting, excessive veneration of Mary (what missionaries sometimes called "Mariolatry"), and saint worship.[19] Priests were poorly educated—and were sometimes illiterate in Arabic or liturgical Coptic—and even bishops drank "arrack" (*'araq*, a hard liquor of the local variety).[20] American Presbyterian missionaries like Lansing found this last indulgence deplorable, since they came from a church that regarded the production, sale, or consumption of alcohol as behavior incompatible with church membership.[21] These points aside, four aspects of Lansing's "narrative of missionary labor in the valley of the Nile" give his account lasting interest.

First, as Lansing traveled from village to village late in 1861 and again in 1862, his chief mode of evangelical outreach was selling Arabic Bibles and Christian tracts.[22] The Copts whom he met were hungry for books and bought Bibles with alacrity. (Lansing claimed that in the first place he stopped, one man "almost snatched the book, saying, 'I'll take it and spend my evenings reading it!' and he kissed it and pressed it to his bosom with evident delight.")[23] Working with an Egyptian assistant, and cooperating with Lord Haddo, later known as Lord Aberdeen (an evangelically minded Briton who had come to Egypt for his health and who had then found his calling as a purveyor of Bibles along the Nile), Lansing stopped in towns and villages, loaded up donkeys with books, and reported large sales at every stop.[24] He went to churches or approached men wearing black turbans (a sign of Coptic identity); to children he sold off "a great many penny tracts."[25] He did not try to sell Bibles to Muslims but happily did so when Muslims approached him. Reflecting on his quick sale of thirty dollars' worth of books to some Coptic "scribes" in Sohag, he noted, "frequently, we found them comparing the prices of our books with what, with them, would be the cost of transcribing and binding them, and of course they consider them very cheap, even when we sell at full cost price."[26] His account captured a moment when Arabic print culture in Egypt was neither a novelty nor a fixture, when the authority of Arabic printed sources was eroding the authority of Arabic oral culture, and when demand for books was soaring. Lansing claims that the Arabic Bible was having an impact. He notes that in some places Coptic priests were beginning to read the Arabic Bible aloud in church, in lieu of the Coptic text, and records that until their relations soured, the bishop of Luxor allowed him to deliver Arabic-language sermons before the Coptic masses.[27] In sum, Copts were proving eager to read or hear about a Bible that they could hope to understand and that resembled oral folk epics (for example, about the Biblical figure of Job [Ayyub]), which circulated among Muslims as well.[28]

Second, Lansing observed and censured the large-scale use of peasant conscription and forced labor, particularly for canal digging and railway building. He was an eyewitness to the kind of strong-arm intervention among *fellahin* that made the regimes of Muhammad Ali and his heirs so notorious in modern Egypt.[29] Lansing issued scathing denunciations of this forced labor and argued that it benefited only Egypt's ruling classes, foreign tourists, and businessmen. "And thus it is," he wrote, "that railroads, factories, fortifications, and palaces, almost without number, are being raised throughout the land. Their towering walls are laid upon the very heart of poor, crushed Egypt. Their stones are cemented with her people's blood." Having seen the line built between Cairo and the Suez, where "10,000 forced laborers, who, from overwork, insufficient food, and the bitter cold of the desert nights, were dying by hundreds," he assures readers that these railways would "enrich a crowd of sycophants and parasites, mostly foreigners."[30] These points suggest that although the American missionary presence may have accompanied and benefited from Western imperial expansion, missionaries themselves were sometimes bitter critics of ruling regimes and Western powers.

Third, Lansing's account offers rare insights into the collision of Protestant, Roman Catholic, and Coptic Orthodox churches—and the competition over Christianity and Christians—that was besetting Coptic culture in this period. American missionary sources from the late nineteenth century through the mid-twentieth rarely mention the presence of Roman Catholics in Egypt, even though Catholic schools and churches operated in some of the same small towns (such as Tahta, near Sohag) where American Presbyterians were active. (Indeed, Jesuit missionaries had been active in Upper Egypt since 1718 and by 1750 claimed some 1,300 Coptic Catholic adherents in places like Akhmim and Girga.)[31] Only Arabic sources, written by Muslim and Christian Egyptians, do justice to illuminating the parallel paths that Protestant and Catholic missionaries followed.[32] As an English-language work, Lansing's account is unusual for noting the widespread Roman Catholic presence in Upper Egypt during the early 1860s. Going into the church in "Ghinneh" (Qena), for example, he found a church worker who archly observed that some of Lansing's books had come from a London press. "This smacked of Rome," Lansing wrote, "and aroused my suspicions, and a few leading questions brought out the following facts, viz.: that this was the church and school of the Coptic *papal* church . . . and that the absent priest was an *Italian*." "Oh, Rome!" he goes on to lament, after hearing children reciting "dead Coptic prayers" in this Catholic church: "For dead Coptic in Ghinneh is the same as dead Latin in the rest of the world. Better [thy] motto might have been: 'anything that will deaden the intellect and crush the soul, and further thy selfish ends.'" Once back in Luxor, he reflected that the job of making the Bible known among Copts was complicated by the need to offset the influence of "Catholic books which the Romish church has palmed off on them, and which they receive as orthodox without knowing the source." Still later, after a trip to Negadeh, he noted that there was a Catholic convent and church but expressed relief upon hearing from the people "that but one man with his family had been perverted."[33]

Finally, Lansing's account shows the difference that foreign consular protections and Egyptian government concessions could make on the ground. For a start, there was Lord Aberdeen, the traveler-turned-Bible distributor: the *dhahabiyya* boat that he used for his book plying was, according to Lansing, on loan from the viceroy himself, who had issued "a firman to all the subgovernors of the Upper country to treat [Aberdeen] as became a royal guest." Mustapha Agha, a Muslim notable in Luxor who served as consular agent for the United States and for several European countries, helped Lansing by enrolling Muslim boys in Luxor's fledgling American mission school, which was temporarily located in the Coptic Orthodox Church. Lansing claimed, too, that one of the wealthiest Coptic landowners of Upper Egypt, Botros Bey of Sheikh Marzuk, had "procured a Russian consular agency for Osiut" (i.e., Assiut)—a purely nominal arrangement—so that his sons would be exempt from the military draft and his family would enjoy "Russian protection." Then there was the "papal" (Roman Catholic) church in Qena. Lansing reported that the Copts of Qena, who numbered some 4,000 people, formerly had no church of their own and had to cross the Nile to reach Denderah five miles away—a difficult journey during the annual floods. He heard that local Copts had managed to get a church-building permit in the time of Muhammad Ali (r. 1805–48) but that he had revoked it when local Muslims protested, claiming that the village was a station on the Egyptian pilgrimage route to Mecca so that a church would pollute the village's precincts. (Securing both government permits and popular Muslim approval for church building was an obstacle for Copts in the nineteenth century and remains a sore point in Egypt today.)[34] But finally Qena got a church—not a Coptic Orthodox Church, but a Catholic one. "The Catholics . . . have a church [in Qena]," Lansing noted, "the permission to build having been secured by the French Consul, and in this they possess a great vantage ground for proselyting [sic] from the Copts."[35]

Of course, the Americans benefited in similar ways: the viceroy Said Pasha, following intercession from the American consul, gave the mission a prime site for one of its buildings in the Muski district of Old Cairo.[36] Likewise, Lansing notes how President Abraham Lincoln, prompted by the American consul-general in Egypt, wrote to Said Pasha in 1861 to intercede on behalf of one of the mission's lay evangelists. (This was a Syrian-priest-turned-Protestant named Faris al-Hakim, whom Muslim authorities jailed, beat, and sentenced to hard labor for trying to defend a Coptic woman who, following her Muslim conversion and marriage, wished to revert to Christianity.)[37]

Lansing's *Ibis* voyages confirmed his sense that Upper Egypt would be a rich field for the American missionaries. His colleagues agreed, and in 1865 they established a permanent station in Assiut, among the largest Coptic population in Egypt. In the long run, this move helped the mission mobilize a grassroots program of Coptic reform and foster the growth of Evangelical Presbyterian congregations under indigenous leadership.[38]

THE AMERICAN MISSION AND ITS EVANGELICAL CULTURE

The American Presbyterians who went to Egypt after 1854 had their place in an Anglo-American Protestant missionary movement that gained momentum during a long nineteenth century that lasted from 1792 to 1910.[39] The earlier date saw the publication of William Carey's *Enquiry into the Obligations of Christians to Use Means for the Conversion of the Heathens*—a treatise by an English shoemaker that inspired widespread Protestant interest in missions to Asia and Africa, and that prompted Carey's own journey as a missionary to India. The year 1910 witnessed the convening of the World Missionary Conference in Edinburgh—an event regarded as a landmark in the history of the Protestant ecumenical movement and as a high-confidence point for Protestant missions.

During this long nineteenth century, American Presbyterians were evangelicals in the core senses of the term: they were social activists who believed that lives could be changed through conversion, individual Bible study, and reflection on Christ and his sacrifice.[40] The American Presbyterians in Egypt were also products of and participants in a wider American evangelical culture. Propelled by laypeople, and not church authorities, this culture had emerged in the United States out of the Second Great Awakening—a period of Protestant religious revival in which "loyalty to a particular church [became] less important than a vibrant religion of the heart."[41] In this period, men and women found leadership roles in Christian voluntary societies that pursued a wide range of social causes, such as abolitionism and temperance. Organized efforts to propagate Christianity grew out of these societies, first targeting Native Americans along the westward-moving frontier before expanding overseas.

The Americans Presbyterians in Egypt were also active in an incipient Protestant ecumenical movement. This movement emerged in a transatlantic context, with Americans closely engaging in discussions with British Anglicans, Baptists, Congregationalists, and others. By the mid-nineteenth century, transatlantic and interdenominational dialogues were translating into cooperative Anglo-American efforts in mission fields abroad. Certainly in Egypt, the American Presbyterians looked to British Anglicans and Presbyterians as natural friends and allies. Indeed, the American Presbyterians in Egypt received explicit instructions from their board in Philadelphia to cultivate "tender and cordial feelings of Christian regard" toward other missionaries from the "visible church"—meaning from Reformed (i.e., Protestant) churches—as a set of guidelines, published in 1861, makes clear. These guidelines urged each missionary to remember that he and the other missionaries "are brethren, that the heathen are around them in the land, that therefore they should bear long with one another, and be kind; and that as far as possible, in all general ways they should cooperate for the furtherance of the Gospel."[42]

But in spite of the evangelical and ecumenical tendencies that they shared with other Protestants in the mid-nineteenth century, the American Presbyterians in Egypt—whose church emerged from a union in 1858 as the United Presbyterian Church of North America (UPCNA)—had some of their own specificities. For a start, the UPCNA was organizationally distinct from the larger Presbyterian Church U.S.A. (PCUSA), which sponsored missions in what is now Turkey, Lebanon, and Iran.[43] Otherwise, the UPCNA in the mid-nineteenth century had three ideological features that shaped the church's mission policies and practices, not only in Egypt and northern India (where mission work had started in 1855) but also in the United States. These were opposition to slavery, support for Bible-centered education, and anti-Catholic sentiment.

Opposition to Slavery

The UPCNA took a strict anti-slavery line. As early as 1800, one of its antecedents (the Associate Church) had declared slavery "a moral evil and unjustifiable" and had withdrawn from the American slave-owning states on the grounds that it did not want slave-owners as congregants. This policy helps explain why the Associate Church (as well as the like-minded Associate Reformed Church) spread westward but not southward from Pennsylvania, and why the UPCNA at its birth in 1858 had a strong midwestern focus but with some congregations scattered further afield in states like Oregon and Colorado. The UPCNA enshrined anti-slavery convictions into its 1858 creedal statement, which declared that slavery was "a violation of the law of God, and contrary both to the letter and spirit of Christianity."[44] When the U.S. Civil War began (around the same time that Gulian Lansing was sailing the *Ibis* in Egypt), the UPCNA decided to organize work to help fugitive slaves. When war ended in 1865, the UPCNA entered the U.S. southern states and developed "freedmen's missions" by establishing schools and colleges for African American males and females in Alabama, Virginia, North Carolina, and Tennessee.[45]

The church's work among African Americans followed a path that was in important ways parallel to the work among Copts. Whether writing about Egyptians or African Americans, church sources stressed the need for education, reform, and enlightenment, and for the cultivation of indigenous leaders and self-reliant congregations. The church historian who published a retrospective survey of the UPCNA in 1958 could have been describing Egypt when he wrote, with regard to the Freedmen's missions, "It was hoped that if a large body of Christian Negroes were given the necessary education, they would in turn undertake the evangelization and uplift of the rest of their own people."[46] The attitudes that American missionaries developed in Egypt toward Coptic reform and evangelization should therefore be understood not only as a response to specific Middle Eastern and Egyptian conditions but also as an organic outgrowth of larger mission philosophies that were evolving in the United States.

Support for Bible-Centered Education

Leaders of the UPCNA emphasized that every believer should be able to read and engage with the Bible. The Rev. William J. Reid, a United Presbyterian pastor in Pittsburgh, clarified this idea in a manual of UPCNA doctrine first published in 1881. To have a "saving faith," Reid advised, "we must study the Bible diligently, and listen attentively and regularly to the preaching of the word." Besides baptism and the profession of belief, he added, "Another qualification of the members of the church is *knowledge*. . . . The ultimate standard of knowledge is the Scriptures. No one who is ignorant of the doctrines of grace, as revealed in the Bible, has a right to a place in the church."[47] Writing in 1894, the UPCNA church historian James B. Scouller attributed the church's emphasis on knowledge to Calvinist values that demanded intelligent Bible reading, that is, "not . . . learning for its own sake, but [learning as an] auxiliary to the advancement of religious truth." Scouller wrote that these values had guided the forebears of the United Presbyterians in America when they "built their schoolhouse near the church, and very often hired the schoolmaster before they hired their pastor."[48] The American Presbyterians in Egypt appear to have followed a similar impulse, by making education and Bible-based literacy a mission priority and by starting schools in towns like Luxor and Assiut before they had functioning Evangelical churches in place.[49]

American missionaries in Egypt were not unique in promoting education in their mission. Protestant missionaries regarded education as an ideal medium for evangelization, not least because—to borrow the words of a missionary to Bengali Muslims, who spoke at a conference in Cairo in 1906—schools "help in breaking down prejudice and banishing fear" toward the missionary message.[50] Phrased more critically, schools provided captive audiences to whom missionaries could convey their ideas. Likewise, American Presbyterians were not unique among evangelicals in valuing literacy for the sake of Bible reading. The idea that the Bible should be accessible to ordinary believers in their vernaculars was a grounding principle of Protestantism during the sixteenth century, and in ensuing generations inspired Protestants to develop many different vernacular print languages. Indeed, this idea was the bedrock of two missions that worked closely with the American Presbyterians in Egypt, namely, the American Bible Society (ABS) based in New York and the British and Foreign Bible Society (BFBS) based in London. By 1922, the latter society alone boasted Bible translations in some 550 world languages.[51]

Yet if the missions of the UPCNA were not unique in promoting education as a vehicle for Bible study, embracing print technologies for the development of Christian literatures, or using schools for evangelization, then their approach to literacy and literary work in Egypt was nevertheless distinctive. For unlike their closest peer among the Protestant organizations in Egypt—namely, the British CMS mission—which focused on urban communities and on formal schooling for children, the American Presbyterians promoted literacy even among adults from the peasantry and working classes. They did so by seeding ad hoc voluntary programs that called upon Egyptians to teach each other how to read. The result was that, in late nineteenth-century Egypt, many Copts appear to have learned to *read* the Bible without ever learning how to *write*. The Rev. Menes Abdel Noor, an Egyptian Evangelical pastor in Cairo, recalled in 2005 that this had been the case with his own paternal grandmother in Upper Egypt. His grandfather (a railway employee who was expelled from his family home for turning from Coptic Orthodoxy toward Protestantism) taught his grandmother how to read (the Bible), yet she never learned how to write.[52] Strikingly, the American mission's emphasis on adult literacy programs persisted into the second half of the twentieth century, when Egyptian Evangelicals and American Presbyterians together launched rural education and literacy projects in Upper Egyptian villages that had remained little touched by either missionary or government schooling. These mid-twentieth-century campaigns had a catchy motto—"Each One Teach One"—but the idea behind the pedagogy was little changed from the late nineteenth century, when the American missionaries had urged newly educated Copts to teach their friends and relatives to read.[53]

Anti-Catholic Sentiment

A deep vein of anti-Catholic sentiment ran through American Protestant popular culture in the mid-nineteenth century, and leaders of the UPCNA helped propel it. This sentiment was grounded in anxieties about American social ills of the period, including widespread urban poverty and alcoholism, which, in the view of Protestant evangelicals, were most pronounced among immigrant Roman Catholic populations.[54] In the particular case of the UPCNA, some of this animosity may have derived from "anti-papal feeling inherited from centuries of persecution in Scotland."[55] Whatever its source, anti-Catholic attitudes explain why the American Presbyterians in Egypt kept their distance from the Catholic missionaries who operated in some of the same places where they were active. Moreover, while the Americans in Egypt often described followers of Coptic Orthodoxy as "nominal Christians" in need of reform, they generally refrained from describing Roman Catholics as Christians or from mentioning Catholics at all.

Anti-Catholic sentiment was particularly visible in Philadelphia, the city that hosted the UPCNA's foreign mission board after 1858. Since the 1840s, Philadelphia had been the center of a nativist "Protestant Crusade" that was responding to an influx of Irish Catholic immigrants. Philadelphia even became the home of an "American Protestant Association," founded by clergymen in 1842 for pursuing what a city historian summarized as "an unremitting ideological war on popery." One of the founders of this association, the Rev. Samuel B. Wylie, was a professor and vice-provost at the University of Pennsylvania and was also a Presbyterian pastor.[56]

In 1870, at the UPCNA's General Assembly, leaders of the church went so far as to declare that the "church of Rome" was not a real church but was instead "the synagogue of Satan" and an "Abomination of the Earth"; on these grounds they concluded that "Papal baptism" was illegitimate.[57] They discussed this issue because American church leaders were beginning to debate the terms on which Catholics should be admitted into the UPCNA (suggesting that some may have been opting to join). In practice, however, and in the long run, the UPCNA appears to have left the question of Catholic baptism and possible Protestant re-baptism to the discretion of congregations, in order to avoid scaring off potential Catholic converts.[58] Indeed, the UPCNA later began to pursue formal missions to Roman Catholic immigrants, especially Italians, in Pittsburgh and other Pennsylvania towns. They thereby engaged in home missions to Catholics just as other Protestant churches, like the Presbyterian Church U.S.A., were doing in the late nineteenth and early twentieth centuries.[59]

The American missionaries to Egypt came out of this Presbyterian milieu where attitudes toward Roman Catholicism were closely tied to Protestant anxieties about immigration, and where church leaders were prepared to deny the very Christianity of Roman Catholicism. No wonder, then, that American missionaries in Egypt avoided contact with the Catholic priests and nuns who during the late nineteenth century were opening many new schools in the country. The sectarian animosities dividing Protestant and Catholic missionaries during this period were compounded by ethnolinguistic distinctions. For whereas Protestant missionaries in Egypt, with few exceptions, were American and British, the Catholics were generally French and Italian.[60]

THE CONTEST FOR COPTS

Upon arriving in Egypt in 1854, the American missionaries decided that the Coptic Orthodox Church was hopelessly corrupt and in need of a Protestant-style reformation. They soon realized, however, that CMS missionaries on the one hand, and Roman Catholic missionaries on the other, had their own ideas about the role and goal of a mission to Copts and were also competing for Coptic allegiances. The result was a contest for Copts that reflected divergent beliefs over the forms that Christian authority and practice should take. In the long run, this competition led to the creation of distinct Egyptian Presbyterian, Episcopal, and Catholic churches, even while stimulating changes among those who stayed loyal to Coptic Orthodoxy.

If American and British Protestants had compared notes with Roman Catholics during the second half of the nineteenth century (or even during the first half of the twentieth), they would have discovered that their attitudes toward their Coptic missions converged on many points. This is no surprise: Protestants and Catholics were drawing on a common pool of information and misinformation about Copts that Europeans had accumulated over the centuries.[61] Both Protestants and Catholics believed that many Coptic priests were barely literate and had a poor grasp of the meanings of Coptic liturgies and saw this as a reflection of the degraded educational and spiritual state of the Coptic population as a whole.[62] They agreed that Copts shared many cultural commonalities with Muslims—pointing, for example, to practices of male circumcision and female seclusion— and regarded this as further proof of Coptic backwardness.[63] Meanwhile, they expressed concerns that their missionary efforts to Copts were hampered by the religious apathy and debauched lifestyles that so many Western Christians exhibited in Egypt.[64] Finally, Protestant and Catholic missionaries tended to interpret Coptic history under Islamic rule as "one long sad record of indignities and persecutions inflicted on the Christians" and sometimes marveled that the Copts had maintained a Christian heritage at all.[65] Gulian Lansing expressed this in 1864 while inserting another sectarian barb. "The more I see of the Copts, and learn of their history," he wrote, "the more I admire the constancy with which they have withstood for the ages the Muslem [sic] power, and of late years the machinations of Rome also."[66]

What Lansing called "the machinations of Rome" was the outgrowth of a movement that was gaining momentum within the Catholic Church in the 1850s (just as the first American Presbyterians were arriving in Egypt). Led by Pope Pius IX (r. 1846–78), this movement aimed to encourage Eastern Christian churches—Armenians, Greeks, Nestorians, and others—to recognize the authority of the papacy in Rome and "return" to the universal church. In an 1846 encyclical, Pius IX had assured Eastern Christians that "We will consider your special Catholic liturgies as entirely safe and protected" if they recognized Roman papal authority; in this way, Copts could become Catholics and retain Coptic liturgies.[67] Of course, Pius IX's overture did not mark the first time that the Roman Catholic Church had appealed to Copts: Vatican emissaries had been attempting to negotiate with Coptic church leaders since 1439, though these earlier efforts foundered.[68] In 1741, the move for union had gained a symbolic boost when the Coptic bishop in Jerusalem professed "la foi romaine" (the Roman faith) and was granted jurisdiction over the Coptic Catholic community.[69] The Protestant mission historian Kenneth Scott Latourette suggested that this jurisdiction was more of an abstraction than a reality and that the Catholic enterprise in Egypt did not really flourish; by 1840, the only Catholic churches in Egypt were in Cairo and Alexandria, and they catered mainly to expatriates.[70] Yet even while granting that the Coptic Catholic population remained small (reportedly numbering 2,100 in Upper Egypt by 1773), the historian Alastair Hamilton has recently argued that counting churches would not have sufficed for gauging the community's size. Muslim rulers were reluctant to issue church-building permits, so that in the eighteenth and early nineteenth centuries, Coptic Catholics in Upper Egypt worshiped in "private houses or in chapels hidden in the hospices belonging to the missions."[71]

The pace of Catholic missions in Egypt accelerated in the mid-nineteenth century as European diplomatic and economic influence grew. But the nature and focus of the missions shifted. Despite Pius IX's calls for continuing negotiations with the ecclesiastical elites of Eastern churches,[72] Jesuits and Franciscans concentrated increasingly on humble Coptic believers, intensifying work that had begun in the early eighteenth century by looking to the small towns and villages of Upper Egypt where most Copts lived.[73] Thus Roman Catholics, like the Americans, increasingly undercut Coptic Orthodox ecclesiastical authority by building communities at the grass roots. In Alexandria and Cairo, Catholic missions increasingly relied on French consular intervention to secure land for schools and churches,[74] and it appears that Catholic missions did the same in Upper Egypt. Thus it was that in 1862 Gulian Lansing had found the Catholic church in Qena where children were learning to recite liturgies in the traditional Coptic (not Latin).[75] Roman Catholics called members of these communities *les coptes unis ou catholiques* (Uniate or Catholic Copts) and distinguished them from those they called *les coptes schismatiques ou dissidents* (schismatic or dissident Copts).[76]

Catholic writers suggested that the Uniate[77] Coptic population grew to 5,000 by 1894, to 25,000 by 1911, and to 39,000 by 1937.[78] Today, the Coptic Catholics who live in towns like Akhmim, Tahta, and Assiut, as well as in Cairo and Alexandria, have a population estimated at 200,000.[79] However, the history of the late nineteenth- and early twentieth-century Catholic missionary enterprise in Egypt is now hard to trace, partly because it was organizationally so heterogeneous, drawing on the efforts of priests, nuns, and laypeople who represented many different mission societies. According to one count, between 1844 and 1943 twenty-three separate Catholic women's missions came to Egypt and operated schools.[80] While the largest numbers of Catholic missionaries to Egypt came from France, and while most Catholic missionaries used French as a lingua franca, the Catholics were also heterogeneous in terms of their national origins, with Italians, Maltese, and Syrians participating, as well as the occasional Poles, Austrians, Britons, and others.[81] (The American Presbyterians, by contrast, came from a small but centrally run denomination and, relative to the Catholics, were culturally homogeneous.) Finally, the Catholic presence in Egypt was pluralistic in terms of its goals. Only certain Catholic missionaries specialized in outreach to the village Copts of Upper Egypt. Most Catholic missionaries in Egypt appear to have dedicated themselves to schools in Cairo and Alexandria, which catered to motley local and expatriate elites. Schools of the latter type represented Franco-Catholic cultural outposts in Egypt and pursued educational missions that were only incidentally related to the mission of making Copts into Uniates. In short, the very complexity and diversity of the Roman Catholic presence in Egypt has made its history harder to grasp. But if one theme stands out, it is that the Roman

Catholics in Egypt had no particular interest in appealing to Muslims and concentrated their missions on Christians—on Copts and other Eastern Christian minorities (both Uniates and "schismatics"), as well as on Latin-rite Catholics.

Initially, members of the CMS in Egypt focused attention on Christians as well. From the moment its first five missionaries arrived in 1825, and until the death of the last of these, John Lieder, in 1865, the CMS concentrated on reviving and reforming the Coptic Orthodox Church. Like William Carey, the English missionary to India who fired the imaginations of so many evangelicals, Lieder was originally a shoemaker. But unlike Carey, Lieder was German, as were his early colleagues in the CMS mission. In this regard, Lieder's presence attests to the vitality of the "Anglo-German evangelical network" of the nineteenth century, when Protestant collaboration within Europe drew upon a sense of community forged partly in opposition to Roman Catholicism, and when German Protestants served overseas on behalf of the CMS.[82] According to Paul Sedra, who has studied the impact of the CMS on the nineteenth-century Coptic Orthodox Church, Lieder brought artisanal values to bear on his mission to Copts by promoting what he regarded as modern values of discipline and industry in the approach to Christian learning. Lieder was instrumental in operating a training college for Coptic Orthodox priests from 1843 to 1848, but reportedly "found their illiteracy in Arabic, Coptic, and English such that substantive instruction could begin only in 1845." The CMS later took some of the credit for influencing the Coptic pope Cyril IV (r. 1854–61), whom Egyptian historians subsequently hailed as the Coptic Orthodox Church's first modern reformer. Among other things, Cyril stressed higher standards for educating the clergy and—in a move that some have called a reaction to the missionary challenge or threat—founded the Great Coptic School (Madrasat al-Aqbat al-Kubra), which educated an important new generation of Coptic laymen.[83] Cyril was also responding to Protestant influence when, to suppress what he regarded as the excesses of idolatry, he allowed his followers to stage public burnings of Coptic icons in Cairo and Assiut, thereby destroying important parts of the Coptic medieval artistic heritage.[84] In sum, the goal for CMS missionaries like Lieder was to cultivate an enlightened and literate clergy whose members could "revive" Coptic Orthodoxy after centuries of languishing, in their view, under Muslim dominion.

The CMS goal was *not* to make Copts into Anglicans. On the contrary, CMS missionaries wanted to keep the Coptic Orthodox Church institutionally intact as "the National Church of Egypt" (to borrow the words of an Anglican admirer, writing in 1897).[85] CMS policy toward the Copts appears to have reflected a prevalent British fascination with the Coptic Orthodox Church—an autocephalic church that possessed distinctive traditions (including an episcopacy) and that had its own history of contention with Roman Catholicism during and after the Crusades.[86] To a large extent, the Coptic Orthodox Church may have reminded Anglicans of their own Church of England and of the challenges that had historically beset its claims to autonomy.[87] Thus while CMS missionaries, as Protestants and evangelicals, shared some common attitudes with the American Presbyterians about church reform, education, and Roman Catholicism, they had no desire to subvert Coptic ecclesiastical authority. The CMS held this position until 1865, when its work in Egypt lapsed, and again after 1882, when the CMS restored its mission in Egypt in the form of a mission to Muslims.[88] In the words of the Rev. Montague Fowler, an Anglican observer writing about "Christian Egypt" in 1901, the CMS in the early nineteenth century still hoped to see the "self-reformation of the Coptic Church."[89]

In the long run, however, and contrary to aims and intentions, the CMS did preside over the creation of a distinct Egyptian Episcopal Church in the Anglican model. It emerged because CMS missionaries needed a church "home" for the small number of Muslims who eventually converted. But perhaps more important, it emerged because CMS missionaries did not want to spurn Christians (including Copts of the Orthodox, Catholic, and Evangelical variety) who became drawn into the Anglican orbit as a result of contacts forged through CMS schools, hospitals, and other activities. By 1922, the Episcopal Church in Egypt claimed 429 members. The church never grew big, not only because the CMS lacked ambitions to expand among Copts but also perhaps because the Anglican Church was compromised by its connections to Britain, which became the colonial occupier after 1882. Matthew Rhodes, an Anglican historian of the CMS in Egypt, has noted that the Anglican Church of Egypt was very "tribalistic" in the sense that its British expatriate members neither socialized nor worshiped with the Egyptian Episcopalians. "Born almost by accident," Rhodes writes, "it remains questionable whether [the Episcopal Church of Egypt] should continue to exist" or whether it should merge into Coptic Orthodoxy or the Evangelical Protestant community. "A more likely scenario is, however, that it will continue like those deposited by other cultures, washed up by the high tide of British imperialism."[90]

Unlike the CMS missionaries, the American Presbyterians had little hope of a Coptic self-reformation. They also had little respect for the hierarchy of bishops that characterized Coptic Orthodoxy and Anglicanism. The Rev. William Reid expressed this sentiment in his manual of United Presbyterian doctrine by asserting that "Episcopacy [meaning church government by bishops], like an absolute monarchy, does not allow sufficient liberty to the individual."[91] This mistrust of the Episcopal system had roots in the dissenting history of the UPCNA's Scottish forebears, who, in the words of one church historian, had waged three bitter struggles in their church life: the "struggle against papacy (the rule of Rome), against prelacy (the autocratic rule of bishops), and against Erastianism (the control of the Church by the State)."[92] But their mistrust of ecclesiastical authority was also distinctly American and in keeping with the populist spirit of nineteenth-century Protestant evangelical culture in the United States, where evangelicals "refused to defer to learned theologians and traditional orthodoxies" and shared an "overt rejection of the past as a repository of wisdom."[93]

The Americans in Egypt had two clear ideas about how church life should work, reflecting their evangelical and Presbyterian sensibilities. First, they maintained that the Bible, like prayer and collective worship, should be presented in plain language that believers could understand. Thus Arabic should be the language of the Bible, prayer, and worship in Egypt, just as English was the primary language in the United States. Liturgical Coptic had no place in their scheme. Second, the Americans believed that members of the congregation should play leading roles in running the church. Laymen, not only clergymen, should make church decisions on local (congregational), regional (presbytery-wide), and national (synod-wide) levels—in an "ascending series of judicatories"[94]—by consensus or voting. Reid, in his manual of doctrine, likened this Presbyterian system to a "government by elders" or to a "republican form of government, [which] unites individual freedom with consolidated power."[95] This attitude toward church government certainly informed the American mission in Egypt. In fact, so natural did these attitudes toward church authority appear that American missionaries seem to have remained oblivious to their particularity and radicalism in the Egyptian context. Writing in 1914, for example, the missionary Rena Hogg claimed that the abiding aim of her father, the Rev. John Hogg, in the earliest years of the American mission was "not to make the Coptic Church United Presbyterian but [simply] to make her Christian."[96]

The American mission in Egypt was four years old when it welcomed its first followers in 1858—a year after its founding missionary, Thomas McCague, had begun to deliver sermons in Arabic.[97] According to Andrew Watson, these adherents included a Coptic grain merchant named Saleh Awad, a Coptic monk named "Makhiel" (Mikhail) from Belyana in Upper Egypt, and an Armenian named Menas Ya-cob.[98] These individuals became the nucleus of the fledgling Evangelical Church.

By 1864, the American mission had assumed responsibility for a girls' school in Alexandria, which it was running on behalf of a Presbyterian "ladies" mission society in Paisley, Scotland. It was also operating a boys' school and a girls' school in Cairo, with a few hundred students attending. An Arabic-language congregation had formed in Cairo in 1863 while the missionaries had started to train a local clergy in the Presbyterian mode. Local "Evangelicals" (as Egyptian Presbyterians were becoming known) were already evangelizing in tandem with American missionaries. For example, Makhiel, the former Coptic monk, was distributing Arabic Bibles and "testif[ying] ... to the doctrine of salvation by Christ,"[99] while another Copt named Awad Hanna was accompanying missionaries on riverboat expeditions, stopping to explain "the rottenness and ruin of the Coptic church" to Coptic villagers and townsfolk who would listen. By this time, too, Andrew Watson claimed, Coptic Orthodox authorities were trying to woo students away from the American mission schools and into a new batch of Coptic schools, going so far as to "kidnap" some for this purpose. They were also discouraging their flock from buying Arabic literature from the missionaries and local evangelists.[100] Orthodox authorities had joined the contest for Copts.

As the mission approached its tenth anniversary in 1864, it was teetering close to bankruptcy. With civil war raging in the United States, the American mission was cut off from funds and could barely pay rents and salaries. The mission was sustained at this juncture by donations from Presbyterian mission supporters in Scotland, an English merchant named Rankin in Alexandria, and, above all, the Maharaja Dhulip Singh (1838–1893).[101] The latter was the son and theoretical heir of the vanquished Maharaja Ranjit Singh (1780–1839), the Sikh leader who had been known as the "Lion of the Punjab." The British in India exiled the young Dhulip Singh to Britain and to boarding school, where he converted to Christianity. He passed through Egypt in 1864 and sought help from the American missionaries in finding a Christian bride. The Americans in Cairo introduced him to one of their students, a pretty girl named Bamba Muller (1847–1887) who was the daughter of an Ethiopian (and by some accounts slave) mother and German father. Following his marriage to Bamba, Dhulip Singh became one of the mission's most important benefactors and, for several years running, gave the mission five thousand dollars to mark the anniversary of his marriage. The "romance of Bamba" became so important to the popular folklore of the American mission that it attained the status of a UPCNA legend and was used in promotional and fund-raising brochures well into the twentieth century.[102] Mission sources typically ended their versions of this "real life" romance with Bamba's move to an English estate, but left out the sad details that followed—including Dhulip Singh's eventual abandonment of Bamba and their six children, his adulterous liaisons and accumulation of debts, and Bamba's early death. (Dhulip Singh himself was a tragic figure who struggled to fit into the Victorian aristocracy while posing as an English gentleman and Sikh maharaja.)[103]

The second decade of the American mission in Egypt opened in 1865 with a few significant developments. The mission sank roots in Upper Egypt by establishing a permanent base in Assiut, where it opened a school for boys and girls. This was also the year when the new Coptic patriarch, Demetrius II (r. 1862–70), launched a campaign to stamp out Protestantism, beginning the decade that Andrew Watson later called "the time of the Coptic persecution of native Protestants." By 1865, the fledgling Evangelical Church of Egypt counted sixty-five members, almost all of them Copts. The Evangelicals in Assiut and its environs were beginning to spread the word among kin and neighbors and to organize prayer meetings where they read and discussed the Arabic Bible. It was around this time (again according to Watson) that Demetrius II found his own brother reading an Arabic Bible that the latter had bought from an American mission bookshop: the incident resulted in a furious row between the siblings.[104] Such an incident, if true, may have signaled to the patriarch the extent of the influence that Protestants were having on Coptic devotional life.

In 1904, Andrew Watson's son, the Egyptian-born Charles R. Watson (who was then serving as corresponding secretary of the UPCNA's foreign mission board in Philadelphia), elaborated on this period of "Coptic persecution." The younger Watson agreed with his father in asserting that Demetrius II and his bishops had found a ready ally in the Egyptian ruler, Khedive Ismail (r. 1863–79), who shared a hatred for the missionaries as foreigners and who proved adept at manipulating "the bigotry and animosity of the Coptic priests to his advantage."[105] Watson père and fils agreed that, rather than targeting the missionaries, who were shielded by the armor of consular protections, Khedive Ismail abetted the Coptic patriarch in the latter's attack on Copts who were turning to Protestantism. "This persecution was not an accidental outbreak of fanatical jealousy and hate," Charles R. Watson wrote.

"It was a deliberate plan in which the government lent its authority and influence to make effective the efforts of the Coptic Church to wipe out Protestantism forever."[106]

According to Andrew Watson, the persecution—or "ecclesiastical warfare"[107]—accelerated in 1867, when Khedive Ismail revoked the exemption that had protected the students of American mission schools from forced labor or military drafts. He did so just as the patriarch (accompanied by a government army contingent) was setting out on a tour of Upper Egypt. Upon arriving in Assiut, the patriarch issued a bull denouncing the Coptic Evangelicals, and this was read aloud in churches to serve as a warning and public shaming. The patriarch sponsored a public burning of the Arabic Bible (also known as the Van Dyck Bible, after its American translator) that had been imported from the American mission press in Beirut.[108] He demanded that Coptic parents withdraw their children from American mission schools or have them face call-ups to work on the railways and had Fam Stephanos, a Coptic tax collector and Protestant evangelist, banished to the White Nile on trumped-up charges. In another case (which suggested that Coptic Orthodox laypeople were supporting the patriarch's efforts) a local Coptic village sheikh accused two Copts of visiting a Protestant's home and subjected them to the bastinado (a beating on the soles of the feet). The beating was so severe that one man died from his injuries.[109] In the town of Kus in 1874, Coptic priests even ordered church members not to sell or rent land to Protestants. Meanwhile, many Copts were attending Evangelical prayer meetings by stealth. The American missionaries looked for help in this period from American and British consuls, to little avail, while John Hogg, on furlough in Britain in 1876, even appealed to Foreign Office authorities.[110] Problems persisted until 1876 when—much to the missionaries' relief—British and French financial interests forced Khedive Ismail to resign following the Egyptian government's fall into bankruptcy.

Reflecting on these events, Andrew Watson observed that the Coptic patriarch and his supporters leveled their harshest attacks against "native evangelists" by "imposing forced labor on them or their children."[111] The fact is that Egyptian men and women were becoming driving forces behind grassroots evangelization, while some were even drawing mission salaries as colporteurs (Bible salesmen) and Bible Women. Historians have overlooked these "native evangelists" because archival or published sources by or about them are lacking and because some may have possessed literacy of the reading-only variety. The task remains to recover their stories by conducting interviews with Egyptian Evangelicals who may have some knowledge of the roles that their grandparents and great-grandparents played

2.1. Three Bible Women, Assiut Conference, 1916. Anna B. Criswell Papers, Presbyterian Historical Society, Presbyterian Church (U.S.A.), Philadelphia.

in the church. Indeed, conversations with a few Egyptian Evangelical pastors suggest that these family histories of the church have been passed down as matters of pride.[112]

In the midst of Coptic Orthodox persecution, the Evangelical community grew in the 1860s and 1870s. Whereas in 1865 the church had had only 69 members, by 1870 it claimed 180 members, and by 1875 it claimed 596. The mission also grew by 1875 to include an American staff of seven ordained men, two non-ordained men, six unmarried women, and nine married women, as well as an Egyptian staff of two ordained men and fifteen presbyterial workers.[113] The American mission in Egypt followed a pattern that was common among Anglo-American Protestant missions in this period: women outnumbered men by fifteen to nine.[114]

Two incidents occurred in 1869 that had symbolic import for the history of the American mission, the Evangelical Church, and Christian sectarianism in Egypt. The first was a case of iconoclasm that occurred when a group of Evangelical youths broke into a Coptic Orthodox church in Assiut in order to burn and destroy its icons—pictures of "Christ, the Virgin and the Child, the prophets, the Apostles, and some of the martyrs."[115] This case illuminated emerging Egyptian Protestant attitudes toward iconography and saint worship as well as the psychological distancing of the Evangelicals from Coptic Orthodoxy.

When Andrew Watson wrote about the icon-burning incident in 1897, he berated the perpetrators by describing their deed as "injudicious" and "disgraceful"—and this, in spite of the disregard that American Presbyterians had for the veneration of images. Watson regretted that American and Spanish consuls had been drawn in to intervene for the youths, after they had first been arrested, judged, and sentenced to prison terms of one to three years, and concluded that their early release after a few months' hard labor was "certainly not in accordance with their deserts."[116] Meanwhile, J. R. Alexander, who arrived as a missionary in 1874 (five years after this incident occurred) and who published a short history of the Egyptian Evangelical Church in 1930, described the deed as the "utterly inexcusable" act of "misguided men" and wrote that they "deserved their punishment." Nevertheless, he noted approvingly that the incident had alerted Muslim law enforcement authorities to the idea that Christianity, as practiced by the Protestants, was "as much opposed to idolatry as Islam and the Kuran [sic]." Alexander also claimed that the episode had kindled in the Muslims of Assiut and adjoining provinces an interest in Christianity, and prompted several to buy Arabic Bibles.[117] Finally and by contrast, Earl E. Elder, who wrote a cumulative history of the mission in 1958, described the iconoclasm in tones of approval. Elder suggested that while the young men may have acted rashly, their aims were ultimately noble, since they wanted to purge church life of extraneous "non-Biblical" features. Elder added that the youths used their jail terms to sing psalms and to make the jail into a de facto "Protestant meeting place." Elder also claimed that the young men had only been sentenced to prison terms after the local Coptic Orthodox bishop threatened to turn Catholic unless justice were served, thereby prompting the Coptic Orthodox patriarch to press for quick action from the Muslim authorities.[118]

Strikingly, Watson, who witnessed the period of "Coptic persecution of native Protestants" first-hand, was very critical of the icon-burning incident and described the young men as vandals, whereas Elder, who wrote in 1958—a time when relations with Coptic Orthodoxy were improving amid the pressures of the Nasser era—was more supportive of the youths' behavior. Yet a fourth perspective came from a memoir published in 2000 by Hanna F. Wissa, whose Evangelical grandfather was one of the icon-burners. Wissa's family liked to think that Bamba, the mission protégé who married the Maharaja Dhulip Singh, asked Queen Victoria to intervene with the consuls to secure the young men's early release. Family legend thus connected the young men to the grand narrative of the mission in its age of empire.[119]

The year 1869 witnessed another, much more troubling event for the American missionaries. This was when one of their own, the Rev. B. F. Pinkerton, seceded from the Presbyterians along with a small group of Egyptian Evangelical pastors and followers from Upper Egyptian towns like Luxor and Mellawi. An observer might now call Pinkerton and his associates premillennialists (in that they emphasized Christ's imminent return) and pentecostalists (given that they let the spirit move them, spiritually and physically, during worship), but the American Presbyterians at the time lacked this vocabulary. Instead, Andrew Watson wrote that Pinkerton's behavior became increasingly erratic such that the other missionaries were at a loss for what to do. "Many of Mr. Pinkerton's motions, exclamations, remarks, sighs, and groans at family prayers, were not only new but often startling, and certainly led both Mrs. Watson and myself to conclude he was losing his mind," wrote Watson.[120] J. R. Alexander later added to this account, recording that Pinkerton had begun practicing faith healing and the laying of lands, and had been engaging in "ecstatic meditation and prayer" that was accompanied by "unusual bodily contortions."[121] According to both Watson and Alexander, the American missionaries greeted Pinkerton's voluntary resignation, on grounds of doctrinal difference, with relief, but their dismay mounted again five years later in 1874, when Pinkerton returned from a trip to the United States armed with funds and plans for organizing his church along the lines of the Plymouth Brethren movement.[122] Alexander wondered in 1930 whether the "beliefs and practices of Plymouthism" had struck a chord among Egyptian Christians, who, along with their peasant forebears, had suffered lives of poverty and hardship. He speculated that they may have welcomed Pinkerton's "jubilant conviction" that the Kingdom was coming. Did they believe, Alexander mused, that as brethren "they would all be equal in position and power, free from domination of Bishop or priest?"[123]

Pinkerton's schism remained traumatic to the Presbyterians because it persisted. (Indeed, some Plymouthite churches—a legacy of Pinkerton's movement—flourish in Egypt today, adding to the internal complexity of the small Egyptian Protestant population.)[124] While some missionaries regarded Pinkerton as deranged, others regarded his breakaway as a betrayal. Thus the missionary Rena Hogg asked in 1914, "How could a Christian deliberately set out on an enterprise whose inevitable outcome would be the creation of division among Christ's people? How could conscience demand his coming to teach to those who were already Christians in heart as well as in name, doctrines which, even had they been true, were of secondary importance, while millions around were living a starved life for lack of the great essential? How indeed could he reconcile his course with the most ordinary code of honour?"[125] Her plaints overlooked the sectarian divisions that the Presbyterians, like the other Protestant and Catholic missionaries, were sowing among Copts. Her objections also seem ironic, given that Presbyterian missionaries of the late nineteenth century were so ready to belittle or deny the Christian content of Coptic Orthodoxy as a way of justifying their Protestant reformation in Egypt.

The Pinkerton episode showed that while the American Presbyterians may have disliked the idea of papacy and episcopacy as a mode of organizing churches, they nevertheless had their own strong ideas about Christian decorum and protocol. For them, Pinkerton's ecstatic mode of worship went beyond the pale. Likewise, in the early twentieth century, the American Presbyterians frowned upon other Americans who trickled into Egypt as members of independent faith missions, including those who later became associated with Pentecostal movements.[126] American Presbyterian sources are as silent about these other evangelical Americans as they are about Roman Catholics, and their silence testifies to their opprobrium.

In 1870, the American Presbyterians decided that the Egyptian Evangelical Church had grown sufficiently to warrant greater autonomy in a system of Arabic-speaking congregations joined in a presbytery. They therefore decided to separate the American mission formally from the Egyptian Evangelical Church, and to cede presbyterial control to the latter. In good American fashion, they wrote a constitution to establish these principles of church government—a document that J. R. Alexander later hailed as a "Charter of Rights," and "unique among the missions in both the Near and the Far East," a document that "opened the way for the Evangelical Church of Egypt to become self-governing and independent." The only catch—and it remained a catch for many decades—was that the missionaries continued to hold the purse strings on money that came from the church in the United States. In 1871, following this reorganization, Arabic became the official language of Egyptian Evangelical affairs. Around this time, too, the church established the custom of giving Egyptian pastors fixed and regular salaries. Alexander praised this last development as an improvement over Coptic Orthodox custom, by which the priests sometimes had to beg for their livelihoods.[127] The provision of salaries, in any case, marked a professionalization of the Evangelical clergy.

In 1878, Khedive Tawfiq (the mild-mannered successor of Khedive Ismail) officially recognized the Protestant community of Egypt as a distinct Christian sect (ta'ifa).[128] This step was small but significant,

since it signaled the legal recognition of Egyptian Protestants as independent from Coptic Orthodoxy, and enabled them to establish
Protestant regulations for marriage and other personal status affairs. Since the Evangelical Church was (and still remains) the largest Protestant denomination in Egypt, the new arrangement gave
Evangelicals a leading role in Protestant dealings with the Egyptian
government.[129] Thus, in 1878, the young Evangelical Church reached
a state of institutional maturity.

CONCLUSION: A COPTIC REFORMATION?

In 1897, Edith L. Butcher, a British Anglican historian of Coptic Orthodoxy, praised English attempts to help the "National Church of Egypt"
instead of "adding to her troubles by attempts to proselytise among
her members." Her comment contained an oblique criticism of the
American Presbyterians who had drawn so many Coptic children into
their schools. Butcher went on to write that although members of the
CMS mission were grateful for the help that the Americans had given
them, these Britons "sincerely mourn the consequent spread amongst
the Egyptians of disloyalty and schism."[130] Another British Anglican,
the Rev. Montague Fowler, was even tetchier about the Americans. In
his overview of "Christian Egypt," published in 1902, he criticized the
American Presbyterians for alleging that Coptic Orthodox schools—
as well as Greek Orthodox and Catholic schools—were being established to compete with American mission institutions. He implied,
in other words, that the Americans had inflated opinions about their
own impact. Fowler also criticized the American missionaries for in-
citing dissension among Copts and dismissing the Christian foundations of Coptic Orthodoxy. Such assertions, he remarked, indicated
that the American missionaries were "lamentably wanting in the true
spirit of Christianity." Noting that the Evangelical Church was growing, Fowler insinuated that he sympathized with the Coptic Orthodox
patriarch's decision to excommunicate Copts who turned Protestant.
"In the opinion of many who are closely acquainted with the conditions of Christianity in Egypt," he added, "the danger to the cause of
Christ arising from systematic proselytising among the Copts is very
great." Fowler suggested, finally, that the Americans had misplaced
goals, and that they should not be making Copts into Presbyterians
when there were so many Egyptian Muslims to convert.[131]

In suggesting that the Americans' claims regarding intersectarian competition were merely the product of a puffed-up self-image,
Fowler was wrong. Others sensed the contest as well. Writing in

1894 about "Catholic France in Egypt," a French writer named Victor Guérin surveyed the Roman Catholic mission schools of Lower Egypt and paused to consider the Jesuit School of the Holy Family in the Muski district of Cairo. Guérin wrote that this school was founded in 1879, expressly approved by Pope Leo XIII, "with the goal of forming among the Coptic nation a clergy destined to maintain Coptic Catholics in the faith, to convert schismatic Copts, and to combat the progress of Protestantism in Upper Egypt." While the school educated a wide range of students in the French-language medium, its special aim was to educate Uniate Copts from Upper Egypt, to train them as teachers, and then to send them back to Upper Egypt, where they could "present a powerful and effective competition (*une concurrence puissante et efficace*) against the American and English Protestants."[132]

For the Coptic Orthodox community, the sense of competition with foreign missionaries was acute. According to the historian Brigitte Voile, the missionaries' "new vision of Christianity" led to one of the major upheavals (*bouleversements*) in modern Coptic history. (Two other upheavals were the disintegration of Coptic village life through urbanization and the "emancipation of the Copts," symbolized by the abolition of the *jizya* tax in 1855).[133] Certainly the harshness of the Orthodox Church's reprisals against Coptic Evangelicals during the 1860s and 1870s testified to these feelings of threat, as did the church's efforts to open Coptic Orthodox communal schools during this same period. According to J. Heyworth-Dunne, a British convert to Islam who in 1938 published a now classic history of modern education in Egypt, Coptic Orthodox educational expansion during the reign of Khedive Ismail was "undoubtedly spurred on by the increasing influence of the American Missionaries in Cairo and Upper Egypt."[134]

In *Two Thousand Years of Coptic Christianity* (1999), the historian Otto Meinardus presents some details of what the Coptic Orthodox reaction to the missionary challenge entailed. Observing that Coptic theological studies lapsed into "almost complete silence" in the 1400s, he notes that theological production waxed anew in the eighteenth century, when Orthodox Church scholars "became more and more concerned with the proselytizing work of the Catholic Church." The field grew more vibrant in the nineteenth century, following what Meinardus calls "the introduction of the printing press by Cyril IV" when Coptic lay intellectuals began to publish works on doctrine and faith. A seminal work of the latter type was called *The Glittering Pearl of the Divine Mysteries*, which "attacked the Protestant theology of the American Presbyterian Mission in Egypt."[135]

Meinardus calls the second half of the nineteenth century a period of "the Coptic Enlightenment" and in so doing follows a path traced by leading Coptic Orthodox thinkers of that period—among them Marcus Simeika, founder of the Coptic Museum in Cairo.[136] One of the prime features of this "enlightenment," as understood by Coptic Orthodox historians, was the development of a laymen's movement that convened the first Coptic communal council, called the Majlis al-Milli, in 1874. This council contained elected representatives who intended, in the euphemistic words of Meinardus, to "share with the patriarchate the burden of supervising the financial and civil affairs of the Copts."[137] Otherwise phrased, the Majlis al-Milli represented an attempt among educated Coptic Orthodox laymen to assert their voice in the running of church affairs; it posed a challenge to the ecclesiastical hegemony of the patriarch and his bishops.

In its conception and scope, the Majlis al-Milli resembled the Evangelical Church's presbyterial structure—and this resemblance was no accident. In a historical and sociological study of the Coptic Orthodox Church, published in 2003, S. S. Hasan observes that "The reaffirmation of the will of the people in church affairs, in modern times, was largely influenced by the example of the American Presbyterian churches in Upper Egypt, which were run democratically." She also suggests that the Protestants posed an even greater threat to Coptic Orthodoxy than did the Roman Catholics: "However much the Orthodox Church objected to the Catholics, their fiercest ire was reserved for the Protestants. The latter were far more aggressive in competing for converts and were scornful of Orthodox ritual, in a way that the more traditional Catholics were not." For this reason, she explains, "The label *Protestant* remains a damning epithet to this day in Orthodox circles."[138]

By working among poor and marginal groups, ranging from orphans to garbage collectors, Protestant and Catholic missionaries also challenged the Coptic Orthodox Church by setting examples for public service.[139] Coptic Orthodox leaders responded by directing new attention not only to elite school-goers but also to the Coptic poor. Efforts that began in 1881 with the establishment of the Coptic Benevolent Society (a society founded, according to the historian Mine Ener, in response to Protestant and Catholic missions) set the foundations for the church's twentieth-century social welfare endeavors.[140]

Paul Sedra has recently argued that the nineteenth-century Coptic "enlightenment," sometimes called the Coptic *nahda* or "awakening," was inextricably tied to foreign missionary interventions. Sedra focuses primarily on the educational methods and programs of British missionaries and their associates in Egypt, and emphasizes their role in propagating a culture of literacy, textual authority, and print culture among nineteenth-century Copts.[141] He suggests that by stimulating popular interest among Copts in the history and traditions of Egyptian Christianity, missionaries helped seed the growth of a modern Coptic cultural or ethnoreligious consciousness—a kind of "Coptism" or "Copticity"—linked to a communally directed sense of social responsibility.[142]

Egyptian Evangelicals participated in this burgeoning Egyptian Christian print culture of the late nineteenth century. Writing in 1925, the missionary J. R. Alexander noted that the work of the missions and the American and British Bible societies had helped spread the Arabic Bible, so that whereas few Christian families had owned a copy of the Bible when the Americans began their work in Egypt in 1854, few families lacked one fifty years later. Alexander remarks that "The Evangelical community, directly and indirectly, has made the Coptic community, next to itself, the best educated and most enlightened part of the population." He notes, too, that Copts were beginning to open their own schools and to promote Bible study, which led to a kind of internal process of evangelization: "Through these various agencies a strong reformation is going on within the Coptic Church and among the Coptic people."[143]

Alexander's words from 1925 reveal an identity shift that had either occurred or was occurring, for he drew an implicit distinction between Egyptian Evangelicals and Copts. The term "Copt," at its core, can simply refer to one of the autochthonous Christian peoples of Egypt (to which indeed the word "Egypt," from the Latin *Aegyptus* via the Greek *Aigyptos*, is related). But at a time when missionaries had made the Egyptian Christian scene more complex, Alexander used the term "Copt" in 1925 to imply affinity only to the Egyptian Orthodox Church. For Alexander, Evangelicals were no longer Copts, even though the vast majority of those who joined the Protestants were indigenous Christians of Egypt. Anecdotal evidence suggests that Evangelicals came to feel this difference as well and at some point began to call themselves *Injiliyyun* (Evangelicals) rather than *Aqbat* (Copts). Their late nineteenth-century excommunications from Coptic Orthodoxy, the trauma of having been denied rites of marriage or burial in family plots, and their treatment as "pariahs"[144] by Coptic Orthodox loyalists and church authorities had made Evangelicals feel that their turn to Protestantism meant an end to their Copticity.

To an observer now viewing the history of the American mission in Egypt against the expanse of the late nineteenth and twentieth centuries, British Anglican fears that American missionaries would weaken the Coptic community appear to have been unfounded.[145] For while American Presbyterian missionaries, along with their Roman Catholic and British evangelical counterparts, did help make Egyptian Christian culture more pluralistic, the Coptic Orthodox Church emerged in the long run from the missionary contest for Copts looking stronger, more culturally vibrant, and more confident than ever before. It did so even as small but thriving Protestant and Catholic churches appeared. Perhaps, then, the American missionaries did help effect something of a Coptic reformation, as they had originally hoped, even if Coptic Orthodox leaders were inclined in moments of bad temper to dismiss the changes that the American missionaries wrought as a "Protestant deformation" of Coptic tradition.[146]

In short, the arrival of the American missionaries meant that Copts gained a new choice in how they would live and practice their Christianity. This element of choice then compelled Coptic leaders of all sectarian backgrounds to rise to the challenge of maintaining allegiances in a competitive market of Christian ideas. The result, in the end, was a rejuvenated and more pluralistic culture of Egyptian Christianity.

CHAPTER 3

The Colonial Moment of the American Mission, 1882–1918

Listen to these statistics. Statistics, did I say? They are the tracings of the finger of God.
—Rev. J. K. M'Clurkin, in United Presbyterian Church of North America, *Foreign Missionary Jubilee Convention of the United Presbyterian Church of N.A.* (1905)

The present political division of the Mohammedan world is a startling evidence of the finger of God in history and an unprecedented missionary challenge to the churches of Christendom.
—Samuel M. Zwemer, *Islam: A Challenge to Faith* (1907)

The Christian conquest of Egypt is no holiday task.
—Charles R. Watson, *Egypt and the Christian Crusade* (1907)

THE PERIOD FROM 1882 to 1918 was an important chapter in modern Egypt, the British Empire, and the Anglo-American Protestant missionary movement. It began with Britain's invasion and occupation of Egypt, and ended with the closure of World War I and the defeat of the Ottoman Empire. Egyptians had to face in 1882 the onset of de facto colonial rule and in 1918 a future in a post-Ottoman world where the symbolic geographic unity of Muslims was gone; the consequences for the formation of Egyptian nationalism were enormous.[1] These were also years when Britain reached its imperial apogee by asserting new territorial claims, particularly in Africa,[2] and when American and British missions experienced an upsurge in ambition and scope. Women were increasingly joining, funding, and setting priorities for missions, while donations to missions were soaring.[3] At the same time, drawing on a slogan that became associated after 1886 with the college- and university-based Student Volunteer Movement (SVM) for missions in the United States as well as its counterpart movement in Britain, many American and British mission supporters embraced the idea that "the evangelization of the world in this generation" would be feasible as never before.[4] These were years when American

and British missionaries gained the confidence to turn their attention to Muslims. By 1900, missionaries were even identifying Egypt
as a "strategic center" for Muslim evangelization worldwide, reasoning that as the home of the venerable university mosque of al-Azhar,
Cairo was a bastion of Sunni Islam.[5]

Bold, brash, and expansive, the spirit of missionary evangelism resembled the spirit of British imperialism in this period and infused
the work of the American Presbyterians in Egypt. However, to say
that missionaries shared the aggressive rhetoric of British imperialism is not to say that missions and the British Empire were wholly co-
terminous or mutually supporting.[6] For a start, in Egypt as elsewhere
in the Muslim world, British authorities often regarded missionaries
as nuisances, more to be appeased and distracted than supported.
Lord Cromer, consul-general of Egypt from 1882 to 1907, was known
for his lukewarm opinions about missionaries and their projects, and
in the Sudan tried to distract missionaries toward work in the south
and away from predominantly Muslim northern regions, where he
believed that missionaries might spark a Muslim anti-British rebellion.[7] Moreover, missionaries themselves reflected a considerable
degree of multinational diversity and this makes it difficult to place
them within the scheme of British imperialism. In Egypt, Americans
and to a lesser extent other non-British Protestants (such as Swedish
and Dutch missionaries) were able to embark on evangelical projects under the British umbrella. So were Catholic missionaries, even
if their relationship to Britain (a nation that had depended largely on
Protestantism for its invention)[8] was ambivalent.

In the late nineteenth century, when the U.S. government had only
a modest diplomatic presence in the Middle East, American missionaries occasionally looked to the British government and its consuls
for protection and help. Like the American Presbyterian missionaries
working in India, American missionaries in the Middle East regarded
Britain as an ally of the Protestant cause and cheered its advances, in
spite of the moral failings that in their view marked so many British
soldiers and civilians in imperial service.[9] Thus American missionaries in Beirut applauded Britain's bombardment of Alexandria in
1882 and greeted the Occupation (in the words of one missionary) as
"another phase of the great, inevitable conflict between Christianity
and Mohammedanism."[10] Likewise, American missionaries in Egypt
praised the beneficence of British rule. In an account addressed to
American churchgoers in 1907, Charles R. Watson, the secretary of
the United Presbyterian foreign mission board, praised the British
invasion of Egypt in 1882 for saving local Christians from Muslim
mobs, and went on to hail the "magnificent British administration"

for promoting Egyptian prosperity and progress in the years that followed.[11]

However, unlike the British CMS missionaries, who returned to Egypt on the heels of the 1882 invasion intending to concentrate exclusively on Muslims, the Americans began to reach out to Muslims even as they continued work among Copts. Indeed, after 1882 the Egyptian Evangelical Church experienced its period of greatest growth, drawing as before the vast majority of its members from Coptic Orthodoxy. Meanwhile, in 1899, following the Anglo-Egyptian conquest of the Sudan, the American Presbyterians expanded southward along the Nile. From Egypt they helped organize Evangelical congregations among Egyptian Christian expatriates in northern Sudan (especially Khartoum), and soon sent missionaries into southern regions where they began to preach among Shilluk and Nuer peoples who practiced local religions.[12] British power made it possible for the American Presbyterians to expand their activities in the Nile Valley with some sense of official protection, and yet the relationship of the missionaries to the empire was of limited relevance in day-to-day work.

In the new *Oxford History of the British Empire* (1999), Andrew Porter argues that "It is . . . impossible to speak in any straightforward way of 'religious', 'ecclesiastical' or 'missionary' Imperialism. Such hard-and-fast categories are almost meaningless." Rather than having been complicit in the empire's aggressive maneuvers, Porter contends, missionaries were often critics of British colonial policies and supporters of society's underdogs—popular advocates, not imperial power-mongers. Reflecting the spirit of recent research on the history of Christian missions and non-Western Christianity, Porter also suggests that missionaries in British imperial territories delivered Christian ideas, which people then reworked to meet their own needs and conditions.[13]

These ideas of choice and cultural autonomy in the missionary encounter may be apropos for regions like sub-Saharan Africa where the "large-scale adoption of Christianity has been one of the master themes" of the region's modern history,[14] and where the turn to Christianity entailed a move from many local and oral culture–based religions into a global and more textually based Christian order.[15] But this benign reading of missionary history is harder to sustain in the case of evangelization among Muslims, particularly during this 1882-to-1918 period of Britain's "New" or high imperialism. In places like Cairo, Tehran, and Lucknow, many Christian missionaries described their missions to Muslims as a return to, or fulfillment of, the twelfth- and thirteenth-century Crusades, and propounded the idea that Islamic societies were backward, ignorant, and poised to disintegrate.[16]

Missionaries in this period were leading proponents of Orientalism: a set of discourses that asserted the corruption and weakness of the Islamic world in order to justify intervention (military, economic, cultural) in its affairs.[17]

It is hard to avoid the term "imperial Christianity" in the context of missions to Muslims during this period because, far from extolling a gentle "gospel of love" (to borrow a phrase used by a later generation of missionaries), American and British missionaries described evangelization, very clearly and on many occasions, as war. They used such rhetoric even while many of their actions—providing free health care in clinics, raising orphans, and so on—demonstrated peaceful forms of social engagement. Muslims in Egypt and other parts of the Arabic-speaking world eventually became aware of this rhetoric, and from about 1930 onward increasingly commented on it. By the end of the twentieth century, some Muslim writers were still commenting on it by pointing to the words and deeds of Protestant missionaries from the era of high imperialism as proof of the implacable hostility of Western Christians to Muslims.[18] Far from associating colonial evangelism with the proliferation of religious free choice, therefore, many Muslims looked back on the age of British high imperialism as an age of cultural onslaught on Muslims. One Muslim critic expressed this sentiment in 1993 by suggesting that Christian missionaries made Muslims doubt their beliefs, civilization, and future, and thereby delivered psychological and spiritual blows that still bruise the Arab world.[19]

Formal British rule over many parts of Africa was so brief within the span of the continent's history that one can arguably call it a "colonial moment."[20] One can speak of a colonial moment in Christian missions as well, as American and British missionaries spread around the world in tandem with British imperialism—and sometimes even edged into the domains of other empires, such as France's North and West African territories. In this period, missionaries often adopted discourses of military expansion—a language of "occupation," mission "fronts," and spiritual weaponry.[21]

Four salient developments occurred in the American mission in Egypt during the "missionary moment" of 1882 to 1918. The first entailed the growth of missionary interest in Muslim conversion—a phenomenon that was central to missionary attitudes toward Christian universality, religious liberty, and belief as a matter of individual choice. The second entailed the growth of the Evangelical Church, largely at the expense of Coptic Orthodoxy. The third related to the mobilization of the American church, which increasingly relied both at home in the United States and abroad in places like Egypt on the energy and commitment of women. The fourth was the growth of Protestant ecumenism, meaning in practice, increased cooperation on the ground between the Americans and their British counterparts. As the twentieth century opened, missionary "statesmen"—leaders in church diplomacy—harnessed this budding ecumenical movement to the cause of missions to Muslims.

THE STATUS OF CHRISTIANS IN EGYPT AND THE CHANGING NATURE OF "DHIMMITUDE"

Reflecting on the status of non-Muslims in 1854, when the American Presbyterians began their mission in Egypt, Andrew Watson noted that Christians and Jews in Egypt had been able to practice their religions and to pursue livelihoods. But that was as good as it got. Otherwise, "the Muslim was everything, before God, before the kadi [Islamic court judge], and before the civil ruler. Christianity and Judaism only existed by a kind of sufferance, and their professors were the objects of opprobrium, hate and ridicule." Watson praised Said Pasha, the grandson of Muhammad Ali who ruled Egypt at that time, for facilitating the missionaries' educational work by providing them with land grants for building schools. But he had nothing good to say about the *'ulama*, the Muslim religious scholars, as a whole. "The mosques were generally the hotbeds of fanaticism," he recorded, "and the sheikhs and learned men were the foremost in opposing the kind treatment of other religionists. The usual manner of speaking of the Christian then was to call him 'that Christian pig'; and the Jew, 'that dog of a Jew.' The title deed of property bought by either Jew or Christian in its description of the buyer used to run thus: 'So and so, the damned, the son of So and So, the damned.'"[22]

The Arabic language had a special term to describe a non-Muslim in an Islamic society like Egypt—a society that was ruled, as Egypt had been since the seventh century, by an Islamic state. The term was "dhimmi," and although Watson did not use it, the situation that he described—including name-calling of Christians as pigs[23]—fit into a recognizable range that one could call "dhimmitude" (that is, the quality, experience, or state of being a non-Muslim in an Islamic domain).[24] The term "dhimmi" (a non-Muslim person) was related, in turn, to the term "dhimma," loosely meaning a pact of protection. Although *dhimma* may have originally had a neutral meaning in the Qur'an and hadith (traditions about the Prophet Muhammad and his companions), suggesting a moral obligation of stewardship for all humankind, the term evolved to carry specific assumptions about non-Muslims.[25] These assumptions became associated with a text of murky provenance called the Pact of Umar, which has usually been ascribed to the caliph 'Umar ibn al-Khattab (r. 634–44), but sometimes to the Umayyad caliph 'Umar ibn 'Abd al-'Aziz (r. 717–20). (In fact, the Pact of Umar appears to have been a legal composite, and may have owed elements to both men.)[26] In the centuries that followed the early Islamic conquests beyond Arabia, the term "ahl al-dhimma"—"the people of the pact"—came to suggest a condition whereby Jews and Christians lived under the authority of Islamic regimes. They were allowed to practice their faiths and pursue livelihoods—much as Watson described it—provided that they recognized the supremacy of Islamic rule and remained loyal to it. Other conditions became attached to their status as *dhimmis* as well. Christians and Jews became subject to a special poll tax, or *jizya*, that was originally meant to contribute toward the cost of defending the Muslim polity (for in fact, *dhimmis* were allowed neither to bear arms nor to serve in Muslim armies). Christians and Jews could not build or repair places of worship without securing permission from Muslim authorities. Christians and Jews were welcome to convert to Islam and to achieve thereby the full social status of Muslims, but they were not allowed to convert between Christianity and Judaism. More generally, those who were born into Islam (as the children of a Muslim father) or who converted to Islam were not allowed to leave its fold or profess disbelief. The reasoning behind this Islamic doctrine was that belief in God was imperative, and that Muhammad had been the last in a long line of prophets, including Jesus, Moses, and others, so that the Qur'an superseded Judaism and Christianity as a more accurate and complete articulation of God's will. In theory, the penalty for Muslim apostasy—usually following opportunities to recant—was death.[27]

In the past twenty-five years, Western historians have vigorously debated the nature of *dhimmi* life in Muslim states, and especially in the Ottoman Empire and Alawid Morocco (which had a large Jewish minority). They have scrutinized the centuries before the rise of the modern nation-state introduced the theoretically egalitarian and religion-blind notion of citizens. Interest in *dhimmi* life has been particularly strong among Jewish historians, who have written in the aftermath of the creation of Israel in 1948 and the dispersion of Jews who lived in Islamic territories. Jewish historians have been deeply divided over the extent to which the "Jews of Islam" flourished or languished under Muslim rule, even though they have generally agreed that Jews in the Islamic world were never persecuted like the Jews of Christian Europe.[28] Their dispute hinges around the degree of humiliation or disability that Jews faced as non-Muslims and the extent to which Jews really *belonged*—that is, not so much how Muslim majorities regarded or treated them but rather how Jews felt about their own life, history, and place among Muslim majorities. This debate may never reach closure because the goal of its striving is so elusive within Middle Eastern history. It involves an attempt to gauge what Bruce Masters has called the degree of "psychological distance" that divided Muslims, Christians, and Jews, the quality of social contact among them, and the question of whether there was much more "to draw them together, beyond commerce or natural disasters."[29]

Debates involving the place of Christians in Islamic history have tended to be less anguished than those regarding Jews, since Christians of the Islamic world (with the notable exception of the Armenians and Assyrians) either remained rooted in the nation-states that emerged from the Ottoman Empire and Iran, or voluntarily emigrated, mostly to Europe, the Americas, and Australia.[30] In the Arab world, Christians also carved out niches in Arab nationalist movements while acknowledging a cultural affinity with Arab-Islamic society. Consider, for example, Michel Aflaq (1910–1989), who was born in Damascus to a Greek Orthodox family and became an ideological founder of the secular pan-Arab Ba'th Party.

Until social circumstances began to change in the nineteenth century, the Copts of Egypt, like Jewish and other Christian *dhimmi* populations throughout the Islamic world, paid the *jizya*, were theoretically barred from military service, and occupied a socially subordinate position relative to Muslims. Yet however disadvantaged the Copts were in Egypt (with opinions varying on this question considerably),[31] they enjoyed a degree of cultural confidence as Egyptians because they traced their roots to the indigenous, pre-Islamic population of the country. They had not been dispersed, nor had they migrated from afar. Rather, Copts lived, as their forebears had done, along the banks of one river, the Nile; they were of the land. The Monophysite creed regarding Christ's nature, which exposed the Copts to Byzantine persecution in the late fifth, sixth, and early seventh centuries, had become a linchpin for a collective identity rooted in Egypt.[32] This experience of persecution by Byzantine Christian authorities tempered any sense of solidarity that Copts might have had with other Christian populations in what became the Islamic empire, and consolidated their identification with Egypt. For all these reasons, Copticity (meaning the quality, state, or consciousness of being a Copt) extended quite smoothly into modern Egyptian nationality, while Coptic historians found space in an emerging Egyptian nationalist history by describing the Copts as a cultural link bridging pharaonic and Islamic Egypt.[33]

Modern histories written by Egyptians have often reflected this interweaving of Coptic communal history with great events of the Egyptian nation. Studies have commemorated, for example, Coptic opposition to the Napoleonic invasion of 1798 and British Occupation of 1882, and Coptic support for the 1919 nationalist uprisings against Britain, as well as the 1967 and 1973 wars against Israel.[34] Copts have also shared Egypt's cultural triumphs. Thus, as one writer has noted, the Coptic patriarch Shenouda III held a "papal celebration" (*ihtifal babawi*) in 1988 when the (Muslim) novelist Naguib Mahfouz won the Nobel Prize in Literature.[35] Yet in the present-day context where Islamist politicians have occasionally called for a return to an Islamic order in which Christians should function as *dhimmi*s, Copts of all sectarian backgrounds have begun to speak up for their citizenship in Egypt—a citizenship that assumes equality with Muslims in terms of civic rights and duties, ranging from national defense to the payment of taxes.[36] Some Muslim intellectuals have lent strong support to this vision of Egypt. Thus the rationale raised in one recent affirmation of unity—in this case by an Egyptian Muslim writing in a volume on "the national role of the Egyptian church across the centuries"—is that Copts and Muslims are "one family" (*usra wahida*) "joined by the unity of land, of goal, and of destiny."[37]

The fact is that for Copts (as for other Middle Eastern Christians and for Jews) the idea of the citizen (*muwatin* in Arabic) is now highly valued, whereas the term "dhimmi" has developed very negative connotations, suggesting a state of humiliation and debility, and not of benign Muslim protection. Thus no matter how natural or ineluctable *dhimmi* status may once have seemed as part of the Islamic social order, and no matter how rosy a picture historians can draw of intersectarian relations in the nineteenth century and before, one would have trouble today finding a Copt who wants to make an official return to "dhimmitude."

THE HATT-I HUMAYUN, RELIGIOUS EQUALITY, AND INTERCOMMUNAL RELATIONS IN EGYPT

An examination of the Hatt-i Humayun, one of the landmark decrees of the Ottoman Empire's Tanzimat ("Reorganization") era, shows the extreme difficulty of assessing Muslim-Christian relations and the nature of dhimmitude in the second half of the nineteenth century. Issued in 1856, the Hatt-i Humayun expanded on an earlier reformist edict, the Hatt-i Sherif of Gülhane of 1839, by promising legal equality for all Ottoman subjects, Muslims, Christians, and "other non-Muslims," "without distinction of classes or religion."[38] In the twentieth century, Western historians of the Middle East hailed these edicts as watersheds that recognized Ottoman peoples as individual citizens and that eliminated the "millet system," by which the Ottoman government had conceived of and interacted with society as a cluster of religious communities, or *millets*.[39] Meanwhile, Protestant missionaries in the Middle East remembered the Hatt-i Humayun as an edict that was intended to open doors not only to religious equality but also to religious liberty, which they interpreted as religious free choice.[40] The edict certainly helped set the tone of expectation that buoyed American Presbyterian missionaries during their first half century in Egypt.

In his chronicle of the CMS published in 1899, Eugene Stock claimed that Britain had pressed for this edict after a series of reprisals against individuals who had been deemed Muslim apostates. One incident occurred in 1843, when "an Armenian and a Greek, who had been lured . . . into professing Mohammedanism, but who had recanted and again embraced Christianity, had been beheaded." Other incidents occurred in 1852 and 1853 when two men, both converts from Islam to Christianity, were executed as apostates in Aleppo and Adrianople. In 1855, Lord Clarendon mentioned these specific incidents while discussing Britain's defense of "Turkey" against Russia in the Crimean War. According to Stock, Clarendon declared that "The Christian Powers are entitled to demand, and Her Majesty's Government to distinctly demand, that no punishment whatever shall attach to the Mohammedan who becomes a Christian, whether originally a Mohammedan or originally a Christian, any more than any punishment attaches to a Christian who embraces Mohammedanism."[41]

In *Christians and Jews in the Ottoman Arab World* (2001), Bruce Masters writes that the Hatt-i Humayun, on the one hand, "dismantled the legal hierarchy governing the relations between Muslims and non-Muslims established by the Pact of 'Umar with the blunt justification that such steps were necessary to save the empire." But on the other hand, the decree "sounded better on paper than was the reality of its implementation in the provinces."[42] British government records show that two years after the decree was issued, a British diplomat reported his visit to the sultan where he expressed "a widespread feeling of disappointment, and almost of despair," that was spreading in Europe over the fact that so "little had been done in execution of the Hatti-Humayoun [sic] since its promulgation."[43] This diplomat's observation indicated that the decree may have been designed more to appeal to or placate European consuls, who were pressuring the sultan for reforms, than to reconfigure intercommunal relations on the ground. Coming at the close of the Crimean War, the decree may have also represented an imperial tactic to preserve the loyalty of non-Muslims in the Balkans and to bolster goodwill from Britain and France, whose leaders were inclined to ward off Russian expansion into Ottoman domains for the sake of maintaining the balance of powers. In a survey of Ottoman history after 1700, Donald Quataert suggests that the Hatt-i Humayun had two other motives as well. It sought, first, to enlarge Ottoman armies by granting Christians "universal rights"—and duties—in order to add them to the pool of potential conscripts, and second, to create a uniform law code for all Ottoman subjects so as "to bring Christians who had become protégés of foreign states back under the jurisdiction of the Ottoman state and its legal system."[44] Quataert is referring to the way local Christian merchants in the nineteenth century had increasingly sought out the protection of European consuls, gained access to the series of legal and fiscal rights known as the Capitulations, and thereby moved beyond the judicial scope of Ottoman authorities.

The Hatt-i Humayun may have only worsened intercommunal relations—to the extent that Muslims became aware of it—by heightening Muslim popular resentment toward local Christians who were moving up in society on the rising tide of European influence.[45] (Indeed, along these lines, Eugene Stock claimed that in Nablus, one of the few towns where the edict was publicized, "riots broke out" in which "the [CMS] Mission-school and agent's house were destroyed with perfect immunity.")[46] Ottoman Christians had been finding new economic opportunities as middlemen in the burgeoning trade with Europe, and new educational opportunities in missionary schools. In the nineteenth century, they had embraced European ideas—many of them a variation on the French revolutionary theme of *liberté, egalité, fraternité*—that were also beginning to influence emergent cadres of Ottoman Muslim (including Egyptian) educated elites. Rank-and-file Muslims may have therefore felt that Christians were forgetting their proper place in an Islamic milieu. Thus the Hatt-i Humayun may have terminated *dhimmi* status as an official legal category without abolishing dhimmitude as a social construct that shaped popular attitudes.

In Egypt, the Hatt-i Humayun may have become more important in retrospect than it was at the time of its issue. Missionaries certainly remembered it. Thus, for example, when the missionary Earl E. Elder wrote a history of the American mission in 1958, he included the story of a Coptic woman who had married a Muslim man and had embraced Islam "for worldly gain," but then wanted, in 1861, to revert to Christianity. Elder mentions that Faris al-Hakim, a Syrian former priest and Protestant evangelist working in Upper Egypt, had nurtured the expectation that the Ottoman "decree of religious liberty" would have some bearing to help with her case, and the missionaries thought so, too.[47] Elder implies that the decree did not help her because a new sultan ascended the throne in 1861 and chose to ignore it.

Strikingly, Iris Habib al-Misri, a leading Egyptian historian of Coptic Orthodoxy who wrote books in the third quarter of the twentieth century, neither mentions the Hatt-i Humayun explicitly nor discusses the elimination of restrictions on *dhimmis*. In 1978, writing Coptic history in the patriotic mode, she instead described the nineteenth-century liberalization of the Coptic condition as an "emancipation from the many Ottoman-imposed restrictions and discriminations." In other words, she blamed the Ottoman Turks (branding them "despotic and tyrannous" rulers) for applying restrictive policies toward non-Muslims, and then praised the modern Egyptian government, beginning in the Muhammad Ali era, for lifting them.[48] In this regard, her book *The Story of the Copts* (a 584-page English abridgment of her multivolume Arabic opus on "the story of the Coptic Church") serves as a reminder that nationalism's pact with history may depend as much on forgetting the past as remembering it.[49] In this case, al-Misri chose to forget or ignore the fact that restrictions on Copts, as a feature of Islamic state policy toward non-Muslims, arose soon after the Islamic conquest of Egypt in 639–42 and predated Ottoman claims to Egypt (1517–1914) by almost nine hundred years.

As the twentieth century ended, Egyptian intellectuals were approaching the question of Coptic citizenship more frankly and were discussing the Hatt-i Humayun decree as a matter of continuing relevance. Their frank appraisals became possible, and assumed new importance, after the regime of Anwar Sadat (r. 1970–81), the Egyptian president who fanned flames of Egyptian sectarian discord while pursuing a disastrous policy of cultivating Islamists.[50] Writing in 1990, the literary and social critic Ghali Shukri connected al-Khatt al-Humayuni (as the Ottoman Turkish decree is known in Arabic) to the liberalizing decrees of Said Pasha (the grandson of Muhammad Ali who ruled Egypt as Ottoman governor). In the mid-1850s, Said had permitted Copts into military service and formally revoked (or in Arabic, "lifted," *rafa'a*)[51] the *jizya* payment for *dhimmis* (which Copts had apparently not paid since 1815 anyway).[52] But Ghali Shukri also pointed to the edict's unfulfilled message of equality—a message compromised, in his view, by the Egyptian politicians who, in 1934, accepted the Humayuni decree but added a list of "Ten Conditions" (al-Shurut al-'Ashara) to restrict the building and repair of churches in Egypt.

In fact, the Hatt-i Humayun had specifically addressed the issue of church building and repairing, by promising that each Christian sect would be able to present its plans for consideration and approval to the Sublime Porte (as Europeans called the Ottoman central government). In other words, the edict had promised good, fair, and efficient government from officials who would "take energetic measures to insure to each sect, whatever be the number of its adherents, entire freedom in the exercise of its religion."[53] The Egyptian government's "Ten Conditions" of 1934 clarified and in practice restricted the edict's words in a post-Ottoman context. These "Ten Conditions," which remain in force in Egypt today, make church building contingent on lack of proximity to mosques and to Muslim populations; the fourth condition even asks whether any Muslims object to a proposed church's construction.[54] (In other words, the stipulations of 1934 guided the law back toward the restrictions on *dhimmi*s that are associated with the Pact of Umar.) Likewise, in a report on the Copts prepared for a human rights group in 1996, the Egyptian sociologist Saad Eddin Ibrahim and his coauthors specifically cited the "Hamiyouni [*sic*] Decree" of 1856 in relation to the "Ten Conditions" for church building of 1934. The authors pointed to ongoing restrictions and hassles that Christians faced in getting government permits for churches, in a context where Muslims faced no comparable restrictions for mosques.[55]

The American Presbyterians began their work in Egypt two years after the issuance of the Humayun decree. And yet, the social climate that Andrew Watson described in his mission chronicle was not one of tolerance and communal harmony. On the contrary, writing in the 1890s about the 1860s and 1870s, Watson suggested that Muslims in Egypt had inflicted a "reign of terror" on local Christians by engaging in chronic intimidation and petty assault.[56] At the same time, he wrote, Muslim sensibilities made it hard for members of the growing Evangelical Church to get government-issued church-building permits. Recalling the 1870s, Watson noted that "no Christian church can be erected in Egypt without a license (though no permission was then required to build grog shops or houses of ill-fame)."[57] Watson suggested that the climate of Muslim hostility reached a peak in 1882 during the popular movement and uprising associated with the Egyptian military officer Ahmad 'Urabi (also known as 'Arabi), when growing animosity toward European merchants and consuls in Alexandria and Cairo combined with what he described as a primordial Muslim contempt for Christians. Watson wrote that when touring Egypt in the winter of 1882–83, he found that, as far south as Aswan, "it was the universal belief among native Christians that unless the British troops had reached Cairo [in September 1882] there would have been a general massacre of them, and a division of their property among the [Muslim] 'believers'. From what is known of Muhammadan fanaticism and hatred in such circumstances," he added, "that is what might have been expected. Many reported that they could hear their Muhammadan neighbors talking together about the division of property of the native Christians."[58] In the same spirit, Archdeacon Dowling of the Anglican Church in Jerusalem claimed more succinctly in 1909 that the Copts "know that if England had not stepped in to suppress the rebellion of Arabi [sic] Pasha, they would have been massacred wholesale."[59] In short, Watson and his missionary colleagues in Egypt later remembered the British Occupation of 1882 as a culminating moment in a history, not of Muslim tolerance toward local Christians but the opposite: what Dowling calls thirteen centuries of Muslim "evils and disabilities" imposed on Copts.[60]

However, the two decades preceding Britain's invasion were also years of growing European economic and diplomatic intervention. Khedive Ismail took loans from European bankers in order to make Cairo into a Paris along the Nile. His extravagance led the Egyptian government to bankruptcy in 1876, and prompted him to sell all of Egypt's shares in the Suez Canal Company to Britain. This sale did not succeed in staving off bankruptcy but became a source of continuing chagrin among Egyptians who believed that Egypt deserved revenues from the canal that cut through its territory. Meanwhile, European bankers stepped in, seized control of government coffers, and called for new taxes for defraying the loans. The rural peasantry and urban laboring classes staggered under these taxes. In their economic distress, the masses lent support to Ahmad 'Urabi, an army officer who called for the end of foreign control and the liberalization of government.

The Urabi Revolt, as the swirl of events that accompanied Ahmad 'Urabi's rise to influence is known, assumed a nativist expression of Egyptian nationalism, taking "Egypt for the Egyptians" as its slogan. Yet while leading historians have scrutinized the Urabi Revolt—in the process cataloguing its elements of class conflict, anti-foreign sentiment, incipient nationalism, changing forms of mass communications, and the like—they have not identified intercommunal religious conflict as a major theme of the movement.[61] Nor have missionaries featured as important players—or even as lightning rods for popular discontent—in mainstream accounts of nineteenth-century social history in Egypt.[62] This absence of attention raises questions about the import and impact of intercommunal strife and missionaries in this period, as well as about the way history has been written. Did missionaries have as negligible an impact as their absence in standard social and political histories suggests? Is a history that relates largely to Copts too marginal or specialized to warrant attention in a general social history of Egypt? Or is it that, as Bruce Masters has suggested, Western historians have downgraded attention to the role of religious communal identities in political affairs out of a possibly unconscious desire to correct for Orientalist presentations of Middle Eastern religion as a wellspring of primordial hostilities?[63]

A look at accounts of Coptic Orthodox Church history suggests, in any case, that the missionary image of the Muslim "reign of terror" did not reflect general conditions for Christians on the ground, at least when considered against the long duration of Coptic experience. Copts have traced a lengthy history of persecution in Egypt, during both the Byzantine and Islamic eras, while the Coptic Orthodox Church has preserved traditions about martyrs who died for their faith.[64] These traditions have depended on perceptions of dark and repressive periods of Coptic history, like the Mamluk era (1250–1517), when, in the aftermath of the Crusades, Christian-Muslim relations in the Islamic heartland deteriorated and Islamic states placed heavier restrictions on Christian communities.[65] During this period, Copts witnessed "killing, seditious uprisings (*fitan*), and internal wars," the destruction of churches, waves of Coptic conversion to Islam, and grinding taxes, while most ominously of all, as a symptom of social malaise, the indigenous Coptic tradition of history-writing lapsed into a silence that lasted till the nineteenth century.[66]

But strikingly, historians of Coptic Orthodoxy, whose emphasis on persecution and suffering has often been so great as to be "strongly misleading,"[67] have not commemorated the mid- to late nineteenth century as a bleak or brutal moment in Coptic history. On the contrary, they have described it as a period of "enlightenment" when Copts experienced a cultural *nahda* (awakening or renaissance) that mirrored the *nahda*s of Egyptian national sentiment and Arabic literature. Some historians have even called this a period of Coptic "emancipation," implicitly equating the Copts' changing conditions with freedom from bondage.[68] Others have pointed out that some Coptic Orthodox leaders, who had their own grievances about foreign meddling in Egypt, counted among 'Urabi's supporters. In this period, too, more Copts joined the landowning classes. This fortified a Coptic elite whose members, in the early twentieth century, were able to participate energetically with Muslims in nationalist activities and parliamentary politics.[69] In short, missionaries may have viewed the disturbances of this period through a Christian sectarian lens, but Coptic Orthodox and Muslim supporters of 'Urabi may have perceived his movement instead as a native Egyptian uprising against the encroachment of foreigners.[70]

3.1. Miss Ethel Weed in Mansura, a predominantly Muslim town in the Delta, c. 1921. Dwight H. and Lucille B. Fee Papers, Presbyterian Historical Society, Presbyterian Church (U.S.A.), Philadelphia.

In sum, to say that the Hatt-i Humayun abolished *dhimmi* status and promoted religious equality is not to say that the edict eliminated intercommunal tensions, anxieties, and hostilities on the ground in the years after 1856. Nor is it to say that the edict abolished dhimmitude, meaning assumptions among Muslims, Christians, or Jews about the place of non-Muslims in Islamic states. On the contrary, the edict may have helped arouse a defensive popular reaction among Muslims who feared or resented the social changes that were occurring. Nevertheless, by setting a tone of expectation (even if primarily among Western observers) regarding human rights and personal liberties, the Hatt-i Humayun was one important factor among others that converged in Egypt during the late nineteenth century to open opportunities for American missionaries. The social and psychological restrictions that had kept Christians and Jews apart from Muslims were also becoming looser or were falling away. A spirit of reform, along with a sense of possibility for positive change, prevailed among intellectuals. Western imperialism was expanding, its presence made manifest on the ground by consuls, businessmen, and tourists. Protestant missionaries, sometimes forming multinational alliances, were becoming more globally ambitious. And beginning with the invasion of 1882, Britain was occupying Egypt and dictating the terms of its governance even while continuing to recognize the legitimacy of the Ottoman Empire and the subdynasty of the Muhammad Ali family.

All of these things together meant that Christian missionary work in Egypt was becoming freer and more expansive in the 1880s than it had ever been since the seventh-century rise of Islam. This meant, in turn, that Muslim evangelization was becoming conceivable, if still not easy. Thus when conversions from Islam to Christianity began to occur, it was significant that the heaviest and most fearsome reprisals came from Muslim relatives and neighbors, and not from courts of law.

The Challenges of Muslim Conversion

Even if missionaries, after 1882, felt more optimistic about the climate of religious freedom in Egypt, and even if they claimed to detect an upsurge of interest among Muslim "inquirers" coming to see them to discuss the Bible and Christian belief, conversions from Islam remained rare. Andrew Watson noted in 1906 that "In 1900, there were six [converts from Islam]; in 1901, there were also six; in 1902, there were eight; in 1903, there were fourteen; in 1904, there were twelve. Two of these have defected to Islam through the threats of friends and Moslem officials." However, what did change significantly after 1882 is that missionaries felt greater liberty themselves, even if assumptions about Muslim-Christian relations persisted among local Egyptians. Missionaries felt freer to speak up, and they were more hopeful that Egyptians would listen. Watson conveyed this idea when he contrasted the early years of the American mission, in the late 1850s, with the situation prevailing in the late 1890s. Muslims in that earlier period, he claimed, had been hostile not only to Christians but also to the mere prospect of hearing about Christianity. Times, he implied, had changed.[71]

The American missionaries' overtures toward Muslims made their first discernible mark in 1866—sixteen years before the British Occupation—when the first Muslim converted to Christianity under their auspices and joined the Evangelical community. A second Muslim man named Ibrahim Musa (who had encountered the Americans at their mission school in Alexandria) converted in 1868 and became a lay evangelist. Then and later, Muslim conversions remained unusual enough to warrant special citation in mission reports.

In 1914, the missionary Rena Hogg tallied Muslim conversions to Christianity as follows: "At the beginning of the Arabi [sic] rebellion the number of Mohammedan converts baptized by the American mission during its whole history had reached but twenty-six. By the close of 1883, twenty-two more had professed their faith in Christ, thirteen of whom had already been baptised, while the remaining nine were still under instruction."[72] (By this stage, the total Evangelical Church membership, drawn almost entirely from the Coptic population, included some one thousand members.)[73] American missionaries hoped that the British Occupation would make mass evangelization and conversion among Muslims more feasible. Along these lines, Rena Hogg quoted from one of her father's letters, written in the immediate aftermath of the 1882 events and reflecting high hopes for what the Occupation might do: "If Egypt is given religious liberty worthy of the name, our success amongst Mohammedans will soon surpass that amongst the Copts."[74]

But neither individual religious liberties nor Muslim conversions ever reached the height that missionaries hoped. Nor did British authorities offer protection to converts from Islam. And so, by the time the World Missionary Conference convened in Edinburgh in 1910, British and American missionaries praised British colonial regimes with striking points of exception. As Brian Stanley has noted, "The only sections of the [Edinburgh conference] report openly critical of British colonial policy related to Egypt, the Egyptian Sudan, and northern Nigeria. In each case, the report complained, the administration was in practice inclined to favor Islam at Christianity's expense."[75] Missionaries sensed that British officials were trying to curry favor with Muslim ruling elites as a way of securing cooperation and facilitating colonial rule. In Sudan and Nigeria, British regimes were also trying to push missionaries away from Muslim populations by enticing them toward thinly governed "pagan" zones where missionaries could help secure colonial rule by proxy.[76] Britain's discouragement of Muslim evangelization was especially galling to missionaries who believed that Islam and Christianity were locked in a great contest for souls being waged on the African continent, and that Britain, as a Protestant power and "the greatest of all rulers of Muslims," had a role to play in facilitating worldwide evangelization by enabling missionaries to move freely and safely.[77] So glaring was the breach in missionary-imperial relations, regarding the relative favoring of Islam and Christianity in Africa, that historians and advocates of missions have continued to discuss it ever since.[78]

If Christian missionaries had an unspoken pact with the British Empire, then its terms went as follows: missionaries were expected to provide the empire with a veneer of ethics, respectability, and moral purpose; to praise British governance among churchgoing audiences at home; and to act in ways that would tacitly support and not compromise British rule on the ground.[79] Thus a writer duly declared, for example, in an 1895 issue of the *Women's Missionary Magazine of the United Presbyterian Church* (published in Pittsburgh, Pennsylvania) that "Under the British occupancy [Egypt] is undoubtedly better governed than in all its history."[80] In return, British colonial authorities agreed to assist or advise missionaries in colonial settings, remove obstacles to their institutional growth, and protect missionaries, as privileged foreigners, from physical harm—if only by achieving an illusion of crushing power that dissuaded "natives" from testing their wrath.[81] British authorities kept up their part of the bargain so well vis-à-vis the UPCNA American Presbyterians in Egypt, Sudan, and northern India that a mission brochure for tourists in Egypt was able to claim around 1922 that "No member of the American Mission in any of its fields has ever suffered from human violence, but one man was killed by a lion in the Sudan."[82]

This bargain and its benefits did not, however, extend to "native" converts, regardless of their religion of origin. For a start, British colonial authorities (many of whom made the cultivation of local traditions into a fetish)[83] often regarded converts as cultural opportunists, underminers of local authority, or deviants from "authentic" cultures.[84] But even from the purely pragmatic view of imperial self-preservation, support for converts—and especially for converts from Islam—would have been unwise, since such a policy would have aroused popular hostility toward British rule, possibly to the extent of provoking collective resistance. (British authorities had learned an important lesson by watching from Egypt, after 1882, as the Sudanese Mahdist movement expanded, fueled in part by popular Muslim hostility toward the increasing presence of foreign Christians, like General Charles Gordon, in the Turco-Egyptian regime. Anti-colonial jihad was a phenomenon that they wished neither to revive nor duplicate elsewhere.)[85] Thus unwilling and perhaps unable to intervene for native converts, British authorities in Egypt, as in other Muslim-majority regions of the British Empire, took a hands-off approach and left former Muslims on their own, much as the Dutch rulers of Muslim Java had done in the eighteenth century.[86]

This refusal to protect Muslim converts came as a grave disappointment to Christian missionaries, who knew that social barriers to Muslim out-conversion were so high as to be nearly insurmountable—and this, even when Muslims privately expressed belief in Christian teachings. Evidence for the sanctions that faced aspiring or successful Egyptian converts from Islam is anecdotal and comes from mission reports, missionary memoirs and chronicles, and books and articles published for mission-supporting audiences. These Muslim convert stories from Egypt describe the trials and tribulations of converts in very similar terms. They also echo a larger body of Muslim convert anecdotes that were recorded and shared by British and American Protestant missionaries working throughout the Muslim world.[87] The Muslim conversion stories in English had a clear purpose: they were intended to inspire and brace mission supporters, who may have wondered why conversions from Islam remained "a saga of the few" despite so much missionary effort, or why missions to Muslims were still worthwhile, and worth funding, from a Christian evangelical point of view.[88]

Islamic law in theory prescribed the death penalty for the apostate who did not recant. But in practice, and judging from missionary records, the law courts in Egypt never imposed a sentence of death for apostasy after 1854, when American Presbyterians started their mission. In any case, courts did not *need* to sentence apostates, because Muslim social solidarity was so strong that families and neighbors took matters into their own hands. In other words, on a day-to-day basis, Egyptian Islam did not function as an autocracy of jurists, who dictated terms from the courts. Rather, from reading missionary accounts about the treatment of converts from Islam, one gets the sense that *ijma'*—a foundational concept in Islamic legal studies, usually translated as "consensus" to suggest the historical accumulation of agreement among eminent scholars—was invested in the Muslim people and had an everyday relevance. Egypt did not have a culture of Islamic inquisition, nor were there Islamic "thought police" roaming the Egyptian landscape. To be a Muslim meant to proclaim one's identity as Muslim, implicitly accepting thereby the foundational creed of Islam: the oneness of God and Muhammad's historic role as God's prophet. But regarding converts, the consensus among Egyptian Muslims was that any Muslim who tried to leave the Islamic fold should be persuaded and, failing that, forced to return.

According to American missionaries, the most formidable sanction facing the potential Egyptian convert out of Islam was the violent rage of families. Men who resisted the imploring of their relatives typically faced assault and battery, kidnaping, detention in a local jail or family home, and threats of poisoning.[89] That some men who professed Christianity were jailed and beaten as a means of persuasion or coercion suggests that local Muslim police officers and the Muslim relatives of aspiring converts may have seen eye to eye. Families may have felt a communal obligation to respond in this manner since the pattern of reprisals appears to have been so routine, even ritualized. In practice, men either caved in and recanted, or fled from home, going to Cairo or, if they were already in Cairo, leaving Egypt in order to construct new identities as Christians.

There is no evidence that death threats against converts from Islam were actually carried out in Egypt, although missionary sources hinted at deaths that occurred under suspicious circumstances. In a book published in 1924, Samuel M. Zwemer, a missionary of the Reformed Church in America, mentions, for example, that during World War I in Egypt "there was grave suspicion that a leading Moslem in Cairo deliberately arranged to have his son meet with a tramway accident rather than permit his public baptism." Likewise Zwemer claims that a Muslim tailor in Denshawai—a man who had been merely an inquirer and not a full-fledged convert—was poisoned by the *'umda* (mayor), who had tampered with his coffee.[90] The few reasonably documented cases of murdered converts came from outside Egypt, for example, from Basra (now in southern Iraq) in 1892. There, a Syrian man named Kamil Aytani, who had adopted the name Kamil Abd al-Masih (meaning Kamil the Servant of Christ) upon his conversion from Islam and who had become an evangelist working with American missionaries, was apparently poisoned after having encountered hostility from local Muslims. He died following sudden and severe bouts of vomiting; Muslim authorities seized his body, prevented missionaries from examining it (notwithstanding attempts at consular intercession), and rushed it off for Muslim burial in a secret location. One of the leading American Presbyterian missionaries of Beirut published a biography presenting Kamil Abd al-Masih as a martyr, while Zwemer, who had known this man, later pointed to his case as well.[91]

But sanctions were not only physical. The male convert from Islam faced disinheritance (on the Islamic legal grounds that a non-Muslim cannot inherit from a Muslim); nullification of marriage to a Muslim woman (on the Islamic legal grounds that a Muslim woman may not marry or remain married to a non-Muslim man); and loss of child custody (again, on related grounds that Muslim minors should not be placed under non-Muslim custody).[92] Converts, in short, lost their families. Beyond these sanctions rooted in Islamic family law, there were also informal sanctions. Muslim employers stripped apostates of jobs, or Muslim neighbors boycotted their businesses.[93]

Since ostracism occurred on many levels, the problem facing the missionaries was what to do with male converts from Islam and how to help them construct new lives as Christians.[94] Converts needed help finding new homes and jobs, as well as Christian wives with whom they could start Christian families. The last problem was particularly tricky, since most Copts-turned-Evangelicals suspected the motives and sincerity of converts from Islam and did not want to marry their daughters to them, fearing that they would recant and pull their children into Islam (since the children of a Muslim father would be deemed Muslim in law, regardless of the mother's religion). According to the biographical profiles of noteworthy Egyptian Muslim converts provided in a collection by the American missionary H. E. Philips, two well-educated converts from Islam found Catholic wives (one of whom was of Syrian, not Egyptian, background), while a third, a police officer, married the daughter of another convert from Islam. In all three cases, the wives of converts from Islam came from marginal Christian communities or backgrounds.[95] J. R. Alexander summarized this situation in 1935 by noting that "Muslim converts feel that they are not heartily welcomed by the Church, its ministry, and its people, that they are regarded with suspicion, that their motives are questioned, that there is very little practical sympathy shown them in their trials." He added that this chilly reception from Evangelical Copts gave Muslim converts another incentive to recant.[96]

This problem among Muslim converts—and their rejection by "Eastern Christians"—was not unique to Egypt. When the journal *The Moslem World* began publication in 1911, it occasionally published articles on this issue. In 1918, for example, an article titled "The Loneliness of the Convert" considered the plight of "a prominent convert from Islam" who declared, "I have been a Christian now for twenty years. Yet I cannot say that I have a single intimate friend among the Christians." A missionary reflected on the "haunting faces" of Muslim converts who sat "in the midst of Christian congregations, with a trace of undefined wistfulness that tells us that they do not feel themselves wholly a part of the worshipping throng."[97]

The sanctions applied to men who left the Muslim fold suggest that, in the Muslim consensual view, sustained conversion to Christianity amounted to social death. Certainly the family who lost the son, daughter, or sibling to Christianity had cause for grieving. Zwemer confirms this notion by mentioning in *The Law of Apostasy in Islam* that in 1909 one Muslim father in Cairo sent out what looked like death notices, edged in black, to announce his twenty-two-year-old son's conversion to Christianity.[98] In a short memoir published sometime in the 1930s as a fund-raising brochure for American churchgoers, Kamil (formerly Ahmad) Mansur recounts that after his conversion to Christianity, he saw his mother just once—and this was in 1925, some twenty-one years after his conversion. Kamil Mansur visited his mother in Sohag (Upper Egypt) while attending a church conference in the town, but left quickly to avoid angering neighbors. Kamil had become a convert through the inspiration of his brother Mikhail (formerly Muhammad) Mansur. The elder brother was an Azhar graduate who converted in the 1890s and became an evangelist for the American mission. There is no evidence that Mikhail Mansur (d. 1918), once a Christian, had any contact with his parents again.[99]

For missionaries, conversion entailed an affirmation of Christian belief and an acceptance of Evangelical (Presbyterian) doctrine, confirmed by baptism; they did not theorize more deeply than that. The missionaries in Egypt did, however, appear to see a distinction between "conversion," meaning a dramatic religious turn from another religion, and "accession," meaning a shift from another Christian sect into the Evangelical Church. In their view, a change from Islam was conversion whereas a change from Coptic Orthodoxy was accession.[100] Yet as their comments on the challenges of Muslim conversion implicitly show, American Presbyterians on the ground in Egypt appreciated that conversion from Islam meant much more than change of faith. They certainly did not regard conversion from Islam as a spiritual flashpoint like the biblical Saul's light-blinded conversion on the road to Damascus (Acts 9:3). Nor did they regard it as did the philosopher William James, whose famous work titled *The Varieties of Religious Experience* (1902) describes conversion as a psychological and spiritual experience, as well as a state of consciousness.[101] Missionaries recognized that conversion from Islam in Egypt entailed a familial and communal rupture and demanded reinvention on the part of the convert: it was a process, not an isolated event, and was an intensely social affair.[102] Some of them might have even acknowledged that conversion was not an abstraction of belief but rather an answer "to problems of self-identification in a shattered social world."[103]

Conversion of Muslim females posed special problems for the missionaries. From the viewpoint of Muslim society, Muslim females who professed an interest in Christianity or, even more, a desire for baptism were easier to handle and were less of a social threat than were males. Most of the females who encountered American missionaries did so in schools or in orphanages, and were generally young and unmarried. (Missionary sources never discuss the issue of Muslim conversion among married women, divorced women, or widows.) Therefore, in a society where fathers or legal male guardians arranged marriages, a young woman could simply be married by proxy to a Muslim. Then she would fall under her husband's authority, and her schooling (and steady exposure to missionaries) would end. This is what reportedly happened to Nafisa, the eldest of four daughters of Ahmad 'Urabi, the Muslim army captain who had given his name to the Urabi Revolt, and who was subsequently exiled to Ceylon. The American mission report for 1883–84 notes that four of 'Urabi's daughters had enrolled in the mission's school in the Harat al-Sakka'in district in Cairo. But Nafisa apparently showed too much

3.2. The Converts' Society/Jami'at al-Mutanassirin (for Muslim converts to Christianity in Cairo), presented to Mr. and Mrs. Fee by its general secretary, Kamil Mansur, August 14, 1923. Dwight H. and Lucille B. Fee Papers, Presbyterian Historical Society, Presbyterian Church (U.S.A.), Philadelphia.

interest in the Bible, so her family withdrew her and her sisters after a month and hired a "Mohammedan priest" to teach them to read the Qur'an. Meanwhile, American women from the mission visited her at home and helped her read "most of the Old Testament and some of the New."[104] Writing in 1971, Elizabeth Kelsey Kinnear (herself a former missionary in Egypt) claimed that Nafisa was soon married off: "The bride had not been allowed to stay long in the school, but she had a Bible in which she read every day. However, her new husband soon put a stop to that."[105]

Missionaries realized that it was almost impossible for Muslim women in Egypt to profess faith in Christ and then to be allowed by their families to pursue a public Christian life, and this raised questions about conversion. Could one count as a convert a woman who attended a mission school, read the Bible, professed faith in Christ, but was never allowed to be baptized—a woman who was then married to a Muslim man and otherwise then led a "Muslim" life? Some missionaries in the early to mid-twentieth century implicitly responded to these questions with answers of yes, and pointed to the existence of "secret believers" or "hidden disciples," many of whom were women.[106] Writing in 1953, the missionary H. E. Philips explained what secret belief could mean and how it could happen even among men: "There are many secret believers in Christ who are thoroughly persuaded that He died for their salvation but who have never had the courage to face the persecutions that await every baptized convert from Islam."[107]

By claiming the existence of secret believers, missionaries recognized a disjuncture between private belief and public religion. They also recognized the possible existence of hybrid Muslim-Christian identities. This line of thinking about the social meanings and manifestations of conversion continued to evolve among missionaries after World War I. By the 1930s, as Muslim popular opposition to missionaries was mounting, some American Presbyterians in Egypt were beginning to discount the importance of formal conversion through baptism as a missionary goal, and to express the hope that many Egyptian Muslims would absorb Christian ethics and values until they became Christian in all but name.[108]

BECOMING EVANGELICAL: COPTS, MUSLIMS, AND THE GROWTH OF THE CHURCH

Outreach to Muslims concerned missionaries deeply in the years from 1882 to 1918, and yet the rate of Muslim conversion remained minimal throughout this period. By contrast, the Evangelical Church of Egypt grew and flourished during this period with new members coming almost entirely from the Copts of Upper Egypt.

In 1880–81, W. W. Barr and Robert Stewart of the UPCNA had set out on a tour of inspection to mission fields in India and Egypt. Upon their return to Philadelphia, they wrote a report in which they reflected on the status of converts who came from assorted Muslim, Hindu, Sikh, and outcaste communities in India, and from the Muslim community of Egypt. "Embracing Christianity involved the loss of almost everything," they wrote, "and endangers life itself."[109] Their comment on the social sacrifice behind Christian conversion begs the question of why, if stakes were so high, people changed religious allegiance at all. The question seems appropriate since American Presbyterians had no desire to encourage cults of martyrs and, unlike the Coptic Orthodox Church, did not extol a church history of martyrdom. Implicit in their comment was also the idea that conditions were not as dire for Copts who joined the Evangelicals. Andrew Watson later confirmed this impression in his chronicle of the mission by noting that while families and Orthodox ecclesiastical authorities sometimes applied sanctions to Copts who turned to Protestantism, Muslim authorities—the ultimate powers in the land—did not care if Christians switched sects.[110] Nor did Muslims care which church a Copt attended.

Missionaries thought it was clear why Copts turned Evangelical: the Coptic Orthodox Church, they felt, was ignorant and corrupt. In the view of United Presbyterian missionaries and church leaders, the life and early career of one of the first Egyptian Evangelicals illustrated the need for reform. Mikhail Yusuf al-Bilyani (1819–1883), or "Father Makhiel" (as Andrew Watson and other missionaries called him), became a Coptic monk as a young man. According to the church historian James B. Scouller, Father Makhiel had reportedly been forced to live as "a horrified spectator of the foul lives of the bishops, their abbots and their associates" and to cope with an abbot in Cairo who was a "Sodomite," who stole money from his own monks, and who had the monks lashed three hundred times each when they tried to lodge a complaint with the Patriarch.[111]

Disillusioned with the church and with the political intrigues of ecclesiastical authorities (which he had witnessed first-hand as the member of a Coptic Church delegation to Abyssinia in 1844), Makhiel became attracted to the CMS missionaries who stressed biblical knowledge. But when the Coptic Orthodox patriarch Cyril IV discovered Father Makhiel's correspondence with Rev. Kruzé of the CMS, Father Makhiel fled briefly to Jerusalem where he met Bishop Gobat of the Anglican Church. He returned in 1855 after Bishop Gobat introduced him to Dr. Philip of the Scottish mission to the Jews in Alexandria; Dr. Philip, in turn, advised him to contact the American missionaries, who had just started work in Egypt. Father Makhiel, whose trajectory illustrated the Anglo-American evangelical network in practice, soon became a dynamic evangelist for the American mission. Father Makhiel was inducted into the Evangelical community as one of the first members in 1858, was ordained the first "native" pastor in 1867, and remained a leading figure in the Evangelical Church and community until his death in 1883.[112]

Most Copts who joined the Evangelicals probably had experiences of church life that were far less sensational than that of Father Makhiel. Many of the earliest members of the community came into contact with American missionaries by attending mission schools or serving as teachers in them. (In fact, by 1882, of the six ordained Egyptian Evangelical pastors, all but Father Makhiel had established contact with the American missionaries by attending or teaching in their schools.)[113] In the early years of the mission, adult women also joined the community after encountering American women who visited their homes. But before long, many Copts turned to the Evangelicals under the aegis of Egyptian evangelists and not American missionaries. Some of these Egyptian evangelists were salaried employees of the American mission, the American Bible Society, or the British and Foreign Bible Society, working as colporteurs and Bible Women. Still others were volunteers.[114]

While some Coptic families disowned children who joined the Evangelicals (judging from anecdotal evidence),[115] the social deterrents were never as high for Copts as for Muslims. Indeed, in many cases, entire households, or clusters of households, turned to the Evangelical Church; Coptic "accession" could be a collective affair. Census data hint at this trend. In some parts of Upper Egypt, where Coptic populations were centered, the growth of the Evangelical Church was significant. For example, according to the Egyptian government census of 1907, Abu Qirqas *markaz* (district) of Minya province, and Abu Tig and Mellawi districts of Assiut province, witnessed considerable growth in Protestant numbers, though this was often concentrated in particular villages. One of the most dramatic shifts, for example, occurred in Qalandul village (Mellawi district, Assiut province), where in 1907 there were reportedly 453 "Protestant Copts" (as the census classified them) relative to 853 "Orthodox Copts," amid a Muslim majority of 3,906 people. In other words, Protestants accounted for more than half of this village's Christian population and one-eighth of its population overall. Similar figures prevailed for Hur, a village in the same district, where the population included 441 Protestant Copts, 830 Orthodox Copts, and 3,065 Muslims. Nakheila village in Abu Tig district of Assiut province had a more complex sectarian landscape: there, the Coptic-Muslim population was divided remarkably evenly, with 6,744 Copts and 6,745 Muslims. Among the Copts, 1,512 were Protestants, 313 were Catholics, and 4,919 were Orthodox, so that some 27 percent of the Christians in the village were not counted as Orthodox.[116]

In most Upper Egyptian villages, Evangelical Church growth was considerably more modest and uneven than the examples cited above. Safania village of Feshn district in Minya province offers an example of how modest growth could be: in 1907, of the village's 247 Christians (who lived amid 3,740 Muslims), only 10 were Protestants.[117] Likewise, while Abu Tig district (Assiut province) reportedly had a total of 3,421 Protestant Copts and 1,689 Catholic Copts relative to 34,242 Orthodox Copts and 95,125 Muslims, 22 of the 36 villages in the district had no Protestants whatsoever. (Similarly, 26 of the villages in the same district lacked Catholics.) This was the case even though every village in Abu Tig district had an Orthodox population of some size.[118] By contrast, many villages in the region just south of Cairo, or in the Delta region of Lower Egypt, had minute Coptic populations as a whole. Beba district of Beni Suef province contained 68 villages but had only a single Protestant Copt (and no Catholics) in its entirety; otherwise Beba district contained 113,295 Muslims and 5,138 Orthodox Copts.[119] American missionaries began work in the Delta town of Tanta in 1892 (and started medical work there in 1897), and yet by 1907 the census only listed 35 Protestant Copts in all of Tanta district—a district of Gharbia province that included 64 villages and that had a Muslim population of 244,701. (The district also contained 84 Catholic Copts and 6,540 Orthodox.)[120]

With its village-by-village roster for the entire country, the Egyptian government census of 1907 claimed that many villages contained a single Protestant Copt. There were places like Gezirat Meteira, in Qus district of Qena province, that reportedly had a lone Protestant Copt among 84 Orthodox Copts and 2,810 Muslims; and Tilt, a village in Feshn district of Minya province, which counted one Protestant Copt among 146 Orthodox Copts and 2,428 Muslims.[121] The historian is left to wonder what that Protestant was doing in Tilt, how that person got there, and why he or she stayed put.

In fact, and assuming that the census was accurate, the lone Protestant of Tilt may not have been as socially isolated as the numbers might suggest. For despite the petty rivalries that sometimes marked relations between different Protestant missions, despite the mutual contempt that placed Catholic-Protestant missionary relations under a steady chill, and despite the annoyance that the Coptic Orthodox hierarchy registered toward both Protestant and Catholic missionaries, it appears that sectarian lines were less important to Egyptian Christians on the ground. Protestant and Catholic missionaries and Coptic Orthodox ecclesiastical authorities did not necessarily replicate their own sectarian biases among the Christians of Egypt.

Scattered hints in missionary writings and church histories suggest, on the contrary, that many Egyptians found their way to the Evangelical Church through the conscious or unwitting mediation, or back-and-forth exchange, of other Protestant and Catholic missionaries, while many Copts gained experience in mission schools (either as students or teachers), which they then brought to Coptic Orthodox endeavors.[122] Even converts from Islam sometimes followed a circuitous route to the Evangelical Church. Consider, for example, the case of one of the most distinguished Evangelical converts from Islam, Mikhail (Muhammad) Mansur, a graduate of al-Azhar who became the imam of the chief mosque in Sohag (Upper Egypt). According to H. E. Philips, Muhammad Mansur reportedly encountered a Muslim convert to Christianity who belonged to the Evangelical Church in

Sohag and, after engaging in disputation with him, became attracted to Christianity. After being denied baptism in a church near Sohag (for reasons that Philips does not explain), Muhammad Mansur went to Cairo where he sought and received baptism from Roman Catholics and changed his first name to Mikhail (Michael). A year or so later he went on pilgrimage to Rome and was blessed by the pope. But then, Philips claims, he became concerned about the Catholic practice of saint worship and sought out the Americans instead. On December 26, 1897, Mikhail Mansur officially joined the Evangelical Church and became a mission evangelist.[123]

Judging from a comment made in 1937 by Donald Attwater (a historian of the Catholic Eastern rite churches), this kind of Catholic-to-Protestant crossover was not uncommon. Attwater lamented that "as we [Catholics in Egypt] lack means to build churches and schools and train priests, Protestant missions reap much of this harvest."[124] But the trend was, in fact, reciprocal. Raymond Janin, a Catholic priest and missionary to Egypt, wrote in 1926 that 30,000 Coptic Catholics had been "reclaimed" (se réclament) from Protestantism even though he also asserted that Protestant influences in Egypt were thwarting Catholic expansion.[125]

Somewhat to the chagrin of missionaries and ecclesiastical authorities, many Copts also married across sect, producing Orthodox-Protestant, Protestant-Catholic, and Orthodox-Catholic hybrid families. Cross-marriage may have become more common with time; certainly by 1888 missionaries observed that Orthodox Copts were following the Protestant custom of organizing Bible study and prayer groups, so that differences in devotional life were becoming less prominent. In contrast to conditions that had prevailed in the 1860s and 1870s, missionaries also reported in 1888 that "There is less ill feeling generally on the part of the Coptic toward the Protestant community."[126]

Writing in 1937, Amir Buqtur, a professor at the American University in Cairo and a graduate of the mission's Assiut College, recalled an aunt and uncle who had had a "mixed" marriage. The aunt was deeply attached to the Coptic Orthodox Church, and his uncle felt the same about the Evangelical. So they baptized their children twice, once in each church, and the aunt took pleasure in thinking that since the Orthodox baptism came second, it "cleansed" the children of the Protestant ritual.[127] Hanna F. Wissa told an identical story about his grandparents.[128] Mikhail Mansur offers another example of a mixed marriage. During his Catholic period, he married a Catholic woman, but she did not follow him into the Evangelical Church. H. E. Philips issued only one terse remark on the subject, saying that this woman "proved to be a faithful wife but a more faithful Roman-ist."[129] In a similar vein, many Copts worshiped with the Evangelicals or sought out their schools and other social services but returned to Coptic Orthodoxy for big life events, such as weddings and funerals. This practice—which persists today[130]—explains the discrepancy in missionary statistics for Egypt, which sometimes distinguished between Evangelical "communicants" or official members, and the much larger Evangelical "community." (Elder wrote, for example, that in 1904 the Evangelical Church had 7,757 members and a community of 29,000.)[131] These trends suggest that sectarian boundaries were not as fixed as the census roster might seem to suggest.

In Egypt, social factors besides the appeal of creed or worship sometimes pulled people to join the Evangelical Church. For example, in a report prepared around 1912, one of the American Presbyterians summarized what an elderly Evangelical churchman, from a village outside Assiut, had told him about conditions for Coptic peasants during the reign of Ismail (1863–79). "There were twenty-one separate taxes which the fellahin were at that time forced to pay to the government," he recorded, and "The Coptic church ruled its members with a despotic oppression similar to that of the government. The elder [who was] then an earnest young Copt became deeply indebted to the priest for prayers [of intercession] and because he was unable to pay the debt the priest seized his land."[132] For this man, the turn to Protestantism may have offered an escape from debt or from the prospect of future debt, and may have reflected not only a change of worship and creed but also a rejection of—and emancipation from—a social order in which ecclesiastical authorities exploited peasants. Of course, Protestant modes of worship had intrinsic political implications. Like other Protestants in Egypt, the Americans and Egyptian Evangelicals stressed the power of individual prayer and sought to instill confidence in the ability of men, women, and children to seek a direct line to God through prayer and Bible study. Presbyterians placed little value on intercession from priests. Moreover, for women, the Evangelical Church may have been particularly empowering. According to Hanna F. Wissa, "It was easier to get to the masses through the women who were thirsty for knowledge and felt it was a way towards emancipation, especially if they were able to go to the American Mission schools."[133] Even Coptic women who did not attend school may have found the Evangelical Church appealing, simply because American missionaries expected women to read the Bible and helped them toward that goal.

Other social factors, many of which are impossible to weigh, contributed to the spread of the Evangelical Church—factors such as the accident of geography (e.g., the accessibility of particular villages to itinerating evangelists), alienation from families (suggesting another way in which a person's religious turn could offer an escape from an earlier self), or the power of personality (e.g., the inspiration of a particular preacher or believer). Missionary sources suggest that this last factor was important for Nakheila, the village eighteen miles southeast of Assiut that registered 1,512 Protestants in the 1907 census. In 1870, one of the first Egyptian ordained pastors, the Rev. Tadrus Yusuf (b. 1840)—a native of Cairo who was a graduate of both the Coptic Orthodox college founded by Cyril IV and the CMS school of John Lieder—went to Nakheila with five Evangelical Church members. The community gained a further boost when one of the village's most prominent and charismatic Coptic laymen—a man named Tadrus Abu Zaqlawi—turned Evangelical with members of his family. According to Elder, from the moment of his public profession until his death, Tadrus Abu Zaqlawi "carried about with him a copy of the New Testament and was ready in season and out to give an account of his faith."[134] The government census provides numbers, but offers no insights into the local antipathies, opportunities, and strains—or even bursts of enthusiasm—that prompted Copts to join the Evangelicals.

If for Copts joining the Protestants became less socially anathema over time, then for Muslims conversion always remained cataclysmic and ruptured individuals from families. There was no possibility (by law) for a male convert to Christianity to marry or remain married to a Muslim woman and thereby create a hybrid family in the way that Protestant, Catholic, and Orthodox Christians could create intersectarian households. Regarding conversion from Islam to Christianity, there was no culture of live-and-let-live among Muslim families, just as there was no culture of religious "choice" in the way that American missionaries understood it.

Given the social sanctions and stigmatization that deterred conversion from Islam, it is no surprise that the first Muslim convert to join the Evangelical Church was a freed slave who made the move in 1866. It is probably a reflection of this man's humble social status that Andrew Watson did not record his name, only mentioning that he "made a simple and earnest profession [of Christian faith], and was faithful in the performance of his Christian duties, and in trying to learn to read, so as to peruse the words of the Saviour in his leisure moments."[135] In many ways, ex-slaves, like orphans, were perfect candidates for conversion, since by definition they lacked families who were apt to drag them back to the Muslim community under threats of death. Disinheritance would not have meant much either, since it was unlikely that they had wealth or property to forfeit. Thus in Egypt during the late nineteenth century, freed Muslim slaves had less to lose (and potentially much more to gain, in the form of a support network and access to free education) by embracing Christianity. And in fact, of the thirty-nine Muslims baptized by the mission up to 1883, twenty-two were former slaves.[136] Four years later, in 1887, Lord Cromer sent twelve freed Sudanese slave girls to the American mission orphanage in Cairo; of these twelve, the missionaries reported, eleven became Christian. The seven or eight who reached adulthood became "household helpers, practical nurses, and teachers' helpers." One became a Bible Woman, while another became matron of the mission's boarding school for girls in Cairo. Only one married.[137] The mission report made no mention of any objections from neighbors or of any social sanctions that had challenged or deterred their conversions.

By contrast, the conversion of Ahmed Fahmy, who was baptized by the Americans in 1877, was passionately contested. Ahmed Fahmy came from a Muslim family of "good position and some wealth"; his father was the chief clerk in a Muslim court of appeal.[138] Ahmed Fahmy's conversion confirmed the missionaries' belief in the universal appeal of Christianity, even for a highly literate Muslim like him who had studied at al-Azhar and who knew some French and English. Ahmed Fahmy also represented a model convert because he withstood his family's persuasion and coercion. Missionaries celebrated his conversion when it occurred, and continued to recount his story over the decades. In 1971, one former missionary still called it "one of the most exciting stories in the mission's history," ranking alongside the story of Bamba, the mission schoolgirl who in 1864 married the Maharaja Dhulip Singh.[139]

Like many Egyptian Evangelicals of the era, Ahmed Fahmy became exposed to the American missionaries by attending one of their schools in Cairo, along with his brothers, Muhammad and Mahmud.[140] In 1875, the mission hired Ahmed to teach Arabic to one of the new women missionaries, Margaret Smith, and they read devotional books together, including a daily chapter from the Bible. "After several months with Miss Smith," Andrew Watson recorded, "he began to ask questions, and finally he became satisfied as to the truth of Christianity." When Ahmed professed faith and underwent baptism in 1877, "news of his defection from the religion of his fathers spread rapidly through the city." Friends and relatives came to plead with him, and when that failed, Watson reported, some of them dressed up as peasants, waited outside the mission house, and kidnaped him. The missionaries appealed to the American and British consuls, who interceded with the khedive and his government to extract information and guarantees for Ahmed's safety. Yet Egyptian authorities reportedly said that Ahmed's father had "a right to retain him," while the consuls declared it "a very delicate case," leaving Watson to conclude that the Egyptian government "would rather have the name of religious intolerance than do justice."[141] Another missionary, Anna Young Thompson, wrote in her diary at the time that Ahmed's father, "Sharif Pasha," sought help against the missionaries from the khedive, who ambiguously declared, "There is freedom of religion; nothing can be done." His father also appealed to the rector of al-Azhar, who reportedly said that Ahmed should be burned.[142] Meanwhile, Watson claimed, the family variously threatened to kill Ahmed (according to one version, by hiring Greek thugs to do him in, and later by threatening to poison him), hired a sheikh to write amulets to restore his Muslim faith, and forced him to sign a document of recantation in the office of the chief of police. Eventually he got word to the missionaries that his Christian faith was intact and escaped to one of their houses.[143] Charles R. Watson concluded in 1907 that the case of Ahmed Fahmy "showed that the day had passed when a Moslem could be legally put to death in Egypt for becoming a Christian, but it also revealed the power of Islam and its relentless hostility toward Christianity."[144]

In many ways, Ahmed Fahmy's experience with family closely resembled that of the Azhar-educated brothers, Mikhail and Kamil Mansur, who joined the Evangelical Church in 1897 and 1901, respectively. In Ahmed Fahmy's case as in the case of the Mansur brothers, relatives seemed to want to frighten the young men into returning to the Muslim fold rather than to harm or kill them. Even American missionary accounts make the families' threats sound staged or half-hearted. (For example, missionaries reported that Ahmed Fahmy's mother warned him not to eat food given by other relatives because there were plans afoot to poison him, while Mikhail Mansur's uncle tried to kill him with a dagger, but failed; afterward, Mikhail Mansur's father urged the extended family to desist from further attacks and to leave the young man alone.)[145] The parents of Ahmed Fahmy and the Mansur brothers appear to have shared the experience of loving and losing their sons. In one small way, however, Ahmed diverged from the Mansur brothers and from most other converts from Islam: he did not change his name upon conversion, to something Christian-sounding like Mikhail (Michael), Murqus (Mark), or 'Abd al-Masih (Servant of Christ). Instead he retained his quintessentially Muslim name, Ahmed, until death. Perhaps the name his parents gave him remained central to his construction of self, or perhaps he clung to it as a link to the life he had lost.

So celebrated was Ahmed Fahmy's conversion that missionaries recorded many details of his experience. From these, one can identify three ways in which his story illuminated larger social trends of the period.

First, when Ahmed's relatives were trying to persuade him to recant (in what missionaries regarded as his house arrest phase), the family enlisted help from Jamal al-Din al-Afghani (1838–1897), who was the most famous activist of the late nineteenth-century Muslim world. Iranian by birth, Afghani traveled throughout the Muslim world from India and Afghanistan to the Ottoman domains, and also spent time in Russia, France, and Germany. He engaged in a famous debate at the Sorbonne in 1883 with the French philosopher Ernest Renan, and disputed the latter's claim that Islam was incompatible with science and reason. Through his writings and activities Afghani also tried to rally Muslims against Western imperial incursions; he is therefore regarded as a major figure in the late nineteenth-century pan-Islamic movement, which had strong anti-colonial dimensions. Along with his erstwhile colleague, Muhammad Abduh (the famous Egyptian jurist-reformer), Afghani is regarded as a chief ideologue of Islamic modernism and as an intellectual predecessor to twentieth-century activists like Hasan al-Banna (founder of the Muslim Brotherhood).[146] Today, Muslim intellectuals, such as the Swiss-Muslim thinker Tariq Ramadan (b. 1962), continue to hail Afghani as a source of inspiration.[147] Afghani's cameo appearance in the Christian conversion epic of Ahmed Fahmy is therefore quite striking: Afghani, a man so closely associated with Muslim anti-colonial activism, tried and failed to bring a Muslim apostate back to the fold.

But perhaps this was not so surprising after all. For though lionized by later generations of Muslims, Afghani, by some accounts, was not much of a believer himself.[148] Andrew Watson dismissed Afghani as a "noted arguer" and wrote that he was "more of an infidel than a Muhammadan," while the missionary Anna Young Thompson, who overheard the discussion that occurred in the mission house, described in her diary the appearance of this "learned Moslim man known as 'The Philosopher' for his much & overwhelming talk & arguments, [a man] from Persia or Afghanistan ... who can argue that there is a God or that there is none." She heard them discussing Christ, Muhammad, the Bible, and Voltaire, and added, "Our friends said these men had no religion, that they were nearly infidels. But Ahmed's father had sent them to talk and he Ahmed was not afraid to answer them."[149]

A second detail in Ahmed Fahmy's story suggests that the idea of Egyptian emigration to America may have been taking hold. One of Ahmed's brothers, Muhammad—a man who vehemently opposed Ahmed's conversion yet who had himself been working in American mission schools for ten years—reportedly accused Ahmed of wanting "to marry an American wife, & go to America & get an education."[150] This suggests that in 1877 there was already a perception in the air of Christian conversion as an avenue to emigration to the United States. Emigration among Evangelicals may have already begun. Certainly by 1882, the year of the British Occupation, and five years after Ahmed Fahmy's conversion, Warda Barakat (a woman of Syrian background who had been among the first seven Egyptians to take communion with the missionaries in Alexandria in 1860) had moved to Illinois with her husband.[151] By the time the missionaries prepared their report for the 1883–84 year, two more Evangelicals had emigrated to America, although these were converts from Islam.[152]

Third and finally, Ahmed Fahmy's life offers a powerful illustration of the global extent and interconnectedness of the Protestant missionary movement in this period. Sensing that it would be impossible for him to pursue a Christian life in Egypt given his well-connected family's resistance, Ahmed accepted an invitation from Lord Aberdeen to study medicine at the University of Edinburgh. (Son of the previous title holder, who had distributed Bibles in Upper Egypt in 1861, this Lord Aberdeen [also known as John Campbell Gordon] later became the governor-general of Canada.)[153] In January 1878, Ahmed left his asylum in the mission buildings of Cairo and, eluding a search party, boarded a boat captained by a friend of the British consul of Alexandria, whereupon he sailed to Scotland. After finishing medical studies in Edinburgh and deciding, in the words of Aberdeen, that "it was useless for him to make the attempt" to go back, "as his life would be forfeited the moment he set foot on Egyptian soil," Ahmed accepted an offer from the London Missionary Society.[154] In 1887, upon his arrival in China, Ahmed founded the first modern hospital in Chang Chew (Zhangzhou), Amoy, calling it Hok-im I-koan, meaning, "The Good News [Gospel] Healing House," and ran it successfully as a medical missionary until his retirement in 1919. Eventually, Ahmed did find an American wife: in 1905, a few years after the death of his first wife, a Scottish woman, in a cholera epidemic, Ahmed married a missionary of the Reformed Church in America and traveled with her to the United States during two furloughs. He never returned to Egypt, and his children became British and American.[155]

Compared to Ahmed Fahmy, the Muslim convert Muhammad Habib was less fortunate, and less committed, but his case also warrants scrutiny. A government-school graduate, Muhammad Habib became exposed to Christianity by Protestants in Mansura. Around 1882, he moved to Cairo and opened a stationery shop. He began to study the Bible and other Christian books and to discuss them with the Muslims around him. Once it "became known that he was rejecting the Muslim faith," Andrew Watson chronicled, his Muslim neighbors tried to persuade him of his errors. When that did not work, they dragged him to the *qadi*'s court and jailed him on the charge of becoming Christian; they also spat upon him and beat him. According to Watson, "His goods were seized, his wife divorced, and he himself sent to the government hospital on the plea that he was insane." The missionaries turned to the British authorities, who promised to intercede only if Muhammad Habib agreed to leave Egypt (since they clearly regarded him as a problem and perhaps agreed with assessments of his mental instability). Thus Muhammad Habib went to Cyprus in 1883. The authorities allowed him to return after a year, but only if he promised to stay away from his old neighborhoods. Missionaries then employed Muhammad Habib at their bookstore in Zagazig, a Delta town, but according to Andrew Watson he fell in with "bad men, became discontented with his one wife, and at least went back, nominally, to Islam" (where, Watson implied, he could resort to polygamy). "His departure, after enduring so much, was a sad disappointment to us all, and a severe trial to our faith in any real conversion from Islam." Andrew Watson's son, Charles, later added in 1907 that the case of Muhammad Habib—and above all, his experience of being unilaterally divorced and consigned to a mental hospital—"was not calculated to reassure [Muslim inquirers] in their hopes."[156]

In 1898, a new mission dedicated primarily to Muslim evangelization arrived in Egypt: this was the "Egypt Mission Band," an interdenominational group of seven men from England and Northern Ireland who had first started open-air prayer meetings in Belfast among Saturday-night crowds. Before long, this organization became known as the Egypt General Mission (EGM), and established a rapport with the American Presbyterians, who helped them rent their first property in Abnoub, a village north of Assiut. The EGM soon shifted its efforts to the Delta region and established bases in various towns such as Zagazig, Ezbet el-Zeitoun, Bilbeis, and Ismailiyya; they also opened a hospital in Shebin el-Kanater. As a matter of policy, EGM missionaries sent all their converts to the Evangelical Church rather than initiating a church of their own. EGM missionaries visited cafés, produced colloquial Arabic Bible translations and Christian texts for semi-literate readers, and in a few places preached from halls that opened onto market thoroughfares.[157]

Writing in 1897, thirty-six years after his arrival in Egypt, Andrew Watson expressed doubt that the steep barriers deterring Muslim conversion would ever fall.

The great difficulty [in the period after 1854] was the non-recognition of the principle of religious liberty by the government officials, except when compelled by pressure from a Christian power through its consul-general. . . . [T]here has always been, and there still is, the Muhammadan *esprit de corps*, that is so strong that a brother will kill his brother and a father his son rather than see them become Christians. Besides, the idea of personal liberty has no place in the Muhammadan system, whether religious or civil.[158]

After 1900, however, the next generation of missionaries, buoyed by the giddy rhetoric of worldwide evangelization, was more optimistic about the potential for missions to Muslims. By the time World War I ended, Charles Watson (who had been a four-year-old child in Cairo at the time of Ahmed Fahmy's baptism)[159] was among those who believed that religious liberty in Egypt could be encouraged or, failing that, legislated through the force of national and international law. Religious liberty, and the lack of it in Muslim societies, was to remain a leitmotif in American evangelical discourses throughout the twentieth century.

WOMEN AND THE MISSIONARY ENTERPRISE AT HOME AND ABROAD

Just as the missionaries' focus on Muslims obscured an almost wholly Coptic movement to the Evangelical Church, so did the predominance of missionary men as policy setters and chroniclers obscure the strong representation of women in the mission field during the 1882-to-1918 period. Likewise, the focus of mission accounts on the work in Egypt obscured the U.S.-based efforts of UPCNA churchgoers, and especially women, to mobilize support for the Egyptian field.[160]

In the early to mid-nineteenth century, as American foreign missions expanded, women ventured abroad as the wives of missionary men.[161] This was the "helpmates" phase of female missionary activity, for while wives were expected to assist their husbands and their missions, sponsoring agencies did not necessarily recognize them as missionaries in their own right. (Indeed, when the United Presbyterian Church published *Rules and Recommendations for Foreign Missionaries and Candidates of the United Presbyterian Church* in 1861, its text addressed men, mentioning "females . . . who go out to the missionary work" [*sic*] as an afterthought.)[162] The U.S. Civil War (1861–65) then gave women their "baptism of power."[163] Forced to support and replace the work of men, women gained confidence and experience. After the Civil War, single women began to enter the missionary force in greater numbers. This trend continued so that by 1890, married and single women together constituted 60 percent of the American Protestant missionaries working abroad.[164] The foreign missions of the UPCNA closely followed this trend. By 1895, the mission in Egypt had a staff of thirty-nine missionaries, of whom twenty-three (59 percent) were women.[165] Unlike their male counterparts, women missionaries were able to open schools and health clinics for women and children, train female evangelists ("Bible Women"), and organize systems of home visiting. Women opened doors to new social worlds.

Even as female missionaries worked abroad, their activities were connected to the efforts of churchgoing women at home, as missionary periodicals attest. In the case of the UPCNA, evidence for women's home-front participation can be found in a monthly journal that was published in 1881 and 1882 (when the church's work abroad was limited to Egypt and northern India) under the editorship of Mrs. Sadie C. Blair of Plumville, Pennsylvania. The journal's name evoked the exoticism of the foreign mission field—it was called *Zenana Workers: A Ladies Missionary Magazine*. The title referred to secluded Muslim and Hindu women—"zenana women"—in the Punjab. By hinting at the work that women alone could pursue in zenanas and harems, this journal embodied the spirit of American Orientalism in this period and offered social escapism and vicarious tourism to the American churchgoing women who read it. In fact, this journal covered not only the church's foreign missions in northern India and Egypt but also some of the church's "home missions." For example, its April 1882 issue encouraged children, through their Sunday school classes, to collect materials for the church's Freedmen's Missions, and especially for the work "supplying the [African American] prisoners of our country with religious reading." The same issue tallied funds that women's groups had raised for foreign missions in March of that year. It reported, for example, that the United Presbyterian ladies of Mexico, Pennsylvania, had raised fourteen dollars, those of Ontario, Ohio, had raised thirteen dollars, and those of Coila, New York, had gathered eighty-two dollars—with this last sum having been specially marked for the mission's girls' school in Cairo, Egypt.[166]

Zenana Workers was ecumenical insofar as it cited efforts of other American Protestant groups. Thus the May 1882 issue praised a Baptist missionary to India who described his "remarkable success among the Telugus . . . having baptized 530 persons, while on a recent tour among the villages." The same issue included a story for children (borrowed from another mission publication) titled "You Won't Eat Me, Will You," which was about the power of the gospel to reform a cannibal king in the Fiji Islands.[167] Items like the last one, which was not too far off in spirit from a novel by Rider Haggard, showed how the genre of popular missionary writing could blur the line between news and adventure stories.

One of the most striking assertions to appear in the journal *Zenana Workers* was the editor's claim in the July 1881 issue that "The world may be evangelized within twenty years." The college campus–based Student Volunteer Movement (SVM) for foreign missions did not adopt "The evangelization of the world in this generation" as its slogan until a meeting in Mt. Hermon, Massachusetts, in 1886. But clearly grand expectations for the global capacity of foreign missions were already in the air when Sadie C. Blair wrote her editorial for *Zenana Workers*.[168] As an ephemeral publication that apparently lasted for just two years (1881–82), *Zenana Workers* captured the mood of the moment when foreign missions were expanding American frontiers abroad, when women were driving support for missions within churches, and when American Protestants had the confidence to assume that dollars and cents would translate quickly into numbers of converts.

Zenana Workers' "mission" as a church journal was eventually overtaken by the *Women's Missionary Magazine* of the UPCNA, which began publication in 1886, one year after the incorporation of the Women's General Missionary Society (WGMS). The WGMS became the dynamo of the UPCNA's social service initiatives. Based in Pittsburgh, the WGMS remained administratively and financially independent from the UPCNA's board of foreign missions, which was led by men (most of them ordained pastors, and many of them with mission experience) from offices in Philadelphia. In the case of the UPCNA, the distance of over 250 miles between the offices of the two boards helped preserve the autonomy—and possibly, too, the vitality—of the women's society, as well as the division of labor between them. The WGMS survived as an independent entity until 1956, long after most other mainline Protestant churches had merged their men's and women's missionary boards.[169]

In the UPCNA, the WGMS assumed responsibility for appointing and supporting single women missionaries in the church's foreign missions, whereas the Philadelphia-based board of foreign missions was responsible for men and married couples. After 1889, the WGMS also assumed responsibility for all medical work, so that it paid the salaries of male doctors to Egypt as well.[170] Meanwhile, the WGMS pursued mammoth efforts within the United States by supporting missions to Native Americans (especially in Iowa and Oregon), African Americans (in states such as Tennessee and Mississippi), and poor whites in the Appalachian and Ozarks regions of Kentucky and

Arkansas. The WGMS also ran an orphanage and a home for the aged, arranged help for financially distressed families of deceased clergymen, and supported temperance work.[171]

The WGMS stood at the apex of a vast network of women's and children's mission societies that were organized within UPCNA congregations across the country. Statistics amassed in the *Women's Missionary Magazine* showed, for example, that in 1893 women's missionary societies were located in places like Houstonville, Iowa (thirty-seven members), Swedenborg, Illinois (ten members), Concordia, Kansas (fifteen members), and Loveland, Colorado (thirty members).[172] In turn, these grassroots women's mission societies formed and supervised children's and young women's mission societies. The Rev. W. E. McCulloch explains in *The United Presbyterian Church and Its Work in America* (1925) how these organizations functioned: "In the Junior Department are the Little Light Bearers, whose membership begins at birth and continues until six years of age; and the Juniors, from six to fifteen years of age. During the first fifteen years of life, our boys and girls are given missionary information, taught to pray and to give in behalf of missions, and are trained in the missionary spirit."[173] These children's missionary societies met every week, usually before and in conjunction with the Sunday school classes that preceded congregational worship.[174]

In 1904, at a conference in Pittsburgh celebrating the UPCNA's foreign missions, Mrs. J. P. White of Topeka, Kansas, urged women to be "agitators" for missions and to mobilize their homes in "our conquest of Egypt and India." She urged mothers to discuss missions during dinnertime and fireside conversations, and not to waste time talking about parties or fancy clothing so that "the children grow up to believe that the evangelization of the world is the supreme duty of life." She wrote, "The United Presbyterian Church is advancing on the forces of Satan, arrayed under Hindu idolatry, Mohammedan fanaticism and Sudanese savagery." "Mothers of this generation," exhorted Mrs. White, "the Master is calling you to train workers for Egypt and India."[175]

This cradle-to-grave engagement with missions may help explain why, by 1910, the UPCNA reported the highest per capita rate of giving to foreign missions, leaving all other major American Protestant denominations far behind. (The UPCNA reported in 1910 a rate of $2.25, compared, for example, to $1.05 for the larger Presbyterian Church in the United States, and just sixty-six cents for the Protestant Episcopal Church in the United States.)[176] Two other factors may also explain the high rate of giving among United Presbyterians: first, the church's encouragement of tithing, and second, the foreign and women's mission boards' policy of urging female missionaries to write frequently to the home congregations and mission board.[177] According to Donald Black, a retired pastor who as a child in the 1920s had participated in a UPCNA junior mission society, the steady flow of news from the mission fields helped make the missionaries' work seem real and vital, and gave members of mission societies a focus for study and prayer. Black recalled that children often knew missionaries by name because they prayed for them during meetings.[178] The papers of Walter and Clara Skellie, stored at the Presbyterian Historical Society in Philadelphia, also give a sense of the flow. Occupying half a cubic foot in the archives, their papers consist largely of letters that the Skellies sent to the Glen Falls, New York, congregation that sponsored them.[179]

Anna Young Thompson (1851–1932), known to her friends as "Anna Y," epitomized and tied together the trends of the times. Thompson arrived as a missionary in Egypt in 1871, and spent the next sixty-one years of her life in that career. Thompson wrote copiously but mainly to, for, and about women and children; moreover, she was a letter writer, not a chronicler, and penned several letters a day.[180] Her newsy missives, published first in *Zenana Workers* and later over the years in *Women's Missionary Magazine*, suggest that Thompson was one of the people who helped bring the mission alive for readers at home by offering steady transmissions from Egypt. However, unlike her male counterparts in Egypt—men like Andrew Watson, Earl E. Elder, and C. C. Adams, who achieved stature in their long missionary careers—Thompson never published a mission history or scholarly book to earn her a place on a library bookshelf and therefore an easy entrée into studies later written on missions.

Anna Young Thompson's life encapsulated the history of the expanding American frontier in North America and, through missions, abroad. Her father was a Presbyterian pastor who had emigrated from Ireland to the United States. As a young child in the early 1850s, she traveled with her family by covered wagon from Pennsylvania to the Oregon Territory, later returning via boat from San Francisco, traveling across the Isthmus of Panama. Sometime around 1870 Anna inquired with the UPCNA about joining a mission to American "freedmen," but after learning that no vacancies were available, she accepted a posting to Egypt instead. Upon arriving in Egypt in 1871, she began to teach in a mission school. This was typical for single women missionaries of the era, since "'to teach' was the female equivalent of 'to preach'" in an age when women were barred from the clergy, "and [it] was therefore an evangelistic mandate."[181] The preponderance of women in foreign missions also helps explain why preaching "in practice was the least important missionary method in the Middle East."[182] In terms of its impact, schooling held first place.

Thompson taught in various mission schools over the years but eventually became the supervisor of Egyptian Bible Women, helping train the female evangelists who made house-to-house visits to women. In this manner she followed a trajectory that was common to American missionary women around the world in this period by moving away from direct evangelical work and toward the administration of work by locals in mission employ.[183] She also became an organizer and leader of the Women's Christian Temperance Society of Egypt and of the interdenominational student group known as the Christian Endeavor Society. Having originally studied Arabic with Ahmed Fahmy, the Muslim man who converted to Christianity in 1877, Thompson developed such strong Arabic skills that she eventually became a language examiner for new missionaries in Egypt. She only stepped down from this role after World War I when, to her dismay, the mission began to teach colloquial and literary Arabic separately by adopting the pedagogical methods of the CMS missionary W.H.T. Gairdner.[184]

In diaries, Thompson recorded frequent meetings with well-to-do American tourists passing through Egypt. Among the more famous tourists she hosted, for example, were Ulysses S. Grant, former president of the United States, and his wife, Julia, who came to Cairo in 1878. Meeting American travelers at luxury hotels, she took them on tours of mission institutions, hoping to generate interest and financial support. Sometimes big gifts materialized. For example, the generosity of two American Quaker tourists, the Fowlers, who had visited Egypt in 1896, enabled the American mission in 1906 to open the Fowler Orphanage, which still operates in Cairo today under the direction of an Evangelical Church congregation.[185]

Thompson was an "indefatigable meeter of trains and visitor of hospitals" who claimed in 1917 alone (as she approached her sixty-seventh birthday) to have visited 656 Egyptian homes. She traveled so much and talked to so many people that she reportedly knew "all the railway officials along the line up country and down, and at every station the window went down so she could call for her old friends and ask about their families. . . . It was not uncommon for her to know the family connections in Egypt so well that she could tell people about relatives they did not know they had."[186] When old age encroached on her health, she insisted on remaining in Egypt because that was where she wanted to die and be buried—that was the place she regarded as home.

Another biographer has described Thompson as a "reluctant feminist in Egypt" who pursued an active and lifelong career as a missionary while "dealing with the reality of [her] own subservient place within the structure of the mission."[187] She acceded to the judgment of a few of the leading missionary men in Egypt who in 1890 canceled her marriage to a much older and twice-widowed missionary man on the grounds that it "would shock the Egyptians, especially the Orthodox Copts, if a man had three wives during his lifetime."Yet with her friend Margaret Smith (the same young woman whose reading of the Arabic Bible had contributed to Ahmed Fahmy's conversion), Thompson staged a sit-in at a Missionary Association meeting in the early 1890s and refused to budge until the men granted voting rights to the women. They behaved like mission suffragettes some thirty years before women in the United States won the right to vote nationally in 1920.[188]

Anna Young Thompson generally avoided criticizing "the mission fathers"[189] in Egypt even while she weighed in on "The Woman Question in Egypt"—as the title of one her articles, published in 1914, suggests. This article considers debates among educated Egyptian men, which Thompson describes as a debate over whether Egyptian women, by unveiling, would come to "enjoy the freedom of European women."[190] Thompson shared a core assumption that ran through the American women's missionary movement in this period—the idea that "women around the world were sisters, but non-Christian religions oppressed them" and that "The liberation of women was an essential part of, a major step toward, the kingdom of God."[191] The study guides used by American women at foreign missionary society meetings explicitly elucidated these points of American goodness in gender relations. Thus a popular guide from the period encouraged women to discuss such questions as, "Among non-Christian religions, which is most inadequate in its estimate of women?" and "In what lands do women eat with their husbands at a family table?"[192] If the attitudes of American Presbyterian missionary women in Egypt qualified in any way as feminism (meaning advocacy for greater rights for women), then it was a distinctly Orientalist feminism, built on the conviction that women in Islamic societies were oppressed and that American women, who were enlightened and liberated, could save them.[193]

Anna Young Thompson had been in Egypt for more than thirty years by the time the UPCNA held its jubilee missions convention in 1904. At that gathering, Mrs. W. W. Barr of the WGMS declared that the United Presbyterian "home" church in 1904 claimed 1,109 local women and children's mission societies with 26,575 members who in the past year had raised over fifty thousand dollars for Egypt and India beyond the church's general budget for foreign missions. Mrs. Barr also reported that in Egypt, the Evangelical Church had 3,302 female members in 1903 (relative to a total membership of 7,324);

5,879 women and girls were attending Sunday morning services; 1,313 women and girls were attending mid-week evening services; and 3,366 were attending women's prayer meetings.[194] Although most of these female worshipers would have been Copts, the lack of statistical specificity regarding Muslim involvement would have enabled Mrs. Barr's audience to retain confidence in the universal approach, appeal, and impact of the mission enterprise in Egypt.

Numbers like these bred confidence, even though they may have been minute relative to Egypt's total population (which, according to the 1907 census, included 11,189,978 people).[195] Statistics gave missionaries a sense of possibility, progress, and purpose, and contributed to the heady optimism that marked Christian missions as the twentieth century began.[196]

CONCLUSION: THE DECISIVE HOUR IN FOREIGN MISSIONS

In 1911, John R. Mott, the American Protestant layman who did so much to promote the ideal of "the evangelization of the world in this generation" among American college students, published a new book. Its title—*The Decisive Hour of Christian Missions*—distilled the feelings of hope, moral purpose, and imminence that the previous decade had given. In fact, in the decade before the onset of World War I there were several important developments that affected the American mission in Egypt.

First, in 1905, Annie Van Sommer and Arthur T. Upson, two British missionaries connected to the evangelical, interdenominational North Africa Mission, founded the Nile Mission Press (NMP) in Egypt.[197] Based in Cairo, though coordinated from Tunbridge Wells, England, this publishing enterprise drew support from leading mission organizations in Egypt—above all, the American Presbyterians, CMS, and EGM, as well as organizations like the Young Men's Christian Association (YMCA) and the British and Foreign Bible Society (BFBS)—to produce an Arabic literature for Muslims. This ecumenical venture gained further momentum in 1906 when Protestant missionaries in Egypt organized a conference in Cairo for workers among Muslims worldwide. Its participants sounded a theme that continued to influence mission work among Muslims for the next twenty-five years: they argued that Cairo was a strategic center and a cultural and intellectual crossroads for Islam, and that it was pivotal for the Christian missionary approach to Muslims.[198] By laying the groundwork for cooperation among missionaries to Muslims, the Cairo conference of 1906 anticipated future ecumenical conferences. In fact, it may have been no accident that Charles R. Watson—who was in 1906 serving as secretary of the UPCNA's foreign mission board in Philadelphia, and whose father, Andrew Watson, presented a paper at the Cairo conference—suggested the idea for the joint Anglo-American missionary meeting that occurred in Edinburgh in 1910.[199]

The World Missionary Conference, more commonly known afterward as "Edinburgh 1910," was hailed at the time as a landmark in Christian cooperation. Historians have continued to hail it; writing in 1952, one called it not a mere conference but "an event in the life of the church," while another wrote in 2002 about its "enduring significance without parallel for twentieth-century Christianity."[200] The conference celebrated and studied Euro-American missions that were mostly in Asia and Africa. (Disapproving of the way that some Protestant churches were evangelizing in countries where Roman Catholicism prevailed, high-church Anglicans had excluded Latin America from the conference's purview.)[201] Attended by members of the American mission in Egypt, among them Andrew Watson and Anna Young Thompson,[202] Edinburgh 1910 also accelerated collaborative efforts among Protestant missionaries who worked among Muslims from Nigeria to India and Java. A key participant in Edinburgh 1910—and the man later entrusted to record its summary account—was W.H.T. Gairdner, who was one of the intellectual and organizational forces behind the CMS mission in Egypt and later one of the first faculty members at the American University in Cairo, which emerged under the leadership of Charles R. Watson.[203] Gairdner recorded in his conference account, *Echoes from Edinburgh*, that "The first day of discussion had reminded the Conference of the vast problem of Islam, that great non-Christian system that strides like a Colossus over half of Asia and Africa."[204] The Edinburgh conference-goers expressed various concerns relating to the Muslim world—foremost among them the "lack of religious liberty"—and encouraged missionaries to engage in the special study of "Islamism—not simply of the Koran, but of the living faith of the people."[205]

The year 1910 also witnessed another signal event for the history of American missions, although it is an event that many historians have since overlooked. This was the publication of *Western Women in Eastern Lands*, a book by Helen Barrett Montgomery, who was a leader in the ecumenical women's foreign missionary movement, later "the first woman president of a major denomination (the American Baptist Convention), and the first woman to translate the New Testament into English."[206] Her book, which surveyed fifty years of American women's involvement in foreign missions, inspired the organization of a Jubilee celebration among American women's foreign missions societies throughout the United States. This roving celebration of lectures and luncheons "gathered thousands of women for celebrations in forty-eight major cities and many smaller locations" during 1910 and 1911, and raised thousands of dollars for the development of interdenominational women's colleges in India, China, and Japan. Dana L. Robert noted that, by stimulating "grassroots unity from the bottom up," the Jubilee of 1910–11 drew on and added to the popular energy of the foreign missions movement among American women.[207]

In 1911, Protestant missionaries to Muslims decided to build on the momentum of the Edinburgh conference and to "join forces" by holding a conference in Lucknow, India, to consider the special "problem" of Islam. R. S. McClenahan, the principal of Assiut College (the leading primary and secondary school for boys run by the American mission in Egypt), pointed to the core of the problem as he saw it. "Islam," his conference paper declared, "is the one religious faith in the world which has shown enough energy to seriously antagonize, attack and corrupt the Christian Church, and even to imperil its very existence."[208] Attended by one hundred and sixty delegates and one hundred and fifty "approved visitors," the Lucknow conference brought together a denominationally diverse group of American, Canadian, British, Danish, and German missionaries to consider "the Pan-Islamic movement and its bearing on missions."[209] Lucknow 1911 refined plans for pooling resources to train missionaries, share advice on methods, and produce a Christian literature for Muslims not only in Arabic but also in languages such as Persian and Urdu that were used widely by Muslims. Conference leaders also resolved to establish a joint international and interdenominational study center in Cairo to train Protestant missionaries in Arabic and Islamic studies for work throughout the Islamic world.

Samuel M. Zwemer (1867–1952), an American who had formerly worked as a missionary in Mesopotamia (i.e., the region that became Iraq after World War I) and the Persian Gulf region (especially Bahrain and Oman), was a leading participant in the Cairo, Edinburgh, and Lucknow conferences. Zwemer became the driving force behind Protestant collaborative missions to Muslims in the early twentieth century, and used missions to Muslims as the rallying point for Protestant collaboration and ecumenism. After Lucknow he established a new quarterly journal, *The Moslem World*, which he envisioned as a kind of missionary analogue to the journal *Der Islam* and *The Encyclopedia of Islam*, both of which remain in operation today. Zwemer acknowledged in his opening editorial that *The Moslem World* was an outgrowth of the Cairo 1906, Edinburgh 1910, and Lucknow 1911 conferences, and explained, "If the Churches of Christendom are to reach the Moslem world with the Gospel, they must know it and know of it."[210] The journal that Zwemer founded in 1911 continues today under the title *The Muslim World*. The tiny shift of the spelling from Moslem to Muslim (which occurred in 1948, and which reflects a more accurate transliteration of the Arabic word *muslim*, meaning one who surrenders to God) had symbolic import, and arguably testified to the change of heart and outlook that was occurring within the missions movement of mainline American Protestantism in the post–World War II period. *The Muslim World* is now an academic journal produced by and addressing an audience of scholars who come from diverse Muslim, Christian, and other backgrounds; its academic constituency today not only lacks an evangelical agenda but might be surprised to learn that the journal's founders once had one.

In 1912, Zwemer moved to Cairo to promote the kind of ecumenical mission to Muslims that missionaries had discussed in Edinburgh and Lucknow. He secured a loose affiliation with the American Presbyterian missionaries and, working with Gairdner of the CMS, established the Cairo Study Centre. This center opened with nine missionary students, among them an Indian convert from Islam who intended to work among Muslims in India and an American missionary who proposed to work among Muslims in China. Zwemer kept a scrapbook to commemorate the early Cairo Study Centre. This scrapbook shows that in 1912–13 he lectured on topics in what he called "Islamics," such as "The Moslem doctrine of God," while Gairdner lectured on such things as "The Phonetics of Arabic" and "Translation, Arabic to English."[211] In these lectures, Gairdner began to lay the foundations for a pedagogical program to teach Arabic, especially colloquial Arabic, to English speakers.[212] When the Cairo Study Centre later merged, in 1920, into the American University in Cairo (AUC), it changed its name to the School of Oriental Studies (SOS). In the long run, Gairdner's program for Arabic study enabled AUC to assume a leading role in Arabic pedagogy for English speakers—a position it continues to hold today, even though the university's connection to missionaries was broken over a half century ago.

Zwemer also became an organizational dynamo behind the ecumenical project to develop Christian literatures for Muslims. In October 1910, on the heels of the Edinburgh conference, he organized the American Committee of the Nile Mission Press in New York City, which was originally envisioned as an American fund-raising source for the NMP. However, the organization changed its name in January 1915 to become the American Christian Literature Society for Moslems (ACLSM) and began to support a range of projects that it deemed worthy.[213] In 1918, for example, it funded the publication of a Chinese version of chapter 2 of the Qur'an (*al-Baqara*, "The Cow"), at the request of a missionary in China named Rev. E. C. Lobenstine. (The minutes explained the rationale for the latter project:"It has been found that printing the Koran in Chinese opens the eyes of Chinese Moslems to the imperfections of the book.")[214] Throughout the inter-war period, the ACLSM remained a major sponsor of the NMP even as it funded other projects. It gave money to the NMP for publishing specific tracts, books, and journals, and also for acquiring a new build-ing site and printing press in Cairo.[215] Meanwhile, the NMP fulfilled the mandate from the Lucknow 1911 conference by publishing mis-sionary tracts not only for Egypt but the entire Muslim world. By 1925 it was sending special consignments intended "for [missionary] work among Arab sailors in a port of British Columbia" as well as for work among Muslims in places like Ecuador, South Africa, and China.[216]

After 1915, wealthy or well-connected Protestant men and women served on the board of the ACLSM in New York City.[217] Rich donors occasionally gave to the ACLSM, but in fact the organization's sup-port base was socially broad and depended on dues-paying members scattered across the United States. The ACLSM also had a few special "ladies' auxiliary societies" working and raising funds on its behalf in places like Poughkeepsie, New York; Newark, New Jersey; and Bal-timore, Maryland. It had a cluster of supporters in Michigan and in 1918 even attracted $5,333 from a group of Dutch-speaking farmers in Sioux City, Iowa, who had donated after Zwemer translated the society's promotional materials into Dutch on their behalf.[218]

Zwemer took an aggressive approach to Christian missionary work among Muslims and published many works in English about Islam, a religion that he described as retrograde, fanatical, and intellectu-ally and spiritually impoverished.[219] Arab Muslim activists became aware of his writings and circulated them, often in translated sum-mary form, long after Zwemer had died. As the twentieth century ended, some Arab Muslim thinkers wrote anti-missionary treatises that portrayed Zwemer, first, and Gairdner, second, as the chief vil-lains in a Christian evangelical and Western imperial plot to sub-vert Islam.[220] In the long run, Zwemer aroused such bitter animosity among Muslims that he proved to be more of a liability than an as-set to the work of Christian missionaries in Egypt and other parts of the Muslim world.[221] Yet in one respect Zwemer was more astute than his colleagues: he recognized the growing presence of Muslim im-migrant groups in the United States and Britain and considered their implications for Christian missions to Muslims as well as for Muslim missions to Christians. He realized in a way that his colleagues did not that the Muslim world could be found in New York, Detroit, and

London, and that Islam was poised to become a missionary religion in Western, predominantly Christian societies.[222]

The second decade of the twentieth century began on a hopeful note for missionaries, since missions were continuing to expand globally, funds were relatively plentiful, and Protestant missionaries were devising new ways to cooperate across denominational and national lines. The ecumenism that missionaries affirmed at the Edinburgh 1910 conference also contained a strong spirit of internationalism. For this reason, the war that began with a gunshot in Sarajevo in 1914 was all the more shattering to missionary morale, since it pitted ostensibly Christian peoples against each other.

Historians of missions have argued that World War I dealt a devastating and humbling blow to the foreign missions movement among mainstream or mainline Protestants who watched as European powers descended into "a Christian civil war."[223] But while the war weakened mainline Protestant missions, it strengthened the evangelical vision of American independent "faith missions," sponsored by conservative, fundamentalist Protestant church groups, who saw in its apocalyptic destruction a sign of the millennium to come.[224] Thus the war helped set in motion a long-term shift in American evangelicalism and the nature of American evangelical missions. For mainline Protestants, World War II later compounded the shock of World War I. Evidence for this changed mood can be found in the bleak tone that pervades the seventh volume of Kenneth S. Latourette's *History of the Expansion of Christianity*, which covers the years from 1914 to the early 1940s, when Latourette was writing. Zwemer had in 1916 published *The Disintegration of Islam* (based on lectures he gave at Princeton Theological Seminary in 1915) but Latourette, while finding hope in the spread of Christianity via missions in Africa and Asia, perceived in 1945 what he described as the disintegration of Christendom in Western Europe following the onslaught of the world wars, the growth of secularism, and the spread of Communist atheism.[225]

The euphoria, confidence, and bravado that had distinguished missionaries after 1882 was subsiding by the time World War I ended. After 1918, American Presbyterians in Egypt showed persistence but greater caution as Muslim nationalists stood up to challenge the aspects of Christian missionary work—notably, evangelization among Muslims—they regarded as not only inappropriate and repugnant but subversive.

Egyptian Nationalism, Religious Liberty, and the Rethinking of the American Mission, 1918–45

> Of course all of us have known that such days as these would come.
> — W. B. Anderson to C. C. Adams,
> Philadelphia, July 13, 1933

> If the only beneficial results of all this anti-missionary agitation are a deeper interest in the welfare of the more unfortunate members of society, an improvement in the working of Moslem philanthropic institutions and an awakening in the Coptic Church, then it will not have expended itself in vain.
> — Cairene [C. C. Adams], "Egypt and Religious Liberty,"
> *International Review of Missions*, October 1933

DURING THE AMERICAN PRESBYTERIAN mission's first sixty years in Egypt, missionaries occasionally endured the vituperation of Coptic bishops and priests and taunts from Muslim crowds. But such events had been isolated and had not tempered missionaries' hopes. The situation began to change in the 1920s when challenges appeared on multiple fronts. Thus, if 1882 to 1918 had constituted a high-confidence period in the history of Protestant missions in Egypt, then the interwar years represented, for missionaries, a period of chronic low-grade anxiety. Missionaries were buffeted by financial troubles and by criticism of foreign missions that emanated from the American "home front"; they were increasingly worried, too, about tightening Egyptian laws and attitudes that restricted their work among Muslims. Against this context, American Presbyterians began to reappraise their mission in Egypt. They also began to articulate ideals of individual religious liberty; to publish statements and reports on the subject; and to strengthen relations with other Protestant organizations that were facing similar concerns about Christian missions in the Muslim world.

The cataclysmic violence of World War I dealt a psychic blow to the foreign mission establishment, which just a few years earlier in 1910 had celebrated Protestant unity at the World Missionary Conference in Edinburgh. The rise of the Bolshevik movement in Russia, with its ideological support for atheism, added to the gloom. In this postwar milieu, an important shift in Protestant missionary thought began to occur, reflecting a change in how missionaries conceptualized the cultural geography of Christian societies. This shift was visible by the time Basil Mathews, a British ecumenical activist, published an account of the Jerusalem 1928 conference of the International Missionary Council (an organization founded in 1921 as an outgrowth of the Edinburgh 1910 conference). Mathews declared that the greatest threat to Christianity came from irreligious enemy forces that were maneuvering within the "citadel" of Christian countries. "Therefore," Mathews concluded, "the Western world is itself a mission field. The home base of missions is not a geographical entity at all, but is simply Christ wherever He lives in human life."[1] This idea gained momentum, and within twenty years Kenneth S. Latourette, the American mission historian and former missionary to China, suggested that the mission-planted churches of Asia and Africa should send missionaries to Western countries, where they were needed.[2]

This shift toward an internal critique of the Christian West was consonant with a more somber mood among American Presbyterians in Egypt. This mood deepened in 1926 when the UPCNA announced a 34 percent cut in the foreign mission budget, along with the recall of fifty missionaries from the Nile Valley and northern India. These retrenchments produced anguish among American Presbyterians in Egypt and led some to feel that home churches had failed.[3]

For Egyptians, and Egyptian Muslims in particular, the decade after World War I brought its own difficult transitions. Foremost among these was the collapse of the Ottoman Empire, which European powers dismantled in postwar settlements. In former Ottoman lands, new political entities emerged, including Syria, Lebanon, Transjordan, and Palestine, which the League of Nations placed under French and British mandates. The independent republic of Turkey also emerged from Ottoman Anatolia and Thrace. Yet while few Egyptian Muslim thinkers lamented the passing of the Ottoman Empire as an administrative entity, many did lament its passing as a symbol of Muslim imperial and cultural unity, and as a counterpoint to Western imperialism. The Ottoman collapse also challenged Egyptian intellectuals to mull over the links that bound Arabic-speaking people together in spite of the borders that cut them apart. Meanwhile, many Egyptian thinkers emerged from World War I deeply frustrated with Britain's continued hold over their country. Britain had tightened its grasp in 1914 by announcing Egypt's severance from the Ottoman Empire (which had aligned itself with Germany and the Central Powers during the war) and by placing Egypt under a military protectorate; at the same time, Britain had elevated the Egyptian khedive (that is, the descendant of Muhammad Ali and the head of the Egyptian ruling family) to the status of king. By war's end, Egyptians were anxious to shake off British control and seize the opportunity for self-determination that President Woodrow Wilson had upheld for colonized countries in his famous "Fourteen Points" speech of 1918.

In 1919, the Egyptian nationalist Sa'd Zaghlul led a *wafd* (delegation) to present Egypt's claims for independence at the Paris Peace Conference. But when Britain thwarted the delegates' efforts to broach Egypt's future in this forum, Egyptians rose in a popular anti-British uprising known as the 1919 revolt. Britain responded in 1922 by declaring unilateral independence for Egypt—meaning a non-negotiated and restricted independence that retained Britain's hold over military and diplomatic affairs. After 1922, Britain also encouraged the drafting of an Egyptian constitution and the establishment of a parliament. In Egypt, the years from 1923 until the military coup and revolution of 1952 are therefore described as a period of constitutional monarchy. Yet this was a highly contentious period in which nationalist politicians, the king, and British authorities were all jockeying for influence, as parliamentary politics degenerated into "personalized programless factionalism."[4]

Important political battles were nevertheless taking place in Arabic newspapers, where Egyptian Muslim nationalists were competing for the attention of growing literate, middle-class audiences. The biggest battle involved Islam: what it should mean in a modern Egyptian society; how the Egyptian government should protect and promote its values; and who should have the authority to interpret it for the sake of public affairs.[5] Nationalists were also debating how Egypt should respond to, borrow from, and in some ways distance itself from the West, that is, from the lands of western Europe and North America, which for more than a century had been exerting a strong cultural, economic, and political pull on Egyptian society. Meanwhile, three main contenders were competing for Muslim authority and popular allegiance in Egypt: the *'ulama* or religious scholars at al-Azhar university mosque; representatives of new Muslim popular groups, such as the Muslim Brotherhood; and Western-educated Muslim intellectuals.[6]

Christian missionaries played a critical symbolic role in these debates about the future of Egypt. In the early 1930s, Egyptian Muslim nationalists from across the political spectrum began to point to episodes of Christian evangelization (*tabshir*) among Muslim youths as evidence for an Islamic social order gone awry. Representatives of different parties or groups seized upon the alleged misdeeds of missionaries to discredit standing governments for inaction while cultivating their own popular followings or claims to leadership.[7] New Muslim organizations like the Young Men's Muslim Association (YMMA) also pointed to missionary incidents in order to spur Muslims into social and political engagement.

Together, these Muslim nationalist groups seriously challenged the future of American Presbyterian activities in Egypt. Yet even in the midst of their criticism of missionaries, Muslims in all these groups insisted that they were opposed to neither the presence of Christian missions per se nor to the Christian provision of charity in Egypt. They maintained, rather, that they objected to Christian efforts to convert Muslim schoolchildren and youths and to criticize Islam in ways that amounted, in their view, to defamation (ta'n).[8] These nationalists did not draw sectarian or national distinctions but described Protestants and Catholics, of French, American, Swedish, British, and other backgrounds, as equally pernicious. In other words, these nationalists pointed to the existence of a unitary Christian missionary problem, and called on the Egyptian government to do its duty (wajib) by protecting Muslim schoolchildren, upon whom they claimed evangelizers (mubashshirun) otherwise preyed.

Public debates over missionaries struck a chord with members of a growing Muslim, newspaper-reading, public, who pressed the government to act. Muslim parliamentarians responded by drafting new laws in the 1930s and 1940s that restricted missionary work by subjecting mission schools to government oversight. Egyptian politicians and journalists described these regulations as part of an effort to protect Egypt from foreign intrusion, to restore national sovereignty and public order, and to guard Islam, which the constitution of 1923 confirmed as the religion of state. In practice, the American Presbyterian missionaries in the 1930s and 1940s found themselves negotiating the enforcement or waiver of new laws by dealing with the petty functionaries of an ever more elaborate Egyptian bureaucracy. While new regulations affected everything from sanitation to recreation, the American Presbyterians were most concerned about laws that forbade them from teaching Christianity to Muslim children in their schools.

This scenario of curtailment was not what missionaries had foreseen during the years of World War I. On the contrary, some missionaries had hoped that in the war's aftermath, a progressive international order would emerge to strengthen individual liberties in Egypt as in America. H. E. Philips, a staunch advocate of the mission to Muslims, was one of these idealists. In 1918, while on furlough in the United States after a stint as a missionary in Luxor, Philips gave a sermon at a church in Topeka, Kansas, and in it suggested that Germany's treatment of Belgium during the war was God's retribution for Belgian atrocities in the Congo. A reporter in the congregation publicized his remarks, whereupon a federal court, acting on the terms of the wartime Espionage Act, had him arrested on charges of treason. As he awaited trial in Kansas facing a possible term in a federal prison, with his case postponed because of the influenza pandemic, Philips reflected on religious liberty in Egypt as it pertained to converts from Islam. "The question of religion is bound to be discussed at the [Paris] Peace Conference on account of the Jewish question and the Armenian question," he wrote in a letter to the UPCNA mission board. "Is not this the opportune time to get the nations protecting the weaker peoples of the earth to openly state that there shall be absolute freedom on the part of these peoples to choose their religion and a guarantee of protection in case of a change from one religion to another? The United States is in a position to tell the Allies what should be done to protect our converts."[9] Philips (who was ultimately cleared of the treason charge) was not the first missionary to express the hope that treaties, or later the League of Nations, would guarantee religious liberty in a country like Egypt. Nor was he the first to be disappointed by the limitations of international law as it pertained to human rights.

Developments in the United States and in the UPCNA strongly affected the American Presbyterian mission in this period, above all in matters of finance. But circumstances on the ground in Egypt—and especially Muslim anti-missionary agitation—were ultimately more important to the mission's day-to-day operation and to the mutual transformations that the missionary encounter produced. While the missionaries helped sharpen Egyptian nationalist consciousness and Muslim identities in the process of provoking resistance, Egyptian Muslim nationalists and activists challenged American Presbyterian missionaries, in turn, to sharpen an ideology of religious liberty. Egyptian Muslim resistance also prompted the American Presbyterians to develop a stronger sense of Christian solidarity with other Protestant organizations that were, like them, beginning to embrace a philosophy of mission that emphasized deeds—social service—more than words as a mode of proclaiming the faith.

Islam, Modernism, and Missionaries in Egypt

The year 1926 was a turning point for Egyptian Muslim nationalist thought—the moment when "the old political universe in which Egyptians had lived before World War I crumbled around them."[10]

Certainly winds changed for Christian missionaries, who began to face sustained resistance to their work.

In 1924, the new republic of Turkey abolished the Ottoman caliphate, thereby eliminating a reassuring symbol of leadership within the *umma*, or universal Muslim community. Responding to these developments, scholars from al-Azhar convened the Cairo Caliphate Conference in 1926 to discuss reviving the institution of rule by a caliph, who could represent and theoretically defend the Muslim people in the post-Ottoman setting. But the conference ended without resolution. The historians Israel Gershoni and James P. Jankowski have observed, "By 1926 the Ottoman religious-political order was dead" and there would henceforth be no "symbolic focal point for [Sunni] Muslim allegiance." These conditions elicited "the birth of a new political universe" in which the Egyptian nation, and not the wider *umma*, became a focus for evolving Egyptian Muslim identities, and in which the burgeoning middle classes exerted a stronger influence.[11] "The entry of these middle strata into the negotiation over national identity," wrote Jankowski and Gershoni in a later study, "was the decisive event shaping the evolution of Egyptian nationalism; it in large part accounts for its relentless Islamicization, Arabization, and 'Easternization'"—and for the growth of psychological distance away from the West during the interwar period.[12] Popular piety would continue to shape the policies and pronouncements of Egypt's ruling elites.[13]

The year 1926 was a pivotal moment in the "struggle over the country's soul" for another reason: conservative *'ulama* lashed out against two Egyptian Muslim thinkers who proposed new interpretations of Islamic tradition.[14] The first thinker, 'Ali 'Abd al-Raziq (1888–1966), was a *qadi* or Shari'a court judge and graduate of al-Azhar who published a book in 1925 called *Al-Islam wa-usul al-hukm* (Islam and the principles of governance). In this book, 'Ali 'Abd al-Raziq dismisses the need for a caliph in the modern age and emphasizes "that Islam as a religion contained no political principles and embodied only spiritual authority and moral guidance affecting man's relationship with God." By using the terms "caliph" and "king" interchangeably, 'Ali 'Abd al-Raziq was also making an oblique thrust against Egypt's King Fu'ad; a monarchy, like a caliphate, he suggests, was irrelevant to modern society.[15] Incensed by the book and supported behind the scenes by King Fu'ad, conservative *'ulama* voted in 1926 to strip 'Ali 'Abd al-Raziq of his position as a *qadi* and place in the Azhar community. The second thinker to challenge the Islamic tradition was the Arabic literary scholar Taha Hussein (1889–1973). In 1926, conservative *'ulama* accused Taha Hussein of heresy for proposing a literary and historicist interpretation of the Qur'an in his book *Fi al–Shi'r al-Jahili* (On pre-Islamic poetry).[16] They objected, for example, to his suggestion "that the existence of Abraham and Ishmael could not be assumed as historically valid by virtue of their mention in the Quran."[17] Taha Hussein's accusers brought him to court, where he was acquitted of heresy; nevertheless, he expunged offending passages from a subsequent edition of his book.

The American Presbyterians in Egypt closely followed the charges that the 'ulama leveled against 'Ali 'Abd al-Raziq and Taha Hussein, and worried about their implications for religious liberty in Egypt. They believed that the charges contradicted the 1923 Egyptian constitution's promise that "freedom of conscience is absolute"—a clause whose inclusion missionaries had supported.[18] Thus, in 1926, J. R. Alexander of the American mission and Charles R. Watson of AUC helped draft a memorandum on religious liberty, which they presented to the British high commissioner. In the memorandum they asked, with reference to both cases, "Does not such procedure on the part of the Government indicate its trend and purpose to prevent the freedom and liberty to the individual and the community that the Constitution provides? In none of these cases did the individuals concerned attack the prophet or the religion of Islam." They continued, "In view of these well-known events may we not be anxious concerning the future of our various missionary endeavors?"[19] The American Presbyterians were concerned for converts from Islam like Hassan Kadri: in 1920, when Hassan refused to recant, his uncle reportedly had him assaulted by hired thugs, registered a charge of insanity against him (so that the uncle could be made his guardian), and then had him arrested on a charge of trading hashish and smuggling; meanwhile, Hassan made plans to emigrate to America and study theology. "We hope he lives long enough to get out of the country safely," a missionary had written.[20]

The Presbyterians may have also understood Taha Hussein's collision with religious conservatives in relation to a culture war that was roiling the American Protestant establishment. Church historians have called this debate the "fundamentalist-modernist controversy" and have connected it to the rise of a persistent conservative-liberal divide within American Protestantism.[21] In the 1920s, Protestants who became known as fundamentalists insisted on the timeless inerrancy of the Bible as the word of God, whereas those who became known as modernists insisted on the Bible's historicity and on "the conscious, intended adaptation of religious ideas to modern culture."[22] In content and timing, the resemblance of this American Protestant debate about the Bible and Christian tradition to the Egyptian Muslim debate about the Qur'an and Islamic tradition is striking.

In the mid-1920s, the fundamentalist-modernist controversy nearly tore asunder the Presbyterian Church U.S.A. (PCUSA), with which the UPCNA (the sponsor of the Egypt mission) later merged in 1958. Consider that in 1925, conservatives within the PCUSA persuaded their church's General Assembly to censure the presbytery of New York for ordaining some ministers who refused to affirm the doctrine of the Virgin Birth (the doctrine that Mary conceived Jesus without a human father). One of the leaders of this effort within the PCUSA was the Presbyterian layman William Jennings Bryan, who in 1925 also served as the prosecuting attorney in the Scopes trial. In that trial, which became a landmark in U.S. legal history, Jennings represented the State of Tennessee in defending a law that forbade state educators from teaching "any theory that denies the story of the Divine creation of man as taught in the Bible," including the theory of evolution, which taught instead "that man has descended from a lower order of animals."[23] In the 1920s, the American Presbyterians in Egypt were concerned about the debates in which the Presbyterians of the PCUSA were embroiled, but managed to sidestep these by sticking to the UPCNA's creedal statement, emphasizing their church's history of union, and judging from missionary correspondence, remaining shy of theological discussion. They did so while remaining leery of Christians whom some of them began to call fundamentalists.[24]

The American Presbyterian missionary Charles Clarence Adams (1883–1948) exemplified the convergence between Protestant and Islamic modernism in this period. In 1908, on his application for missionary service, C. C. Adams described himself as an avid Bible reader since childhood. Asked whether he believed "the Scriptures of the Old and New Testament to be the word of God, the only infallible rule of faith and progress," he responded with an unqualified yes.[25] Yet by the 1920s and early 1930s, Adams had come to regard modernism as a positive development and to connect it with the idea of reform (and Reformation) that was so closely associated with the theological history of Presbyterianism. It was probably for this reason that Adams became such an acute observer and admirer of kindred trends in Islam, and why he published in 1933 a study of the Egyptian Muslim reformer Muhammad Abduh (1849–1905) that also discusses the controversies of 'Ali 'Abd al-Raziq and Taha Hussein. Titled *Islam and Modernism in Egypt: A Study of the Modern Reform Movement Inaugurated by Muhammad 'Abduh*, this book is still cited by historians. In it, Adams defines modernism in Egypt as "an attempt to free the religion of Islam from the shackles of a too rigid orthodoxy, and to accomplish reforms which will render it adaptable to the complex demands of modern life."[26] His private correspondence with the UPCNA mission board secretary in Philadelphia shows that Adams was a supporter of Egyptian Christian modernism, too, and wished that the Cairo Evangelical Theological Seminary, at which Egyptian men were trained for the Evangelical (Presbyterian) pastorate, would engage more energetically in modernization and reform.[27]

Missionaries like Adams may have admired modern Muslim thinkers who brought critical reason and historical analysis to bear on Islamic tradition, but the feelings were not necessarily reciprocated. In fact, intellectuals like Muhammad Husayn Haykal (whom Adams also discusses in *Islam and Modernism in Egypt*) emerged in the early 1930s as critics of Christian missionaries and called for tighter government regulation over missionary schools and social services. Often recognized as the author of the first modern Arabic novel (*Zaynab*, 1914) and the first modern biography of the Prophet Muhammad (*Hayat Muhammad*, 1935), Muhammad Husayn Haykal (1888–1956) began to insist in the early 1930s on the relevance of Islamic culture and values for Egyptian society. Haykal did so while supporting the idea that religious thought should be subject to scientific rationalism, and that religious observance (for example, in the payment of *zakat* or alms, which the Qur'an enjoins as a Muslim duty) should be subject to personal discretion—ideas that prompted a biographer to describe him as a Muslim secularist for approaching religion as "a matter of personal faith in which the believer is responsible to God alone, not to religious officials such as the 'ulama of al-Azhar."[28] In his biography of Muhammad, which many Muslim readers at the time interpreted as signaling his "fundamental shift from a Western orientation to an Islamic one,"[29] Haykal makes many remarks about the "intense fanaticism" and hostility of Christian missionaries toward Islam, and concludes that "Western imperialism supports with its power the proponents of this slander (*ashab hadhihi al-mata'in*) in the name of freedom of opinion."[30]

Even Taha Hussein weighed in to criticize missionaries, though he offended some Muslim activists by minimizing the threat that the isolated conversions of missionaries posed.[31] In their criticism of missionaries, Muslim modernists found common ground with the 'ulama of al-Azhar, with whom they otherwise had ideological differences. Together the 'ulama and Muslim modernists articulated views about the Islamic integrity of Egyptian society that met with a groundswell of popular support.

Among Egyptian Muslim nationalists, an upsurge in anti-missionary rhetoric after 1927 accompanied and spurred the emergence of new forms of Muslim social activism. Unlike earlier Islamic charities that relied on wealthy donors, many of whom established *waqf*s or

Islamic endowments, and even unlike some of the Muslim and Coptic benevolent societies that formed among educated elites in the late nineteenth century,[32] the new Muslim organizations of the post–World War I period drew on a broader, middle-class base of support. They also developed outside the precincts of established institutions such as al-Azhar, embraced publishing technology for the dissemination of ideas, and extolled a philosophy of communal self-help. Significantly, these organizations imitated many Christian missionary methods for the sake of Muslim social outreach: they were as likely, for example, to sponsor football matches as to organize study groups for the discussion of scripture.[33] Finally, these organizations formed branches not only in Cairo but also in towns ranging from Aswan to Alexandria. Whereas opposition to Christian evangelization had, in the past, been sporadic and atomized, the rise of these new societies meant that opposition to missionaries could be coordinated nationally.

The most formidable Muslim group to develop in this period, from the American Presbyterians' point of view, was Jami'at al-Shubban al-Muslimin (literally, "Society of Muslim Youth"), which debuted in November 1927. In English translation, this organization was commonly known as the Young Men's Muslim Association or YMMA, and the resemblance of its name to the Young Men's Christian Association or YMCA was telling. Like the YMCA, which under American leadership after World War I had developed an active presence for Egyptians in Cairo, the YMMA functioned as a social, cultural, and athletic club for well-educated young men of the upper middle classes.[34] However, unlike the Cairo YMCA, whose leaders, as a matter of policy, welcomed non-Christians as members, the YMMA appealed exclusively to Muslims.[35] The society's charter expressed an aim "to promote Islamic values and knowledge suited to modern times" while selectively borrowing from the cultures of the East and West. Later, in 1930, YMMA leaders adopted more specific resolutions that included counteracting Christian missionary work, appointing members to attend Christian missionary lectures for the purpose of surveillance, and pressing the government to strengthen the Islamic content of school curricula. Its board members were highly educated men (some of them with advanced degrees from universities in London, Paris, and Vienna) and they had powerful government contacts. For example, one was the director of primary schools in the Ministry of Education, and another was a member of parliament.[36]

Other new Muslim groups copied a different Christian missionary technique, namely the free distribution of tracts. Both the Jam'iyat al-hidaya al-islamiyya (Association of Islamic Guidance) and the Islamic

Home Mission of al-Faydiyun gave out Islamic tracts on the train between Cairo and Alexandria, in a region where American Presbyterians since 1912 had operated a railway car in order to evangelize among Muslim villagers.[37] Egyptian Muslim activism was not unique in taking this direction: comparable organizations had flourished in India from 1874, when Tamils in Madras established the Hindu Tract Society with the aim of counteracting Christian missionaries and promoting Hindu revival. Historians of Christianity in India suggest that tract societies played an important role in seeding modern Hindu nationalism in the late nineteenth century.[38] Likewise, the parallel movement in Egypt helped cultivate Egyptian Muslim nationalism during the twentieth century's interwar era.

In retrospect, al-Ikhwan al-Muslimun, or the Muslim Brotherhood, founded in 1928, was the most important Muslim activist organization to appear in the late 1920s. It remained a vital force in Egyptian Muslim society throughout the twentieth century, persisting despite periods of heavy government repression, and went on to spawn offshoots throughout the Muslim world. Because it gained such a large following in the 1930s and 1940s among the Egyptian Muslim middle and lower-middle classes, and because its leaders made opposition to Christian missionaries one of the movement's earliest rallying cries, its role in anti-missionary activism cannot be underestimated. Nevertheless, American and British Protestant missionaries in Egypt did not register its existence as a discrete organization for many years, probably because they retained a deep fascination for al-Azhar and expected the greatest challenge to their work to come from that direction.[39] John S. Badeau, for example, who arrived in Egypt in 1936 and became dean and later president of AUC, had the impression, as he recorded in memoirs, that the Muslim Brotherhood "did not emerge on the popular scene" until after World War II. Alluding to the organization's roots in the lower-middle classes, Badeau added, "Had one been in government one would have known it, but they were not particularly talked about. One did not have friends who were Muslim Brothers."[40]

The founder of the Muslim Brotherhood was a schoolteacher named Hasan al-Banna (1906–1949), who had joined the YMMA while studying in Cairo in 1927 and admired its programs and aims.[41] But Banna "had a profound belief in the piety of the masses," in the words of a biographer, and felt that another organization was needed—something that could reach beyond the educated elites of the YMMA to embrace the Muslim rank and file. As if to illustrate his support for a meritocracy of the pious, Banna appointed a carpenter as one of his deputies and a *makwagi* (professional clothes ironer) to lead the organization's first school. Meanwhile, he began to promote the idea of Muslim mission or *da'wa*, from an Arabic word meaning literally "call" or "invitation." In this regard, Banna was building on ideas that had been articulated earlier by the Egyptian-based Syrian thinker Rashid Rida (1865–1935), whose encounters with Christian missionaries before World War I had prompted him to theorize about Islam's missionary impulse.[42] Under Banna's leadership, the Muslim Brotherhood embarked upon activities—such as offering adult education programs to combat illiteracy and sponsoring youth clubs—that closely resembled the activities of the American and British Protestant missionaries in Egypt. Even the organization's summer camps for children, which proliferated in the late 1930s,[43] replicated the Vacation Bible Schools of the American missionaries.[44] By preaching in cafés, too, the Muslim Brotherhood copied a favored technique among American- and British-sponsored colporteurs or Bible salesmen.[45]

The Muslim Brotherhood first emerged in Ismailiyya, a town in the Suez Canal zone that was inhabited by many foreigners who worked for the French- and British-owned Suez Canal Company. The foreign presence in Ismailiyya may indeed have spurred the establishment of this organization, which from its inception had strong anti-foreign dimensions.[46] Yet it was also significant that Banna came from the Delta, and that in his formative teenage years in the early 1920s, while he was a student in Damanhour, he had witnessed the expansion of Christian missionary activities among Muslims in the region. In his memoirs, Banna recalled the presence of three young women from what he described as the "evangelical Injiliyya mission" (*al-irsaliyya al-injiliyya al-tabshiriyya*), which "descended upon" the region. He wrote that under the leadership of a "Miss White," the missionaries tried to propagate Christianity among Muslims by opening a girls' school that taught embroidery, as well as by offering medical care and housing orphans. Banna and a friend responded by starting a "reformist society" (*jam'iyya islahiyya*) in al-Mahmudiyya, his hometown, to counteract the Christian missionaries while providing Muslim charity as an alternative. "We waged a meritorious combat against their message," he wrote, "and the society of the Muslim Brothers later followed it in this struggle."[47]

The Injiliyya mission to which Banna referred was probably the American Presbyterian mission and the associated Evangelical Church, *al-Kanisa al-Injiliyya*. The "Miss White" was probably Florence Lillian White of Grove City, Pennsylvania, who joined the American mission in Egypt in 1919, at age twenty-two. "Miss White," as the minutes of the American Missionary Association also called her, worked in the Delta for the next few years, helping superintend the mission's school for girls in Tanta in 1923 and serving on the committee to administer mission accounts in Delta stations. According to her personnel file, Florence White "retired" after just seven years, in 1926, because the mission deemed her "unacceptable as a worker"; in fact, the termination of her service coincided with a spate of missionary cutbacks that the church undertook amid a funding crisis.[48] Thus it appears that Banna apprehended the American missionary presence at the moment of its greatest expansion in the early 1920s, when the mission's staff was at its largest and when mission stations were opening in the small and almost entirely Muslim towns of the Delta, far from the Coptic communities of Upper Egypt where Evangelical congregations were thriving.[49]

In the late 1920s, Muslim activists also gained important forums in the Arabic periodical press. Political parties like the Liberal Constitutionalists (associated with Muhammad Husayn Haykal) and the Wafd (associated with Sa'd Zaghlul) had their own newspapers, but now the leaders of new Muslim organizations were initiating journals, too. The founders of the YMMA, upon its inception in 1927, started a weekly journal called *al-Fath* (The conquest); its editor, Muhibb al-Din al-Khatib, later helped Hasan al-Banna start *Jaridat al-Ikhwan al-Muslimin* (The Muslim Brotherhood newspaper) in 1933.[50] The historian Ami Ayalon has remarked that as late as 1881, Shaykh Husayn al-Marsafi of al-Azhar had "strongly criticized the rapid spread of printing [as] a modern device that compromised traditional values."[51] But in 1930 even the *'ulama* joined the fray by establishing Azhar's own journal, *Nur al-Islam* (Light of Islam).

In this atmosphere, the printed page was becoming a pulpit, and its audiences were growing. Thus in 1928, when Samuel M. Zwemer caused an uproar by distributing Christian tracts within the Azhar courtyard, Muslim nationalists and members of the YMMA were ready and able to issue a loud call for action. The incident with Zwemer was the spark that lit the tinder: it set off a round of Muslim anti-missionary agitation that prompted the Egyptian government to place Christian missionaries under tighter restrictions.

Samuel M. Zwemer and the Power of the Printed Page in the World of Islam

During a long career, first as a missionary to what is now Iraq and the Gulf States, later in Cairo as a "missionary-at-large" to the Muslim world, and finally as a professor of Christian missions in the United States, Samuel M. Zwemer made his name as an advocate of Christian missions to Muslims. He published extensively; traveled tire-lessly in order to preach, lecture, and raise funds for mission causes; and played a leading role in consolidating the Protestant ecumenical movement. Born in Michigan to immigrant parents, Zwemer spoke Dutch as his mother tongue and belonged to the Reformed Church in America. From childhood he was also fluent in English and German.[52] Like the American Presbyterians in Egypt, Zwemer forged close ties with British Protestants, and above all with two CMS missionaries, his wife, Amy (née Wilkes), whom he met in Basra, and his colleague in Cairo, W.H.T. Gairdner, with whom he developed a program for missionaries to Muslims. However, unlike the American Presbyteri-ans in Egypt, Zwemer had language skills that enabled him to build bridges to the Dutch Reformed missionaries of Southeast Asia and to keep abreast of trends in German missions.[53] As a result of these contacts, Zwemer developed a sense of Protestant world mission that went beyond the Anglo-American circuit. He also developed a sense of the Muslim world that ranged from Detroit (which hosted a grow-ing Arab immigrant community) to Jakarta in the Dutch East Indies. More than most of his missionary contemporaries, Zwemer recog-nized that Christianity and Islam were globally diffuse religions and that they could not be confined to either Europe and North America (in the case of Christianity) or Asia and Africa (in the case of Islam). Over a long career, however, Zwemer's ideas about Islam and Chris-tian missions to Muslims showed little evidence of growth: he stuck to the idea that Islam was backward and that Christians should ap-proach Muslims head-on.

Zwemer was a driving force behind the American Christian Litera-ture Society for Muslims (ACLSM), the organization founded in New York City in 1915 to fund missionary publishing for Muslims.[54] The ACLSM defined its purpose as "spreading . . . the Gospel through the printed page wherever Moslems are found" and called print "the ubiq-uitous missionary."[55] In 1922, while living in Egypt and serving as the ACLSM's honorary field secretary, Zwemer helped prepare a report titled *The Power of the Printed Page in the World of Islam*.[56] Declaring that "One common fact at once emerges: *The Moslem World is learning how to read*," the report suggested how missions could produce literature for Muslim readers living as far afield as Algeria, Burma, and Borneo, and speaking languages as diverse as Azerbaijani Turkish and Chi-nese.[57] Yet while Zwemer and his colleagues were hailing the rise of literacy and print culture as an opportunity for Christian outreach to Muslims, few missionaries—Zwemer included—had yet appreciated that rising literacy rates and burgeoning print cultures could equally serve as tools for Muslim resistance to Christian missionaries.

There were early rumblings of this development, as illustrated by an episode that occurred in 1910. Writing in this year to UPCNA administrators in Philadelphia, Thomas J. Finney of the American Presbyterian mission reported that some Muslim readers had taken offense at an article titled "The Muslim Idea of Prayer" that appeared in the August issue of *al-Murshid* (The Guide), the mission-sponsored Arabic journal of the Egyptian Evangelical Church.[58] Written under the editorial supervision of an Egyptian pastor named Mitri al-Diwayri, this article quoted from a book published in 1895 by a CMS missionary in Iran, W. St. Clair Tisdall, who had discussed Muslim procedures for prayer "in order to show how puerile and formal they are."[59] The minutes of the Missionary Association reported in October 1910 that a Muslim protest "was taken up by the Nationalist newspapers and agitated to such an extent that the Government made representations to the British 'Charge d'Affairs' [so] that the Khedive's Cabinet felt it necessary that the Murshid be discontinued in the interest of public tranquility." Thus the Egyptian government shut down *al-Murshid* but, following the intercession of the American consul, allowed the missionaries to launch a new journal in its stead. The missionaries called the new church journal *al-Huda* (meaning, almost synonymously, "The guidance").[60] Finney translated the words of one Egyptian Arabic newspaper, which had declared after the incident that "The only thing we can do and do effectively if we are true Moslems, is to make sure that no boy or girl of Moslemeen [i.e., the Muslims] is allowed to enter the American Schools."[61]

The *Murshid* affair passed quickly and no Muslim boycott ensued. Writing a chronicle of the mission in 1958, Earl E. Elder recalled simply that the episode had had "one salutary reaction" by publicizing Protestant mission schools to Muslim newspaper readers.[62] But in fact, the episode had a deeper import than that. It showed that Muslims were beginning to judge and respond to Christian missionaries not only on the basis of what missionaries said or did in fleeting encounters, but by what they wrote and left standing in print. In the particular case of *al-Murshid*, Muslim readers probably became aware of the article about Muslim prayer because missionaries sent it to them. Indeed, even by the 1930s, the ACLSM in New York was giving an annual grant to the Protestants in Egypt so that free copies of the Evangelical Church magazine—by then, *al-Huda*—could be sent to Muslims for the sake of evangelical outreach.[63]

Muslim awareness of Christian missionary writings sharpened so that by the late 1920s, educated Muslims were reading not only the tracts that American and British missionaries published with Muslims in mind—tracts with titles like "Pray without Ceasing" and "Taking Hold of God" (by Zwemer), or "The Sinlessness of the Prophets" and "The King of Love" (by the CMS missionaries W.H.T. Gairdner and Constance Padwick)[64]—but also the journals, manuals, and narratives that they published for fellow missionaries and mission supporters. In a sympathetic account of the YMMA published in 1932, Georg Kampffmeyer, a German philologist of Arabic, confirmed that language posed no boundary. Educated Egyptian Muslim men were reading missionary texts in English, German, and French, and these texts made them feel as though Islam were under attack.[65]

The works of Zwemer were squarely part of the missionary oeuvre that contributed to Muslims' perceptions of Christian assault. Zwemer hammered on a set of themes about Islam and Muslims in all his published and unpublished works, and this gave his writings an interchangeable quality. For example, in *Islam: A Challenge to Faith*, published in 1907, Zwemer stressed his views on Islam's flawed human, not divine, origins, as well as its backwardness and unsuitability for modern times. "Islam as a religion is doomed to fade away in time," Zwemer concludes, "before the advance of humanity, civilization and enlightenment." For proof, he suggests, Christians needed only to look at the "intellectual, social, and moral conditions" of modern Muslim societies, as for example in the Arabian peninsula, to perceive the "inadequacy of the religion of Mohammed."[66] In this book as in other writings, Zwemer questioned the behavior of Muhammad, relative to Jesus, and claims that many Muslims privately found Muhammad embarrassing.[67] He made similar claims in *Mohammed or Christ* (1915), *The Disintegration of Islam* (1916), and *Across the World of Islam* (1929). Given how potentially offensive to Muslims Zwemer's writings were, and how successfully he broadcast them in speech and print, it is no surprise that one of the first things that al-Azhar's journal, *Nur al-Islam*, published upon its debut in 1930 was an Arabic translation of a Zwemer article from *The Moslem World*, which outlined Muslim regions that missionaries still needed to "occupy." Following the translation, *Nur al-Islam* included an exhortation of its own, urging Muslim readers of Zwemer's article to rise up against the danger of Christian missions.[68]

It was a portent of things to come that the same American missionary records that discussed the affair of *al-Murshid* in 1910—namely, Thomas Finney's correspondence and the minutes of the Missionary Association—also noted the visit to Egypt of Zwemer, who was at that time still associated with the Arabian Mission of Basra and the Gulf. In a letter to Charles R. Watson in Philadelphia, Finney sounded a note of caution, confiding that Zwemer's lectures to American missionaries and Egyptian Evangelical pastors made a "decided impression except [that] several of the [Egyptian] pastors thought it dangerous for him to talk on the question of work among Moslems." Referring again to the Egyptian Evangelical clergy, Finney wrote, "Our pastors are exceedingly afraid these times lest the Moslems rise to persecute them as leaders of the church."[69] But the American Missionary Association minutes for October 1910 praised Zwemer without hesitation and also shared his rhetoric of Christian militancy: "We have felt keenly the stimulus of his presence, and of his ideals of the Conquest of Islam; and we would aid and encourage him in his large plans, and trust that all his and our enterprises looking toward this end shall enjoy perfect affiliation and co-operation."[70]

A year later, Zwemer arrived in Cairo. During the next seventeen years he was able to work independently in Cairo, because a woman belonging to the "Southern Presbyterian Church" in the United States served as his "special sponsor" and provided his salary.[71] At the same time, his home church, the Reformed Church in America, retained him as a "missionary-at-large," the United Presbyterians paid for his housing in Cairo, and the ACLSM in New York gave him an annual budget for travel. Meanwhile, Zwemer cooperated with the American Presbyterians in evangelical work among Muslims in Egypt, for example, by supervising lay evangelists (including Mikhail Mansur) and meeting with Muslim inquirers. From 1915 until 1928, Zwemer also served as chairman of the World's Sunday School Association's Committee for Moslem Lands.[72] The director of the NMP in Cairo once dubbed Zwemer "The Whirlwind," and the name fit the man who gave 192 fund-raising talks during a trip to the United States in the summer of 1921 and who, on a trip to Iran, India, and Ceylon in 1928, logged 15,295 miles and spoke ninety-five times in one hundred days.[73]

Zwemer quickly earned a reputation within Egypt's Muslim community. He reportedly became so well-known in Cairo for his Arabic tract called "Do You Pray?" that "people began to use this as a title and he would be pointed out in the street with the words, 'There goes "Do You Pray.""[74] In 1914, the missionary J. H. Boyd in Tanta wrote to Charles R. Watson in Philadelphia to report that some Muslim leaders were organizing a society for persuading Muslim converts to Christianity to return to Islam. Boyd added, "Dr. Zwemer is back and hard at it again. . . . Certainly the Mohammedan leaders do not rejoice over his return. To them he is a sort of nightmare."[75] Another missionary noted Zwemer's exceptional ability to draw Muslim crowds to public lectures,[76] while a third—a young man named James K. Quay, who later left the American Presbyterian mission for the Cairo YMCA—remarked in 1920 that after less than a decade in Egypt, "I am almost certain he is known to more Egyptians than any other American. I meet his acquaintances in trains, street cars, shops, everywhere."[77]

But by the early 1920s, American Presbyterians in Egypt were confessing to mixed feelings about Zwemer's activities. In 1921, Russell Galt, an AUC professor, alerted the head of the UPCNA foreign mission board in Philadelphia to "Dr. Zwemer's agitation, which has so angered the older missionaries, and which has been carried on by him in an unwise manner."[78] Others expressed "considerable impatience" with his "methods," as well as frustration with his protracted absences from Egypt—that is, with the way Zwemer was constantly sweeping into Cairo and out again for the sake of his missionary globe-trotting. Yet even as some of the American Presbyterians were expressing a desire to terminate his informal affiliation with their mission, others professed admiration for his work and approach.[79] In any case, by 1928, Zwemer had earned such a reputation for his headlong pursuit of Muslim evangelization that his fracas in al-Azhar did not entirely surprise his detractors or admirers.

Accounts of Zwemer's incident at al-Azhar—what happened and what it meant—diverge in Christian and Muslim sources. One of the most candid accounts from an American Christian perspective came from Charles R. Watson, president of AUC. Robert E. Speer, one of the towering figures in the American foreign missions movement, wrote to Watson asking whether it was true that Zwemer had been forced out of Egypt. Watson confirmed that Zwemer had encountered "difficulties."

> He visited the Azhar, taking Dr. and Mrs. Hill and Mr. and Mrs. Davis, to show them the place. He had some controversial Arabic tracts in his pocket and his statement is that individuals in the mosque asked him for copies of any literature he had. He gave them out and one of them was carried to a fanatical sheikh in the mosque who was lecturing. He created a scene shouting and tearing up the leaflet. There was something of a commotion but the party got out safely. The Azhar authorities contend that they have a signed agreement from him because of a former difficulty, that he would not distribute literature in the Azhar. Anyhow, some pressure was brought to bear and while he was not put out of the country, it was thought wise to relieve the situation by having him slip away.[80]

Zwemer left for Cyprus and returned two weeks later, but he soon left Egypt permanently to become a professor of missions at Princeton Theological Seminary. Watson concluded that Zwemer's behavior at al-Azhar had been "extremely unwise" and that following Egyptian press coverage of the International Missionary Council conference at

Jerusalem in 1928 (where mission leaders had declared the cause of advancing religious liberty a top priority),[81] it "seemed to support the impression that some concerted program was formed for the forcing of Christian propaganda upon Moslems."[82]

In a study of Christian missions in Egypt, published in 1988, an Egyptian writer named Khalid Muhammad Na'im provided one of the clearest summaries of the Zwemer incident from a Muslim point of view. Drawing on contemporary Arabic newspapers, Na'im traced the story to 1926 when, he wrote, Zwemer secured a permit from the Egyptian ministry of Muslim religious endowments to enter mosques. Zwemer then entered al-Azhar and distributed evangelical pamphlets to students. According to Na'im, the major conflict erupted on April 17, 1928, when

> Zwemer went to al-Azhar a second time with three foreign missionaries, one of them a woman. Together they entered the study hall of Shaykh Surur al-Zankaluni, when he was explaining a chapter of the Qur'an—namely *Surat al-Bara'a* [or *al-Tawba*; chapter 9, "Immunity" or "Repentance," on dealing with idolaters]. Zwemer and his group began to distribute three evangelical tracts which included Christian explanations of *'Ayat al-Kursi* [the "Throne Verse" from the Qur'an, 2:255] and of the names of God. . . . In the halls of al-Azhar, this dangerous work stirred up its students, who numbered nearly 3,000.

Following the uproar that ensued, Na'im continued, a group of *'ulama* presented a petition of protest to the government, which responded by prohibiting Christian missionaries from distributing evangelical tracts in streets and public places. Meanwhile, newspapers took up the cry, while a few poets composed *qasida*s (Arabic odes) calling on Zwemer and the missionaries to go. Na'im concludes that this episode reverberated for a long time and alerted the Muslim public to the dangers of missionaries.[83]

Asked years later about the incident, H. E. Philips (one of the American Presbyterians who had gone on record as an admirer of Zwemer's techniques)[84] told a story that was similar to Watson's (except that Philips made no suggestion of "unwise" behavior). Philips commented that after some bad publicity died down, "that was the end of the matter for Dr. Zwemer" although afterward a Sudanese Muslim student at al-Azhar—a man who had been in the courtyard at the time of the episode—"became a staunch Christian and was killed in a street accident some time later."[85] J. Christy Wilson, Zwemer's biographer and successor at Princeton Theological Seminary, used Philips's anecdote to end the story of the Azhar affair on a note of evangelical success. But for Muslims Zwemer's story did not end there and in that way. On the contrary, for Muslims the episode went down in infamy; writers of Arabic anti-missionary treatises were continuing to mention it fifty, sixty, and seventy years later.[86] In the long run, this episode came to epitomize for Muslim activists the Christian assault on Islam: in their renditions, Zwemer invaded al-Azhar, a venerable precinct of Islam, and tried to strike at its heart. Muslim accounts thereby challenge Christian missionary narratives that dismissed the episode as a fleeting disturbance.[87]

Yet Christian missionary sources also challenge the account presented in Muslim anti-missionary texts, which portray Zwemer's distribution of tracts in al-Azhar as a sudden affront and as a one-time (or, according to Na'im's more detailed version, two-time) affair.[88] Reports of the British and Foreign Bible Society indicate that Zwemer was visiting al-Azhar and distributing Arabic Bibles in 1915, accompanied by Mikhail Mansur. In 1916 he visited al-Azhar and distributed New Testaments in Malay and Javanese to Southeast Asian Muslim students: "He says that each time he visits the Javanese they entertain him well, and have prayer with him before he leaves."[89] In the early 1920s he was visiting al-Azhar with Kamil Mansur and wrote, "Scarcely a week goes by when I am in Cairo without visiting the Azhar, either alone or in company with tourists, missionaries, and students of our theological seminary." He noted that within three months, and with the help of the American Bible Society, he had placed "nearly a dozen" Arabic Bibles in the hands of Azhar professors, along with "over 150 copies of Matthew's Gospel" among Azhar students.[90] In 1924, following a tour of mission fields in India, Egypt, and Sudan, W. B. Anderson of the UPCNA mission board in Philadelphia recorded, "We visited the Azhar with Zwemer and Miss Helen Martin. It is a wonderful sight." Anderson added, "We went freely about the students and spoke with them, and evidently Zwemer is much loved by many. He spoke freely to them and gave tracts and gospels to many as we went along. He said this would not have been possible five years ago."[91]

These missionary accounts suggest that Muslims in al-Azhar, like the American Presbyterians, were divided in their opinions about Zwemer. Certainly in 1924, W. B. Anderson and Zwemer himself felt warmly received during visits to the institution, regarded some of the faculty and students as friends, and felt free to hand out Christian literature. It appears, therefore, that the salient feature of Zwemer's encounter at al-Azhar on April 17, 1928, was not that he distributed Christian tracts but rather that Muslims rose up to protest against it.

Hawadith al-Tabshir: The "Missionary Incidents" of the Early 1930s and Their Political Aftermath

In the five years after Zwemer's melee in al-Azhar, Christian missions in Egypt came under the withering scrutiny of Muslim nationalists, while "missionary crimes" (*jara'im al-mubashshirin*) roused heated discussion in the Egyptian periodical press. And yet, Arabic journals and newspapers in the early 1930s did not focus on the misdeeds of individual foreign missionaries, who remained peripheral to their stories; rather, they focused on Egyptian Muslims and Christians who crossed the missionaries' paths. Four incidents provoked particular agitation in the press and added fuel to Muslim anti-missionary activism. These were the cases of Fakhry Farag and Kamil Mansur, in 1930; of Yusuf 'Abd al-Samad, in 1932; and of Turkiyya Hasan, in 1933. The following sections examine each case, as well as the reactions and consequences they elicited. By the time these scandals subsided in 1933, popular protest had made a difference: the Egyptian government stood ready to carry out what one newspaper called its duty "to protect the religion and morals" of Egypt by passing laws restricting missionary activities.[92]

The Fakhry Farag Affair

Fakhry Mikha'il Farag was a medical doctor who belonged to the Coptic Catholic Church. Soon after AUC opened in 1920, he began to participate in the university's Extension (public outreach) Program by giving lectures on sexually transmitted diseases and sexual hygiene to male audiences consisting of AUC students, visitors from other institutions (such as al-Azhar and the police training school), and interested members of the general public.[93] But on February 4, 1930, Dr. Fakhry moved beyond this repertoire by giving an Arabic public lecture at AUC titled "Shall Women and Men Be Equal in Their Rights and Duties?" Addressing an audience estimated later to have included 1,200 men and women, most of them Muslims, he argued strongly for women's equality. According to an internal AUC report, Dr. Fakhry's remarks caused offense when, more than an hour into his talk, he addressed his own Coptic Catholic community, "charging them with having surrendered what were the rights and privileges of women all over the world to a system which gave the woman only half the rights of man in society." He was referring to the fact that Coptic communities in Egypt, Catholics included, followed Islamic laws of inheritance that gave female heirs half the share accorded to males. At that moment, the AUC report claimed, the audience entered a state of "intense excitement." Afterward, some Muslim men went to report the event to newspapers, which picked up the story.[94] The journal *Kawkab al-Sharq*, for example, expressed its surprise that the Americans had allowed this man to "preach" in a way that "venereal-ized" and "syphilized" his hearers and disgraced Islam.[95] Following an investigation, the authorities arrested Dr. Fakhry in April and charged him with the crime of defaming (*ta'n*) Islam. He was placed on trial, where, on May 25, 1930, judges acquitted him of the charges.[96]

A historian of AUC attributed the uproar over Dr. Fakhry's lecture to the presence of 400–500 students from al-Azhar who pounced on the doctor's critique of Islamic law and women's rights. The event also occurred at a time when Hasan al-Banna was beginning to expand the Muslim Brotherhood and to agitate against Christian missionaries.[97] But while AUC helped Dr. Fakhry by providing money for his bail and legal defense, the university's own records suggest that AUC leaders were eager to distance themselves from the controversy.[98] Henceforth AUC became more cautious in its public programs and implemented "steps . . . to guard against such an incident recurring in the future."[99] As for Fakhry Farag, American sources observed that he emerged from the trial a broken man, "nearly flattened out by the experience," and died soon thereafter.[100]

Fakhry Farag was neither a Protestant nor an evangelist, while the institution where he spoke, AUC, was not formally part of the American Presbyterian mission. But Muslim nationalists and activists were not interested in, or convinced by, such fine points. Detecting a unitary threat from *mubashshirin* (an Arabic word that was able to cover both foreign missionaries and local evangelists) and making few distinctions among "Christianizers" (*munassirin*), whether of the Protestant or Catholic variety, they connected Fakhry to the American missionary enterprise.[101] In the Fakhry affair, as in the three incidents that followed, the American Presbyterians found themselves implicated in and affected by episodes for which they did not feel culpable.

The Kamil Mansur Affair

Kamil Mansur, the Egyptian convert from Islam to Christianity, had been working with the American Presbyterian missionaries since 1918 as a lay evangelist to Muslims.[102] In this capacity, Kamil held Monday night meetings for inquirers—people curious about Christianity or the Evangelical Church—at an American mission building in the Ezbekiyya district of Cairo. At one of these meetings on April 7, 1930, a dispute arose during a lantern slide lecture about the life of Jesus. Later, American missionaries and journals like *al-Fath*

4.1. Kamel Eff. Mansour (Kamil Mansur), n.d. (c. 1920?). Dwight H. and Lucille B. Fee Papers, Presbyterian Historical Society, Presbyterian Church (U.S.A.), Philadelphia.

(the organ of the YMMA) agreed on the outlines of what happened. Namely, following the lecture, a few Muslim men went to the police to register a charge against Kamil Mansur for vilifying Islam, but the police rebuffed them. The accusers then resorted to the newspapers, which took up the case. Spurred by the press, the Egyptian government moved into action.[103]

One of the newspapers that reported the case was *al-Siyasa* (the organ of the Liberal Constitutionalist party), which ran an article titled "Armed Evangelism in the House of the Americans." According to *al-Siyasa*, Kamil Mansur had told his audience that he was a Muslim who had "left darkness for the light" by turning to Christ; that the Qur'an contained mere "superstitions and stories" that clashed with the modern age; and that Muhammad had been incapable of performing miracles like Jesus.[104] *Al-Siyasa* and *al-Fath* described his words in similar terms: they called it defamation (*ta'n*) of Islam and aggression (*i'tida'*) against Egypt's religion of state.[105] Linking the cases of Fakhry Farag and Kamil Mansur together, and referring occasionally to the earlier incident involving Zwemer at al-Azhar,[106] both papers began to publish a spate of articles on missionary institutions and "crimes" (*jara'im*), and the dangers they posed to young Muslims.[107] They urged the government to do its duty by punishing Kamil Mansur and by suppressing the "organized assault on the Islamic religion" that missionary societies were pursuing.[108] Meanwhile, students at al-Azhar went on strike. In the words of Khalid Na'im, whose study of Egyptian anti-missionary activism starts from the premise that Christian missions posed a "grave threat" to Egyptian society, Azhar students called on the rector of al-Azhar, Muhammad al-Ahmadi al-Zawahiri, and the interior minister, Mustafa Nahhas Pasha, to bring the "heretic" (*maziq*), Kamil Mansur, to justice.[109]

Egyptian authorities responded within a week of the incident, on April 13, 1930, by ordering Kamil Mansur's arrest on charges of "insolence" (*tatawul*) toward Islam.[110] Released on bail after two weeks in prison, Kamil eventually faced trial where, on December 1, 1930, a court cleared him of the charges.[111] He resumed his career as an evangelist in Egypt and was still working with the American Presbyterians in 1954, when the mission marked its centennial in Egypt.[112]

After the trial, J. W. Acheson, the secretary of the American Presbyterian mission, attributed Kamil Mansur's acquittal to the misstep of a high-ranking Egyptian official who, he claimed, had damaged the prosecution by announcing that the accused was guilty even before the trial began.[113] It may have helped Kamil Mansur's defense that the Americans called on officials from the U.S. State Department, the British Foreign Office, and the Church of England (including the Archbishop of Canterbury) to register concern about the case.[114] In a study of "the political problem of missionaries in Egypt in the 1930s"—a study that considered the case of Kamil Mansur among others—the historian B. L. Carter suggests that although the British authorities regarded Christian missionaries as "a nuisance and at times an embarrassment," they nevertheless felt obliged to look out for them, since they ultimately had to answer to the British Parliament, which was always "ready to listen to the Anglican church."[115]

Meanwhile, Egyptian parliamentary factions and two contenders for the rectorship of al-Azhar (namely, Shaykh Muhammad Mustafa al-Maraghi and Shaykh Muhammad al-Ahmadi al-Zawahiri) used the case to jockey for public favor and political influence.[116] The case also touched a popular nerve at a time of widespread public dissatisfaction with the "unpopular and undemocratic government" of Prime Minister Sidqi Pasha.[117] Reflecting on this case, J. W. Acheson concluded that Egyptian "political intrigue [had been] making use of religious intolerance at our expense."[118]

The case of Kamil Mansur ultimately compelled the American Presbyterians, along with their British missionary colleagues in Egypt, to think more deeply about religious liberty—what it was and how to promote it. Missionaries were concerned when the first judge assigned to Kamil Mansur's case rejected the defense lawyer's claim that Egyptian law guaranteed full freedom of religious expression, by reportedly declaring, "A person who is employed for the purpose of [Christian] evangelization (*tabshir*), especially in a country whose inhabitants are not heathen, has no liberty and no opinions."[119] At the same time, the case sharpened popular Muslim concerns about missionary efforts to "Christianize" Muslims (*tansir al-muslimin*) and stimulated discussions about the social protections and services that the Egyptian government should offer Muslims.[120] Among members of the YMMA and Muslim Brotherhood, the episode sharpened a growing consciousness of the need for an Islamic mission to Muslims at home and non-Muslims abroad. Indeed, throughout 1930, as the case against Kamil Mansur progressed, the journal *al-Fath* ran a series of articles under the headline "Islam Needs Propaganda and Evangelism" (*al-Islam fi haja ila al-da'aya wa'l-tabshir*).[121] At the same time, the journal reported the activities of groups with names like the Society to Protect the Noble Qur'an.[122] The latter society aimed to promote Quranic knowledge among poor Muslims from the Delta to Aswan, much as American Presbyterians and Egyptian Evangelicals had been doing since the mid-nineteenth century, but with regard to Bible reading among Coptic peasants.

The Case of Yusuf 'Abd al-Samad

In January 1932, an eighteen-year-old Muslim youth named Yusuf 'Abd al-Samad declared himself a Christian. Noting that Yusuf was a student at AUC, Arabic newspapers like *al-Siyasa*, *al-Balagh*, and *al-Jihad* asserted that American missionaries had subjected him to "magnetic hypnotism" (*al-tanwim al-maghnitisi*) and other ruses to lure him from Islam.[123] Meanwhile, the newspaper *al-Kashkul* blamed AUC. Calling the university a "hole of snakes and vipers," this newspaper claimed that AUC's teachers were really preachers who thought "that Egypt is one of the dark countries where Red Indians used to live before Christianity" and who routinely attacked Islam in an effort to woo Muslim youths to Christianity.[124]

American Presbyterian sources maintained, by contrast, that what some of the Arabic newspapers attributed to "magnetic hypnotism" was merely Yusuf's persistence in professing Christianity in the face of heavy pressures to recant—pressures that included beatings at the hand of his father and death threats. But the American Presbyterians also maintained that they had nothing to do with either Yusuf or his conversion. They pointed instead to a husband-and-wife team of independent evangelists who worked in the outlying Ma'adi district of Cairo. Four years earlier, in 1928, Charles R. Watson of AUC had tried to find out who this couple was and what they were doing in

Cairo. He had learned then that the husband, Erian Butros, was an Egyptian who had traveled in the United States, while his wife was American, and that together they had started a "Gospel Messengers' Bible School in Cairo."[125] It was apparently at this "Gospel Center"[126] that Erian Butros and his wife encountered Yusuf 'Abd al-Samad, who had reportedly begun to attend their Bible classes in September 1931. This couple had neither institutional nor social connections to the American Presbyterians in Egypt. Nevertheless, in the view of Arabic newspapers that reported on the scandal, the fact that Mrs. Erian Butros was an American appeared to confirm the outlines of a unitary American scheme for Christianizing Muslims.

As the press coverage around the case intensified, the secretary of the American mission, J. W. Acheson, asked the American wife of Erian Butros to prepare a statement narrating her version of events. In contrast to the Egyptian Arabic newspapers that presented Yusuf's father, al-Hajj 'Abd al-Samad, as an upright Muslim who had his son's welfare at heart, Mrs. Erian Butros suggested that the father was a tyrant who, upon hearing that Yusuf had embraced "Christian convictions," "gave him a number of severe beatings, threatening his life continually." Yusuf sought refuge with Mr. and Mrs. Butros, but when he was walking with them in the street two days later he was seized by two policemen accompanied by a detective and a cousin. "My husband demanded a warrant of arrest," noted Mrs. Butros (whom Acheson's papers never identify more fully by name), "whereupon the policeman No. 3875 grabbed him and yelled to the other policeman to arrest him marching them both to the police station of Meadi and lodged a case against my husband for abuse." When Yusuf's father arrived at the police station, she continued, the father "attacked him [Yusuf] violently" and threatened to kill him. "He turned to me most abusively as an accursed Christian, daughter of a dog and daughter of a pig, and promised me death if it took him years to carry it out. To my husband he was even more abusive and threatening and rushed at him with a big stick. This happened in the Police Station with several witnesses present."

The next day, she wrote, Yusuf declared to the authorities that he was a Christian and that he did not want to return to his father. Mrs. Butros then reported the case to the American consul and was reassured when an Egyptian told her that since Yusuf was already eighteen years old, he had reached the age of majority and would be "free to change his religious convictions and also free to leave his father's house" pending a declaration of faith before the appropriate Cairo authorities. In practice, however, Yusuf was shuffled before different officials, where instead of recanting (as his father expected) he repeated his Christian profession. Finally, Mrs. Butros testified, al-Hajj

'Abd al-Samad and his helpers grabbed the young man and pulled him out of the building, and the police stood and watched as Yusuf screamed for help. When pressed to explain, the (Muslim) subgovernor told Mrs. Butros that Yusuf had been given over to his father for "protection." "He admitted that 18 is the legal age to change one's religion but remarked that it was applied to Christians to become Moslems and no precedent going the other way has been established."[127]

Three aspects of the incident, as related by Mrs. Butros, concerned the American Presbyterians: first, the complicity of the Muslim police in returning Yusuf to his father despite the latter's abuse and threats; second, the unwillingness of the authorities to acknowledge the sincerity of Yusuf's statement of faith; and third, the lack of legal procedure for registering conversion from Islam to Christianity. As the subgovernor reportedly told Mrs. Butros, the procedure available for recording Christian conversions to Islam in Egypt was not intended to work in reverse, regardless of what the Egyptian constitution said about freedom of conscience. Their fears were not assuaged when Ismail Sidqi Pasha, the prime minister, suggested in a private discussion with mission representatives that Muslims, if anything, had the right to freedom *from* Christian evangelism. Afterward they recorded Ismail Sidqi's comment that "while evangelistic work might be [acceptable] in primitive countries like Tanganyika, it was not suitable in a Moslem country like Egypt, especially as Egypt is firmly attached to a religion of its own, and is civilized."[128]

The American Presbyterians detected an upsurge of popular Muslim hostility toward missionaries in the aftermath of the case. In March 1932 a missionary wrote to a colleague describing what had happened to two Egyptian Bible Women in a Muslim Delta village across the Nile from Mansura. The two women had started a "Street Sabbath School" for poor children several months earlier, and it typically attracted forty to fifty Muslim women and children on any given Sunday. But one day the Bible Women arrived in the village and "were met with a group of children and men armed with sticks and handfuls of mud" and were "literally driven out." The missionary added, "

> There has been quite a little disturbance here in Egypt the past few months. It started over a young Mohammedan who had been baptized last summer, not by our Mission however, but by an Egyptian (married to an American woman) living in Cairo and doing missionary work on their own. Mansura is one of the outposts, and always ready to seize an opportunity to make trouble, so we have felt it here a little more than in some places—that is, the opposition that has arisen from this incident. It is chiefly political as a great

many people realize, but we live on the edge of a volcano and never quite know when there may be an outbreak.[129]

Reflecting on the case of Yusuf 'Abd al-Samad, the press coverage it had generated, and the Muslim opposition it had aroused, J. W. Acheson, in a letter to W. B. Anderson, attributed the rise in anti-missionary agitation to the YMMA. He added that (James A.) Pollock, one of the missionaries based in the Delta region, "sent me copies of hand bills which were being distributed there in which the missionaries are called 'vile criminals' and the Muslims are urged [to] 'make war against them.' Crowds on the streets were shouting down the missionaries and the police were taking no notice. Some stones were thrown at the Mission by one group of demonstrators."[130]

In a book written in the late 1980s that charted the growth of Egyptian Muslim efforts to "combat Christianization" (*muqawamat al-tansir*) during the years from 1927 to 1933, Khalid Na'im describes the "agitational activity" (*al-nishat al-istifzazi*) of missionaries along with Muslim reprisals that followed. He cites a number of incidents that occurred shortly after the case of the "hypnotized" youth (i.e., Yusuf 'Abd al-Samad, though Na'im does not identify him by name): for example, in Wajh al-Birka, on February 20, 1932, a mob attacked an evangelist with a stick; in Sohag, on February 22, 1932, a Muslim mob attacked a missionary riverboat (which, he claimed, had been used to lure Muslim children); and another instance around the same time (in an unidentified location) when missionaries held a public prayer in front of a YMMA building, prompting its members to disperse the missionaries with sticks and stones.[131] Judging from Khalid Na'im's account, the case of Yusuf 'Abd al-Samad stood out for Egyptian Muslim audiences by drawing attention to the "crimes" of missionaries vis-à-vis Muslim schoolchildren, and prompted them to press the Egyptian government to promote Islamic education as a prophylactic against loss of faith.

On a practical level, popular Muslim hostility to missionaries in the wake of the Yusuf 'Abd al-Samad incident changed some of the ways that missionaries worked. A. W. Keown-Boyd, the British official in the "European Department" of the Egyptian Interior Ministry who was responsible for liaising with Egypt's foreign communities, acknowledged this in April 1932. Addressing S. A. Morrison of the CMS, Keown-Boyd wrote, "I think that you, the Missionaries, will agree that you are faced by a crisis in your work greater than any that has arisen in the last ten years in Egypt. A series of incidents, Abdel Samad, Wagh el-Birka, Tahta, Sohag, Tewfikia, have been exploited in the press, discussed in Parliament and bandied from mouth to mouth throughout the country till today such general feeling has been aroused that it is in fact unsafe to carry on open evangelization in Egypt." He added, "I understand the attitude of the central Government to be as follows:—'Egypt, by her Constitution, is a Moslem state and the Government can brook no interference with Moslem rights or prestige. . . . Proselytizing involves criticism, or unfavourable comparison of the Moslem religion with other religions, and is therefore in the popular view a derogation from Moslem prestige. This popular view the Government is bound to endorse." Keown-Boyd advised missionaries to avoid any open-air meetings or other "causes of friction."[132] In 1915, an American Presbyterian missionary had organized a series of evangelical "tent shows" among Muslims in the Delta.[133] But by 1932, as Keown-Boyd's letter suggests, tent shows were out of the question.

The fate of Yusuf 'Abd al-Samad is unclear. Although this young man professed Christianity for a moment in 1932, the silence of the missionary sources regarding the outcome of his case suggests that he remained a public Muslim in the end. Noting that the government was continuing to investigate his case under pressure from the YMMA, J. W. Acheson speculated, "It is quite probable that the boy will be judged mentally unbalanced and the case filed. The agitation is rapidly being forgotten." Meanwhile, Acheson added, "Our religious teaching in the schools is almost certain to come up for further investigation, but there have been indications of reaction in our favor, and whatever may be the motive there are more inquirers than ever."[134]

The Case of Turkiyya Hasan

Turkiyya Hasan was a fifteen-year-old Muslim girl attending the Swedish Salaam School in the Suez Canal town of Port Said when an incident catapulted her into the national limelight. On June 11, 1933, Turkiyya defied her Swiss teacher in the classroom, the teacher beat her, and in the scuffle that followed neighbors and police came to investigate. Turkiyya later claimed that she had been resisting the teacher's efforts to foist Christianity upon her. Newspapers ranging from the secular-leaning *al-Balagh* and *al-Siyasa* to the Islamist *al-Fath* and *Nur al-Islam* hailed Turkiyya as a heroine for remaining true to Islam, and connected the incident to the spate of "crimes" that missionaries had been perpetrating among Muslim children in schools.[135]

The Swedish Salaam Mission was an evangelical and nondenominational mission that, despite its name, had no formal sponsorship from a church in Sweden. It drew upon a foreign staff that in 1924 included women of Swedish, Finnish, English, and Swiss origin.

Lacking steady income, it relied on what its missionaries regarded as answers to prayers. In the case of the Salaam mission, these "answers to prayers" came from donors in the Nordic countries; from Britons and other Europeans who either worked in Port Said or passed through as tourists on steamships; and from supporters in North America, most of whom appear to have been Scandinavian immigrants. In practice, the Salaam mission in Port Said operated an institution that contained both a school and what its founder called "a home for destitutes." Located next to Port Said's red-light district, this institution reached out to poor Muslim children from a neighborhood where many relied on the prostitution economy. Some of these children were orphans according to the Egyptian Islamic, but not Western, understanding of the term, insofar as they lacked legally recognized fathers.[136] (For example, in a brochure about the mission written around 1924, Maria Ericsson cites the case of one fatherless girl in the school whose mother was a servant in a brothel, and of another girl who came from a "bad home" and whose "parents did not live together.")[137] Thus Arabic sources referred to the Salaam school as an orphanage even though the Salaam missionaries did not use that term for the institution themselves.

Turkiyya Hasan was one of the socially ambiguous children in the charge of the Swedish Salaam Mission and was an orphan in the Egyptian Islamic sense of having no legal father to protect her. Perhaps it was no accident, therefore, that the newspaper *al-Balagh*, upon elevating her as a Muslim heroine for withstanding a Christian attack, identified her more fully as Turkiyya Hasan Abu Yusuf. The longer name, suggesting that she had a father named Hasan and a paternal grandfather named Abu Yusuf, enhanced her patronymic and hence social integrity.[138]

Feted by the press, Turkiyya supplied more information about the Salaam school missionaries and their ways, alleging, for example, that they put copies of the Qur'an in lavatories and that they Christianized children by changing their Muslim names to Christian ones—for example, by making a Saniyya into a Marta, a Nabawiyya into a Leah, and so on.[139] Meanwhile, Turkiyya bolstered her claims regarding the missionaries' attempts to convert her by producing a letter that Maria Ericsson, the head of the Salaam school, had sent her the previous year. (It was written in English and was presumably translated for Turkiyya.) "My dear Turkya," Ericsson had written, "will you be among those who are washed in the BLOOD of the LAMB (Rev. 7:14) [sic]? Are you ready when the Lord your Saviour comes? He is coming soon. It was for me that Jesus died on Calvary, that is what my heart sings, can you join me in this song?"[140] Although Ericsson was originally from Sweden, she had sent this letter to Turkiyya from Flint, Michigan, where she had contacts with evangelical Protestants, some of whom shared her premillennial views about the imminent coming of Christ.[141] For Egyptian Muslim activists, this small detail of the letter's provenance may have confirmed a sense that the case of Turkiyya Hasan, like the case of Yusuf 'Abd al-Samad, was part of a larger American missionary plot. If these activists had only known that Ericsson's contacts included the native Michigander Samuel M. Zwemer, who was listed as the "Field Referee" for the Salaam mission in one of its promotional brochures, then their suspicions would have grown stronger.[142]

The messianic zeal of Ericsson's letter was enough to convince Keown-Boyd, the British official in charge of European community affairs in Egypt, that Turkiyya's allegations had some substance. Keown-Boyd sent a photograph of this letter to the Inter-Mission Council, an organization to which the American Presbyterians belonged, and asked for an explanation. Did Ericsson's letter "contain a true, right and balanced exposition of Christian doctrine," he inquired, and did the council consider "it right or desirable to subject young Moslem Egyptian women at the physically and mentally susceptible age of 15 to influences of this kind"? Finally, he asked the members of the Inter-Mission Council what they proposed to do to "control and regularize the activities of the Salaam School at Port Said and of similar institutions in Egypt which do not apparently owe allegiance to any responsible body, particularly in view of the danger to missionary work and Christians in Egypt arising out of the recent unfortunate incident at Port Said."[143]

Keown-Boyd's last question was the trickiest. For in fact, the Inter-Mission Council, which the American Presbyterians had helped found in 1920 as a cooperative consultative body for Protestant organizations in Egypt, did not include the Pentecostal and independent faith missions that had emerged in Egypt during the early twentieth century.[144] The three primary members of the Inter-Mission Council upon its debut were the American Presbyterians, the CMS, and the EGM, bolstered by AUC, the YMCA, the NMP, and a few smaller organizations.[145] The Inter-Mission Council did *not* include the Swedish Salaam Mission, which Maria Ericsson, a former missionary to the Maghrib and a self-declared born-again Christian, had founded in Port Said in 1911. Nor did it include the Pentecost Faith Mission and missions of the Assemblies of God and Seventh Day Adventist churches, which by 1925 were together supporting twenty-six American workers in Egypt (relative to 159 workers from the American Presbyterian mission, not including Presbyterians at AUC and the YMCA in Cairo).[146]

The reality was that Protestant missionary activity in Egypt was, and had for long been, a free-for-all, and that the Inter-Mission Council represented only one stream—albeit the mainstream—of the Protestant missionary presence in Egypt.

Consequences

If the American Presbyterians felt some ambivalence about the Swedish Salaam Mission and its theology, structure, and methods, then the intensity of the Muslim public reaction to the Turkiyya Hasan affair made it clear that consultation was imperative. After all, the same newspapers that covered the scandal involving the Swedish Salaam School were portraying the American Presbyterians as predators engaged in"vile trickery"(*hila mardhula*).[147] On June 29, 1933, for example, *al-Balagh* published a photograph above a caption reading, "Some of the children whom American missionary women were enticing with sweets and fruit in order to spread the Christian faith in Beni Suef."[148] (Stories about Americans distributing sweets to draw children may have arisen from an experimental program started in 1932 by the Cairo YMCA, during which a group of youth volunteers"regularly visited orphanages, distributed fruit and candy and played games and told stories to the boys" from "underprivileged" parts of the city.)[149] American Presbyterian missionaries also reported facing trouble from Muslim crowds. One missionary nurse reported that in Cairo, on June 18, 1933 (exactly one week after Turkiyya Hasan's incident in Port Said), "a bunch of rowdies" prevented her from working at a maternal and infant care clinic that catered to Egyptian women who had been abandoned by their husbands. As part of the routine in this clinic, missionaries usually tried to teach women ten verses from the Bible.[150]

Much more worrying to the American Presbyterians was the way that newspapers pursued a case against an adult woman, Nazla Ibrahim Ghunaym, an orphan (whose father was dead but mother was living) who had attended the school of the EGM missionaries in Zeitoun and then worked for four years as a teacher in the Swedish Salaam School in Port Said. During her time with the missionaries Nazla Ibrahim Ghunaym had converted to Christianity, joined the Evangelical Church (as EGM converts generally did), and married an Egyptian evangelist named Zaki Isra'il al-Fayumi. A few days before news of Turkiyya Hasan reached the press, Nazla Ibrahim Ghunaym and her husband experienced the birth of their first child. Nevertheless, under pressure from the newspapers, a Shari'a court issued an order rejecting Nazla's conversion to Christianity, nullifying her marriage to her non-Muslim husband, and ordering her return to a Muslim male guardian, namely, to a grandfather in Damietta.[151] *Nur al-Islam*, the journal of al-Azhar, dismissed her conversion as the result of "magnetic hypnotism," while *al-Balagh* claimed that missionaries had married her off to a Christian evangelist as a ruse for conversion: neither paper entertained the idea that her conversion might have been the product of reason, free will, and conviction.[152] Meanwhile, missionaries insisted that her marriage was valid and that her case belonged within the jurisdiction of the Protestant sect, which had its own communal courts. It is unclear from Egyptian or missionary sources how the case was ultimately resolved. But for the American Presbyterians the case of Nazla Ibrahim Ghunaym sharpened concerns about the status of religious liberty in Egypt.[153]

The American missionaries were also keenly aware of the fact that in June 1933, Shaykh Mustafa al-Maraghi, the former rector of al-Azhar, who aspired to regain this position, established an organization called Jami'at Muqawamat al-Tansir, which attracted wide support in the aftermath of the Turkiyya Hasan affair.[154] Although the name of this organization translated literally to mean "Society for Combatting Christianization," it became known in English sources as the "Society for the Defense of Islam."[155] According to Khalid Na'im, the goals of this society included combating apostasy or heresy (*ilhad*), refuting missionaries' arguments, publishing exposés of missionary activities, informing Muslims about missionaries' "repulsive methods" (*asalib khabitha*), and raising funds to house neglected children in orphanages where they could receive an Islamic schooling "far from the accursed (*la'ina*) mission schools."[156] In the words of another Egyptian writer, one of the society's main aims was to win back swerving Muslims.[157] At this juncture, Maraghi did not advertise his own earlier encounter with a Christian mission institution. This had occurred in 1916, when, as Grand Qadi of the Sudan, Maraghi had enrolled his daughter, 'Azza, in the CMS girls' school in Khartoum.[158]

Prompted not only by Keown-Boyd's inquiry but more urgently by the rising tide of Muslim anti-missionary activism, the American Presbyterians and their colleagues on the Inter-Mission Council arranged to meet the principal of the Salaam school and the Swiss teacher who had beaten Turkiyya. Together they went to the Ministry of the Interior and spoke to Keown-Boyd, who presented the Swiss teacher with two options: leave Egypt at once or face trial "for having contravened the law forbidding corporal punishment in schools." The Inter-Mission Council advised the Swiss teacher to leave, whereupon she traveled to Palestine. In an internal memorandum, C. C. Adams of the American Presbyterian mission later recounted these developments to the head of the mission board in Philadelphia. But rather than seeing the case of Turkiyya Hasan as an incident of coercive conversion, Adams dismissed it as the case of an unruly student who had refused to participate in the mandatory "Christian religious exercises" of a mission school and who may have been "instructed by parties outside to make such a scene" for the sake of Muslim agitation.[159]

In a historical study of orphans in Egypt, Beth Baron has observed that the case of Turkiyya Hasan cast a critical light on the Egyptian government's ability to protect the most socially marginal and vulnerable Muslim children and, by extension, its ability to protect Islam, the religion of state.[160] Certainly in the aftermath of the case, the Society for the Defense of Islam and kindred organizations rallied to establish Islamic orphanages under government protection. In one case, in Kafr al-Zayyat, a Muslim mob besieged an institution run by French Catholic nuns; eventually, when no police came, the nuns were forced to hand over the orphans in their care.[161] Thereafter Egyptian authorities took control and began to remove abandoned, neglected, or otherwise fatherless Muslim children from the care of all Christian missions, not only in Port Said but also in places like Assiut, where the American Lillian Trasher ran a large orphanage under the sponsorship of the Assemblies of God church of North America. These measures guaranteed that Muslim orphans would remain Muslim orphans, not least because Islamic law did not recognize adoption in the Western sense of familial transfer to nonbiological parents. Ultimately, Baron suggests, the Turkiyya Hasan case spurred the Egyptian state in the 1930s "to take greater control of education, health, and social services through new or expanded ministries," measures that ultimately led to "the creation of a welfare state."[162]

In a study of the genesis and early development of the Muslim Brotherhood, Brynjar Lia has noted that opposition to missionaries also galvanized the Muslim Brotherhood in the second half of 1933; indeed, in this year alone the organization more than doubled its branches in Egypt. (Lia did not mention the Turkiyya Hasan incident, but the connection to the events of June, 1933 was surely there.) Opposition to Christian missionaries "became the objective of the Society's first organized campaign," while a plan to counteract missionary activities was at the top of the agenda for its first conference, held in 1933. At this conference, the Muslim Brotherhood articulated plans for establishing new Muslim schools and shelters for the destitute, forming local village patrols to warn Muslims against contact with Christian missionaries, and "rescuing" Muslim children from mission schools. As part of the campaign against missionaries, the Brotherhood also began to petition the government to increase the Islamic educational content of government schools.[163]

Meanwhile, the Turkiyya Hasan affair also elicited a response from the Corps of the High 'Ulama of al-Azhar, who were concerned not only about missionary doings but also by the rapid expansion of the Muslim Brotherhood. According to the historian Umar Ryad, "The public role of the scholars of Al-Azhar as 'protectors' of Islam was threatened"; otherwise phrased, Azharites were trying to stave off competition from Banna and his popular movement. Thus on July 17, 1933, the rector of al-Azhar, Muhammad al-Ahmadi al-Zawahiri, issued a manifesto warning against missionary institutions and activities. Zawahiri went a step further in September 1933 by issuing a fatwa condemning Muslim parents who enrolled their children in mission schools.[164] Zawahiri's behavior illustrated, once again, how Christian missionaries played a proxy role within struggles for power and legitimacy that were occurring among Egyptian Muslim leaders.

Following her moment of glory in the Arabic press, Turkiyya Hasan went on to a career that was typical for an orphan woman of her era—she became a hospital nurse—and then disappeared from the public record.[165] Before long, the Swedish Salaam Mission disappeared from the record as well. At some point it joined the Inter-Mission Council, since this organization's minutes for March 20, 1941, list the Salaam mission as a member.[166] But the track ends there: no references to this mission recur after World War II. One can only surmise that the Salaam mission did not long outlive its founder, Maria Ericsson, who was already sixty-nine years old in 1933 when the Turkiyya Hasan scandal occurred.[167] Meanwhile, history and memory conspired to play their own tricks on the missionary past. In an Arabic treatise called "Ruses and Corrupt Methods in the Call to Evangelism" (*Al-Hiyal wa'l-asalib al-munharifa fi al-da'wa ila al-tabshir*), written in the late 1990s, an Islamist writer named Mustafa Fawzi 'Abd al-Latif Ghazal refers to the Salaam school incident in Port Said while excoriating AUC and its ongoing "Christianizing" designs vis-à-vis Muslim students. Dimly recalling the case, but not the name, of Turkiyya Hasan, Ghazal connects the Port Said scandal to an ongoing American scheme for the subversion and conversion of Muslims—and this, even though the American Presbyterian mission had no contact with the young woman.[168]

Attention to missionary scandals dissipated in newspapers as the year 1933 wore on. Keown-Boyd explained more fully to a leader of the Inter-Mission Council that the Egyptian Public Security Department had warned the newspapers to stop issuing reports about missionaries that had been "fabricated or exaggerated: this news was likely to arouse hatred of a section of the community and cause disturbance of public order: breaches of the peace had in fact ensued." The Public Security Department therefore issued a warning that "Any paper which in the opinion of the Department repeated the offense would be referred to the Parquet for inquiry with a view to trial and punishment." Keown-Boyd suggested that under Egyptian law the missionaries could, in theory, pursue charges of libel against newspapers like *al-Balagh* but that it would probably be better to avoid the publicity.[169] Meanwhile, in August 1933, F. Scott Thompson of the American Presbyterian mission observed that the Inter-Mission Council needed to consider ways to exert some control over small missionary groups that did not belong to the organization. "Indiscretion on the part of any," he reflected, "brings reproach and blame to us all."[170]

By the end of 1933, the social landscape facing missionaries had dramatically and irrevocably changed. Amid the uproar over evangelization, Egyptian Muslim nationalists and activists had reached some consensus in identifying Christian missionaries as a threat to national sovereignty and social integrity and calling for government regulation over mission institutions. "There is no doubt," an article in *al-Balagh* had declared, "that the government can bar those missionaries from the Capitulatory rights that are so copious for them" and "likewise that the government can establish schools to welcome the children of the *umma* [meaning the Muslim community]."[171] At a time when Islam in Egypt was increasingly providing "the basis for the new common national culture uniting elite and mass,"[172] government restrictions on missionaries were bound to have popular appeal.

In 1934, the Egyptian parliament took the first step toward reining in missions by passing Law 40 to regulate "free schools" (meaning foreign private schools), which administered the government examinations that were required for entry into public higher education.[173] "Private education is full of shortcomings," an article in *al-Siyasa* declared with reference to this law, "so the government needs to exert greater control."[174] Leaders of the American Presbyterian mission, whose schools had offered government examinations for twenty-five years, were worried about Law 40. It required them to open their schools to Egyptian inspectors, provide information on staff and prove their credentials, and meet guidelines regarding the sanitation and layout of its facilities by ensuring, for example, that a building had separate entrances for boys and girls if it was used by students of both sexes.[175] (In fact, government inspectors had been requiring infrastructural changes even before this law was officially passed. In July 1933, at the height of the anti-missionary agitation, a missionary reported that the government had required the school in Simbelle-wein, near Mansura, to "install water in the new boys building."[176] The missionaries did not object to the government's efforts to improve school quality, but they did feel that the government was enforcing rules selectively as a way to restrict their activities.) According to Jirjis Salama, who in 1963 published a history of foreign education in Egypt, Law 40 ultimately forced the American mission to close many of its rural schools, since it lacked the means to make the structural changes that government inspectors demanded.[177] In a provision that was only fully implemented in the late 1940s, following further legislation, Law 40 also stipulated that it was illegal to teach a student a religion other than his own, even if his guardian gave permission.[178] Missionaries expressed fear that inspectors would use Law 40 to discriminate against them or force them to teach "Koranic study," since the government (under pressure from Muslim activists) had increased the Islamic studies content required of Muslim students for government examinations.[179]

Meanwhile, restrictions on missionary work began to arise from other quarters of the Egyptian bureaucracy. In 1936, for example, the Egyptian government began to require new missionary doctors to pass a medical examination, entailing a fifteen-day series of written, oral, and practical tests, before they could work in Egypt. Charles Laughead, fresh out of the University of Iowa medical school, failed this examination three times before passing. "We have no way of finding out the amount of inadequacy on my part which contributed to the failure," Laughead reflected. But he also confessed to having felt subject to discrimination: "Passing is sixty per cent I am told. It may be one hundred per cent for foreign doctors and probably is if they don't want you. I was quite conscious of an unfriendly attitude from some of the examiners." One official even asked if his medical certificates were genuine.[180] Still other pressures came from the Egyptian passport bureau. In 1938 C. C. Adams, who was serving as secretary of the American mission, noted with foreboding that an Egyptian had replaced a Briton as the official in charge of issuing visas within the Ministry of the Interior.[181] Within a year, Adams reported that the "sheer routine" of his tasks had increased "because of the additional work in connection with passports." It was not only that bureaucratic delays grew longer; it was also that Egyptian officials began to challenge visa applications for American missionaries who were proposing to do jobs, like nursing in mission hospitals, that could be "Egyptianized." The intensification in bureaucratic wrangling was one factor that prompted Adams to resign from the mission and accept the deanship of AUC's School of Oriental Studies.[182]

For Egyptian nationalists, the signing of the Anglo-Egyptian Treaty in 1936, which provided for the withdrawal of most British troops in Egypt, confirmed a sense that sovereignty was within reach. Yet, although textbooks point to this treaty as a significant moment in Egypt's political history, American Presbyterians were far more concerned about the Montreux Convention, signed in May 1937.[183] This convention set out terms by which Egypt, over the course of twelve years, would phase out the Capitulatory system for foreigners, leading to the "submission of foreigners wholly to Egyptian law in Egyptian courts."[184] Missionaries pointed to Montreux when the Egyptian government announced, late in 1937, that it was abolishing customs exemptions for charitable institutions—thereby making AUC, for example, pay taxes on imports of laboratory equipment for science classrooms.[185] In a similar context, missionaries pointed to the way in which the Egyptian government broadcast the Qur'an regularly on the national radio but refused to permit broadcasts from the Bible.[186] "If I read the signs of the times aright," wrote H. E. Philips a week after the Montreux Convention was signed, "in Egypt the program of the Government is going to make Mission work exceedingly difficult."[187] Two years later, in 1939, the missionary F. D. Henderson remarked, "It does not require a drunk king to see or a prophet to interpret the handwriting on the wall." The future of American mission schools in Egypt was in question, he added, and "it is doubtful if [the schools] will be allowed to exercise much direct Christian testimony after the twelve years of transition following Montreux."[188] In 1940, another missionary reported that the minister of education had advised him that, in the wake of Montreux, freedom of religion "would not be interpreted to mean that foreign schools were free to require Muslim children to study a religion other than their own."[189]

A Different Landscape: Rethinking the American Mission after 1932

After 1932, the schools of the American Presbyterian mission faced a decline in enrollments. Missionaries attributed some of the decline among Muslim students, particularly in Vacation Bible Schools, to anti-missionary agitation. But they also pointed to financial distress: Egyptian parents were finding it harder to pay tuitions.[190] The American Presbyterian mission was also financially pinched. Compounding the mission's beleaguerment was the Layman's Report, a stiff critique of American Protestant foreign missions that was published in New York in 1932, when anti-missionary agitation was at its height in Egypt.

As the Depression took its bite in the United States, donations to American religious institutions plummeted by an average of 36 percent.[191] The UPCNA suffered its share of this cut. According to one

4.2. Egyptian Evangelical family having worship. "The father is employed by the American Bible Society." Dwight H. and Lucille B. Fee Papers, Presbyterian Historical Society, Presbyterian Church (U.S.A.), Philadelphia.

missionary, UPCNA church donations in 1934 had dropped 37 percent relative to 1925; according to another, the church's budget for foreign missions in 1937 was down 90 percent relative to its high of ten years before.[192] Deficits gutted programs; for example, in Fayoum in 1932—around the same time that a group of Muslim youths had attacked a lay evangelist with stones and bricks—the mission was running short on funds to support four village schools.[192] In this period the mission closed many such schools throughout Egypt and passed others to the Evangelical Church, whereupon they became "synodical schools" and fell under closer government oversight.[194] Likewise, in 1937, budget cuts forced the mission to close work in three stations.[195] Whereas there had been 217 missionaries in 1924, the number was down to 174 in 1939.[196] The mission's secretary wrote, "We grieve over the sacrifice of work which has been built up by faithful toil across past years and which we feel has been making valuable contribution to the progress of the Kingdom here."[197]

To make ends meet, the mission also laid off Egyptian evangelists by releasing those it deemed the "less fit" among workers. This cost-cutting tactic was very American and offered further evidence for what Andrew F. Walls has described as the business-inspired model of American missions, with its corporate ideal of efficiency.[198] Within the Egyptian Evangelical Church, the salaries of pastors had, in many cases, been falling into arrears as local congregations struggled to tithe and as the church synod was "driven almost to desperation by its finances."[199] Yet what looked financially prudent to the American missionaries looked merely heartless to Egyptians. Earl E. Elder explained in 1937 that "The [Egyptian Evangelical] synod . . . is much more group-minded [than the American mission]. It feels a moral responsibility for those who long ago dedicated their lives, whether of one or ten talents, to Christian service." Rather than eliminating church workers for the sake of a budget, Egyptian church leaders expressed a preference for halting the ordination of new seminarians, "caring first of all for those advancing in years, and waiting for better days."[200]

During the 1930s and 1940s, money was a source of continuing tension between the American mission and the Evangelical Church. If most of the Egyptian pastors had had their way—judging from what the American missionaries wrote about them—they would have cut costs by striking out funding for Muslim evangelization, which they regarded as fruitless and incendiary.[201] It was no accident that after 1932 the American mission, *not* the Egyptian synod, provided the money to pay for Kamil Mansur, the Muslim convert to Christianity who worked as a "special worker" to Muslims.[202]

In any case, by 1934 Muslims were no longer listening as readily to American missionaries or Egyptian evangelists as they had been ten or twenty years before; missionaries suggested that the anti-missionary agitation had scared many Muslims away.[203] By 1938, on weekly trips to Alexandria, Kamil Mansur was attracting audiences consisting mostly of "unattached Copts," and the same was true for his work in Cairo.[204] In some cases Muslim inquirers were facing persecution. In 1939, H. E. Philips reported, "one of [Kamil Mansur's Muslim] inquirers was arrested and bandied back and forth between police stations and parquets for a matter of two days because he was found with a Christian tract in his possession. It was the same tract that caused the imprisonment of one of the Nile Mission Press colporteurs in Cairo. It is a very harmless publication but for some reason it seems to have stirred a great deal of opposition."[205] Much to the missionaries' disappointment, moreover, some of the Muslims who approached them were only interested in emigrating to the United States. In 1933, before the scandal of Turkiyya Hasan hit the newspapers, W. T. Fairman had reported a "good year" for Muslim inquirers: one hundred and thirty Muslim men had approached the mission in Cairo. "But some did not continue for any extended period," he admitted, "and ceased to come when they found we were only teaching them Christian Truth and that the statements of the native press that we were paying large sums of money to converts and giving them good positions and sending them abroad were not true."[206] Likewise, in 1937, H. E. Philips reported that most of the scant number of Muslim inquirers for that year included "the two frequent types, either wanting to get a passport out of the country or to get a job."[207]

Egyptian Muslims may not have been interested in American Christianity, but they were certainly interested in American movies and opportunities—and even in American oddities and inconsistencies—as newspapers of the period suggested. In 1930, for example, at the height of the coverage regarding the defamation case of Kamil Mansur, *al-Siyasa* published critical, front-page articles on the United States considering the plight of the Native Americans, who were consigned to reservations and denuded of rights, and noting the wide accessibility of alcohol, despite the official policy of Prohibition.[208] Two years later, as the uproar over Yusuf 'Abd al-Samad was raging, *al-Siyasa*'s literary supplement published an item on marriage in America. "America does not cease to toss us a marvel (*u'juba*) every day," it wrote.

> For some years now we have heard about civil marriage, and then about experimental marriage. And now we hear about a new kind of marriage—it has broader limits and greater freedom than its predecessors. This type is called sexual partnership (*musharaka jinsiyya*) or natural relations (*'ishra tabi'iyya*); no clergyman comes, no government record is made; rather it is limited to the desire of the partners in remaining in a conjugal relationship. This type is spreading quickly especially among male and female students. And what is the opinion of Egyptians on this one?[209]

In 1933, at the height of the Turkiyya Hasan scandal, *al-Balagh* evinced a similar delight in the American bizarre when it published a photograph from the Chicago Exposition showing a girl with hair two meters long, and another of a stunt showing a young man and two women, clad in swimsuits, forming a human pyramid atop a bicycle on a California beach.[210] In this manner the Egyptian press was evincing Occidentalism—an imaging and stereotyping of American society that provided a foil for Egypt's self-construction.[211]

In fact, some of the strongest interest in America—and in emigration to its lands—was coming from Azhar's journal, *Nur al-Islam*, as well as from *al-Fath*, the journal of the YMMA to which Hasan al-Banna, the founder of the Muslim Brotherhood, also contributed.[212] Like *al-Siyasa* and *al-Balagh* in this period, *al-Fath* and *Nur al-Islam* published articles on Muslim societies all over the world, from Yugoslavia and Djibouti to the Philippines. Yet the vision of the Muslim world (*Dar al-Islam*) conveyed in *al-Fath* and *Nur al-Islam* also embraced western Europe and the Americas, historic centers of Christianity. Thus *al-*

Fath alerted readers to Muslim immigrants in London (where a new mosque was being built) and South Shields (a port town near New-castle-upon-Tyne that had a community of Yemeni dockworkers); likewise, it considered whether Muslims could legitimately apply for citizenship in France, where the state was not Islamic.[213] *Nur al-Islam* profiled British converts to Islam, some of whom worshiped at a mosque in Woking, Surrey, and also published an article on Algerian and Moroccan factory workers living in France.[214] Similarly, through its coverage of the Americas, *al-Fath* helped Egyptian Muslims realize that it might be possible to go to the United States, make money, and stay Muslim. In an issue published in August 1930, which ran an article titled "Zwemer's List" (invoking Samuel M. Zwemer) about the ruses of Christian missionaries who allegedly tried to bribe poor Muslims in Baghdad to convert and who compiled fake lists of Muslim converts to impress church donors at home, *al-Fath* published two items about America. First, it noted that a branch of the YMMA had been started in Boston, Massachusetts, and that its members had sent $315 to al-Hajj Amin al-Husayni in Jerusalem, as aid for Arabs who were "wretched and disaster-stricken" (*mankubin wa-ba'isin*). (In the early 1930s, the "Judaization of Palestine" [*tahwid Filastin*] competed with Christian evangelism as one of *al-Fath*'s primary concerns.) Second, this issue of *al-Fath* relayed news from *al-Bayan*, an Arabic newspaper published in New York City, to the effect that Muslims had built a mosque in North Dakota.[215]

Thus by the 1930s, the American Presbyterian missionaries were not the only mediators of America in Egypt: Hollywood, consumer commodities (such as Ford automobiles, which were often featured on the advertising pages of Arabic newspapers), and news from emigrants were becoming more important. John L. McClenahan, whose father had left the American Presbyterian mission in order to help Charles R. Watson found AUC, recalled that during his childhood in Cairo in the 1920s, many merchants in Khan al-Khalili, the bazaar next to the mosque of al-Azhar, claimed relatives in America. "'Welcome!' they cried. . . . 'You come from California? I have a nephew there, a friend of Rudolph Valentino. And an uncle in Chicago. But only come in. I have everything you desire—brasswork, perfume, alabaster. Only enter and be my guest.'"[216]

For American missionaries, the Coptic scene was also becoming a cause for hand-wringing. An internal report acknowledged in 1939 that the "Evangelical Church is not growing as formerly. The number of adherents won from the world is, each year, smaller than the number of its baptisms (infant) [*sic*], and, Alas! In many places it is not holding its own sons and daughters in its churches—they are reverting to the ancestral Church or to the world."[217] Sounding just like his father, Andrew, who had described the Coptic Orthodox Church as a "mummified" church in 1897, Charles R. Watson admitted in 1936 that he thought the Coptic Orthodox and other Eastern churches were still "as dead as door nails" because their very orthodoxy was stifling. (Watson added, "It is a word of warning to mere orthodoxy anywhere. The Spirit of God is life, life, life.")[218] However, contrary to Watson's assertion, the Coptic Orthodox Church *was* changing in this period, by embracing practices that missionaries had introduced—for example, by imitating the sermons, hymns, and Sunday school programs of the Protestants, and the catechism classes of the Catholics. During the interwar period, S. S. Hasan has observed, "The missionaries sparked church reform [among the Coptic Orthodox] by giving the example of energetic churchmanship." To a large degree, she suggests, the reforms worked insofar as they staunched the flow of Copts to the Evangelical Church.[219] Another missionary had testified to this trend in 1937; not only were some Evangelicals turning back to Coptic Orthodoxy, he wrote, but in some places the Coptic Orthodox Church "seem[ed] as evangelistic as our own church in the same town."[220]

Anti-missionary agitation, economic distress, and concerns about the future of the Evangelical Church battered the morale of the American missionaries. But so did the "Layman's Report on Foreign Missions," also known as the Hocking Report, after its editor, the Harvard professor William Ernest Hocking. Funded by the Baptist layman John D. Rockefeller Jr., this inquiry came from a desire to understand why younger American Protestants were not as committed as their parents had been to foreign missions.[221]

The report, which appeared in 1932 in several volumes accompanied by a summary titled *Re-Thinking Missions*, focused on mission case studies in India, Burma, China, and Japan. But in fact, the report was relevant for Egypt in two important ways. First, by 1932, Christian missions in places like China and India were facing forces of anticolonial nationalism that were very similar to those buffeting Christian missions in Egypt, while evolving relations between foreign missions and indigenous mission-planted churches resembled the American Presbyterian–Egyptian Evangelical relationship as well.[222] Second, Rockefeller borrowed the title of the report's summary, *Re-Thinking Missions*, from an article that Charles R. Watson, the former UPCNA foreign mission board secretary and founder and president of AUC, had published in the *International Review of Missions* in January 1932.[223] In this article Watson had pointed out that many Egyptian Muslims were traveling to Western countries, and some were starting families there, so that lines between the West and the non-West were blurring. Missionaries were also changing: some were beginning to prefer social service over preaching and were no longer viewing schools and hospitals as mere "bait for evangelistic fishing." Watson confessed, too, that his own ideas about Islam had changed, so that while he retained his Christian convictions, he recognized the values inherent in Islam more than he had done in his younger days.[224] This expression of respect for non-Christian religion and for social service as Christian witness stood out in Watson's article and harmonized with the Layman's Report. It was no accident that Rockefeller had seen a connection.

As the distillation of the Layman's Report, *Re-Thinking Missions* connected the decline in church donations among mainline Protestant churches to a changed mood in American society. "The old fervor appears to have been succeeded in some quarters," it suggested, "by questioning if not by indifference." *Re-Thinking Missions* advocated greater reconciliation with non-Christian faiths and practices, recommended that missions concentrate primarily on ameliorating social conditions and not on gaining converts, called for closer ecumenical cooperation and an end to "narrow denominationalism," and suggested that Christianity should grow within indigenous cultural traditions and not as a foreign transplant. It also argued that missionaries should respect diversity of opinion and, implicitly therefore, diversity of religious belief.[225] In his history of American missionary thought, William R. Hutchison noted that the report accurately reflected the view of Hocking, the report's editor, who dismissed the kind of "parochialism that in effect denies the God-given right of others to hold a similar loyalty to their own religious systems." The report was also significant for suggesting that missionaries should be humanitarian ambassadors, not soldiers or salesmen. But Hutchison observed that ultimately, and theologically, "The question of Christian finality—whether Christianity is one version of divine truth or is ultimately the only version—was the do-or-die issue in this debate."[226]

The Layman's Report became the talk of the town among the American Presbyterians in Egypt and was discussed at missionary meetings and in private letters.[227] Many were distressed by its support for a kind of Christian relativism. The secretary of the mission, J. W. Acheson, declared coolly of the report that "The theology, in spite of its literary charm, is impossible."[228] Ella Barnes, who ran the mission's Fowler Orphanage in Cairo, was more expansive. To a friend she wrote, "Its criticisms of missions did not disturb me much, they have all been heard before, but to realize that that many men and women of American Christians (so-called) could sign their names to statements placing our Lord Jesus Christ on a level with leaders of other religions, and presume to re-write the Great Commission, well it put me to bed with a head ache, and a heart wound, and a soul chill."[229] Exchanging thoughts about the report with a missionary in Egypt, W. B. Anderson, the normally mild-mannered head of the UPCNA foreign mission board and himself a former missionary to India, denounced it in 1933 as "the most subtle and skilful [sic] flank attack on the essentials of the gospel of Christ that has been made within my memory."[230]

The Layman's Report also jarred the American Presbyterians because it forced them to engage in much larger debates about Christianity that were brooding over the American landscape. The Missionary Association of Egypt implicitly referred to these debates in the official response to the report that it prepared for the UPCNA mission board by expressing regret that the report emphasized theological questions "on which the thinking of the home church is so seriously divided." It continued, "Our Mission has been happily free from doctrinal controversies and divisions, and we hope that it may continue to be so. In a spirit of mutual forbearance and respect we probably hold about as wide a range of opinions on theological questions as is represented by the workers in good standing in our home church."[231]

The Missionary Association report was referring to the fundamentalist-modernist controversy. The UPCNA had managed to sidestep this controversy in the 1920s, but the Layman's Report—which in words of Charles R. Watson represented the modernist "left wing" of American Protestant thought—forced them to confront it anew.[232] The Layman's Report widened the gap between American Protestant conservatives and liberals, and eroded the consensus that had marked the foreign missions movement in its heyday from the 1880s to World War I.[233] It was a watershed, a moment of "transition within the Protestant establishment."[234] The transition had long-term significance for the UPCNA Presbyterians and their successors, who found themselves pushed or moving leftward as the twentieth century progressed, toward a vision of Christian witness that emphasized social action over evangelism.[235]

Notwithstanding the challenges that were besetting the mission in the 1930s, a few missionaries insisted on the continuing relevance of Muslim evangelization and Christian conversion. J. R. Alexander was eighty-three years old when he prepared a policy suggestion for mission schools late in 1932, in light of the anti-missionary agitation. "Let us restate the objective of the Mission," Alexander wrote. "It is to evangelize Egypt. In the future it is, especially, to evangelize Muslim Egypt. All that has been done in the past is only preparatory to this great, this stupendous objective."[236] Alexander issued a plea asking the mission to continue funding schools in the predominantly Muslim Delta region—the very region where the Muslim Brotherhood was mobilizing its base. Throughout the 1930s and 1940s, H. E. Philips sounded a similar tone. "From the beginning," Philips wrote in 1937, "our Mission has declared that its policy and purpose in raising up an Evangelical Church has been to secure eventually the Evangelization of *all* the people in Egypt." On many occasions, Philips expressed deep frustration with the Evangelical Church, suggesting that its pastors were shirking their Christian duties by avoiding outreach to Muslims.[237]

Quietly, however, some missionaries in the 1930s were beginning to move toward an understanding of mission that utterly rejected polemic and emphasized social service (or what some called a "gospel of love") as a mode of Christian witness.[238] The American Presbyterian mission in Egypt, from its inception in 1854, had always engaged in social service, for example, by treating the sick or teaching children in schools. What was new about some of this mission service in the 1930s was its degree of professional specialization.

Two missionaries, Davida Finney and Milo McFeeters, exemplified this new trend. Davida Finney was a second-generation American Presbyterian missionary in Egypt. (Her father, Thomas J. Finney, was the missionary who alerted the mission board to the controversy of *al-Murshid* in 1910.) In the 1930s and 1940s, when the mission was focusing most of its work on Cairo and other town centers, she launched initiatives to open libraries and promote literacy in Upper Egyptian villages. She also worked to develop materials for semi-literate readers—especially women—with an aim to promoting the retention and development of literacy. In 1933 she published tracts with titles like "The Care of Children" and "The Mother and Her Family," which discuss subjects ranging from infant nutrition to household finances.[239] Milo McFeeters came to the mission in the 1920s with a background in farming and joined the staff of Assiut College. From 1928 until his retirement in the early 1950s, McFeeters developed an experimental dairy farm, where he bred imported American Jersey cows with their local Egyptian counterparts, thereby producing cattle whose milk yields were dramatically larger. In 1949, McFeeters finished a 349-page work on dairy cattle, which was translated and published as an Arabic textbook.[240] Both Finney and McFeeters worked closely with Evangelical communities but pursued projects that had a broadly Egyptian social relevance.

In hindsight, it is possible to say that regardless of whether the American Presbyterians in Egypt responded to the Layman's Report with ire or equanimity, the mission in the 1930s was already changing in ways that the report recommended. Establishing rural libraries, fostering the development of adult literacy, and breeding dairy cattle, as Finney, McFeeters, and others were doing in the 1930s, represented efforts to ameliorate Egyptian living standards and not to add up converts. In the long run, the American mission in Egypt confirmed the observation made by John R. Fitzmier and Randall Balmer, who wrote in a study of U.S. Presbyterian churches that the Layman's Report "both called for and accurately predicted enormous changes in missions policy" in Presbyterian missions worldwide.[241] The fact was that the Layman's Report, with its attention to missions in colonial contexts, was both prescient and timely for the American Presbyterians in Egypt. With anti-colonial nationalist sentiment on the rise and restrictions on missionaries mounting, a mission of social service was becoming more feasible than a mission of religious conversion.

William Ernest Hocking, the Harvard professor who edited the Layman's Report, may have been largely forgotten as a "giant" among early twentieth-century American philosophers,[242] but the study he edited holds its place in the intellectual history of American religion. (The report remains controversial, however, among mission advocates, some of whom continue to deplore what they see as its endorsement of Christian relativism.)[243] Yet, Hocking's role as a public philosopher went beyond the Layman's Report to intersect with the American Presbyterians in Egypt in another respect: he offered the missionaries direct advice on approaching the issue of religious liberty. His support may explain why none of the American Presbyterians in Egypt lambasted Hocking personally, as did some Presbyterians in the United States, even though many disliked or felt uneasy with the Layman's Report itself. In fact, in 1930, around the time when the cases of Kamil Mansur and Fakhry Farag were unfolding in Cairo, Hocking participated with Charles R. Watson in a conference on religious liberty in New York. This conference seeded a report on the status of religious liberty in the Middle East that appeared in 1938 and that included an assessment of the Egyptian anti-missionary agitation of the early 1930s. Neutrally titled *Some Aspects of Religious Liberty of Nationals in the Near East*, this report pointed to the discrepancy between the Egyptian constitution's affirmation of "absolute" freedom of conscience and the lack of a legal procedure for registering conversions out of Islam.[244]

In June 1930, Hocking also wrote to S. A. Morrison of the CMS and advised the Inter-Mission Council against seeking support for religious liberty through treaties or international law. Hocking warned, "If the liberty of religious propaganda is abetted by a Western government, it becomes associated with the interest of that government." He warned, too,"Religious liberties clash, and when they clash the burden of proof rests on the alien religion. In the presence of the new national impulses of the East my tendency is to think that the ideal content of Christianity will best find its way across, for a period at least, through the more informal methods of conversation, discussion, literature, philosophy, as borrowed and adapted by the native seekers and leaders. Am I wrong about this?" Meanwhile, Hocking suggested that missionaries should seek to earn the Egyptian government's goodwill by appealing to its national pride and sense of fairness.[245]

In many ways, the approach that Hocking suggested coincided with the path that the American Presbyterians took. In the years from 1930 to 1933 when anti-missionary agitation was flaring, leaders of the American mission stayed silent in the face of press attacks, even as they followed the news closely and maintained contacts with British, American, and Egyptian authorities. They appealed to the magnanimity of the Egyptian government and tried to show their respect for Egyptian law.[246] Meanwhile, they continued to think about religious liberty, and what they thought it should mean, both in Egypt and universally. In October 1932, in the aftermath of the Yusuf 'Abd al-Samad affair, they gathered with members of the Inter-Mission Council and remarkably, too, with members of the smaller Protestant faith missions—all momentarily united by the urgency of the situation and by the sense of common threat—to formulate "a statement of the motives and principles" for Christian mission work in Egypt. Their statement went through many drafts until it was printed and presented to the Egyptian government in 1933.[247]

A few points in the statement stand out. First, "It is a fundamental conviction of our religion that individuality, as part of the Divine order in creation and providence, should be held in reverence." Thus the statement affirmed the Anglo-American missionary belief in the primacy of the individual over the social collective—a belief that challenged Egyptian Islamic legal and social assumptions.[248] Second, "That we are impelled by our religion not only to respect all men with their beliefs and institutions, but also to love and serve them, is shown by the works of mercy and philanthropy in which Christian missions have engaged in all countries." The statement explained that the signatories sought not to exploit the poor, sick, or ignorant, as critics in Egypt had charged, but to demonstrate "the disinterested love which God has put in our hearts for our fellow men." It defined its missionary service as "the highest service of love" and a "witness by word and deed to what has redeemed and regenerated our own lives." These words, with their emphasis on humanitarian service, matched the spirit of the Layman's Report.

Signaling a commitment to interfaith amity, the statement endorsed the conclusions of a conference held in Delhi in 1924 and attended by leaders of India's Hindu, Muslim, Sikh, Parsi, and Christian communities. It quoted from this conference's resolutions upholding the highest standards of tolerance and respect for other religions, rejecting compulsion in religion of any kind, and affirming unencumbered freedom of a person or people "to hold and give expression to his or their beliefs and follow any religious practice," including rights of both conversion and reconversion. It averred that "every individual is at liberty to follow any faith and to change it whenever he so wills, and shall not by reason of such change of faith render himself liable to any punishment or persecution at the hands of the followers of the faith renounced by him."

The statement continued by expressing the hope that the Egyptian constitutional guarantee of freedom of conscience would be absolute, and included two articles that were specific to conditions in Egypt. Article II declared, "We deplore the absence of any legal procedure for a change of religion similar to that provided by the official circular issued by the Ministry of Justice, No. 2466 (28-2-13) for the embracing of Islam." Article V declared, "We agree among ourselves that as far as lies within our power no one shall enter any school, boarding school, hospital, dispensary, orphanage, welfare center, establishment for higher education, or other institution of ours without knowing that it is Christian and that Christian teaching has a central place in its life." In other words, Article V affirmed that the mission of Christian missionary institutions was to proclaim a Christian message, and signaled that non-Christians should be prepared to enter Christian mission schools with that understanding.[249]

This statement accomplished two things: it enabled the American Presbyterian missionaries to articulate an official philosophy of religious liberty, and it strengthened ecumenical relations among the foreign Protestant organizations in Egypt. But it had no discernible impact on the Egyptian government, which never implemented a procedure for registering Muslim conversions to Christianity, and which continued to elaborate restrictions on religious instruction in mission schools. Missionaries had to grapple with the fact that the Egyptian government was subjecting religious liberty to the preservation of an Islamic public order, and was drawing a connection, as the newspaper *al-Balagh* had done in 1933, between "resisting evangelism and defending the peace and security of the country."[250] Indeed, in 1940, the Egyptian government passed a law requiring Qur'an study for all Muslim students in all primary schools in Egypt—Christian mission schools included.[251] In 1940, parliament considered a draft law to ban the spread of religious propaganda outside mosques and sanctioned spaces, for the sake (as its sponsor explained) of preserving religious beliefs and public tranquility given that the constitutional freedom of religions had been "abused." In 1942, Earl E. Elder described the admonition of the minister of education, who at meetings with missionaries had stipulated a "principle of public order" such that "No religion other than their own shall be taught to students, not even with the formal consent of their parents."[252]

In 1932, when anti-missionary agitation was simmering, Elder had warned his colleagues that "Very few Muslims object to Christian teaching but the day may come when they shall and when the government will prevent us from teaching Christianity to non-Christians. This will mean that our Christianity will have to be caught rather than taught from our schools."[253] Ten years later, in 1942, the day he predicted had come.

Conclusion: The Mission by War's End

World War II depleted the staff of the American mission and halted some of its work. In 1941, for example, a staff shortage forced the mission to shut its girls' school in Alexandria—a temporary closure that became permanent as time passed. In summer 1942, as Rommel's Afrika Korps marched into Egypt from Libya, the American Legation in Cairo advised the missionaries to evacuate the country, prompting most of those remaining to take refuge for some months in Khartoum.[254] Otherwise, the dislocations of wartime were not decisive for the mission in Egypt. More important, in retrospect, was the mission's decision in 1944 to sell or lease one of its two riverboats—a steel-hulled *dhahabiyya* called *The Witness*, which it had acquired in 1917. The release of *The Witness* marked the end of an era: it meant that the mission was giving up its effort to evangelize along the length of Egypt's Nile.

"For almost thirty years," wrote Earl E. Elder, "*The Witness* sailed back and forth from Aswan to below Sohag, some 275 miles, serving as the headquarters for the itinerant missionary or missionaries visiting the churches, encouraging pastors, meeting non-Christian inquirers or casual acquaintances."[255] *The Witness* had been well-used in its early years when new American Presbyterian missionaries had been required, as part of their Arabic language course at AUC's School of Oriental Studies, to spend four weeks visiting villages on a riverboat or bicycle tour. Reflecting in 1920 on a trip of this kind that he undertook near Benha, in the predominantly Muslim Delta, Henry Rankin praised the hospitality of all the farmers, shopkeepers, and others whom he met, and looked forward to taking another trip on *The Witness*. Rankin wrote, "I did not enter a single village where I was not treated with the greatest kindness."[256] By 1944, however, the welcome from Muslims had dimmed, and random "itinerating" (to borrow the missionary term) no longer seemed wise or productive. Financial cutbacks, staff shortages, the changed mood within missions (as exemplified by the Layman's Report of 1932), Muslim agitation along with the formation of groups like the Muslim Brotherhood, and Egyptian government restrictions had together pushed the mission toward retrenchment. Against this context the Missionary Association decided that it could not afford to make repairs on the riverboat. Thus in 1944 it released *The Witness* to the alumnae association of the mission's American College for Girls (ACG). Docked in the wealthy Cairo suburb of al-Ma'adi, *The Witness* became a place for what Elder described as social "retreat."[257]

By 1944, the American mission roster had diminished considerably. While there had been 217 missionaries in 1924 and 174 in 1939, there were only 66 in 1944, consisting of eight ordained men (ministers of the church), four unordained men, thirty-one unmarried women, eight wives, and fifteen short-term appointments.[258] The American mission still had two hospitals, in Tanta and Assiut, as well as six clinics and dispensaries, and it still ran several schools—such as Assiut College and its female counterpart, Pressly Memorial Institute (PMI), the Buchanan Girls' School in Luxor, and the ACG. Together, in 1944, its schools claimed a total of 5,304 students, of whom 3,595 (68 percent) were Christians.[259] But this, too, marked a sharp decline from 1925, when the mission had reported 13,706 enrollments.[260] Moreover, by this time American mission schools were catering increasingly to Egyptian elites, whereas the Egyptian government was teaching the masses. H. E. Philips acknowledged this trend in 1939 when he wrote that there were then 374,292 girls in Egyptian government schools, compared to just 3,208 girls in American Presbyterian institutions, along with 4,933 girls in the synodical schools of the Evangelical Church.[261]

By 1944, the Evangelical Church was small but thriving. It claimed 164 ordained ministers, more than 300 congregations, and 24,504 "communicants."[262] Yet relations between the Evangelical pastors and American missionaries remained tense, since differences of opinion persisted over how to spend money. Some Egyptian pastors, like Mitri al-Diwayri (who was the editor of the Evangelical Church journal, *al-Huda*), were heard to make nationalist, anti-foreign, and implicitly anti-missionary remarks.[263] In 1939 a missionary attributed some of this ill will to an article that a colleague had published in *United Presbyterian*, the UPCNA's journal in America. Egyptian pastors felt that this article treated the Evangelical community in a patronizing and demeaning manner by representing them "as a group of savages with tails running around bare-footed."[264]

On an ecumenical level, however, relations among Protestants were stronger than ever. In 1944 the American Presbyterian mission finally joined the Near East Christian Council (NECC), an organization founded in 1927 through the efforts of the International Missionary Council. (As president of AUC, Charles R. Watson had played a leading role in the NECC's creation, but the American mission had stood apart for many years, claiming that membership fees were too high.)[265] The inclusion of the UPCNA mission of Egypt within the NECC signaled an end to denominational isolation and brought the American Presbyterians of Egypt into closer contact with the PCUSA Presbyterians of Lebanon—a move that anticipated the merger of their churches in 1958. At the same time, during the war, plans advanced for establishing the World Council of Churches (WCC)—plans that the Presbyterians enthusiastically supported.

Yet ecumenism had limits. In the 1940s the American Presbyterians in Egypt had little contact with the predominantly French and Italian cadres of priests, nuns, and lay workers who sponsored Catholic missionary activities.[266] In 1933, as the Inter-Mission Council prepared its statement on religious liberty, R. S. McClenahan of AUC had approached Catholic missions to see if they would like to sign on to the effort. McClenahan reported at the time, "The Roman Catholics do not propose to share in any of these matters as they feel that the events of the past summer do not concern them. They claim that by an agreement made between the Jesuits and the Ottoman Empire some two hundred years ago the Roman Catholic church does not seek to evangelize the Moslem population, but confines her efforts in evangelization to work among Christians. Therefore we cannot expect that the Roman church will participate in any agreement that may be drawn up unless future events bring about a change of attitude."[267] But judging from the commentary about *al-tabshir wa'l-tansir* (evangelization and Christianization) that appeared in the Arabic press, Roman Catholic missions had more in common with their Protestant counterparts than they realized—at least in the view of Egyptian Muslims. Nevertheless, the common experience of Muslim opposition did not bring Catholic and Protestant missionaries in Egypt together in the interwar era. Cooperation had to wait until the decade following the Suez Crisis of 1956, by which time most foreign missionaries had left the country.

By the time World War II ended, a global Christian culture was emerging, and non-Western churches were reaching maturity. Illustrating this trend was a spate of international Protestant conferences in which American Presbyterian missionaries and Egyptian Evangelical Church leaders participated, in places like Los Angeles, Rio de Janeiro, and Tambaram (near Madras).[268] The Tambaram meeting, in 1938, was particularly important, though Christian scholars differed in assessing its long-term significance. Tambaram was where the Dutch missionary Hendrik Kraemer presented his still-cited rebuttal of Hocking and the Layman's Report (later published as *The Christian Message in a Non-Christian World*), contributing to a persistent debate over Christian exceptionalism.[269] But others later hailed Tambaram, first, for confirming that the goal of European and American missions should not be—or should not have been—to establish "outposts of Western Christianity scattered throughout the world," and, second, for affirming the importance of interfaith dialogue rooted in the belief that "God is not left anywhere without a witness."[270]

The American Presbyterian mission in Egypt was an integral part of these church developments. But by 1945, new political currents stood poised to sweep over the mission. Decolonization was on the horizon throughout the British and French empires. Zionist settlement in Palestine was increasing, while Jews were reeling from the Holocaust in Europe. And the Egyptian populace was ready for change. Economic conditions alone contributed to a sense of malaise: "Per capita income may have been 20 percent lower in 1945 than in 1900; half of the decline had occurred during World War II."[271] Against this context, many segments of the Egyptian public were disillusioned by elite politics but at the same time hopeful that the future might bring something better. Reverberations from all these trends, together with the emergence of Israel in 1948, the Egyptian Free Officers coup of 1952, and the rise of the United States as a global superpower, would dramatically change the social standing of the mission in Egypt.

CHAPTER 5

The Mission of the American University in Cairo

> If missions help to make history, world-history also reacts
> on the world-mission, deflecting the currents of its effort,
> giving definiteness to its ideals, causing modifications in its
> methods.
>
> —W.H.T. Gairdner, *Echoes from Edinburgh* (1910)

IN 1916, Charles R. Watson sent a letter to the United Presbyterian Church of North America, resigning his position as secretary of its foreign mission board in Philadelphia. With the strong support of this church and its missionary wing, Watson had been laying the foundation for a Christian university in Egypt. He was resigning to devote himself to fund-raising, finding a site in Cairo, and securing approval from British authorities who had imposed a wartime protectorate on Egypt. In his resignation letter Watson reflected, "I cannot feel that I am severing my connection with the missionary cause that has occupied my interest and strength during the past fourteen years. I think of myself as rather being called from a more general service of the missionary work of our Church to a more specialized form of a missionary effort which aims to present Jesus Christ, in a strategically vital way, to the great Moslem world."[1] Watson's efforts culminated in the establishment of the American University in Cairo (AUC). To anyone who knows anything about AUC and Egypt today, this bold linkage between the university and Christian mission may come as a surprise.

AUC opened its doors in 1920 as a result of Watson's efforts. Yet from the moment of its debut, Watson insisted on AUC's complete independence from the American Presbyterian mission, much to the dismay and anger of some of the missionaries who had been involved in the university's early planning. Watson did, however, actively support AUC's inclusion in the Egypt Inter-Mission Council, an interdenominational forum for the major Protestant missionary organizations in Egypt, and made AUC the host of an Arabic training program for Christian missionaries to the Muslim world. Moreover, during his years as AUC president (1920–45), Watson participated actively in many Protestant ecumenical organizations such as the World's Sunday School Association (WSSA),[2] the International Missionary Council (IMC), and the Near East Christian Council (NECC). In fact, Watson helped establish the latter two organizations, which evolved into the World Council of Churches (WCC) and Middle East Council of Churches (MECC), respectively.[3]

Within American missionary and Egyptian Evangelical circles today, Charles R. Watson is not remembered as a missionary figure, perhaps because his university became a secular institution.[4] Nevertheless, Watson was an active participant in the Anglo-American missionary movement of the early twentieth century, and his ideas, set out over a long career in books, pamphlets, and private papers, mirrored many of the major themes, tensions, and changes that distinguished the mainstream American Protestant culture of his day. Thus a study of Watson's life, and of the university that he founded in Cairo, casts light on the intersecting histories of Christian evangelism, Egypt, and the United States during the first half of the twentieth century. It shows how a project that began with a desire to convert Muslims led to the transformation—or perhaps one could say, the conversion—of Watson's own ideas about modern Christianity and the role of an American educational presence in Egypt.

The story of Charles R. Watson straddles three periods in the missionary encounter in Egypt: the years before World War I, when missionaries were at their most optimistic and expansive; the interwar era, when Muslim anti-missionary agitation forced missionaries to change goals and tactics; and the post–World War II period, when the emergence of Israel and the Arab-Israeli conflict placed new strains on American relationships with Egypt. His story ran parallel to the experiences of James K. Quay (1887–1981), an ordained United Presbyterian pastor, veteran of the Arabic program for missionaries at AUC, and religious secretary of the Cairo Central branch of the Young Men's Christian Association (YMCA), who briefly tried to teach Christianity to AUC students as a personal favor to Watson. Charles R. Watson struggled until the end of his career to define the mission, or missions, of AUC. His struggle contributed to the redefinition of AUC as an educational and cultural bridge between the United States and Egypt and to a larger rethinking of American Protestantism and its missionary engagement.

Watson, the Church, and the Missionary Movement

Born in Cairo in 1873, to longstanding members of the American mission, Charles Roger Watson was a child of the missionary movement. His father, the Rev. Andrew Watson (1834–1916), and his mother,

Margaret McVickar Watson (1836–1929), joined the mission in 1861 and stayed in Egypt until their deaths.[5] His father became the mission's first chronicler, publishing its fifty-year retrospective in 1897, and was also a missionary "pioneer" to Sudan, having visited Khartoum in 1899 on the heels of the Anglo-Egyptian conquest in order to initiate an American Presbyterian mission to the country.[6] Andrew Watson appears to have maintained close and cordial connections to British missionaries in Egypt—not surprisingly, given that he had been born in Scotland and only emigrated to the United States as a teenager. These connections to Britain and Britons may have helped cultivate the strong spirit of Protestant ecumenism that distinguished the thought and career of his son, Charles.

Like the sons of many leading American missionaries to the Middle East in this period,[7] Charles R. Watson attended Princeton University (where he distinguished himself in oratory contests)[8] and received a bachelor's degree from the institution in 1894. His personnel file for the UPCNA states that he also received a master's degree at Princeton after writing a thesis on French analysis of English literature. After graduating, he taught French first at Ohio State University and later, while studying at Princeton Theological Seminary, at Princeton University's "Scientific Department." He briefly taught French and Greek at the Lawrenceville School, an elite boys' boarding school in New Jersey. He then continued his studies for the pastorate at Allegheny Theological Seminary in western Pennsylvania and, in 1899, took a position as minister of Allegheny's United Presbyterian Church. The location had symbolic significance, for it was the Presbyterian community of Allegheny (the sister town of Pittsburgh) that had resolved, at a meeting in 1853, to send missionaries to Egypt.[9] In 1900, Watson became pastor at the United Presbyterian Church in St. Louis, Missouri.

Watson moved into mission administration in 1902, when he accepted a position as corresponding secretary of the UPCNA's foreign mission board. He spent the years 1903 and 1904 abroad, inspecting the church's operations in northern India, Egypt, and the Sudan, and drew on his experiences to write his first three books. These were *Egypt and the Christian Crusade* (1907), *In the Valley of the Nile* (1908), and *Far North in India* (1909).[10] (The last of these, an account of the UPCNA mission in the Punjab, was cowritten with William B. Anderson, a former missionary to India and Watson's colleague at the board in Philadelphia.) In these books Watson surveyed missions in a plain-language, travelogue format that was designed to fire the imaginations of American churchgoing readers and generate financial and moral support.

During his years as foreign board secretary, Watson enthusiastically participated in and organized activities that gathered leaders from mainline American Protestant churches. He was eager to build bridges to Britons as well. Thus in 1906 Watson suggested on behalf of the American Foreign Missions Conference the idea for a joint meeting with British missionary societies—a meeting that reached fruition in the World Missionary Conference held in Edinburgh in 1910.[11] Participants emerged from Edinburgh convinced the future for missions was bright and boundless, especially in this age when British imperial power was helping Protestant missionaries pursue missions in colonized lands.[12]

Confidence was buoying Protestant missionaries as plans for the university in Cairo took shape. Watson shared this optimism, and thought, too, that the British occupation of Egypt was a boon to the Christian cause since it guaranteed religious liberties that were essential for evangelizing in an Islamic society. He also believed that Americans, with their growing prosperity, had a special mission to serve in the world.[13] Writing in 1907, he observed, "These great resources which have been suddenly opened up and which make Americans wealthier, as a class, than people in Europe, must be in God's plan. These great resources are meant by Him to be used, not wasted; wisely invested, not foolishly spent."[14]

THE AMERICAN UNIVERSITY MISSION: EARLY DEBATES

Although AUC was the product of the Christian missionary movement, its missionary character was contested from the start. For while Watson assumed that the university would be autonomous from the American Presbyterian mission in policy and oversight, American missionary leaders in Egypt expected that the university would be an extension of their mission and that it would use education to foster the Egyptian Evangelical Church. A confidential memorandum from the mission asserted, along these lines, that the mission had prepared early plans for the university so that it would complete its "system of Protestant higher education in Egypt . . . and . . . draw the sons of enlightened Copts and Muslims to Evangelical learning and Evangelical truth."[15]

The American Presbyterian missionaries had good reasons for assuming that the new university would be integral to their work. For a start, their association had been considering plans for a Christian college or university in Cairo since 1899, when the missionaries appointed a committee for this purpose. By 1915, these plans were being listed in mission reports under the rubric of "Christian University for Egypt." The fact that the UPCNA had officially endorsed the university plan, that Watson developed the plan while he was responsible for the UPCNA's foreign mission secretariat, and that Watson raised much of the early funding for the university from United Presbyterian donors only reinforced the expectation of interconnection.[16]

The idea for a Christian university in Cairo had other antecedents, too. Among these were discussions that had been occurring since 1906, when American and British Protestants had gathered in Cairo to discuss the challenges of mission work among Muslims. Conferees raised the idea of pooling resources, especially in training Christian workers for Muslims and developing printed materials in Islamic languages. Indeed, at the Cairo conference in 1906, the British CMS missionary D. M. Thornton (1873–1908) had pointed to the challenge posed by Cairo's venerable Islamic institution, al-Azhar, which trained thousands of men from the far corners of the Muslim world. Thornton had asked his colleagues, "Ought not the Christian church in East and West to be able to cooperate in the gradual formation of *an international and interdenominational Christian university in Cairo* within easy reach of the Azhar?"[17]

This idea for educational cooperation among missionaries to Muslims gained a boost at the Edinburgh 1910 conference, and grew clearer at the conference held in Lucknow, India, in 1911, which specifically dealt with missions to Muslims.[18] Samuel M. Zwemer of the Reformed Church in America emerged from Edinburgh and Lucknow determined to fulfill this plan for the cooperative training of missionaries to Muslims. Thus, in 1911, Zwemer moved to Egypt, established an affiliation with the American Presbyterian mission, and worked with the British CMS missionary W.H.T. Gairdner (1873–1928) to open the Cairo Study Centre by devising a program for missionaries studying Islam and Arabic. While Gairdner developed the language curriculum, Zwemer offered lectures on Islamic doctrines, practices, and texts.[19] Watson shared with Gairdner and Zwemer a belief in Cairo's strategic import for global missionary action and in the desirability of Anglo-American cooperation. Therefore Watson ensured that AUC, at its inception, incorporated the Cairo Study Centre. Renamed the School of Oriental Studies (SOS), this AUC program trained American, British, and continental European Protestant missionaries in Arabic until the mid-1950s.[20] The program's scholarly attention to colloquial Arabic was radical for its time but had a practical purpose: it was meant to equip missionaries to speak the language of ordinary Egyptians, whether in public sermons or face-to-face. Thanks to Gairdner, AUC became a pacesetter in the pedagogy of colloquial and modern standard Arabic for English-speaking learners.[21] In the mid-1960s this SOS Arabic program was refashioned as the Center for Arabic Studies (CAS) and then in 1967 as the Center for Arabic Study

Abroad (CASA), which today offers advanced, intensive Arabic training to American graduate students and Middle East area specialists.[22] Through CASA, Gairdner's legacy in Arabic education endures.

Watson valued the ecumenical, interdenominational outlook of the SOS, which matched the Protestant vision that he promoted in published writings and private letters.[23] Thus while Watson emphasized the university's American-style curriculum and school culture, and while he took a very American attitude toward the business of fund-raising for institutional development,[24] his own ecumenical impulses led him to resist binding the university exclusively to the American mission and to the United Presbyterian church in which he claimed membership. This was the case even though he hired a few leading American Presbyterian missionary scholars and administrators for AUC,[25] retained close ties of friendship with the mission board leaders of the UPCNA, and worked closely with the American missionaries, particularly through his participation on the Inter-Mission Council (and, notably, on its committee for mission relations with the Egyptian government). Watson was free to operate AUC independently of the American mission because the UPCNA General Assembly (the church's highest judicatory) had, in 1915, passed responsibility for the incipient university from the church's board of foreign missions to the university's board of trustees, which was interdenominational insofar as it included members of the Reformed Church in America.[26]

Watson's approach to the university led to strains with the American mission. Within just two years of the university's opening, tensions had become so obvious that Watson agreed to hold diplomatic negotiations with representatives from the Missionary Association. His fiercest critic was the Rev. J. R. Alexander (a contemporary of Andrew Watson), who had written in 1915 to the Philadelphia mission board expressing concern that the university-in-the-making was moving out of the control of the American mission and into murky (by which he meant interdenominational) waters. Alexander claimed that the idea for the university had originally been his own but that the project had been delayed after 1899 because of a lack of financing. He reminded the board that "The idea was that it should be a missionary University. . . . [I]ts professors were to be missionaries and its object the salvation of the souls of its students as well as their instruction in secular and professional studies." But without direction from the mission, he feared, the professors may "scarcely regard themselves as missionaries of the Cross but rather as teachers of Science and Research, and they may even become such as those at [the American University in] Beirut, its president included—good men, but they do not preach Jesus Christ and Him crucified [sic] to their students."[27]

The meetings in 1922 ended with the rift as wide as ever. According to Watson, Alexander and a few of his like-minded colleagues demanded substantial missionary representation in the trusteeship and administration of AUC, as well as a voice in determining the university's Christian policy. When Watson refused to accede to their demands, the missionaries accused him of misrepresenting the university's educational mission as Christian in a bid to appeal to American Presbyterian donors. Writing to W. B. Anderson, his friend and successor as foreign board secretary in Philadelphia, Watson described himself as "flabbergasted" by the missionary demands. He confided,"If they had proposed a control of the University on the field which was interdenominational in character, which meant anything at all but mere absorption in the [American] Mission, I would not have been so surprised nor felt so aggrieved."[28]

Mission-university relations remained chilly after this episode and led to a mutual sense of wariness and ideological distance. Writing in 1924 about his visit from Philadelphia to inspect the American mission in Egypt, W. B. Anderson noted that the missionaries had been behaving very coolly toward the "young men" (i.e., young American faculty members) at AUC."They [meaning AUC faculty] feel that they have been turned out into the cold because of the sins of the institution that they represent. Some of their staff do play cards and some do dance, some smoke, [and] two of the members of their staff who are short term men should not have been sent out." (Anderson may have been implying that the last two drank alcohol, behavior that the UPCNA, as a matter of policy, condemned as incommensurate with church membership.)[29] Nevertheless, Anderson noted, the AUC dean had assured him of plans to screen prospective faculty members more thoroughly in the future. Otherwise, he added,"The University seems ready to go to almost any length in the matter of cooperation that will not mean surrendering its independence." Anderson hoped that the mission and university could reach some cooperative agreement or friendlier detente.[30]

And indeed, around 1926, the mission prepared a report that took a more conciliatory tone even while minimizing AUC's relevance for the Evangelical community. It wrote, "The University cannot, without violence to its methods and objective, frighten its student body with such advanced Christian teaching, such appeals to devotion and service, and such a practice of religious ordinances as are suited to the development of Evangelical students who have been trained in lower Mission and Synodical schools."The report claimed that only 8 (out of some 180) AUC students were members of the Evangelical Church of Egypt, and that 19, or approximately 10 percent, came from"Evangelical homes." By contrast, it emphasized the mission's own strong record at Assiut College, where 231 students were official members of the Evangelical Church, and where 58 of the older students were "pledged to enter Christian service" by seeking careers in the clergy.[31]

Following Anderson's visit, Watson took pains to clarify and defend the university's Christian character, even in the "college program" that catered to local Egyptians. The college accounted for the strong majority of AUC students, was separate from the missionary-oriented SOS, and was the university's original raison d'être. In a letter to Anderson at the UPCNA offices in Philadelphia, Watson affirmed the strong Christian credentials of the staff, noted that Bible study and daily chapel attendance were required of all students, and described the four-year cycle of religious and ethical studies in the curriculum. This cycle included a year studying the Bible, a year studying the life and teaching of Jesus, a year devoted to comparative study of Christianity and Islam (including the study of modern Christian missions), and a year examining Christian principles of faith and life. Yet Watson emphasized the need for caution. Pointing out that nearly 60 percent of the Egyptian college students were Muslims, he observed that it would "be very easy to lose them all overnight by some tactless and un-Christian attack upon their religion." Watson concluded that "we"—meaning AUC, missionaries, or Christians in general—had to find a new approach to spreading Christian values that would go beyond "mere talk and harangue."[32]

What was it, exactly, that divided Watson from the American mission in the early years of AUC? It would be a mistake to conclude that the missionaries had a Christian vision for the early university and that Watson and his AUC colleagues did not. It would be a mistake, that is, to accept the word either of early AUC critics, like J. R. Alexander, or of John S. Badeau, a former missionary to Iraq and Watson's successor as AUC president, who suggested in his memoirs that AUC was founded simply because Egypt needed a modern university—making no reference to the university's roots in the missionary enterprise.[33] Watson definitely had a Christian vision, although this vision shifted significantly over the course of his career and contributed to or facilitated the university's long-term secularization.

Watson's "Conversion"

By the time AUC opened its doors in 1920, three things set Watson apart from the American missionaries. First, Watson had an internationalist vision for the Christian missionary enterprise: "a moral vision of one world that emerged after the horrors of World War I and that stemmed from the idealism of Woodrow Wilson's Fourteen Points."[34] He placed little store in Christian sectarianism, or its American Protestant version, denominationalism. By contrast, some leaders in the American Presbyterian mission in Egypt were more isolationist, even relative to missions in other parts of the Middle East, and more protective toward the culture and doctrines of the UPCNA. These differences of outlook help explain why Watson, during his years as AUC president, became a founding member and leader of the NECC at a time when the American missionaries in Egypt refused even to join this organization, citing financial reasons. It also helps explain why Watson, unlike the American missionaries, was so actively engaged in the work of the IMC as coordinated through offices in New York and London.

Second, Watson was born in cosmopolitan Cairo, not Kansas or Iowa, and may have been frustrated by the small-town origins and down-to-the-ground focus of the American missionaries. In many ways, the gulf between Watson and the missionaries was social. Watson's papers at AUC suggest that he valued friendships with leaders in the Anglo-American Protestant missionary movement—men like John R. Mott, Robert E. Speer, J. H. Oldham, and others—who were regarded as missionary statesmen of the day. Watson enjoyed socializing with Egyptian prime ministers and pashas, American and British diplomats, church-minded business tycoons (like John D. Rockefeller Jr.), and distinguished academics from Egypt, the United States, and Europe. His social ease, polish, and skill in what one would now call networking helped him raise the money that built AUC. Watson became an "insider" in the high social tiers of the Anglo-American Protestant missionary movement and in the world of Anglo-American–Egyptian diplomacy, even as he became increasingly peripheral to the American mission and Evangelical Church in Egypt.

Third, Watson became ever more uneasy about American missionary approaches to Muslims in Egypt. His dissatisfaction was already becoming evident by the time AUC made its debut, and grew more pronounced with time. Watson increasingly disliked Christian polemical approaches to Muslims, regarding them as incendiary and counterproductive; in this regard, his private disapproval extended to Samuel M. Zwemer, who helped establish AUC's programs in "Islamics."[35] Watson saw shortcomings in American society, and in Christianity as traditionally practiced; he recognized strengths in Islam and in Muslim culture, and sympathized with Egypt's nationalist aspirations. He slowly abandoned the crusader rhetoric of his early days, and even his faith in the desirability or necessity of formal Christian conversions. But what he retained throughout his tenure as AUC's president was the idea that his American university could be a laboratory for applying modern American Christian values to Egypt and that it could aid and accelerate the country's development. Watson appeared to believe that his university could communicate modernity, Christianity, and American culture as parts of a single message.

A look at his early career as the corresponding secretary for the UPCNA foreign missions would have shown little sign of the evolution in Watson's thinking to come. In 1908, for example, more than a decade before AUC opened, Watson cited biblical passages while exhorting his fellow Presbyterians to support the speedy evangelization of Egypt—a task that he, like many evangelicals before him and after, had interpreted as Christ's command.[36] (These passages were "And Jehovah shall be known to Egypt, and the Egyptians shall know Jehovah in that Day" [Isa. 19:21], and "Say not ye, There are yet four months and then cometh the harvest? behold, I say unto you, Lift up your eyes, and look on the fields, that they are white *already* unto harvest" [John 4:35].) At the same time, he sounded familiar missionary and Western imperial refrains of the period (refrains that persist among U.S. evangelicals and empire builders in the Middle East today) by pointing to social ills that missionaries in Egypt could address in the midst of their ministry: above all, political tyranny and corruption, the oppression of females, and ignorance leading to religious fanaticism.[37] Also like many American missionaries before him and after, Watson conflated American ideals (especially democratic government and openness to social and technological innovation) with the Christianity he planned to purvey.[38] In this regard Watson was an Orientalist in the sense conveyed by Edward Said: Watson presented the Muslims (as well as the indigenous Christians) of the Middle East as so backward that Western intervention—in this case, American missionary intervention—appeared to be both an obligation and act of charity.[39]

These attitudes were still evident in the report that Watson prepared in 1916 for an interdenominational American Protestant conference on world religions. Watson chaired the committee on "Mohammedanism" and Christian approaches to it. The report that came out of these meetings described Islam as a formidable adversary, a "fortress," precisely because its social systems were so coherent. But Christianity had things to offer Islam. These offerings included "The right of all to education," the recognition "that women are people among the people in the world, not existing simply because of and for their sex," the means to understand unfathomable human suffering, "an emphasis on the ethical nature of God and upon the real nature of sin," and the freedom of scientific investigation. "There have been conflicts between so-called religion and so-called science," the report concluded, "but Christendom has always recognized that the world is a subject for study in the most absolute sense, and that it is man's duty to seek to fathom its mysteries, and to make ever clearer its workings as those of God."[40]

Some of the convictions articulated in this report—above all, the universalist interpretation of religion, faith in the intrinsic harmony of science and God, and belief in the socially ameliorative and progressive applications of Christianity in everyday human affairs—persisted in Watson's writings across the years. All of these features, and above all the tendency to value "good works . . . over professions and confessions," make Watson look like an exemplar of the liberal Christian modernist that William R. Hutchison describes in his book *The Modernist Impulse in American Protestantism* (1976).[41] But in many other ways, Watson's convictions changed substantially once he assumed the AUC presidency in 1920.

Like his father before him, Charles R. Watson regarded the Christian mission in Egypt as universal and sought to reach out to Muslim students.[42] Yet as time went on the practical work of running an American university in an overwhelmingly Muslim country like Egypt, and his own active interest in religious liberty, compelled him to respect the religious and communal identities of AUC's Muslim students and to moderate the overtly Christian nature of the college program. Thus the practical requirements for attracting and maintaining a diverse student body led to the diminution of the college's Protestant agenda. Similar processes were beginning to occur in American higher education at large—at private universities like Princeton, Yale, Chicago, and Stanford, and at state universities (e.g., in North Carolina)—as institutions that had deep Protestant roots enrolled ever more diverse student bodies (which, in the American case, included Catholics and Jews especially).[43] This process of removing religious patronage from education is commonly called "secularization," but Watson would have hated the term. He deplored what he called "the acid of secularism,"[44] and, like many missionaries of his era, regarded secularism as a modern evil on a par with materialism, communism, and godlessness.

In practical terms, the political imperative of respecting Muslim sentiments within AUC became more pressing in the late 1920s and early 1930s, when there emerged a cluster of Muslim societies—above all, the YMMA, the Society for the Defense of Islam, and the Muslim Brotherhood—that sought to displace or counteract Christian missionary influence. Driven by news reports that accused missionaries of defaming Islam and converting Muslim youths through subterfuge, the anti-missionary agitation of these years prompted Egyptian Muslim parliamentarians to place tighter controls on school curricula, particularly in matters of religious instruction.[45]

Watson watched with grave concern as AUC became embroiled in accusations about missionary "crimes." First, there was Zwemer, the advocate of missions to Muslims and a faculty member at AUC's SOS, whose distribution of Christian polemical tracts in al-Azhar set off a public outcry in 1928. Watson confided to his friend Robert E. Speer at the time that Zwemer's behavior at al-Azhar was "extremely unwise" and gave an impression of Christians foisting propaganda on Muslims. "Reverse the situation, and I am quite sure we would not tolerate or be pleased with the distribution of Moslem literature on our own campus."[46] AUC also found itself implicated in the scandal surrounding Fakhry Farag, whose public lecture on the social and legal status of women in Egypt, delivered at AUC, led to his arrest in 1930 on charges of defaming Islam. Then, too, there was the scandal involving the former AUC Muslim student Yusuf 'Abd al-Samad, who apparently converted to Christianity in 1932 through the efforts of an independent Egyptian evangelist. The newspaper *al-Siyasa* accused the Americans of committing a crime by converting the young man through hypnotism, and asked "What will the government do to protect law and religion?"[47] Finally, in the middle of 1932, there was a fourth case involving a Palestinian student named Abd al-Qadir al-Husayni who, after failing his courses, stood up at a graduation ceremony and quoted from books in the SOS library in order to claim that AUC was an enemy of Islam.[48]

Commenting on this affair involving Abd al-Qadir al-Husayni, John S. Badeau later recalled that one Arabic newspaper wrote that "the only way [AUC] could get students to come there was to provide the free services of prostitutes." Watson was outraged, especially when the editor of this newspaper, whose son was an AUC student, showed up at a university tea party. Watson asked this editor how he could eat AUC's cake and drink its tea after insulting the university so gravely; the man replied that it was nothing personal, it was only journalism. "Dr. Watson said afterward to us, 'If this is journalism, I am going to do something about it.' He brought out Dr. Lyle Spenser, Dean of the School of Journalism at Syracuse University, to survey the situation, make suggestions, and start us on the road to teaching journalism."[49] Thus the anti-missionary agitation of the early 1930s prompted AUC to offer the first journalism program in Egypt. Ironically, a biographer of Hasan al-Banna, founder of the Muslim Brotherhood, argued that Banna was open to Western influences and innovations by noting that in 1939, he "proposed to send a number of his journalists to the American University in Cairo for training in modern journalism, as he considered the press to be 'the strongest weapon of propaganda.'"[50]

The anti-missionary campaign of the early 1930s also galvanized Watson with regard to the promotion of religious liberty. He became actively involved in the effort of the Egypt Inter-Mission Council to draft a statement on religious liberty, to promote religious liberty in international forums (especially the League of Nations), and to raise awareness of religious liberty issues among U.S. State Department and British Foreign Office officials.[51] In this manner, Watson functioned as a kind of diplomat for the missionary cause, just as he had done after World War I by representing Anglo-American Protestant missionary interests at the Paris Peace Conference.[52] The diplomat in him was responsible, too, for respectful overtures to the Egyptian prime minister, Ismail Sidqi Pasha, during this tense period (overtures that prompted the prime minister to respond with equal courtesy)[53] and for consistent efforts to invite government ministers to preside over AUC graduations.

The anti-missionary campaign changed AUC's curriculum. Writing in 1933 to a leader of the Missionary Education Movement in the United States, Watson acknowledged, "The whole attack upon us last year has made us do some careful thinking as to our policy." While AUC was a private institution and could theoretically teach Christianity "aggressively," it was also accepting government subsidies for half of its college program (i.e., for the "government course" that enabled students to follow the Egyptian government–accredited curriculum and therefore qualify for government jobs). Watson felt that this acceptance of government subsidies obliged him to reconsider the university's approach to religious education.

> I have felt that I ought to imagine myself as Minister of Education in Egypt. I should ask myself what is fair and impartial for an Egyptian Minister of Education in respect to religious education in a country whose State religion is Moslem and whose taxes are drawn from a population 12/13ths of whom are Moslem. Here I feel that we have a different mission to Egypt as an American and Christian institution. It is to work out a line of character training studies which one would feel it was fair to impose on Moslems coming to a Government school.

Watson suggested that the best way to provide an education that would avoid the pitfall of secularism and inculcate belief in God, while still appealing to Christian, Muslim, and Jewish students, would be to emphasize social ethics and to "keep off all theology with respect to Jesus," even while recognizing that the life of Jesus could serve as a valuable role model.[54] Meanwhile, he sent a circular to all AUC staff, clarifying the university's position on the government grants: "Our participation in this [government-supported and government-accredited] system of education is a token and proof of our identification . . . with the problems of the country. . . . Every state has the right to determine its own educational system." For all these reasons, AUC wished to adopt a "sympathetic and cooperative" attitude toward the government program.[55]

James K. Quay and the Cairo YMCA

In 1928, Watson was facing a temporary staff shortage at AUC and wrote to the director of the Cairo Central YMCA to ask if one of its workers, James K. Quay, could step in. He needed someone to teach AUC's "character-training program" for fourth-year students in the government-subsidized track, and wanted someone who could slip easily between English and Arabic. "We do not call it Bible Study," Watson explained, "for it is not always that, but the program includes Bible study, study of the life of Jesus, Christian Sociology, comparative religion, philosophy and suggestions [sic] which generally determine the Christian viewpoint."[56] This was the course that the Muslim anti-missionary agitation of the early 1930s later forced AUC to revise.

Watson had good reasons for seeking out Quay. Like Watson, Quay was an ordained pastor of the UPCNA. He joined the American mission in Egypt in 1919 after having served as a YMCA army and navy chaplain in California. Beginning in 1919, he studied Arabic for two years at AUC's SOS, taught in the American mission boys' school in Cairo, and then worked in villages south of Cairo, where he conducted evangelistic work.[57] Yet when American YMCA workers opened a "Cairo Central" branch for Egyptians in 1923 (at a time when the city's British-led Anglo-American branch catered only to foreigners), Quay decided that he wanted to work there. With the blessing of the American mission, he assumed a position as the YMCA's "religious secretary," initially with a mandate to reach out to Egyptian Evangelical men who were beginning to migrate into Cairo from villages. Watson helped obtain Quay's financial release from the American mission, at first by securing him a grant for the 1925–26 year to develop Christian literature for Muslims as set out in a report that Zwemer, Gairdner, Watson, and others had produced in 1922.[58] Quay and Watson also knew each other from preaching at the American Church in Cairo, participating jointly on the Egypt Inter-Mission Council (representing AUC and the YMCA, respectively), and sharing the experience of being ordained United Presbyterian ministers who stood outside the circle of the American mission.[59] These bonds explain why, following the approval of the YMCA director, Quay agreed to Watson's request in 1928 to teach at AUC in the 1928–29 year.

The experience teaching what was variously known as AUC's "character-training," "Bible," and "Ethics" class was one of the most traumatic of Quay's career. Judging from diary entries that he recopied afterward (perhaps to use as lecture notes), the experience pushed Quay to revise his idea of Christian mission.[60] He later described this mission as an effort to cultivate, through the example of Christ and Christianity, "the outreach of the human heart for God no matter by what name it was called."[61]

In his diary Quay recorded how, in September 1928, be began to approach his AUC "Ethics" class, which contained fifteen Muslim youths, by discussing friendship, citizenship, marriage, and other social values and institutions. A sense of camaraderie developed until one day, with Christmas approaching, his Muslim students came to class bearing presents for Quay aloft—a big brass bowl, an incense burner, and more. Quay wrote that he was deeply touched.

But then, in January, Quay decided it was finally time to spring Christianity upon them. His diary entry for January 13, 1929, noted, "It didn't work. This morning I carried to class an armful of New Testaments. I said to them, 'Fellows, we have been talking about some of the great principles of moral character. For the remainder of the term I want you to study with me some of the high points of the life of Jesus, who, so far as my own experience goes, is the source of these principles. I am going to hand you these testaments now. They cost very little and you may pay for them when you wish.' As they filed out at the close of the hour, all but two of them laid down, not the money, but the books and walked out in silence."

"It has been a different class since the New Testament episode," Quay wrote in May. "Gone is the happy spirit of good fellowship. They endure the class because they have to. And this is what I read in their faces: 'He really wasn't our friend after all. He only wanted to win us away from the faith of our fathers and make Christians of us.'" Quay decided that if AUC asked him to teach the class again, he would use his growing workload at the YMCA as his "alibi."[62] Meanwhile, around the same time, Quay observed that Muslim participation in the Cairo YMCA was declining, leading him to wonder whether there was a "general stiffening of Moslem resistance to Christianity."[63]

In 1930, the YMCA surveyed all its work in Egypt in a three-volume report. Writing in his capacity as the religious secretary of the Cairo

Central branch, Quay set out a clear policy statement that distinguished the YMCA from the Evangelical Church and the American Presbyterian mission. "Religious controversy has no place in this program," he wrote. "The Protestant community accuses us of being non-religious and the Muslim community suspects us of trying to proselyte for Christianity and both are wrong. We try to present a phase of Christianity which we believe the Protestant community has largely overlooked, and we hope to win the Moslem, not away from his loyalties to the things that are good in Islam, but to an acquaintance with Christ as the giver of life abundant. His religious affiliation is his own affair."[64]

When Quay had first arrived in Egypt in 1919, he had described himself as a great admirer of Samuel M. Zwemer—even if it was true, as Quay wrote at the time, that Zwemer was "the kind of fellow to start something big and get you all tied up in it and then walk out from under it and leave you suspended in thin air."[65] Like Zwemer, Quay had thought of himself as a missionary to Muslims, believing, as an associate observed in 1921, that Copts were a "brow-beaten race" and that the Coptic Orthodox Church would "never win the Moslem to Christ."[66] Yet by 1930 (almost two years after Zwemer left Egypt under the cloud of his melee in al-Azhar), Quay's attitude toward his own Christian mission in Egypt was taking a significant turn. He was beginning to listen to Muslim students at the YMCA who explained that the explicitly Christian features of the organization (ranging from the pictures on the walls to the prayers that ended meetings) made them feel uncomfortable. He began to entertain the idea that he could make some of these youths "Christian Muslims," and that they, in turn, could make a "Muslim Christian" out of him.[67]

Looking back on his career in 1960, when he was seventy-nine years old, Quay recalled experiences that included his debacle in AUC's "Ethics" class. He observed that many Muslims in Egypt had come to mistrust Christian missionaries who presented themselves as if "they were the sole custodians of the truth." He acknowledged, too, that when he retired from Egypt in 1947 after some twenty-eight years, he had "no Moslem conversions and baptisms" to his name. Nevertheless, he added in a letter to the YMCA archivist who had asked him to submit his memoirs, "A discerning Moslem reader will perceive that evangelism of the Moslem has also been my motive. He might go so far as to say that I was all the more dangerous because of the friendliness of my approach. In this I would agree with him."[68]

To the list of things that Quay and Watson shared in common, two more may yet be added. First, the attitudes of both men toward Christian missions to Muslims evolved dramatically over the course of their careers and largely as a result of encounters with or reactions from Muslims. As time went on, both men acknowledged the great devotional virtues inherent in Islam, and agreed that personal ethics and genuine faith were more important than one's religious label as Muslim or Christian. Second, both men insisted to the end of their lives that they had a Christian mission to fulfill in Egypt, even if that mission remained unclear to them.

RETHINKING THE MISSION IN EGYPT

By the 1930s, as the tide of Muslim populist and anti-missionary sentiment was rising, Watson was well along in his reassessment of Christian missions. He had already begun, in 1927, to criticize American "Christianity's failure to make good,""to solve social problems," and to become engaged in"internationalism," and had connected these shortcomings to the"general lack of enthusiasm for [Christianity's] propagation"among American audiences.[69] In 1930, writing again to his old friend in the ecumenical movement, Robert E. Speer, Watson admitted that Christian missionaries to Muslims still needed to find a way to prove the consequences of Jesus for their lives."Now here is the real difficulty of missionary work,"Watson reflected."No amount of historical evidence will prove Christ's resurrection, if Christians go on living exactly as though He were dead and fast locked away in the grave."[70]

In January 1932, Watson published "Rethinking Missions," the article that inspired John D. Rockefeller Jr. to name the chief volume of the Layman's Report for Foreign Missions *Re-Thinking Missions*.[71] In the United States, this report elicited some enthusiastic praise (most famously, from the writer and disillusioned former missionary to China, Pearl S. Buck) and some scathing denunciations (with leaders of the southern-stream Presbyterian Church likening the report to snake venom).[72] Like the Edinburgh 1910 conference, *Re-Thinking Missions* marked a watershed in the history of American Protestantism and the missionary movement—but a watershed of a different kind. It marked a dawning skepticism among Protestant intellectuals about the moral verities of the past, a greater willingness to acknowledge publicly the goodness in other, non-Christian religious systems, and an implicit critique of the missionary connection to Western imperialism.[73] In the words of two historians of American Protestantism writing in 1991, *Re-Thinking Missions*, with its"liberal theological platform,""did more than exacerbate tensions between fundamentalists and modernists; it also formulated the outlines of a substantive criticism of an ethos dear to many Presbyterians in the middle decades of the twentieth century—middle-class, capitalistic, Protestant, American." By the 1960s (a generation after Watson's death), this criticism had contributed to the decline of "the self-confident assertions about evangelism, American righteousness, and the superiority of Christianity" and had prompted mainstream American Presbyterians to "discard both the militant rhetoric and the exclusive truth claims" of older missions while pursuing missions in the form of humanitarian aid.[74] Watson's engagement with Rockefeller in the planning stages of the report, and his inadvertent contribution of its title, serves as another example of how Watson played a small but important role in the larger drama of American Protestantism that was unfolding during his lifetime.

Watson told Rockefeller that he had one main concern about *Re-Thinking Missions*, or the Hocking Report, as it has often been called: it was widening the ideological cleavages among American Christians and was giving Christian fundamentalists a foothold from which to continue their "machine gun firing." He thought that the report made its greatest contribution by stimulating debate and removing the "smug satisfaction" of missionaries, and he hoped that it would lift hostilities toward "non-Christian faiths." Watson also shared the report's enthusiasm for social service as a form of Christian witness. He assured Rockefeller, "You have rendered a supreme contribution to the Kingdom of God."[75]

In 1934, at the Foreign Missions Conference of North America, Watson gave a talk that demonstrated the extent of his own "rethinking." Recognizing the new world conditions that were challenging missions—and above all, steep drops in funding prompted by the Depression and by flagging American popular interest, along with rising tides of anti-colonial nationalism—Watson suggested that missionaries in foreign fields needed to revise their approach. For a start they should abandon the cultural arrogance that had played its part in stimulating nationalist hostility. He advised missionaries to "clothe the entire missionary enterprise with a new spirit of humble, deferential service" and implied that they should abandon the idea of "nailing spiritual scalps as trophies upon the walls of home churches." Evangelistic work, which Watson defined broadly as "our total presentation of Christ to the non-Christian world," needed to be less dogmatic and more spiritual, by which he seemed to mean more amenable to local adaptation. "As for the missionary," he wrote, "let him be the servant of Jesus Christ, ever ready to be all things to all men: let that suffice for him."[76] Watson's paper reportedly "created a sensation and prolonged applause" at the conference and was reissued in a condensed version for a wider American audience interested in mission affairs.[77]

By this time Watson was moving away from the idea that formal conversion should be a goal of the Christian mission to Muslims. In a booklet that he prepared in the mid-1930s for AUC donors in the United States, Watson explained more clearly the university's religious policies. "What do we mean by 'Christianity' anyhow?" he asked. "Judging by those who visit us [in Cairo], there are more than 57 varieties. Some of these we would neither endorse nor consider worth imparting to others." (Watson's American readers would have caught his pop-cultural reference to the Heinz pickle corporation, whose labels touted "57 varieties." Heinz was based in Pittsburgh, the same town that claimed the headquarters of the UPCNA.) He elaborated thus:

> In our policy, we put the emphasis on *content* and not on *label*. If we can get the Moslem lad to accept the content of Christianity, Christ's revelation of God, Christ's invitation to fellowship with God, Christ's way of living, Christ's ideals of uprightness and personal morality, Christ's love of others and sacrificial service—we are glad. If the content of Christianity is in his life, the label will take care of itself. Some day, some one will come along and give him a name that will distinguish his brand of life from the ordinary brand of a Moslem world. *Christians were not any less Christian before they were called Christians at Antioch.* It is a question whether they were any more so afterward. At any rate we are supremely interested in content, not in labels.

Watson also emphasized the importance of what he called "voluntariness" in religious practice, for the sake of religious liberties, and rejected the idea that Christianity could be canned and passed on "like rations to a soldier, all packed up and sealed, complete."[78]

He then went on to criticize more specifically the old goals of conversion and sounded a theme that pervaded his writings in the 1930s: the idea that American society was itself deeply flawed. Parodying mission reports to American church audiences that sent news items along the lines of, "Ahmed was converted last month and this month he was baptized and joined the Church," Watson stressed that the turn toward Christianity should not be regarded as an event but as an ongoing process. It was not a matter of conversion leading, as if in a scripted production, to "*Exit Ahmed! Finished!*" Rather, "Our Ahmed is just like your boy John," facing difficult questions about his faith. "Ahmed," the archetypal Muslim student, "admits that Moslem society is all wrong, but he doesn't see that the Christian social and economic order is in keeping with the teachings of Jesus either."[79] The best AUC could do, Watson concluded, would be to introduce students to the model of behavior embodied by Jesus, and then let them go and grow in their own way.

In 1937, Watson published *What Is This Moslem World*, a book that reflected a significant shift in his target audience. Recognizing that Muslims were reading what he wrote, he framed his preface in the form of a letter, first addressing "My Moslem Friends" before turning to "My Fellow Missionaries" and, from there, "To All." The book begins with an apology to Muslims for the "harsh and unfair" portrayals of Islam that often surfaced in Western literature. Signaling a sharp turn from the spirit of his earlier books (most notably his 1907 book, *Egypt and the Christian Crusade*), he noted, "Love is the heart of the gospel we are supposed to be carrying. There were times when we forgot this and thought it was truth, and we wielded the sword of truth with all the merciless zeal of a crusader."[80]

In *What Is This Moslem World*, Watson acknowledged that nationalist pressures were making it harder for missionaries to operate, so that missionaries had to recognize their status as guests in the Muslim world as never before. But believing that Christianity still had an important message to offer, he urged missions to demonstrate a love for humankind and thereby, perhaps, to transform the Muslim conception of Allah by manifesting "a God of love" through social action. He added that missionaries also needed to recognize that Muslims had a commitment to their community and not only their faith, so that a Muslim's conversion to Christianity could be seen as tantamount to treason, a betrayal of family and friends. Implicitly suggesting, again, a move away from the goal of conversion, Watson argued that social service was the appropriate aim for Christian evangelism. Missionaries should work to eradicate illiteracy, reduce infant mortality, eliminate endemic diseases like bilharzia and trachoma, and improve living standards overall. Meanwhile, he suggested, missionaries also had to work to counteract the "undesirable elements" emanating from Christian communities—whether these be from Greek "grogshop keeper[s]," from Hollywood movies (whose influence in the Middle East, as a mediator of American culture, Watson had long recognized),[81] or taverns and dance clubs that Egyptian expatriates encountered in Europe and North America. Is it any surprise, he wondered, that Muslims failed to embrace Christianity en masse, considering the people and ways of Christian life that they encountered?[82]

In the "new day" of the 1930s (a period that coincided with the New Deal policies of the Franklin D. Roosevelt administration in the United States), Watson believed that civic involvement was also important to Americans as well as Egyptians. Americans needed to temper their "higher individualism into higher socialism" and into a greater "government-mindedness" (for a start, by voting in elections).[83] Civic participation and social service should go hand in hand for missionaries as well.

This vision of social service found its expression in AUC's Extension Program, started in 1924, which Watson regarded as a showcase for the university's civic involvement. Watson affirmed in a 1934 article that the "hand of God" ultimately determined the pace and nature of social progress in the Moslem world as elsewhere, but maintained that missionaries should nevertheless extend their own "helping hand" wherever possible. And despite the hostility toward foreigners (including missionaries) that nationalist activities often evinced, Egyptian nationalism could have a positive role to play here as well. For nationalism, he wrote, "puts a nation on its tip-toes of expectancy," "awakens the mind to inquiry," and "under the hand of God, may [also] prove to be a mighty power for progress."[84]

REACHING OUT: AUC's EXTENSION PROGRAM

During Watson's tenure as AUC president, the Extension Program offered services that reached out to rich and poor, educated and illiterate, male and female Egyptians alike. For affluent and educated Egyptians, AUC sponsored a series of public lectures, delivered by scholars, government officials, and medical doctors, on topics that ranged from "Egypt and Freedom of Speech" to "The Water Which We Drink" and "The Legacy of Coptic Culture and Art." In 1933, before the Egyptian government nationalized the airwaves, AUC also sponsored radio lectures on health and science issues—for example, on "Radium and Its Powerful Properties" and "Unfriendly Germs and How to Avoid Them." The university hosted many distinguished Egyptian speakers through its lectures, among them the feminist Huda Sha'rawi (in the 1929–30 series); the nationalist and social philosopher Salama Musa (in the 1932–33 series); and the Arabic literary-scholar-turned-education-minister Taha Hussein (in 1944).[85] In the 1940s the program began to show American popular films for audiences of Egyptian "ladies," with the cultural and social context of each film explained.[86]

From 1937 to 1939, AUC also rented its Ewart Hall auditorium to the Egyptian Broadcasting Service for the monthly radio concerts of Umm Kulthum. These concerts helped consolidate Umm Kulthum's reputation as the leading female singer of Egypt and the Arabic-speaking world, and burnished AUC's reputation in the long run.[87] But in fact, the concerts led to a bitter debate with Egyptian Evangelical pastors who objected that AUC, ostensibly a Christian university, was propagating songs that planted lustful thoughts in the minds of men and thereby led them astray. The pastors argued, moreover, that Umm Kulthum's concerts were sullying the reputation of Christians in Egypt. Watson argued otherwise: he maintained that the university was helping redeem love songs of their bad reputation while recognizing "that the love of man for a woman is a God-given instinct." The conflict drew little interest from American missionaries, and some (like the missionary scholar C. C. Adams) spoke out to support Watson against the pastors.[88] The dispute ultimately ended on a chilly note in 1939, with an agreement to disagree for the sake of maintaining the semblance of Christian unity in Egypt, and confirmed the growing rift between AUC and the Evangelical community.[89]

The Extension Program also took an early lead in sex education. Beginning as an AUC pilot program in 1922, Dr. Fakhry M. Farag (the same Coptic Catholic man who was later charged with defaming Islam in 1930) offered free public lectures in Arabic on sex education and sexually transmitted diseases. Accompanying these lectures was a subtitled screening of *The Gift of Life*, described as "a biological moving picture film of four reels on sex education purchased from the American Social Hygiene Association." In 1925–26 alone, Dr. Fakhry gave nine lectures in Cairo with a total attendance of 2,900, and four off-site lectures in Tanta (through cooperation with the American mission hospital of Tanta) with 1,100 attending. In 1925–26 AUC also held separate screenings and lectures for the fourth-year class at al-Azhar University, the Police School, the Qadis' [Islamic judges'] School, and the Kasr el Aini Medical School.[90] An Extension Program report to Watson, dating to the mid-1930s, stated that over four hundred "Azhar sheikhs" attended one screening of *The Gift of Life*. Describing a scene that is hard to imagine today, the report claimed, "The climax came when the leader of this most conservative group led his fellow [Azhar] students in three cheers for America and science."[91]

Watson was aware of and concerned about prostitution in Egypt and its consequences for public health—hence the public showings of *The Gift of Life*. Some of Watson's missionary colleagues—above all, Arthur T. Upson, the British director of the NMP—had been involved in efforts to address and deter the sex trade, particularly among British troops who were stationed in Egypt during World War I.[92] Combatting the sex trade was also a major concern of the YMCA in Egypt, whose leaders noted that Egypt was a "clearing-house" for European child prostitutes who were then deployed to Mediterranean ports ranging from Marseilles to Beirut.[93] In 1932, responding to an investigative inquiry led by the Egyptian government regarding the merits of either licensing or abolishing prostitution, Watson came down strongly on

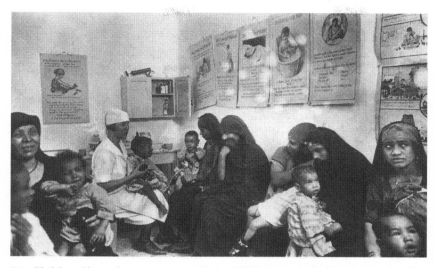

5.1. Child welfare class, Assiut, c. 1920s. UPCNA Board of Foreign Missions Photographs, Presbyterian Historical Society, Presbyterian Church (U.S.A.), Philadelphia.

the side of abolition. He argued that licensing would place prostitutes under the power of potentially exploitative special police, and would facilitate the traffic in women and children. Noting the prevalence of part-time prostitution among women who needed to support their families, he encouraged job-training efforts for former prostitutes in the event of a ban, as well as wage increases for women in general. He also advocated the creation of confidential, no-questions-asked clinics for treating those who contracted diseases.[94]

Foremost among AUC's services for the poor was the Child Welfare Clinic, which provided infant and maternal care. In 1928 alone the clinic reportedly treated more than two thousand cases a month.[95] Watson regarded the clinic as part of the front line in the struggle against infant mortality and debilitating diseases such as trachoma, which was a leading cause of blindness in Egyptian children.[96] Writing in 1934 that there could be "no progress [in Egypt] without higher standards of national health," he noted that "Egypt has the unenviable distinction of having a greater percentage of its population blind or afflicted with eye trouble than any other nation in the world." Watson regarded trachoma-induced blindness as something that was not a matter to be left to destiny, since a simple human act—the washing of a newborn's eyes—could so easily deter it. According to Watson, the challenge for staff at the clinic was to overcome an Egyptian "superstition" that held that it was unlucky to wash a baby until it was forty days old.[97] A report from around 1929 suggested that"The best proof of the success of this phase of the Extension work is the fact that the Egyptian government has recently set aside the sum of approximately $150,000 for opening up similar child welfare clinics throughout the city of Cairo. This also illustrates the principle of the University; namely, not to superimpose our Western ideas on an Eastern people, but merely to help the Egyptians help themselves."[98] Later, the Cairo YMCA did its part to publicize the issue by offering lectures with such titles as "How Can We Save the Fourteen Million Egyptians Suffering from Trachoma?"[99]

AUC's Extension Program was also active in what it called "Village Work" for the improvement of public health among peasants, and initiated a series of annual Village Health Contests to incorporate students into the program. A report from the mid-1930s showed that the contest aimed to encourage public service in the spirit of noblesse oblige, by drawing in young men who otherwise spent summer vacations puttering around their family estates. The first of these contests was held in 1926–27 "to illustrate the texts 'Swat the Fly' and 'Drink Only Clean Water.'" Later themes included "Keep clean, especially the children," and "Drink well or filtered water, not canal water."[100] In 1929–30, the program also held an Eye Hygiene Poster contest to illustrate ophthalmic care to villagers. The university invited students from leading government schools and from al-Azhar to participate in these contests and held a formal prize-giving ceremony, to which government officials and journalists were invited. According to the report for 1929–30, the "Under-Secretary of Public Health, Dr. Shaheen Pasha, wrote an open letter to the Minister of Education urging that this plan be made general in all government schools."[101]

Watson took pride in believing that AUC could function as "the servant of its community."[102] In 1937, addressing "Moslem Friends" in *What Is This Moslem World*, he pointed to the Extension Program as evidence"that the Christian missionary movement of today represents a sincere and unselfish desire to offer you the best that Christianity possesses and to do this in a courteous and fraternal spirit."[103] The family metaphor was telling: Watson felt that AUC belonged in, and belonged to, Egypt.

AUC's Mission

In *What's the Big Idea*, a promotional booklet prepared for American audiences around 1942, Watson called AUC a"bridge of friendliness" between the United States and Egypt, and stressed its international as well as inter-religious dimensions. The big idea behind AUC, he wrote, was to deliver America's "great resources of practical knowledge and of Christian dynamic" for the sake of Egypt's advancement. Even here, Watson affirmed that AUC's educational and social mission had a distinctly religious, that is to say, Christian, component.

But not all the staff of AUC agreed with or promoted this vision. Consider Amir Boktor (1896–1966), a native of Upper Egypt and graduate of Columbia University's Teachers' College in New York. Boktor joined the AUC staff in the early 1920s and served on the faculty until his death in 1966. Boktor's writings show that he was a believer in AUC's *educational* mission and enthusiastically embraced modern American educational techniques. With Watson's support, he founded AUC's bilingual quarterly, *Journal of Modern Education* (called in Arabic *Majallat al-Tarbiya al-Haditha*), in 1928. During his long career at AUC, Boktor published many books in Arabic and English. His Arabic works alone include a travel account of the United States, a study on Denmark and its public schools, a work on the "art of marriage," and a popular overview of the biological principle of heredity, called, "You and I, Where Did We Come From?"[104] Boktor also wrote occasionally for the Egyptian press, in one case, at the time of the Scopes trial in 1925 to ridicule former U.S. presidential candidate William Jennings Bryan and other creationists who opposed the teaching of human evolution.[105]

Boktor was the product of a Coptic family and of a mission-school education, and yet he illustrated a possibility that Watson had recognized: namely, given religious liberty, an individual could exercise the freedom not to observe or proclaim a religion.[106] The issue of Boktor's faith became a matter of concern when Watson and his closest associate, R. S. McClenahan, were considering him for an AUC deanship in 1937. Asked to write a letter stating his religious beliefs, Boktor explained his belief that religion and prayer should be private, not collective, affairs. He noted that his parents, who were Coptic Orthodox Christians, had granted him religious freedom as a youth and had accepted his turn toward the Evangelical community during his student days at Assiut College, the premier secondary school of the American mission. But Boktor wrote that after years of observing the sectarian bickering of his Coptic Orthodox and Evangelical relatives, and the behavior of Evangelical pastors, "I have almost been forced to come to the conclusion . . . that some of the pastors and members of the Egyptian Evangelical Church are more archaic and backward in their general beliefs as well as their attitudes towards others, than Moslems and Copts." On his attitude toward Christian teaching at AUC, he repeated what he had said publicly at many faculty meetings: "In brief I believe that direct teaching of Christianity to our Muslim students has done us more harm than good. Praying over their heads in Assembly exercises may benefit one; but I have a conviction that it makes ninety-nine hostile to Christianity."[107] Following this exchange, McClenahan ultimately concluded to Watson that Boktor was not really a *kafir* or infidel as some had said of him, but was a man of high moral standing who believed in God, though without emphasizing Christ. McClenahan expressed hope to Watson that Boktor would change his views.[108] Meanwhile, it appears that they promoted Boktor anyway.

The case of Boktor serves as a reminder that Watson did not and could not dictate terms of thought to his faculty, who represented the university to students, just as he did not and could not dictate ideas to students (even if he did try to shape their characters and outlook). While it is clear that Watson approached AUC with a Christian agenda, it is unclear how influential his approach was, and what elements of his mission the staff and students apprehended, accepted, or absorbed.

Watson, in any case, never lost his faith in the university's potential for Christian service—even if he felt that the mood in America had turned against foreign missions.[109] In 1944, the year before he stepped down as AUC's president, Watson expressed hope that the United Nations, as the successor to the League of Nations, would enshrine and support a wide platform of human rights, and that its promotion of religious liberty would enable the missionary movement to persist. But he warned that future missionaries in Egypt would need to identify more closely with Egyptian national interests, acquire stronger Arabic skills, and cultivate relations with Egyptian officials as well as with other Christians (and above all, with leaders of the Coptic Orthodox Church, if only to promote Christian unity). Emphasizing again the missionary imperative to harness Christian service for the betterment of everyday life, he added, "Must we not add to our gospel of individual salvation the neglected gospel of social and national salvation?"[110]

In 1945, Watson retired to Ardmore, one of the affluent Philadelphia suburbs, located along the Main Line of the Pennsylvania Railroad, which gave "mainline Protestantism" its name.[111] Watson died there in retirement in January 1948, several years before the United States fully supplanted Britain as one of the "Great Powers" of the Middle East. He also died four months before the emergence of Israel, the Arab-Israeli conflict, and the Palestinian refugee problem. He was therefore able to retain, to the end, his faith in what he regarded as America's fair-minded intentions in the Middle East.

The United States may have had wealth, know-how, and a "Christian dynamic,"[112] but in Watson's view, the country was also unhampered by imperial entanglements."With scarcely an exception,"Watson had told a *New York Times* reporter in 1928,"America is in favor throughout the Near East and particularly in Egypt. There is a feeling that the future lies with America, because of its enormous resources and its progressive spirit. Many Egyptians are coming to America to study. American institutions in Egypt are looked on with favor, whether educational, missionary or commercial. I cannot help ascribing the remarkable growth of our own institution, the American University in Cairo . . . to the prestige of America and the good-will of Egyptians towards America."[113]

Watson sounded similar notes in a sermon he delivered to a Presbyterian congregation in New York City in 1934: "With this new day that has dawned comes an opportunity for serving these people [in Egypt] such as Christianity has never had before. But it is high-grade service and an entirely unselfish service that is required, for Europe has so often exploited the lands of the Near East that suspicion is easily aroused. Here America holds an unusual advantage, for none may accuse her of any desire for territorial aggrandizement."[114]

Even so, AUC was becoming more involved with the U.S. government, and therefore implicated in its regional politics, during the last years of Watson's presidency. In April 1943, Watson's deputy, John S. Badeau, expressed the desire to remain "scrupulously free from direct relationships with the United States government" for the sake of continued institutional neutrality and the university's public image in Egypt.[115] Yet just a few months later, as World War II raged, AUC signed an agreement with the U.S. War Department to teach correspondence courses in mathematics, science, and English to American military personnel passing through the Middle East.[116] Relations quickly strengthened so that in 1945, Watson was able to report that the university had been "accepted by the [U.S.] Department of State for the training of its consular men who intended to specialize in service in the Arabic-speaking areas."[117] (Presumably AUC's ties to the American government grew stronger years later when, in 1961, Badeau became the U.S. ambassador to Egypt.)[118]

By the 1940s, missionary enrollments in the SOS, the program originally founded for training Christian workers to Muslims, had fallen. Together with C. C. Adams, the scholar of modern Islamic thought and former missionary, who served as the SOS dean, Watson had been worrying about its future. To keep the Arabic program alive, Watson began to welcome the enrollment of U.S. diplomatic personnel. Likewise, Watson and Adams welcomed expatriate employees from oil companies like Shell and Anglo-Egyptian Oil Fields, which were approaching AUC for Arabic training.[119]

A report that Watson prepared in 1945 for the American Legation in Egypt signaled the university's weakening connection to missionaries. Modifying a passage from his brochure *The Big Idea* (published around 1942), Watson's report in 1945 called AUC a "bridge of friendliness" between Egypt and the United States, but excised one additional passage from the original—namely, the phrase that called AUC a bridge between "Western Christianity and Moslem lands."[120] Thus Watson presented AUC as a bridge of nations, not religions. Meanwhile, Watson embraced AUC's ambassadorial role in carrying "the cultural, educational, and democratic ideals of America" to the peoples of Egypt and the Middle East as a whole.[121]

In 1956, eighteen years after Watson's death, AUC officials presided over the ceremony to inaugurate the new academic year. Much to the surprise of one of the professors, who had been at AUC since 1920, "no prayers were said at the opening assembly" even though university officials had not formally declared a change of policy.[122] In making a change like this one, AUC may have been following the cue of universities in the United States, where secularization was the mood of the times. But also important was the need for deference to the Egyptian government—a trend that had been evident since the early 1930s and that became imperative in the aftermath of the Suez Crisis. Still another factor appears to have been AUC's growing affinity with the U.S. government, and its increasing reliance on U.S. government sponsorship or aid.[123] Friendly relations with both the Egyptian and U.S. governments proved, in the long run, to be critical to AUC's political and financial survival. Likewise, the revision of AUC's mission away from religious and toward cultural transmission enabled the university to flourish long after the Six-Day War of 1967, by which time the association of American missionaries in Egypt had already disbanded.

Conclusion

The *Oxford English Dictionary* defines conversion as the act of turning toward or into something else, or, when applied to a building, of structural adaptation for a new purpose. In these two senses of the term, the missionary encounter in Egypt "converted" Watson and AUC, but without overturning Watson's personal faith.

AUC was a product of the missionary movement, and its founder, Charles R. Watson, conceived of the university as a Christian endeavor. And yet, AUC moved away from the American Presbyterian mission as soon as it opened in 1920. In many ways, AUC had more in common with the Cairo Central YMCA, an organization that was also in some measure both American and Christian, and that sought to cultivate diverse Egyptian constituencies while promoting ideals based on ethical living and civic engagement. Leaders of both organizations perennially struggled to define the Christian component of their work. "What is the essential Christian element that at all costs must be maintained?" an internal report of the Egypt YMCA had asked in 1930. It answered its own question by acknowledging, "The problem is baffling, in the extreme. . . . [We are] grappling with it daily, hourly and amid misunderstanding, criticism, and oft-times divided counsels of . . . Christian friends."[124]

Meanwhile, Egyptian political pressures in the 1930s, Watson's growing disillusionment with Christian evangelism as previously practiced, and the shrinking of AUC's missionary ties and constituencies converged and paved the way for the steady elimination of AUC's Christian character.[125] Certainly the need to modify Christian instruction for the sake of retaining a predominantly Muslim student body had parallels with other mission-founded institutions in the Islamic world, such as the American University in Beirut and the American College for Girls in Istanbul.[126]

Watson developed and retained a lifelong interest in and commitment to the Anglo-American missionary movement, and he contributed substantively to the process of rethinking that affected this movement in the 1930s. He was an important figure in the ecumenical movement. Yet his efforts have been largely forgotten: he is completely absent from a dictionary of the Presbyterian and Reformed tradition in America, published in 1999.[127] At the same time, after AUC's debut in 1920, some older American Presbyterian missionaries came to regard Watson as something of a renegade, so that he became forgotten in the circles of the American mission and Evangelical Church as well. He is remembered, however, by the retired missionary Willis A. McGill, who was born in Egypt, served as a missionary there from 1937 to 1977, and knew Watson and his children well. In a conversation in 2005, McGill described Watson as a "very astute person" who "had his hand on the pulse of the Arab Middle East" and who "was doing his very best to fulfill the call of Jesus Christ." But when asked whether AUC during Watson's tenure tried to distance itself from the American Presbyterian mission, McGill had just three words to say: "It sure did."[128] Nowadays, at least when speaking to Egyptian Evangelical pastors, one senses that the historical links between AUC and the American Presbyterian mission have been largely forgotten.

What indeed was Watson's and AUC's mission? Was it cultural (in the sense of being American), religious (in the sense of being Christian), social (in the sense of working for the advancement of Egypt), or political (in the sense of propagating democratic or national values)? The case of Charles R. Watson and AUC shows how difficult it is to define the American missionary enterprise in this period precisely because its activities were so broad and because its participants described their mission in a weave of religious, cultural, and political terms.

The missionary enterprise is also hard to pin down because it was constantly evolving. During the interwar era, Watson changed, Egypt, the United States, and the world changed, and mainstream American Protestant culture changed as well, so that in the convergence of these currents, AUC moved toward a model of education that stressed a mission of social service and national development.[129] The history of AUC thus reflects the transition of American Christian missions toward forms of social engagement that became associated, in the second half of the twentieth century, with nongovernmental organizations (NGOs).[130] Such agencies privately struggled, much as the missionaries in Egypt had done, to reconcile their altruistic ideals and notions of giving with the realities of their own political and economic power.[131]

Turning to the Life of the Church: American Mission in an Age of Egyptian Decolonization and Arab-Israeli Politics, 1945–67

> However much people talk about Moslem evangelization in conferences in New York, the fact of the matter is that most of us go for months without ever mentioning the subject of religion to a Moslem.
> —Bradley Watkins to Glenn Reed, Luxor, January 20, 1946

> Feeling has been quite anti-American, but so far the surplus of goodwill built up toward America in the past has prevented anything more than an occasional shout of "Jew" at Americans, and a number have been stopped and asked for their passports by the police.
> —J. W. Acheson to Glenn Reed, Cairo, June 10, 1948

EGYPT HAD BEEN technically independent since 1922, a constitutional monarchy since 1923, and a member of the League of Nations since 1937. Yet by the time World War II ended in 1945, Egyptian nationalists felt that the country was still lacking some basic trappings of sovereignty. Britain continued to maintain troops in the Suez Canal Zone and to sideline Egypt in international affairs, while foreigners in Egypt ran businesses and schools that functioned like metropolitan outposts. Thus as the tide of decolonization began to sweep across the British Empire, Egyptian nationalists were eager to purge foreign influence and assert full independence. This was the mood in Egypt after 1945, and it had critical consequences for the American Presbyterians, who became subject to new policies that sought to reduce missionary numbers and bring mission work under government oversight.

Egyptian nationalists had been trying to rein in missionary activities since the 1930s. And yet, it was only in the mid-1950s, following the Free Officers coup in 1952 and the ascension of Gamal Abdel Nasser (1918–1970) within the revolutionary circle, that the Egyptian government gained the upper hand. The Nasser regime forced

Christian missionaries to abandon teaching Christianity to Muslim pupils, or else face deportations and the seizure of schools. Since the mid-nineteenth century, American Presbyterians in Egypt had regarded schools as a primary site for conveying their Christian message to Muslims. Circumstances now forced them to revise their expectations. In 1956, Glenn Reed, a former missionary to Sudan and UPCNA mission executive, acknowledged that his own expectations had dramatically changed. Amid a discussion regarding whether the Presbyterians should comply with new Egyptian laws on education or abandon work in Egypt entirely, Reed argued for staying. "As for me," Reed told his colleagues, "I am willing to pay any price, short of denial of my faith, for maintenance of contact with Muslim people, for I believe that only through contact will Muslim people ever be confronted with the person of Jesus Christ."[1]

Reed's declaration reflected the sense that mere residence in Egypt could be a mode of Christian witness, on the grounds that how one lived as a Christian could make more of an impression than what one believed. Reed's statement also harmonized with the views of the Anglican "missionary to Islam"[2] and later bishop, Kenneth Cragg (b. 1913), whose book, *The Call of the Minaret*, appeared in 1956. Cragg's book inspired the younger Presbyterian missionaries in Egypt,[3] and epitomized the mood of Anglo-American missions at a time when Britain's moment as a great power in the Middle East was ending.[4] Addressing a Christian audience about the potential of approaching Muslims, Cragg wrote that "no Christian mission is constituted in its success, and none, therefore, is invalidated by numerical failure. The whole point of the argument has been missed if it is not clear that there is a Christian obligation to Islam that neither begins nor ends in how Muslims respond. It is rooted in the nature of Christ and his Gospel."[5] *The Call of the Minaret* reflects a kind of postcolonial evangelicalism that was politically pragmatic and at the same time reflexive, insofar as it stressed that "respectful witness" affirmed a Christian's own faith. Cragg pointed out that missionaries, in any case, could not know what impact Christianity might have on Muslims, either in the short term or long run. "All that Christ will be to Muslims," Cragg advised, "only Muslims can declare."[6]

In the postwar period, American missionaries in Egypt were disadvantaged not only by the mounting tide of anti-foreign, nationalist sentiment that pushed new laws into place, but also, for the first time, by U.S. foreign policy. Following the debut of Israel on May 14, 1948, the American Presbyterians in Egypt took pains to express their support for the Arabs of Palestine and their opposition to the U.S. government's unqualified support for Israel. The American missionaries' vocal, pro-Arab stance helped them weather the first Arab-Israeli war of 1948–49, the Free Officers revolution of 1952, and the Suez Crisis of 1956. But in the wake of the June or Six-Day War of 1967, as Egypt and the Arab world reeled from massive defeat, popular anti-American sentiment spiked. Convinced that all Americans in Egypt—missionaries, diplomats, and business executives alike—were becoming unprotectable, authorities in both the Egyptian government and the U.S. Department of State ordered Americans to leave Egypt at once. On June 21, 1967, the missionaries Martha A. Roy and Willis A. McGill reported from the distance of New York City on the circumstances of their evacuation, observing, "For the first time in our 113 years [as a mission] in Egypt, we do not have a single American present in Egypt."[7]

The American missionary encounter in Egypt from 1945 to 1967 can be studied as a cluster of critical moments, when Egyptian and Middle Eastern politics burst over the missionaries' work. Four moments stand out: the late 1940s, which coincided with the emergence of Israel; the years from 1952 to 1955, when the Free Officers staged their revolution and implemented socialist and nationalist reforms; the Suez Crisis of 1956 and its aftermath; and the period surrounding the Six-Day War of June 1967. Egyptian national and pan-Arab politics bore heavily on the mission in these years, forcing it to retract. At the same time, subtle changes in the internal dynamics of Egyptian and American Christianity occurred, and affected how Christian communities related to each other, what mission work entailed, and what it meant to be evangelical (or Evangelical) in Egypt. John G. Lorimer, who arrived as a young missionary in Egypt in 1952, suggested in retrospect that the circumstances of the 1950s and 1960s prompted American Presbyterian missionaries to focus less attention on institutions like hospitals and more on "the life of the church," by which he meant the devotional and communal life of Egyptian Christians.[8] By the time the Six-Day War broke out in 1967, meetings for Muslim inquirers were a distant memory, while missionaries were no longer actively seeking to draw Copts to the Evangelical Church. Indeed, the social scene had changed so much—and so dramatically relative to the situation in the late nineteenth and early twentieth centuries—that American missionaries and Egyptian Evangelical pastors were cooperating in rural development projects with the Catholic, Orthodox, and other smaller Protestant churches their predecessors had once regarded as rivals.[9]

1945–1952: Educational Nationalism, the Arab-Israeli Conflict, and Religious Rights

The years from 1945 to 1952 saw three key developments with regard to Christian missions in Egypt. These were the tightening of Egyptian legal restrictions on mission schools; the rise of Israel, the Palestinian refugee crisis, and the Arab-Israeli conflict; and the ratification of the UN's Universal Declaration of Human Rights (UDHR). In retrospect, the UDHR, which affirmed values of unfettered religious freedom, is most striking given the *lack* of impact that it had on Christian missions in Egypt. Near the end of this period, the American Presbyterians also experienced a wave of retirements among missionaries who had arrived in Egypt before World War I, when opportunities had seemed abundant.

The year 1945 marked the start of an "era of intense political and economic nationalism" in Egypt. This nationalism coalesced in a law of 1947–48, which "required that at least 40 percent of the board members of companies be Egyptian, 51 percent of the stock of new companies be held by nationals, 75 percent of the white-collar employees be Egyptian and receive 65 percent of the salaries, and 90 percent of the workers be Egyptian and receive 80% of the wages." (This new corporate code left many companies scrambling to comply with its terms of Egyptianization.)[10] Nationalist policymaking also gained expression in cultural realms, where Christian missionaries were strongly affected. Above all, new policies set out to rein in mission schools as places where young citizens were made. Thus economic or business nationalism, and cultural and educational nationalism, proceeded hand in hand in the late 1940s.[11] The CMS missionary S. A. Morrison drew this connection by stating that the Egyptian government had interpreted its new corporate code to force the hiring of Egyptian *Muslims*, leading "minorities" to feel "a gradual closing to them of all doors of employment."[12] In his view, the Egyptian government was interpreting national culture to mean Muslim culture.

In an Arabic history of foreign education in modern Egypt written in 1963, Jirjis Salama argued that mission schools had been an obstacle to national cohesion in the first half of the twentieth century. Mission schools had not only trained elites who went on to work in foreign companies, Salama reasoned, but had also removed children from Egyptian national culture by teaching them to think and speak in English and French.[13] In 2004, another Egyptian historian published a two-volume study of foreign influence in Egypt after 1882, in which he argued, similarly, that the activities of merchants, diplomats, missionaries, and other foreigners were mutually reinforcing in purpose and impact. Yet Christian mission schools, this writer argued, were particularly dangerous to Egypt because their evangelization sought to breed "divisions in the ranks of Islam" (*al-taffaruqa fi sufuf al-islam*) and to capture Egyptian hearts and minds with Western ideas.[14] Both authors claimed that foreign education, including mission-school education, had thwarted the fulfillment of Arabic as a national language for true Egyptians.[15]

By 1945, Egyptian nationalists remained dissatisfied with what they regarded as missionaries' continued attempts to propagate Christianity, whether by requiring Muslim students to participate in Christian instruction and prayer or by refusing to ensure that Muslim students were schooled in Islam. Although Law 40 of 1934 had declared it illegal to teach a student a religion other than his own, even with his guardian's permission, and had stipulated that a child must be educated in his father's religion, some missionaries had circumvented this restriction. By 1947, for example, the American mission boys' school at Luxor was simply dismissing Muslim pupils during the periods devoted to Christian instruction, and was letting them go their own way.[16] Therefore, the government issued a new law—Law 38 of 1948—which reiterated the ban on exposing non-Christian students to Christian teaching or worship and stipulated that students must receive instruction in their own religion, while also requiring all foreign schools to teach Arabic, Egyptian history and geography, and civics up to government standards.[17] Egyptian nationalism had by this time acquired a strong religious element that reflected the values of the Muslim middle classes.[18] As the twelve-year interval following the Montreux Convention stood to expire (and therefore as residual Capitulatory privileges stood to lapse), the Egyptian government now had the power to cancel visas for missionaries whose institutions were in breach of the law.

In various ways, the Egyptian government had already been making its force felt among the missionaries by the time it passed Law 38 of 1948. In 1947, for example, missionaries reported that the Egyptian Christian headmaster of their school in Benha—a school that had in any case been closed for two years—was facing trial for having refused to provide classes in Qur'an study for Muslim students. The Americans interpreted this case as a sign that the government might strike first against Egyptian nationals, before facing American nationals head-on.[19] Around this time, the missionary Bradley Watkins reported that although the mission's boys' school in Luxor had been complying with the Egyptian government law stipulating that Arabic teachers had to be Muslim[20] (a law that implied, as Watkins pointed out caustically, "that Christians are not qualified to teach this sacred language"), the school had not been teaching Islam to Muslim students. But in 1947, some of the Egyptian Christian teachers in Luxor began to press the mission to comply after they were told at a national teachers' union meeting that the Ministry of Education would withhold a supplementary stipend for which Egyptian educators qualified, unless their school offered Islamic education for Muslims.[21]

The mission was feeling these pressures at a time when Egyptian officials were beginning to reject some applications for missionary visas. In 1947, for example, J. W. Acheson reported that Madam Zahia Marzuk, a "domineering" woman and "an American-trained Muslima" in the Ministry of Social Affairs, had rejected the visa application of "Mrs. Armstrong," who was expected to work at the mission's Fowler Orphanage in Cairo. Madam Zahia faulted the mission for not registering the orphanage under a law that had been passed in 1945 to place philanthropic institutions under government oversight. Acheson noted that none of the Christians missions had registered, not only because the purpose of registration was unclear but also because the American mission raised its funds from overseas and had thought (or, more accurately, hoped) that the law did not apply to them. Yet by this juncture Acheson acknowledged the power of Madam Zahia by remarking, "There is no denying she has the whip hand." At the same time Acheson reported that another government bureau had rejected the visa application of a missionary nurse, a "Miss Gordon," whom the mission wanted to appoint as a hospital administrator. The bureau justified its action by noting that the Montreux Convention of 1937 had frozen missionary expansion; therefore, since Miss Gordon's proposed job had not existed on the mission roster in 1937, this was a new job and should be filled by an Egyptian.[22]

By the time Law 38 was passed, the American missionaries knew that the Egyptian government was becoming more exigent, and yet, with their British Anglican counterparts, they still sought to avoid the law's full weight. They addressed a joint Anglo-American appeal to the government, which acknowledged that "the education of children cannot be complete, nor their characters properly formed, without the knowledge of the Creator and of the moral law under which our lives on earth are set," but which then explained their conviction that a Christian missionary school should not "be required to give instruction in religious beliefs other than those for which the School itself stands." The missionaries and government ultimately settled on a compromise. On August 27, 1949, the Ministry of Education sent a note confirming that mission schools "could ask parents to arrange their child's religious education" off school grounds, but advised that they should release Muslim students at fixed times for this purpose.[23] On October 12, 1949, the minister of education arranged a meeting to discuss the new law with Earl E. Elder of the American mission and the Anglican bishop, Geoffrey Allen, as well as with three Catholic bishops, whose schools in Egypt were also affected.[24] The convening of a single meeting for American Presbyterians, Anglicans, and Catholics suggests that the Egyptian state was beginning to deal with foreign Protestants and Catholics on common terms, and that the experiences of Protestant and Catholic missionaries were visibly converging.

There was one clause of Law 38 that the mission could not, or did not try, to avoid: namely, the stipulation that primary schools could no longer operate within the precincts of churches but must have separate buildings. This clause had implications for education in villages, where Evangelical communities had sometimes pooled scant resources to start their own schools. As the American missionary E. M. Bailey observed at the time, "Few village congregations will be able to rent and fewer to build their own buildings." Yet he noted, "For some years I have been considering, and urging at times, that the church might well take another line entirely, and rather than trying to bear the load of formal education called for by the government, let the government do that entirely and add to it a really good program of religious education, given upon Friday and Sunday afternoons when the children are not in school."[25] In time, Christian communities—not only Evangelicals but also Orthodox Copts and Coptic Catholics—did do this by focusing their educational efforts on Sunday schools and other programs that catered explicitly to Christians.[26]

The missionaries were coming to terms with Law 38 just as the Arab-Israeli conflict erupted. Indeed, in the records of the mission that are now preserved in Philadelphia, the missionaries' letters about educational policy are interleaved with their letters lamenting or lambasting U.S. government policy toward the conflict. There appears to have been some consensus among them in deploring the actions of the Truman administration. In January 1948, an interdenominational committee of mission supporters—including an elderly Samuel M. Zwemer, as well as an official from the UPCNA foreign missions board—"resolved" that the partition plan for Palestine in 1947 amounted to an "injustice done to the Arabs." Later, they criticized the Truman administration for lending instant and unqualified support to Israel following its declaration of statehood on May 14, 1948.[27]

Missionaries expressed their concerns in both public and private. In a letter to President Harry S. Truman sent three days after Israel's declaration of statehood, the secretary of the American mission, Earl E. Elder, urged the U.S. government to reconsider its policies in the Middle East given the "ill-will already aroused against America by recent actions of our Government in connection with Palestinian affairs." An enclosed statement from the mission added, "Considering the fact that the Arabs constitute a majority of the population of Palestine, we believe that they have been unjustly treated in the arbitrary partitioning of that country in spite of their protests. We further believe that false hopes have been raised for Jews entering Palestine. Many of them have previously been victims of anti-Jewish atrocities elsewhere, and it is exceedingly unwise to lead them to believe that a Jewish State in Palestine, with aggrieved neighbors on its borders, will solve their problem." The mission sent this statement to Egyptian English and Arabic newspapers, where it was published; later, Egypt's government-controlled radio station broadcast the statement in English and Arabic versions.[28]

Helen Martin, director of the ACG, privately conveyed her thoughts about Israel in a letter to the mission board in Philadelphia. "I think that it is true to say," she wrote, "that the great majority of the Americans resident in this part of the world are shocked beyond measure at the very inept and even disgraceful conduct on the part of our Government in connection with the Palestine situation." Comparing the Arab struggle against the Jews of Israel to the American independence struggle against the British, she concluded, "The Palestine Arabs, both Christian and Muslim, believe that they are fighting a desperate battle for their home land against a foreign invader, as truly as our revolutionary fathers believed that they fought for the freedom and integrity of their home land."[29]

The American mission also expressed support for Palestinian refugees by offering social services. Drawing on its experience in promoting literacy campaigns in Upper Egyptian villages, the American mission worked with the United Nations Relief and Works Agency (UNRWA) and the Society of Friends (Quakers) to initiate literacy campaigns among Palestinian refugees in Gaza, Lebanon, Syria, and Jordan.[30] The mission appointed an Egyptian Evangelical woman, the daughter of a convert from Islam,[31] to organize these Palestinian literacy programs according to the "Laubach Method" (named after a former missionary to the Philippines). This program worked under the motto "Each One Teach One" by engaging newly literate adults to teach others how to read. Davida Finney, the missionary in charge of literacy programs in Egypt, visited Gaza in 1952 when 1,800 Palestinian refugees in the program were teaching 9,000 others how to read; she wrote that she came away from her visit to the Palestinians "greatly impressed with their intelligence, warm enthusiasm and energy."[32]

Another American missionary, John A. Thompson, who had been teaching at the Cairo Evangelical Theological Seminary, traveled to Gaza in 1949 to distribute relief supplies from the UPCNA in coordination with the Society of Friends. He later recalled that United Presbyterian churches in the United States and Evangelical churches in Egypt had raised thousands of dollars for this effort, and that Jane C. Smith, one of the American missionary nurses from the mission's

Child Welfare Center in Cairo, also worked for a time on transfer in Gaza."The refugees are friendly, remarkably free from bitterness, and for the most part resigned to the loss of their homes, lands, and possessions,"Thompson wrote."Many of them think that America and Great Britain are largely if indirectly responsible for their defeat and expulsion." He added,"I am grateful to God and to the Quakers for the opportunity to help these wronged and exiled people. In such a situation the testimony of Christian deeds is stronger than that of words."[33]

AUC officials also spoke out. Although Charles R. Watson died a few months before the emergence of Israel, he went on record in 1947, in mainstream newspapers and church journals, expressing concern over the future of Palestine. In a letter to the editor published in the *New York Times* on December 5, 1947, Watson concluded,"It is difficult to imagine how the U.N. can in the long future maintain its reputation for equitable and even-handed justice in defending the democratic principles of letting majorities rule and letting the majority in any nation decide upon its own preferred form of government, when one of its initial decisions contravenes both these principles and subjects the wishes of 1,306,000 Arabs to the wishes of 640,000 Jews."[34] John S. Badeau, a former missionary to Iraq and Watson's successor as AUC president, took a similar line. In a newsletter addressed to the university's alumni and friends, and written on the day of Israel's debut, Badeau wrote that"The Arab world is aflame with resentment from one end to the other and the creation of a Zionist state can only be accomplished by protracted bloodshed.... Palestine, as the first great Arab cause, is setting up chain reactions that may be the determining factors in the shape of the new Middle East."[35] Badeau also sent a long telegram to President Truman protesting U.S. policy and then released a copy of the text to the Egyptian press, where it had an "enormous impact.""It was not sent for that sake; it was not a public gesture; we felt this way very strongly," Badeau recalled years later. He added,"The Prime Minister ... came to my office in AUC to call on me, which was very unusual indeed, and to express the gratitude of the Egyptian government for the stand we had taken."[36]

In *The Arabists*, a critical study of American Middle East specialists published in 1993, the journalist Robert D. Kaplan suggests that American Presbyterian missionaries entertained feelings of"romance" toward Arabs and the Palestinian cause. John G. Lorimer reflected a similar sentiment when he observed in 1994 that American Presbyterians in the Middle East developed"a profound and somewhat romantic love for the peoples and the lands in which we served."[37] In the second half of the twentieth century, successive Egyptian governments registered these feelings of pro-Arab sentiment among the

American Presbyterians, and the result was a degree of goodwill that helped mitigate otherwise restrictive policies. Lorimer has pointed out, for example, that from 1948 until the 1970s, pro-Palestinian pronouncements helped the American missionaries negotiate the bureaucratic maze of Egyptian residency permits and work visas. He recalled one occasion when the renewal of his own residency permit was in jeopardy: an Egyptian Christian employee opened a file, pulled out the carbon copy of a letter that Lorimer had written to President Lyndon Johnson early in 1967 objecting to American Middle East policy, and presented it to Egyptian officials, who responded by renewing his permit.[38] In a similar vein, a historian of AUC observed that statements like Charles Watson's, backed up by John Badeau and the university presidents who followed him, helped save the university from nationalization in the Nasser era.[39]

Robert D. Kaplan has described "American missionary colonies in the Moslem world" as "the secret drivers of America's Middle East policy since the end of World War II."[40] A historian of American missions in the Middle East pointed similarly in 1986 to a kind of "Protestant diplomacy" among some U.S. Presbyterians who functioned as an informal "lobby for Arab causes within American opinion and governmental policy."[41] These claims notwithstanding, the American missionaries in Egypt were not diplomatic powerhouses. Rather than feeling well connected and powerful, missionaries in Egypt felt alienated and vulnerable—alienated from U.S. foreign policy in the Middle East, and vulnerable to the dictates of the Egyptian government.

Meanwhile, missionaries continued to discuss religious liberty, or what they perceived as the lack of it, in Egypt. Along these lines in 1946, S. A. Morrison wrote, "Whatever the Constitution may say, religious liberty is not yet a reality in Egypt."[42] By the time the 1940s ended, restraints on missionary work were becoming tighter. And it made no difference to the circumstances of missionaries in Egypt when, on December 10, 1948, the General Assembly of the United Nations adopted the UDHR. Article 18 of this declaration guaranteed that "everyone has the right to freedom of thought, conscience and religion; this right includes freedom to change his religion or belief, and freedom, either alone or in community with others and in public or private, to manifest his religion or belief in teaching, practice, worship and observance."[43]

The American Presbyterians in Egypt, along with their British Protestant colleagues, had held out high hopes for this document. They had been trying to promote religious liberty for years, believing that laws and treaties could make Christian conversion socially and legally easier for Muslims. Missionaries regarded Egyptian religious liberty not just as an abstraction of rights but as something that could lead to a kind of free market of religious ideas. Furthermore, they privileged the autonomy of individuals over the authority of families and neighbors, and believed that men and women should be able to choose and change not only their private beliefs but also their public identities as Christians, Muslims, or otherwise. They even supported the individual's right to disbelief.[44]

After World War II, American and British mission societies represented by the NECC closely followed the drafting process of the UDHR. At NECC meetings, they discussed the report of the Lutheran missionary O. F. Nolde, who was representing the interests of the WCC and the IMC at the UN, having secured a consultative status in the United Nations Educational, Scientific and Cultural Organization (UNESCO). But in 1947, Nolde warned missionaries that he was "concerned with Human Rights in the large rather than with Religious Liberty, which is only one detail of the larger problem," and that "It is felt that the problem of religious liberty in Muslim lands can best be approached by other methods than attempts at legislation."[45]

The American Presbyterians in Egypt may have also held out hopes for the UDHR because some of them had encountered one its chief architects in Egypt. This was Charles Malik, a Lebanese Christian of Greek Orthodox background who worked closely with Eleanor Roosevelt on the document.[46] While living in Cairo as a young adult, Malik had befriended James K. Quay, the former member of the American Presbyterian mission and ordained minister who became a leader of the Cairo YMCA. In memoirs of his career in Egypt, Quay proudly claimed that he had helped the young Charles Malik to appreciate the power of prayer and to move away from agnosticism and toward an appreciation of Christ. Quay described Malik as "the most brilliant mind I have ever encountered," and noted that he left Cairo to pursue a doctorate at Harvard under the supervision of William Ernest Hocking—the same scholar whose *Re-Thinking Missions* rocked the Protestant mission world upon its debut in 1932.[47] Yet while Charles Malik may have crossed paths with, and been influenced by, American Presbyterians in Egypt, the document that he helped produce had no discernible impact on the mission after 1948, even though Egypt (along with forty-eight other Muslim majority states) ratified the UDHR.[48]

After 1948, barriers to conversion from Islam to Christianity remained as high as ever in Egypt. The Egyptian government made no moves to enable Muslim converts to Christianity to register their change of religion so that they could marry, inherit, and follow other family-law procedures according to the norms of the Protestant sect (*ta'ifa*). Likewise, Egyptian law continued to forbid Muslim women from marrying Christian or Jewish men, notwithstanding Article 16 of the UDHR, which declared that "Men and women of full age, without any limitation due to race, nationality or religion, have the right to marry and to found a family."[49]

Reflecting on religious liberties after the UDHR had been passed, S. A. Morrison claimed that Egyptian Christians continued to face discrimination in many spheres of life—in everything from gaining access to radio air time to securing permits for building new churches. And while Egyptian law forbade mission schools from teaching Christianity to Muslims, he argued, "Christian children in government elementary schools are commonly induced to attend Islamic lessons on the plea that their knowledge of Arabic will benefit." Morrison ultimately concluded that the UN's human rights documents "lack[ed] teeth."[50] Nevertheless, he expressed concern over what he described as "the prevailing defensive negative attitude of the Christian communities" in the Middle East. Only by participating in civic affairs, he argued, could Christians help advance "Arab civilization" and promote the liberties enshrined in the UDHR.[51] Meanwhile, faced with the "problem of presenting Christianity to the Muslim world" in the midst of the accumulated mistrust of the centuries, Morrison argued that Christians should turn to schools, hospitals, and other welfare institutions but should not expect to be able to convey their message explicitly through Christian worship or scripture study. They should rather try to make their impact "by the whole atmosphere of the institution" and by demonstrating high character, freedom, and self-discipline: "It is hoped that the Muslim will through these channels catch a glimpse of the living Christ at work."[52]

Meanwhile, in 1951, a mission newsletter reported to supporters in the United States that "The big news all round the mission these days is sailings and farewells." About a third of the mission "force" was leaving permanently, while in some places, it announced, "the furlough or retirement of several from a small station nearly puts an end to our occupation of that area. Three stations next year will have only one woman. . . . Most notable perhaps of the farewells was a series in Assiut which is saying goodby [*sic*] to four men whose mission service in that one station totalls [*sic*] about 140 years."[53] This newsletter confirmed that a generational shift was occurring.

In sum, during the period from 1945 to 1952, the Egyptian government was setting the terms on which Christian missionaries could continue in Egypt, evangelical contacts with Muslims were diminishing, and an older cadre of missionaries (including men and women who had known the mission at its moment of greatest expansion in the

1920s, and who had then witnessed the anti-missionary agitation of the 1930s) were retiring. If the American Presbyterian mission in Egypt was beginning to resemble something from the Social Gospel movement—the early twentieth-century movement among some liberal American Protestants that had privileged social reform in this world over soul winning for the next[54]—then it was in good measure because political realities in Egypt were pushing them in that direction. In practice, this meant that young missionaries arriving in Egypt did not come expecting to evangelize in the way their predecessors had done.

THE FREE OFFICERS COUP AND ITS CONSEQUENCES, 1952–56

On January 26, 1952, the missionary Earl E. Elder stood with colleagues on a rooftop in Cairo and watched Shepheard's Hotel—an institution long favored by Western tourists and expatriates—burning down.[55] Meanwhile, Helen Martin, director of the mission's elite ACG, huddled with her female boarding students, later describing her fear as a mob tried to vault over a wall.[56] This was "Black Saturday" in Cairo: a day of anti-British riots and attacks on foreign-owned businesses and institutions ranging from Barclays Bank and the Opera Cinema to a wine shop in Bulaq. "The destruction to this city is unbelievable," a confidential mission memorandum remarked afterward; "one must actually see it to comprehend what has happened."[57] Rioters were venting anger over events of the day before, when British troops in the Suez town of Ismailiyya had clashed with Egyptian police, causing the deaths of some fifty Egyptians and the injury of dozens more. Later, political analysts connected Black Saturday, as an expression of popular dissatisfaction and unrest, with the Free Officers coup that occurred on July 23, 1952, and that overthrew Egypt's constitutional monarchy. Yet while the coup brought a revolution to Egypt, the impact of the changed regime on the mission remained limited until 1956, when the government enforced a law about private schools that compelled American missionaries to reappraise their purpose in Egypt.

Egypt had been ripe for revolution in 1952. Poverty had been deepening, so that while urbanization and literacy rates had grown, standards of living had faltered. "Indeed," observed one economic historian, "the life of the rank and file was probably harsher in 1952 than it had been before World War I."[58] (An American YMCA administrator who arrived in Cairo in 1951 recalled his surprise that "The disparity between the rich and the poor of Egypt was even greater than in China," where he had worked for thirty-three years.)[59] Egyptians also felt humiliated by the country's performance in the first

6.1. Assiut College, dairy cows, n.d. UPCNA Board of Foreign Missions Photographs, Presbyterian Historical Society, Presbyterian Church (U.S.A.), Philadelphia.

Arab-Israeli War of 1948–49, when the Egyptian military had been so poorly prepared that its leaders "needed to borrow road maps of Palestine from Cairo's Buick dealer."[60] Egyptians were jaded from years of parliamentary factionalism and disliked the behavior of King Farouk, who had a reputation for debauchery that included consorting with other men's wives. Rumors circulated, too, claiming that King Farouk and his cronies had skimmed off money from military budgets in 1948 and had then supplied Egyptian troops with shoddy weapons. For a young army officer like Gamal Abdel Nasser, whose family had pressed its way from the rural peasantry into the urban literate classes, and whose military unit had found itself besieged by the Israeli army in the Falluja enclave near Gaza, the sense of disgust for the old regime was acute.[61]

Policymakers in the U.S. government viewed Black Saturday and later the Free Officers coup through the lens of cold war politics. Convinced that Egypt might veer toward the Soviet camp, and deaf to the protestations of Egyptian officials who explained that Egypt's concerns about Britain's footholds in the Suez Canal Zone far exceeded its interest in Soviet communism, U.S. State Department functionaries tried to attract Egyptian support by holding out promises of "technical aid." At first, in the early months of 1952 (i.e., after Black Saturday but before the Free Officers coup), the U.S. government gave Egypt $10 million for agrarian projects as part of the Point Four program, conceived by President Truman, which sought to deter the spread of communism by offering money and technical advice to developing countries.[62] In 1951, when discussions about Point Four aid for Egypt were continuing, American Presbyterian missionaries hoped to become involved through their cattle-breeding project at Assiut College. U.S. government attitudes toward aid to Egypt were already cooling, however, and nothing came of that idea. Nevertheless, in 1952, the mission succeeded in securing a grant of $154,000 from the Ford Foundation to experiment in breeding Egyptian village cows, through artificial insemination, with American Jersey bulls for the sake of increasing milk yields, and to breed chickens and goats as well.[63] This collaboration with the Ford Foundation signaled that the American mission was poised to expand its contact with private foundations, international agencies, and nongovernmental organizations—a development that anticipated policies of the 1960s, when the social service affiliate of the Egyptian Evangelical Church developed joint projects with UNESCO and CARE to install latrines and irrigation water pumps in Upper Egyptian villages.[64]

In June 1952, one month before the Free Officers coup, the mission had also submitted another proposal to the Ford Foundation, this one for a project at the ACG to develop a home economics program. A core part of the program entailed a "Country Life Course," which grew out of ideas first proposed by Wendell Cleland, former director of the AUC Extension Program who had left Egypt to work for the U.S. State Department. The Country Life Course described prospective students as "Young women who are themselves landowners, or who are the daughters or wives of landowners." The course aimed to inspire these women to engage in improving "their own farm hamlets; to induce some of them, at least, to live on their land, i.e., in an attempt at a beginning of a solution of the absentee-landlord problem; to train a group of *volunteer* social workers." Besides training landowning ladies to teach ignorant Christian villagers about the Bible, the course also proposed to advise them on how to build a comfortable country villa.[65] The Ford Foundation awarded the college a generous grant to implement this project. But by the time the Free Officers enacted their Agrarian Reform Law later in 1952, radically redistributing land so that 1 percent of the population would no longer control 70 percent of the arable land, the Country Life Course had lost its constituency.

Land reform, followed by radical tax reform, gutted the old elites and made the landowning classes as passé as the former regime. As John S. Badeau explained, "The landowner was the government; the landowner was the Parliament. If you take away his land, you take away his power."[66] Badeau was inclined to accept the argument that land reform hit Coptic elites harder than Muslims, noting, "Robbed of one position of power, the Copt did not quite know whether he was going to find another position of power in the new regime," especially since there were so few Copts in the Egyptian army.[67] Political sensitivities have deterred historians from studying the impact of land reform on the Egyptian Evangelical Church, although the impact appears to have been substantial. One Egyptian pastor stopped abruptly after saying that the reforms eliminated the church's most stalwart and generous supporters in Upper Egypt.[68]

Many missionaries and church leaders nevertheless sympathized with land reform and its effort to address the gross inequalities that had compounded poverty and high rates of infant mortality, while leaving some two-thirds of the Egyptian population malnourished.[69] One of land reform's most vocal supporters was Henry Habib Ayrout (d. 1969), an Egyptian-born Catholic priest of Syrian family origin and the author of *The Egyptian Peasant* (first published in French in 1938, translated into English thereafter, and published over the years in revised versions). Ayrout admired and sympathized with Egyptian peasants, observing in his book, for example, that, "The enormous economic and political pyramid of Egypt presse[d] down upon the fellah with all its weight."[70] Egyptian authorities appreciated Ayrout's support for land reform after 1952, and later (following passage of a law that required all schools to appoint Egyptian nationals as directors) recognized Ayrout as an "Egyptian" so that he could run a Jesuit college in Cairo. The Ford Foundation was impressed with him, too, and awarded him a grant to develop an artisanal training program in Abu Qirqas, near Minya.[71] American Presbyterian missionaries also admired Ayrout: in the 1950s and 1960s, his book, *The Egyptian Peasant*, was "required reading" among them.[72] Ayrout appears to have played an important role in building Protestant-Catholic goodwill on the ground in Egypt.

What Ayrout was to the Catholic community in Egypt, Samuel Habib (1927–1997) was to the Evangelical. The dynamic "Reverend Sam" later identified 1952 as the year when he found his true calling. That was when he agreed to work with the American missionary Davida Finney in launching a new rural literacy and development project. Arriving in a village called Nazlat Hirz, near Minya, he later recalled that its poverty hit him "like a ton of bricks." The village lacked readily accessible clean drinking water; endemic diseases abounded; and adults often lived just forty or fifty years.[73] In the early 1950s, when the Egyptian government forced philanthropic societies to register themselves officially, Samuel Habib registered this project as a new organizational entity, which became known, after 1960, as the Coptic Evangelical Organization for Social Services, or CEOSS. Working through CEOSS, Habib continued to promote literacy programs while spearheading rural health and publishing projects, and by establishing a press (still active today) called Dar al-Thaqafa (Culture House). At the same time, on the pages of a CEOSS journal called *Risalat al-Nur*, he began to call for gender reforms within the Evangelical community—calling, for example, for eradicating clitoridectomy, eliminating midwives' virginity tests for newly married young women, and removing the partition barriers that traditionally separated men from women in church pews. Under his leadership, CEOSS also cooperated closely with the Egyptian government in encouraging family planning in rural areas by distributing contraceptives to married Muslim and Christian women.[74]

The American missionaries generally supported the socialist reforms that the Egyptian government promoted after 1952 because they recognized that these were attempts to improve conditions for average Egyptians. This may help explain why the American mission initially coasted along after the Free Officers coup. But equally important to their smooth experience, at first, was the tone set by General Muhammad Neguib, who emerged as the leader of the revolutionary circle to assert himself as prime minister (1952) and then president (1953) of Egypt. After Neguib was pushed out of power, American Presbyterians remembered him gratefully for having visited a number of their institutions, including Assiut College, their hospital in Tanta, and the Buchanan Girls' School in Luxor.[75] Adib Najib Salama, a Coptic Catholic who published a history of the Egyptian Evangelical Church in 1993, recorded that General Neguib gave a speech at the Luxor school in which he thanked the Americans for their good work and said, "I myself attended American schools in Khartoum when I was small."[76] S. A. Morrison observed in 1954 that Neguib had had an inclusive vision of Egypt, and made pronouncements such as, "Minorities are precious things. They are like salt in food."[77] The American journalist Edward Wakin made a similar observation in 1963, writing that "Naguib, whose Christmas card depicted a Christian church, a mosque and a synagogue side by side against a Cairo background, used to turn up at services in the various Christian churches. One Yom Kippur he attended services at the Ismailiyya synagogue and one Christmas Eve in the Evangelical Church."[78] American missionaries found Neguib's Muslim catholicity reassuring; perhaps this is why E. M. Bailey reported in the mission's newsletter for 1953 that "Generally speaking, there has been a degree of religious freedom this past year which has not been seen for some time in Egypt. In fact some of the more pronounced of the critics of Gen. Naguib charge that he is too friendly."[79]

In this respect, the younger officer, Gamal Abdel Nasser, who supplanted Neguib in 1954 (first, by staking claims to the prime ministership, and later, in 1956, to the presidency), was a very different man. Wakin has suggested that while Nasser had no particular antipathy to non-Muslims, neither was he fond of them; his regime observed little besides the requisite "exchange of curtsies" with Christian leaders. Wakin speculated that Nasser's indifference may have been the product of his family connections to Beni Mor, a village two miles northeast of Assiut where one-third of the residents were Copts, where the big landowners were Copts as well, and where, according to Wakin, the clergy were uninspiring, craven, and petty. During childhood visits to Beni Mor from Alexandria, Wakin surmised, the young Nasser must have been unimpressed by the Copts whom he saw. In any case he appointed very few to leadership positions, while even in growing departments such as the Foreign Ministry, the number of Coptic employees fell markedly relative to conditions before the Free Officers coup.[80]

In the early years of the Nasser era, American missionaries detected the first signs of how the authoritarian state's expanding system of surveillance would affect their work on the ground. In 1955, several government inspectors came to look at a youth center that the mission had recently started in the Dokki district of Cairo; a missionary later reported that the inspectors had seemed friendly enough. But then, on March 22, 1955, police appeared during a film screening and ordered the missionary in charge, Willis McGill, to shut the center because it was not registered with the Ministry of Social Affairs. When McGill asked for an official document to justify the measure, the officers replied, "We are secret police. We write nothing." When he protested, they merely said, "Do as you like. Only know this, that we have already issued an order to the Police Post nearest your house that your Club is not allowed to operate and that they should use force, if necessary, to keep it closed.'"[81] This time, as on future occasions when authorities insisted on permits, the missionaries did not claim to detect any anti-Christian impulse, per se, emanating from the authorities. Rather, they seemed to interpret these measures as part of the encroachment of the Egyptian state, which was seeking to control, and possibly suppress, all forms of assembly. Ruth Nolin, who worked at Tanta Hospital, described a climate of pervasive surveillance as well: she recalled "being afraid of even private conversations with fellow workers" since they "had been encouraged to inform, particularly on foreigners."[82]

In the early years of the Nasser era it was becoming clear to missionaries that their foreignness was a liability. In the Arab world, anti-missionary nationalism gained a significant boost in 1953 with the publication of an Arabic work titled *Al-Tabshir wa'l-isti'mar fi al-bilad al-'arabiyya* (Evangelism and imperialism in the Arab world)—a work that appeared in at least six Arabic editions over the next thirty years, as well as in Russian, Persian, and Turkish translation. Its authors were two Lebanese Muslims, Mustafa Khalidi (a former professor of obstetrics at the American University of Beirut) and 'Umar Farrukh (a specialist in Islamic history and Arabic poetry). This book, which portrayed Christian missionaries as cultural subversives and political infiltrators, seeded a postcolonial Arabic genre of Muslim anti-missionary treatises. Although Khalidi and Farrukh shared a vision of pan-Arabism that stressed the fellowship of Muslim and Christian Arabs, by the end of the twentieth century their book had become a touchstone for Islamists from Saudi Arabia, the Gulf States, and Egypt who argued that Christians in Arabic societies should know and stay in their subordinate place vis-à-vis Muslims.[83] The book's debut in 1953 was timely: it appeared just five years after the emergence of Israel, and one year after the Free Officers coup, when pan-Arab nationalism was ascendant and popular Arab resentment against Western intervention in the Middle East was intense.[84]

Khalidi and Farrukh argued that Christian missionaries were the most powerful and dangerous agents of Western imperialism, and that mission institutions (schools, hospitals, bookstores, and so forth) were tools for the Western assertion of political and economic hegemony over the Middle East. They described missionaries as latter-day Crusaders, "distinguished by their intense animosity toward Arab Muslims, and by their apparent animosity toward the people of different Christian sects as well."[85] They applied these arguments to Protestants and Catholics and to American, British, French, and Italian missionary groups; they even applied them to the Soviets, whose leaders, they claimed, promoted missionary activities in the Middle East despite their regime's official atheism. Khalidi and Farrukh claimed that "spreading the religion [of Christianity] was very much a secondary matter in all the evangelical movements" and that political and economic agendas were foremost.[86] They concluded by asserting that Western Christian evangelism was a "danger to the existence of the eastern peoples" and that it would lead to either cultural "survival or extinction."[87] Their message to Arab governments was clear: clamp down on missionaries, once and for all, for the sake of cultural integrity.

In 1954, as he was preparing to write a centennial history of the American mission in Egypt, Earl E. Elder expressed some concern about Khalidi and Farrukh's book, which cited the work of one of his colleagues. (This was Anna Milligan, who worked in the UPCNA foreign board in Philadelphia. In 1921 she had published *Facts and Folks in Our Fields Abroad*, describing Egypt as a land "where ignorance was so dense it was all but absolute, [and] where the truth of the Gospel must of necessity be held up before minds blinded by the half truths of Islam or distorted by a degenerate [Coptic Orthodox] church.")[88] Elder concluded that missionaries would have to be supremely careful about what they wrote, since unfriendly forces might be watching them. "Indeed we live in a very sensitive world," he observed, "even more sensitive than it was 15 years ago."[89] Elder realized that, far from being a record of church life of interest only to Christian insiders, mission history might draw the attention of unsympathetic or hostile Muslim audiences who might read it and respond. He understood that mission history in Egypt had become deeply political. S. A. Morrison noted the book by Khalidi and Farrukh as well and connected it to government policies—such as tightening visa restrictions for missionaries—that were confirming Muslim public opinion rooted in a mistrust of Christian evangelism.[90]

Perhaps the Egyptian government was responding, in part, to the call of Khalidi and Farrukh when it announced Law 583 on December 4, 1955. Writing in 1994, Lorimer described this law as a "critical challenge" to the mission and as a watershed;[91] it left the missionaries reeling.[92] Law 583 was much like Law 40 of 1934 and Law 38 of 1948.[93] Law 583 declared, in Article 17, that a private school in Egypt must "teach the subject of religion to its Egyptian pupils, each in accordance with his own religion and following the syllabus set by the Ministry, and it is not permitted for the school to teach its pupils any religion other than their own or to have them participate in the religious exercises of a religion other than their own, even [if] this is approved by the pupil's guardian."[94] By this time, the American mission was educating over seven thousand students, of whom approximately three thousand were Muslims. In some of the mission's nineteen schools, Muslims accounted for more than two-thirds of total enrollment.[95] As 1956 began, missionaries braced themselves to confront a law that they knew the Egyptian government, this time, would enforce.

Suez and After

The Suez Crisis was precipitated on July 26, 1956 (a few months after Britain withdrew its last troops from the Suez Canal Zone), when Nasser nationalized the Suez Canal Company, which French and British business interests had controlled for nearly a century. The event turned into war late in October, when Britain and France, together with Israel (which was retaliating for Egyptian-supported raids into its territory), launched a campaign of ground war and aerial bombardment. Fearing an escalation of the conflict within the framework of the cold war, the U.S. government called on the aggressors to back off. The Suez Crisis signaled the end of Britain's regional dominance—even if that closure had been in the works since end of World War II—and the rise of the United States.[96] It also confirmed Nasser's reputation as the most charismatic leader in the Arab world, and emboldened the Egyptian government to purge what it regarded as vestiges of foreign control. Thus the Egyptian government hastened to nationalize foreign businesses ranging from department stores and textile factories to banks. It also sequestered and later officially "Egyptianized" (massarat) the assets of many British-, French-, and Jewish-owned enterprises.[97] Together, these measures prompted the exodus of Jews, Greeks, Italians, and members of other jaliyat (minority or expatriate communities), who did not claim Egyptian nationality.[98] In fact, the Suez Crisis had far-reaching consequences for Christian missions and churches as well, and entailed parallel processes of nationalization.

Even before the crisis, there were signs that the Egyptian government was determined to have its way with Christian missions. In January 1956, missionaries noted with apprehension a report in the Egyptian Gazette that stated that officials in Alexandria had declared themselves ready to seize any mission schools that did not comply with Law 583 concerning religious instruction for Muslim students.[99] Conversations with Egyptian officials led missionaries to believe that the government would no longer allow the status quo ante, whereby missionaries had released Muslim students during periods of religious instruction while making Muslim parents responsible for Islamic instruction. They understood that the government was declaring itself—not parents—the guardian of Egyptian children insofar as Islamic learning was concerned.

By May 1956, the secretary of the mission, E. M. Bailey, was grasping for ways that American mission schools could avoid teaching Islam on their premises. In a letter to Donald Black, the secretary of the foreign mission board in Philadelphia, Bailey tossed out several ideas. Noting that many institutions in Egypt (including Islamic schools supported by the Ministry of Religious Endowments) barred non-Muslim students from enrolling, he suggested that the mission could try to refrain from accepting non-Christians. He then suggested that the American mission could simply close all its schools, but quickly dismissed this idea as financially impractical on the grounds of advice from a lawyer, who had warned that any mission school that closed might have to pay indemnities to former employees. (Later Bailey also acknowledged that such action would probably lead the Egyptian government to revoke visas for "more than half of the Mission.")[100] More wildly, he suggested that the mission could make all its schools into kindergartens and universities, where no religious instruction would be required. Bailey's letter conveyed a sense of desperation.

In official exchanges with the Egyptian government, Bailey was more cool-headed. In May 1956 he wrote to the minister of education explaining that the American mission, as a Christian organization, did not feel that it should be required to teach Islam in its schools. He asked that the government continue the earlier policy of allowing Muslim parents to assume responsibility for their children's religious education, and noted that under the previous arrangement, 88 percent of Muslim students from mission schools had passed the government examination in Islamic studies—a rate that compared very favorably with the national average. Significantly, several smaller Protestant organizations—British, American, and Dutch—became signatories of Bailey's letter as well. Yet, a hint of the old rivalry surfaced later when an American mission report claimed that Catholic missionaries had remained aloof from deliberating with the Protestants: "[We] were warned by many people that the Roman Catholics would be perfectly happy to see us go out on a limb, close our work and leave Egypt, leaving them with a free field and whatever arrangements they could make."[101]

In spring 1956, the American mission drafted an Arabic letter to Muslim parents, explaining that enrollment of their children would be contingent on the Egyptian government's allowing parents to assume responsibility for religious teaching. Bailey heard that Catholic schools were intending to circulate a similar letter.[102] The point, in any case, was moot. In May, an official from the Ministry of Education announced that the government would not allow foreign schools to discriminate against students on account of their creed—a statement that missionaries understood as meaning that the government would not allow them to deny enrollment to Muslims.[103] Around this time, too, the Americans followed with consternation the case of the Egypt General Mission (EGM). Having decided that instead of complying with Law 583 they would close two of their schools, in Port Suez and Ismailiyya, EGM missionaries notified the Ministry of Education accordingly. "The reply was a squadron of police who took over the property, and would not even permit the missionaries to enter the residence there," an American mission report declared. "After protest by the British Embassy, the [EGM] missionaries were permitted to work for two weeks clearing the residence of personal effects and taking an inventory of the mission property. The property, according to the Government, has not been confiscated or expropriated, but has been 'requisitioned.'"[104]

By the time the UPCNA board of foreign missions sent two of its executives to Cairo from Philadelphia, in June 1956, the American missionaries were in a state of crisis over how to respond to Law 583. By this time, they had already sought advice from Henry Byroade, the American ambassador in Cairo, who displayed the obsessive interest in Soviet expansion that was a trademark of the U.S. government. He urged the Americans to keep their schools open, but gave missionaries the impression that his knowledge of American institutions was restricted to AUC and the ACG. According to a mission report,

> He said the American Mission Schools are the best thing America has in Egypt. . . . He pointed out that we cannot compete with Communism in the Near East in the sphere of economics—the trade pattern is against us there. The main area in which we do have something to contribute is that of ideology and culture, and at that point our American Mission Schools are performing an invaluable service. The Embassy then, and in a later contact, pointed out that if we close our schools and pull out, a quick offer will come from behind the Iron Curtain to provide teachers and other cultural agents to fill the gap.[105]

Meanwhile, the American missionaries also conferred with Muslim alumnae of the ACG as well as with Evangelical pastors. The alumnae urged them to comply with the law, reassured them that teaching Islam to Muslims would not be so onerous, and emphasized that Muslim students might then benefit from Christian missionary activity. One of the Evangelical pastors later said regarding the Egyptian authorities, "We cannot blame them for this decision [of requiring Islamic instruction for Muslims as a mode of ethical education], for it is something that they have learned from the missionaries."[106]

During a collective debate among the American Presbyterians that elicited "great anxiety and soul searching,"[107] the missionary Walter Skellie tried to devise a list of pros and cons for complying. He concluded that to teach Islam to Muslims would be to "compromise our conscience" but that the only alternative was for the missionaries to leave Egypt. With that, they would then lose everything—their schools, their opportunities, and their possibilities for cultural and spiritual influence. After much discussion, missionaries voted, thirty to twelve, in favor of complying with the law on teaching Islam. The mission report noted that the lack of unanimity caused no rancor; there was simply widespread relief that a decision had been made. On July 3, 1956, three weeks before the nationalization of the Suez Canal, leaders of the American mission signed a formal agreement with the Egyptian Ministry of Education agreeing to comply with the law, but with the understanding that the government would not later require mission schools to provide mosques or places for Muslim prayer.

A report from the mission concluded that "even this decision is a bitter cup," and added, "In a real sense our missionaries are forced to carry on their work constantly hedged about by increasing restrictions in a new kind of imprisonment. They need our constant sympathetic prayers."[108] Afterward, Donald Black, the secretary of the foreign mission board, set about explaining the policy shift to American supporters in the United States. He sent a letter to all the American pastors of the UPCNA, first explaining that the subject was "extremely confidential," that it should not be shared with the press, and that "extreme care should be exercised in any writing to the field" because "mail censorship is still practiced in Egypt." Black tried to explain why the mission in Egypt, "faced with one of the most critical situations in its history," agreed to teach Islam to Muslims. Rather than resist the law and lose schools to the government, Black wrote, the mission decided to remain in Egypt, to preserve points of contacts with Muslims, and to act upon the "conviction that Christian missionaries, as guests in a land, should submit themselves to 'the ordinances of man for the Lord's sake' (1 Pet. 2:13)."[109]

In retrospect, a mission report on the year 1956 noted that there were other clauses of Law 583 to which the American schools had been forced to respond. For example, the law stipulated minimum standards for playground space per child. Unable to meet the minimum in all its schools (and sensing again that the Egyptian government would be more likely to enforce the playground clause within foreign institutions), the mission secretary speculated that they might have to cut enrollments. But this was of minor concern, and the secretary noted that the missionaries generally thought that most of the law's provisions were good and would improve the educational system.[110] It was only the clause about religious teaching that had bothered American Presbyterians; indeed, its implementation dealt them an existential blow.

Conditions for the Protestant missions grew more ominous as 1956 wore on. In August and September, missionaries noted that the Egyptian government was invoking laws about church permits and rights of assembly in order to threaten some churches with closure. Missionaries and Egyptian Christians had been complaining about the difficulty that Christians faced in securing church permits since the nineteenth century, and the difficulty had never abated.[111] Thus in the nineteenth and early twentieth centuries, some Egyptian Christians had secured municipal building permits instead of church permits (since the latter could only be issued by the rulers of the Muhammad Ali dynasty); they had then erected meeting halls where they gathered for worship, Bible study, and the like. In other cases, they had rented buildings or organized meetings in private homes. But Egyptian authorities now demanded to see documentation. The Americans Presbyterians noted the case of Wilbur Skaggs, an independent American missionary who, sometime that summer, had been called before the police about his rented meeting hall. Unable to produce a church permit, Skaggs began reporting to the police in advance of every worship meeting, by identifying speakers and topics. But in August, police told Skaggs that this would no longer suffice and that he and his colleagues could no longer assemble. Meanwhile, the pastor of one of the Evangelical churches in Cairo approached the mission to seek its church permit, which police had demanded to see; the mission secretary knew of a property deed, written in Italian, that had been registered with the American consul many years before but did not know whether that church had ever secured a khedivial or royal decree.[112]

After Britain, France, and Israel launched attacks on Egypt in late October, the ground shifted even more. Many Catholic schools either had French teachers or taught in the French medium; the Egyptian government therefore associated them with France. Hence, after the onset of the "Tripartite Aggression," the Egyptian government nationalized all Catholic schools that did not operate under Vatican auspices,[113] though many Catholic schools, in any case, lost their core constituencies as minorities and expatriates flooded out of the country. The Egyptian government also deported Britons. These deportations ended the Egypt General Mission and terminated the work of the Church Missionary Society, British and Foreign Bible Society, and Nile Mission Press in Egypt. (With the approval of Egyptian authorities, the BFBS later transferred custodianship of its work and assets in Egypt to the American Bible Society.)[114] The government also froze the bank accounts of British missions. That November, lacking access to their funds, the few remaining British missionaries had to turn to the Americans for loans so that they could buy airplane tickets and leave.[115] The sudden depletion of Protestant missionaries prompted E. M. Bailey to observe, in December, that it "looks as if Willis [Mc-Gill] and I will be the Egypt Inter-Mission Council before long."[116] By this time there were seventy American Presbyterian missionaries on the ground in Egypt (including wives, but excluding workers on furlough). Twenty-nine were in Assiut, twenty-one in Cairo, six in Tanta, three in Fayoum, Minya, and Luxor, and two in Mansura.

Three stations—Alexandria, Benha, and Beni Suef—contained only one woman in each.[117]

The American missionaries watched what had happened to their British colleagues and feared that it could happen to them. John G. Lorimer wryly observed, "One of the ladies of our own generation, when it appeared that some would have to leave the country at the time of the 1956 war was heard to say: 'If they are going to throw us out, I hope it's before I waste the best years of my life studying this awful language [Arabic].'"[118] Meanwhile, missionaries accelerated efforts to transfer mission properties to the control of the Evangelical Church[119] and, sensing that official connections to the United States were no longer advantageous, began to urge the Evangelical Church to go its own way.[120] Developments in the newly independent Sudan sharpened their concerns. In February 1957, American missionaries in Khartoum had been summoned to a meeting at the Ministry of Education; when they arrived and saw a large array of Sudanese authorities, including southern province governors, and found themselves guided with other Protestant and Catholic missionaries into a big conference hall, "We knew then," a missionary reported, "that this was going to be IT." Indeed, the Sudanese minister of education thanked them for their efforts in the past but announced a new policy: "the time has come that the Government herself takes full responsibility for the national education in the South."[121] He declared, in short, the nationalization of all mission schools in the southern Sudan—a measure that anticipated the Sudanese government's wholesale expulsion of foreign missionaries in 1964.[122]

These developments were in the air in 1957, when the Egyptian church became independent of the UPCNA. In theory, independence meant that the Evangelical Church would be able to make creedal decisions and set church policies for itself; in practice, independence sought to ease the Evangelical Church's relations with the Egyptian government. Sensing the mood of the times, Evangelical leaders christened the independent church the "Coptic Evangelical Church in the Nile Valley." Their insertion of the adjective "Coptic" was meant to signal, as a leader of the Evangelical community later explained, that "we are here and we are of here."[123] The name, in other words, was a plea for indigenousness—a bid to distance the Evangelical Church from the foreign mission that had seeded it—although it was *not* meant to signify closer identification with Coptic Orthodoxy. Henceforth the Evangelicals became the only Protestant community in Egypt to include the word "Coptic" in their church name.[124]

Meanwhile, the American Presbyterians were becoming distracted by changes occurring within the church in America. In 1958, the

UPCNA merged with the larger Presbyterian Church in the United States to create a new denomination: the United Presbyterian Church in the U.S.A. (UPCUSA). In line with a decision made by the PCUSA in 1956 to ordain women as ministers of the church, the new UPCUSA also allowed for the ordination of women.[125] Meanwhile, the new church refashioned its missions into something called the Commission on Ecumenical Mission and Relations (COEMAR) and, in a nod to the changing times, began to call its overseas missionaries "fraternal workers."[126]

The metaphor of siblinghood in the phrase "fraternal workers" was a sudden change. In a policy paper written in 1955, Donald Black had considered the relationship of the UPCNA to each of its mission-planted churches abroad—in Egypt, Sudan, Ethiopia, India, and Pakistan—and had written, "Our destiny and labor abroad is inseparably linked to that Church which is the result of our evangelical missionary effort. Regardless of its difficulties and imperfections, it is our child."[127] Likewise, writing for an audience of missionaries in 1957, E. M. Bailey still described the UPCNA, relative to the Egyptian Evangelical Church, as "the Mother Church in America."[128] The emphasis on parity appeared after 1957 in official publications. Thus a history of the UPCNA, published in 1958, described the new Coptic Evangelical Church as an "independent sister church," citing the minutes of the American church's General Assembly.[129] Similarly, John Coventry Smith, a former Presbyterian missionary to Japan who became head of COEMAR, explained the status of the former mission churches to American audiences by saying, "They are not now our children. They are our sister churches in Christ and join us in being witnesses to the whole world."[130]

The question of paternalism and parity took many years to resolve, not least because the American church retained important levers of power by making grants to churches in its former mission fields.[131] (At root was what the missiologist Jonathan Bonk calls "affluence as a Western missionary problem.")[132] Donald Black described his own encounter with this issue when he visited American missionaries in the southern Sudan in 1956. Two years earlier the Egyptian Evangelical Church had sent its first missionary, Suweilim Sidhom, to work with the American Presbyterians in that district.[133] "There was a car at the station, a station wagon which had been a gift from a congregation [in the United States] to one of the women. Should they let Suweilim drive it? His driving skills were unknown. Suweilim was probably the only missionary in that mission who did not have access to a car. No one questioned his ability to effective mission work," Black recalled, "he was [just] caught in a group where some were more equal than others."[134]

In some respects, the disappearance of the UPCNA and its board of foreign missions, followed by the emergence of COEMAR with its official discourse of fraternalism or sisterhood, suggest that 1958 was a moment of closure in the mission's history. Certainly the archival record ends in 1958, since the papers for the UPCUSA missions (i.e., the COEMAR papers) are neither fully catalogued nor open to researchers. Drawing largely on memoirs and interviews, one can nevertheless identify four developments that stand out in the late 1950s and early 1960s.

First, in 1958, the Egyptian government announced another law—Law 160—that targeted foreign schools. Law 160, which was actually implemented in 1962, stipulated that the directors of all schools in Egypt had to be Egyptians.[135] To comply with Law 160, the American mission transferred all of its remaining schools to the authority of the Coptic Evangelical Church and appointed suitable Egyptian directors. Yet the transitions were sometimes difficult for the Egyptians involved as well. In a study of the ACG that drew extensively upon interviews with former teachers, graduates, and principals, Christine Sproul has noted that Egyptian alumnae resented the first Egyptian director, a woman who held degrees from the University of Colorado and the University of Wisconsin, so that she lasted just three years in the job. The alumnae found her style too autocratic because she made decisions that had previously been submitted to the alumnae advisory council.[136] With Egyptianization, the consultative American style of administration was giving way to concentrated authority.

Second, in the post-1958 period the American missionaries began to engage in a kind of self-effacement, partly for the sake of political expediency. They began to give full credit to Egyptian Evangelicals even in projects where American missionaries were actively involved. This was especially the case with the rural literacy and development projects that came under the CEOSS umbrella. To some degree, missionaries wrote themselves out of the record, and this makes their work after 1958 more difficult for the historian to trace.[137] Meanwhile, as missionaries stepped into the shadows, the Evangelical Church of Egypt and other independent Protestant churches in the Middle East assumed an increasingly prominent role in the NECC, which missionaries had founded in 1927. From 1962, Middle Eastern church leaders began to shift "mission organizations out of the regular membership . . . putting them into a section known as the Commission on Outreach and Witness."[138] In 1964 this trend was confirmed when church leaders retained the NECC acronym but changed the organization's full name to the Near East Council of Churches.[139]

Third, the spirit of ecumenism grew even stronger as the American Presbyterians in Egypt began to develop friendly relations with a broader range of Protestants, including Pentecostals, as well as with Roman and Eastern rite Catholics.[140] Evangelicals began to collaborate with other Egyptian Christians on a wider range of social projects and to participate in international ecumenical forums, above all the NECC (which was recast in 1974 as the MECC) and the WCC.[141] The dramatic improvement in Protestant-Catholic relations, in particular, was not only the outgrowth of the Second Vatican Council of 1962–65 (which initiated new Catholic efforts to promote ecumenical and interfaith understanding)[142] but also, and perhaps more important within Egypt, a response to conditions on the ground. Lorimer, whose own daughter later worked for a Catholic organization near Minya, suggested that as Egyptian Protestants and Catholics "of every stripe" sensed that they were "minorities of a minority," vis-à-vis Orthodox Copts and the Muslim majority, they "realized that [they] had much in common, and found various ways to be helpful to each other."[143] Tensions occasionally surfaced, though these tended to be between the leaders of Evangelical and Orthodox communities. (Evangelicals resented it, for example, when Bishop Samuel of the Coptic Orthodox Church approached American Presbyterians in order to seek Coptic Orthodox representation on the governing board of CEOSS.)[144] By contrast, Coptic Evangelicals and Catholics began to find that they had more in common, and their relations steadily improved, largely because of a shared perception that the Orthodox Church behaved like a heavyweight among Egypt's Christian communities.[145]

Fourth, even as there was a growing global ecumenical impulse among Egyptian Christians of the kind that set them on the "road to internationalism,"[146] the churches were turning inward. The Coptic Orthodox Church was moving toward greater communal introspection, reflecting a sense that Egyptian Christians needed to look out for themselves. Thus under the patriarch Cyril VI (r. 1959–71), Orthodox Copts revived pilgrimage to monasteries, the study of early church martyrs, and the production of hagiographical literature, taking refuge in a kind of Coptic neo-traditionalism.[147] The Orthodox Church also developed its own social service network. In the process, S. S. Hasan has argued, "The Coptic Orthodox Church took upon itself the role of bolstering the battered self-image of Egyptian Christians as well as of equipping them with the values and skills that would enable them to succeed economically despite discrimination."[148] Protestants turned inward, too. Lorimer recalled that his work as a missionary began to focus more pointedly on the Evangelical community, adding,

"The much larger world of the Coptic Orthodox Church was on the periphery of our service, and the infinitely larger world of Islam was even more so."[149] In 1975 Bernard Quick expressed a similar idea but with greater frustration, writing that the Evangelical Church was "extremely conservative, pietistic in terms of emphasizing the inner life of the Christian and serving, basically, its own constituency."[150] To some extent, American Presbyterians were turning inward in the United States as well. In 1986 Donald Black explained why the leaders of COEMAR, the new mission venture of the UPCUSA, became so actively involved in American social affairs: "Church people discovered that the former foreign mission concern for approaching Muslims or Hindus with the gospel was now a matter of neighborhood evangelism." In the 1960s, therefore, American Presbyterians began to press churches into community service as clinics, tutoring centers, and food banks, even as some church activists were becoming involved in opposition to the Vietnam War.[151]

Meanwhile, many more Egyptians were emigrating to the United States. The American missionaries were helping to send Evangelicals to American seminaries, while American YMCA workers, with the explicit support of Nasser, were helping to raise scholarships to send Egyptians to the United States for higher degrees. (In 1960, for example, a YMCA report noted that Nasser had authorized sending six hundred Egyptians to the United States.)[152] As the 1960s advanced, the Americans in Egypt were also continuing to trace titles for mission properties and buildings, calculate and pay off property taxes, and draft legal documents to transfer assets to the Evangelical Church.[153] Finally, by the mid-1960s, tensions between Israel and its neighboring Arab states were escalating, and U.S.-Egyptian relations were withering.

These tensions were affecting the American mission and Evangelical Church in 1965, when the Second Vatican Council issued *Nostra Aetate*, a landmark decree that revisited the "relation of the Church to non-Christian religions." *Nostra Aetate* recognized the "spiritual patrimony" linking Christians and Jews, deplored the history of anti-Semitism, and ascribed blame for the crucifixion of Jesus to the sins of humankind, declaring that "what happened in His passion cannot be charged against all the Jews without distinction, then alive, nor against the Jews of today."[154] Pressed by the politics of the Arab-Israeli conflict, which created a new climate of anti-Semitism in Egypt, Egyptian Evangelical leaders struggled to respond to the Vatican's exoneration of Jews, which had been widely advertised in the Arabic media. Around this time a leading Egyptian Evangelical pastor gave a sermon that was a case study in contradiction: on the

6.2. Assiut College, American missionary and Egyptian pastor planning a field trip for the students, c. 1965. UPCNA Board of Foreign Missions Photographs, Presbyterian Historical Society, Presbyterian Church (U.S.A.), Philadelphia.

one hand he welcomed the prospect of cordial Christian-Jewish relations and advised Christians of the imperative to love all peoples, "even the Jews," but on the other he confirmed the guilt of Jews for goading Pontius Pilate to keep Jesus on the cross. "And from this we see," he concluded, "that the Jews are the ones who crucified Christ with their guilty hands and wicked hearts, and their whole history is one of killing the prophets whom God sent among them. All this does not prevent us from loving the Jews but we cannot change history."[155]

When students at PMI, the mission's college for girls in Assiut, asked the missionary Kenneth Bailey to clarify the Vatican ruling, he explained "that the question of the responsibility of the Jews for the death of Christ was not a political question, but should be understood theologically and should not be attributed to succeeding generations of Jews." He added, "Everyone in Pilate's court who was responsible for sending Jesus to the cross are still blamed by the Pope. But God, the righteous judge, will neither blame their children nor their grandchildren, let alone their descendants 2,000 years later." News of Bailey's explanation circulated in Assiut, and reached the secret police, who interpreted it as a "pro-Israeli anti-Arab statement by an American." The result was that when Bailey's visa expired, Egyptian authorities refused to renew it and gave him ten days to leave the country. His career in Egypt ended, Bailey moved to Beirut to teach theology.[156]

By the mid-1960s, leaders of the Evangelical Church were increasingly eager to distance themselves from Americans; their social credibility as Egyptians was at stake. Far from providing a "security blanket" relative to the Muslim majority,[157] contact with Americans in a period of growing anti-American sentiment had begun to leave Egyptian Evangelicals badly exposed.

1967: THE CONCLUSION

The son of an American missionary, who grew up in Cairo in the 1920s, later reflected that during his childhood, the Arabic word Amrikani—"American"—had been for Egyptians "the superlative in war, art, politics, and automobiles."[158] But by the 1960s, the missionary Bernard Quick claimed that the positive reputation had eroded so much, as a result of the American government's support for Israel, that the Evangelical Church's connections with the United States were no longer a source of prestige. Quick wrote that America's reputation worsened until, by the mid-1960s, "it got so embarrassing for the Evangelical Church to be associated with Americans" that they asked the American missionaries not to attend synodical meetings.[159] The missionary Kenneth E. Nolin told a similar story. As "the situation became more intense" on the eve of the 1967 war, he recounted, it became increasingly "awkward" for Egyptian Evangelical pastors to have Nolin visit their homes. Evangelicals could not afford to be seen with Americans.[160]

The changed mood and circumstances of missionary work in Egypt prompted the American Presbyterians to decide, at their annual meeting in the winter of 1966–67, that "the time had come to disband." As John G. Lorimer recalled in 2004, they "saw no point in continuing."[161] Thus the small group of remaining missionaries voted to dissolve the Missionary Association, which their predecessors had established in 1870.[162] By this time, Americans were no longer controlling schools or other institutions, since Egyptian laws had already engineered their Egyptianization.

An interview with a former director of the ACG in Cairo showed how the political strains in this period pressed on Egyptians as well.

Farouza Barsoum, who ran the ACG from 1965 until late in 1967, re-called that she had "faced growing anti-American sentiment from Ministry of Education officials" who pressured the school to follow a strict government curriculum that was at odds with the school's liberal arts philosophy. People accused her "of 'being an American' because of her support of the American programs and style of edu-cation." According to Barsoum, "Tensions increased to such a degree in the spring of 1967 that, when the lights were on in the school, out-siders would accuse ACG of making signals to the enemy."[163]

In May 1967, Egypt asked the UN Emergency Force to leave the Sinai peninsula (where it had been seeking to maintain the shaky peace in the aftermath of the Suez Crisis) and declared a blockade of Israeli shipping through the Straits of Tiran. Many interpreted the measure as a buildup to war. As the U.S. government confirmed its support for Israel, anti-American sentiment peaked within Egypt. Farouza Barsoum recalled that the situation grew so strained that "the bus drivers [at the ACG] requested that the name of the school be painted off the side of the buses, as they could not guarantee the safety of the students. At the same time the administration decided to paint out the name of the school from the roof of the administration building for the same reason."[164]

On June 5, 1967, the Israeli military launched a preemptive strike on Egypt and destroyed 80 percent of the Egyptian air fleet while it was still parked on the ground. In the six-day war that followed, Israel made dramatic territorial gains at the expense of Egypt, Jordan, and Syria, by seizing the Sinai peninsula, the Gaza strip, East Jerusalem, the West Bank of the Jordan River, and the Golan Heights. The war also pushed out new waves of Palestinian refugees. The Six-Day War delivered Egyptians and Arabs a devastating defeat.

On June 5, Martha Roy and Willis McGill were among the hand-ful of American missionaries remaining in Egypt. In an account of events written from New York City two weeks later, they described the "paroxysms of rage" and the "hate America and kill Americans line" that overtook many Egyptians in their despair, prompting the U.S. Embassy to fan out into Cairo that night to collect all Americans for evacuation. The last Americans included the general manager of American Express as well as Miss Ellen Van Dyck, the eighty-two-year-old granddaughter of the American missionary translator Cor-nelius Van Dyck (1818–1895), after whom the Van Dyck Arabic Bible is known.[165] After spending several hours gathered in the basements of the Nile Hilton and the now defunct Nile Hotel, hearing the muffled noise of shouts and gunshots outside, the last Americans left Cairo under cover of darkness. A convoy of Egyptian police escorted them to the train station, and to Alexandria, where officials confiscated their residency permits before placing them on a ship bound for Cyprus and Greece.[166]

This was a moment of rupture that left no American missionaries resident in Egypt. During the yearlong hiatus that followed, the UPCUSA and Coptic Evangelical Church reached an agreement: henceforth American Presbyterian missionaries would only go to Egypt at the invitation of the Evangelical Church. Those who returned as guests of the Evangelical Church saw changes. Before the war, for example, Marjorie Dye had been working with CEOSS literacy projects from a base in Minya; when she returned in 1969, she had to work from Cairo, because from 1967 until 1973 the Egyptian government restricted Americans from going "to the villages." There was, however, a positive side to this development. "Because of the political situation," she explained, American connections to the Evangelicals had "cast a shadow on the entire program for some time. The removal of all foreign personnel, however, demonstrated that CEOSS was a truly indigenous organization."[167]

Paths changed for others as well. Martha Roy, who was born to missionary parents in the Delta town of Tanta in 1913, regarded Egypt firmly as her home and had spent only four college years in the United States when the Six-Day War uprooted her. In 1967–68, a year of forced exile in New York, Roy studied for a master's degree in musicology at Columbia University, where she began to develop a specialization in Coptic liturgical music.[168] Upon her return to Egypt in 1968, she continued studying music at the Coptic Institute for Higher Studies in Cairo. Thirty years later, in 1998, she and two colleagues—one Coptic Orthodox, the other Roman Catholic—finished compiling, annotating, and translating the Coptic Orthodox liturgy of St. Basil. Published by the American University in Cairo Press, it was a highly ecumenical venture. "We have heard that Pope Shenouda [the patriarch of the Coptic Orthodox Church] is very pleased with it," she remarked in 2005, from her room in an assisted living facility in Cairo.[169]

For their part, leaders of the Evangelical Church responded to the Six-Day War of 1967 by energetically emphasizing their support for Egypt and the Palestinians, and by conducting mass prayers for the Arab armies. Cooperating closely with other Egyptian and Middle Eastern churches, they sent statements to influential people, including the Catholic pope, the UN secretary general, the Archbishop of Canterbury, and the president of the Palestine Liberation Organization (PLO), to protest Israeli policies and to "announce intense disapproval for the U.S. and Western provision of aid to Israel." They emphasized their "commitment and fealty" (al-'ahd wa'l-bay'a) to

President Nasser and, through the forum of the NECC, provided aid to Palestinian refugees.[170] At conferences and in sermons, Evangelicals also tried to distinguish the Israeli state and modern Zionist thought from biblical Israel and Zion.[171]

In retrospect, it is difficult to know whether the deeds and statements of Evangelical pastors reflected a genuine sense of pan-Arab solidarity and opposition to Israel, a desire to win favor among Muslims by proving loyalty to a national cause, or a response to pressure exerted upon them by the Egyptian government. Conversations with Egyptian pastors and American missionaries suggested that some combination of these three factors was influencing Evangelical statements about the 1967 war and the Arab-Israeli conflict in general. It appears, too, that just as the Arab-Israeli conflict served as a crucible for pan-Arabism in the post-1948 period (helping to paper over the ideological and economic differences that otherwise distinguished Arab states from each other), it also served as a crucible for Christian solidarity in the Middle East (helping to smooth the tensions that continued to affect, for example, the relationship between leaders of the Evangelical and Coptic Orthodox churches). The conflict gave the countries of the Arab League an excuse to meet and talk, and the same could be said of the church groups in the NECC.

The Middle East at large is still grappling with the 1967 war, and so are American Presbyterians, who have been struggling since 1967 to achieve consensus while setting church policies toward Israel and the Palestinian refugees. John Coventry Smith, the head of COEMAR who went on to become president of the WCC, observed in his memoirs that "In 1967 the Six-Day War left us struggling to find ourselves in its aftermath. The Christian community, including its leadership, was utterly unprepared for the questions that this raised. We did not have a clear theological position about the Jews, the foreign mission wing was sympathetic with the Arabs, and the national mission wing had friends in the Jewish community and tended to side with them."[172] Smith's memoir appeared in 1982, but his summary still rang true a generation later, in 2006, when an acrimonious debate, involving a dispute over whether to divest from companies that facilitated the Israeli occupation of the West Bank, roiled the American Presbyterian community.[173]

The Six-Day War of 1967 ended the American missionary presence in Egypt, but a new beginning soon followed. Those who eventually returned to Egypt came as guests of the Evangelical Church—and in some sense, too, as guests of the Egyptian government. John G. Lorimer reflected that while "it was not exactly comfortable to be an American in the Middle East" in 1967, he felt very welcome upon his return. Indeed, "a year later as some of us returned," he wrote, "we learned that the government authorities had called in our Egyptian colleagues and asked, 'What did we do to offend the missionaries? Please let them know that we know the difference between politicians and missionaries and that we appreciate their work. Tell them that they will always be welcome.'"[174] Egyptian authorities appeared to recognize that the American Presbyterian missionaries were Egypt's allies and advocates, and that the missionaries (regardless of the influence they either exerted or lacked) were prepared to challenge the policies of the U.S. government and, more narrowly, the American church.

After 1967, the missionaries who returned to Egypt consciously focused on service to Christian communities and more pointedly on the "life of the church." They did so even as private foundations, nongovernmental organizations, and international agencies were proliferating as providers of "development aid," and as church groups of various national origins and orientations (such as German Lutherans) were becoming more involved with the Evangelical Church.[175] American Presbyterians were no longer the sole partners of the Evangelical community, nor were they the Evangelical Church's only benefactors. Moreover, even as some American Presbyterians were pursuing social justice issues at home and abroad, interest in foreign missions was further declining among mainline Protestants. This disengagement was reflected in the way that leading research institutions began to eliminate faculty lines for mission historians and individual church congregations withdrew from foreign mission activities.[176] These changes left American Presbyterian leaders and missionaries to mull over what the church's "errand to the world" should now be, and where it should go.[177]

Conversions and Transformations

I recall an incident in Assiut [around 1912] during the holy
season of Ramadan, a time when Moslems fast during the
day and spend nights eating and visiting friends. Father and
I were walking through the streets during this season and
a stranger, an Arab, came out of his door and invited us to
come into his home and share his supper. While we were
eating, he described a scene he had witnessed during his
childhood, the pursuit of the first Christian missionary in
Assiut—a Scot named John Hogg [1833–1885]—by a mob. He
had been insulted, jeered, and stoned by the crowd, but Dr.
Hogg, we were told, never turned aside, never raised a hand
to protect himself, or even showed anger. He simply went
his way, straight and dignified. At this point in the story, our
host stopped, looked toward heaven, and exclaimed, "I hope
to see that man in Paradise." As we walked home, I turned
over his remark in my mind and said to Father, "Dad, you've
always taught me that I must believe in the divinity of Christ
if I hope for salvation. Does our Moslem friend have any
chance at all of seeing Dr. Hogg in heaven?" Father thought a
moment. "I'm not at all sure that he won't," he said.

—William U. McClenahan, *G.P.* (1974)

None of the [Muslim] boys in my group was ever baptized
but I am morally certain that in the lives of them there was
a new understanding of God and a new realization of the
meaning of prayer and an appreciation too of the message
of Christ. What the good Lord will do with them on the
day of judgment is not for me to say. Whatever may be the
kind of heaven to which I shall be admitted after death I
shall confidently expect to see my Moslem friends there
too. Indeed I believe that I am a broader and much more
understanding Christian because of my intimate contacts
with these Moslems who believe as firmly in God as I do
and who pray diligently or more so than I do.

—James K. Quay, "Service in Egypt
from 1919 to 1948" (1975)

WHAT HAPPENED

Viewing the long stretch of the mission's history, from 1854 to 1967, four periods stand out. The first extended from 1854 to 1882, and began when American Presbyterians, inspired by the idea of universal evangelization, initiated their mission in Egypt. Constrained by social strictures against conversion from Islam, the Americans focused mostly on Copts and set out to trigger what they hoped would be a reformation of Coptic Orthodoxy. They slowly drew a following and began to organize the Egyptian Evangelical Church, which emphasized the primacy of the Arabic Bible for worship and encouraged laypeople to participate in church affairs. In the long run, their efforts spurred Coptic Orthodox leaders to rise to the competition and enact reforms—such as incorporating Arabic sermons into collective worship—as a way of retaining followers.

The second period began with the British Occupation of 1882 and ended with World War I. This was the mission's colonial moment—its period of greatest expansion and self-assertion. The mission intensified work among Muslims but also, thanks to the growing number of women in the mission, among females. The mission enjoyed not just the protection of the British authorities and the advantages of the Capitulations but also robust financial support from the church in the United States. This was the period when the mission had the greatest freedom to maneuver. Thus it was possible, in ways that later became inconceivable, for a missionary to stop in a Delta village and distribute tracts to local Muslims.

The third period, from 1918 to 1945, was an age of chronic anxiety. The mission faced economic retrenchment as a result of the world Depression, so that the mission was forced to reduce its own size. Also, beginning in the late 1920s, Muslim nationalists seized on the Arabic periodical press to publicize a series of missionary "crimes" involving the conversion of Muslim youths and what it claimed was defamation of Islam. New organizations like the YMMA and the Muslim Brotherhood emerged, copying some features of Christian missionary organizations (such as their youth clubs) while urging the government to restrain Christian missions. The Montreux Convention, signed in 1937, began a phasing out of the legal and fiscal privileges that had helped the mission to flourish. By the time World War II began, the Egyptian government was restricting missionary visas and imposing regulations on mission schools that ranged from the details of sanitation codes to the content of curricula.

The fourth period, from 1945 to 1967, which included the Free Officers coup and revolution of 1952, was one of Egyptianization, meaning the steady assertion of policies intended to reduce foreign influence and place Egyptians in charge. It was also a period shaped by the Arab-Israeli conflict. With its ever more elaborate bureaucracy and (after the rise of Nasser) increasingly authoritarian tendencies, the Egyptian government invoked laws to regulate which missionaries could get residency permits, what and how mission schools could teach, where Christians could worship, who could run institutions, and even how much playground space a school had to provide for each child. The greatest moment of reckoning for the missionaries occurred in 1956, when the government enforced a law that required Christian mission schools to hire Muslim teachers to teach Islam to Muslim students on their premises. Another law, enacted in 1958 but imposed in 1962, required the mission to place Egyptian directors in charge of its institutions. Amid these changes the mission accelerated the transfer of properties to the control of the Egyptian Evangelical Church. As anti-American sentiment intensified near the end of 1966, the American missionaries voted to dissolve their Missionary Association, months before the outbreak of the Six-Day War prompted Americans to evacuate Egypt.

A MISSION TRANSFORMED

In 2006, the eighth volume of *The Cambridge History of Christianity* appeared. Titled *World Christianities*, it covers the century from 1815 to 1914 and dedicates a third of its 683 pages to "the new Christian churches outside Europe" that were the product of missionary efforts. One of its editors observes that assessing Christian history during this period was hard because so much of religious belief "lies in the human heart beyond historical observation and generalization." He concludes, "It is difficult to define a criterion for the success of religious faith; how many Christians got to heaven is known to God alone."[1] The editor's remark may reflect an assumption that the history of world Christianities has had a bearing primarily on Christians and their inner religion. The experiences of the American Presbyterians in Egypt suggest instead that missionary encounters, as episodes in world history, broadly affected institutions, social practices, and ideas, exerting influences that went well beyond the range of professing Christian communities.

In Egypt, the American missionary enterprise had a strong impact on Muslim communities. This was not only because missionaries provided schooling and health care to Muslims who sought their services, but also because missionaries inadvertently stimulated forms of social activism that sharpened Muslim political consciousness. At the same time, and in tandem with other Protestant and Catholic societies, the American mission accelerated a nineteenth-century contest for Coptic allegiances that inspired reforms in the culture of Coptic Orthodoxy, gave rise to a new Evangelical Church, and shaped a pluralistic culture of Christianity in Egypt. Conditions in Egypt also changed the American Presbyterians, by forcing them to rethink the methods and goals of Christian mission, to define a philosophy of religious liberty, and to cultivate relations with British Protestants that grew into an ecumenical movement. In sum, the counting of baptisms and bodies in churches cannot alone measure the impact of an encounter that elicited striking cultural "conversions" or transformations among Egyptians, Americans, and others.

Kenneth Cragg has described the story of Muslim converts to Christianity as a "saga of the few," and if one thinks in terms of Egypt's aggregate population, the same phrase could apply to Egyptians who turned from Coptic Orthodoxy to Protestantism.[2] In 1859, five years after the Americans had launched their mission, missionaries claimed four adherents of a Reformed (i.e., Protestant) creed: these were the first members of the budding Evangelical community. Almost a century later, in 1957, when the Egyptian Evangelical Church became independent from its American sponsor, American Presbyterians pointed to an Evangelical Church membership of 26,663 official communicants, representing 196 congregations.[3] Considered next to Egypt's total Coptic population, estimated at nearly two million in 1960, or next to the total Muslim population, estimated at just over twenty-four million for that same year, the Evangelical Church's membership was minute.[4] The size remains small even if one acknowledges that many more Copts attended Evangelical services than official membership tallies suggest.[5] On the other hand, the scope and impact of the missionary encounter appears much larger if one includes the number of Muslims, Copts, and others outside the Evangelical community who attended the mission's schools; read its publications; attended its Vacation Bible programs, Sunday schools (including its "Street Sunday Schools," which offered poor children makeshift instruction in urban alleyways and courtyards), and public meetings; sought treatment in its clinics and hospitals; and participated in its rural development programs. The encounter also had reverberations for Egyptians at some remove, including those who listened to imams, priests, journalists, and community activists when they declaimed against the mission's evangelism.

The history of the American mission in Egypt was not merely a history of religion and religious practice: it was a history of ideas, and ideas have power. That may explain why some local leaders reacted so viscerally to the mission's activities. The American Presbyterians believed, for example, that literacy should be universal; even peasants should read. They then went about devising pedagogies and literatures for the semiliterate, even as they tried to appeal to social elites. Just as radically for Egypt, they believed that women belonged in church as much as men, that women should study the Bible as much as men, and that worship should be genuinely collective, with men, women, and children gathering together. Hanna F. Wissa reflected that his mother, the nationalist Esther Fahmy Wissa (1895–1990), flourished in the Pressly Memorial Institute, the mission's college for girls in Assiut, because "The missionaries encouraged their pupils to debate and to think and to give their opinions without fear."[6] They encouraged laypeople to participate in running the church, and presented their own Missionary Association as a model for government, by drawing up a constitution and charter of rights that provided for regular elections. In 1954, when the mission celebrated its centennial in Egypt, the president of the Missionary Association was a woman: this was Davida Finney, who helped establish the rural literacy program that later evolved into CEOSS.[7] (Finney was not the first woman to hold this elected position; several women had held this distinction before her.)[8] Over the years, Egyptian Copts and Muslims alike found many of the missionaries' ideas and practices compelling, and that is perhaps why the missionaries seemed so subversive and threatening to Coptic Orthodox patriarchs and to men like Hasan al-Banna, the founder of the Muslim Brotherhood.

In 1935, the missionary J. R. Alexander wrote that the Evangelical Church was "really a small reformed Coptic Church in Egypt, with a sprinkling of converted Jewish, Greek, Syrian, and Muslim elements."[9] Although converts from Islam were only one part of this "sprinkling," American missionaries had devoted considerable effort to the evangelization of Muslims, especially in the fifty years between the British Occupation of 1882 and the rise of anti-missionary agitation in the early 1930s. In 1953 H. E. Philips, who had joined the American mission in 1908 as a strong advocate of Muslim evangelization, looked back on this effort when he published *Blessed Be Egypt My People* (referring to Isaiah 19:25). In this volume, Philips paid tribute to the approximately two hundred Christian converts from Islam who were still living in Egypt, and profiled six individuals, including the brothers Mikhail and Kamil Mansur. Philips expressed hope that the stories would inspire readers and show them the "almost insuperable difficulties that face those who seek to evangelize Muhammadans."[10] At the same time, pleading for the worth of an effort that appeared to have had such modest yields, he announced to his readers that there were many Egyptian believers in Christ who kept their identities secret because they feared the wrath of their Muslim community.[11]

One year after Philips published his tribute to converts from Islam, S. A. Morrison, a member of the CMS mission that had dedicated itself to Muslim evangelization in Egypt since 1882, surveyed conditions for Christian missionaries in the Middle East. "So great is the psychological strain to which the baptized convert from Islam is subjected, and so complete the severance from the community which follows his public confession of faith," Morrison wrote, "that some Christian leaders advocate the cessation, at least for the present, of the baptism of converts, and prefer that the 'followers of Jesus' remain as a leavening force among their own people."[12] Two years later, in *The Call of the Minaret*, Kenneth Cragg also grappled with the ethics of baptizing Muslims, recognizing that they would be vulnerable not only to accusations of apostasy but also to charges of "cultural displacement" or "repudiation."[13]

This idea of refraining from Muslim baptism, with the social interests of Muslims at heart, came out of an interpretation of the missionary landscape that had been many years in the making. During the interwar years Morrison had cooperated closely with American Presbyterians on the Inter-Mission Council and had helped draft a statement of religious liberty with other Protestant missionaries in Egypt in 1932. But by the time he wrote in 1954—six years after the UN issued the UDHR—he had no illusions about the direction in which Egypt was going, and no expectation that Egyptian laws would be liberalized to lift sanctions against leaving Islam. It was not merely that Egypt was institutionalizing Islam, Morrison knew; it was also that the Christian missionary enterprise had been so closely associated with British imperialism and Western colonial hegemony, that Egypt's search for national sovereignty demanded a withdrawal of certain perquisites (such as the right to set school curricula or to acquire residency permits and visas) that had enabled foreign missions to flourish. Egypt's search for sovereignty also entailed an affirmation of community borders that drew on the tested frameworks of Islamic tradition. Once an advantage for Christian missions in the late nineteenth century, Western imperialism had become a liability by the mid-twentieth.[14]

With missionaries pushed onto the defensive, the ground was prepared for a new form of Christian-Muslim encounter. This was what became known, in the second half of the twentieth century, as "interfaith dialogue," and it assumed two things: first, that participants would begin from positions of faith, and second, that participants would aim not for persuasion and capitulation but for mutual self-affirmation.[15] After 1956, Kenneth Cragg became most closely associated with a Christian variant of interfaith dialogue known as "respectful witness" to Muslims, and this idea gained an enthusiastic following among some of the younger American Presbyterians in Egypt, who regarded themselves as Cragg's "disciples."[16] Yet however esteemed "respectful witness" was among the American Presbyterians in the late 1950s and 1960s, missionary accounts from this period, as well as conversations with former missionaries, give little evidence that much formal dialogue with Muslims actually occurred.

Respectful witness was nevertheless important to the American Presbyterians as a theoretical framework for approaching Muslims because it signaled a readiness to discuss Christianity openly and without deception. The American Presbyterians had no intention of pursuing "stealth missions" as some American evangelicals (for example, the Southern Baptists) later did in parts of the world that restricted missionary activity.[17] Nor did the Presbyterians recruit volunteers from America to come to Egypt on tourist visas for evangelical "relays," as the interdenominational North Africa Mission (NAM) tried to do in Algeria after 1977, when the Algerian government revoked that organization's legal status.[18] On the contrary, like the Egyptian Evangelical Church and CEOSS, the American Presbyterians aimed to respect and conform to Egyptian laws, even if they privately wished that some laws might be changed.

In the century after 1854, American missionaries had often called Egyptian Christians (Orthodox Copts and Evangelicals alike) "timorous" or "timid" for refusing to evangelize among Muslims.[19] They had remained largely blind to the long history of *dhimmi*s in Islamic societies.[20] But by the 1950s American missionaries and mission leaders were finally acknowledging how perilous it could be for a native Christian to evangelize in an Islamic society. Donald Black recalled, for example, that when he visited Egypt in 1956, as secretary of the foreign mission board of the UPCNA, one of the American mission schools had recently dealt with the case of "a Christian [Egyptian] girl student [who] had witnessed her faith to another [Muslim] student. The latter reported this talk to her parents, who then went to the government, and the Christian student had to be expelled. Her education was finished. The school was reprimanded for letting this happen. The schools were not to be considered instruments of evangelism."[21] Perhaps the Americans in the 1950s were finally recognizing the dangers of Muslim evangelization now that their own visas and residency permits were in jeopardy—and now that Egypt could so easily deport any missionary who disturbed the government's sense of public order.

Charles R. Watson, who had resigned from the foreign mission board of the UPCNA in 1916 in order to launch AUC, had steadily insisted that American Presbyterians should respect Egyptian laws as a measure of good faith and citizenship. Feeling no need to rack up converts,[22] Watson set out to make his university into a bridge linking the United States (with its Christian society) to Egypt (with its Islamic society). Earlier in his career as foreign mission secretary, he had likened missionary work in Egypt to a modern crusade, but by the 1930s his tone had changed. In 1937, addressing his "Moslem Friends" in the book *What Is This Moslem World*, he apologized for the "harsh and unfair" things that Christians like himself had written about Islam in the past, and vowed to pursue instead a "gospel of love" that would demonstrate Christianity selflessly, and in "courteous and fraternal spirit and in the fullest cooperation with your own progressive leaders."[23] Watson later confided to a colleague that he was hurt by the review of his book that appeared in a Christian missionary forum "where it was stated that I did not recognize the weakness of Islam and its need for Christianity."[24] Watson struggled, to the end of his days in Egypt, to define a mission that could be intrinsically Christian while respecting the social and legal principles of an Islamic state.

Writing in 1994 about his own missionary career in Egypt, which had stretched from 1952 to 1970, John G. Lorimer reflected, "No Christian missionary, I believe, can serve for long in a Muslim society without experiencing ambivalence about his relation to Muslims and the validity of his mission in a Muslim world." Lorimer then evoked Charles R. Watson, who "had, in his younger days, spoken of Islam in the derogatory language typical of the era" but who by the end of his life "viewed the relationship differently." Lorimer also quoted from a eulogy that was delivered upon Watson's death in 1948: "Charles Watson," the eulogist had declared, "was not one of those who saw in the Christian church everything good and in Islam everything bad. He preferred to call himself one of those who saw everything good in the God and Father of our Lord Jesus Christ, not a little of whose goodness had overflowed into the Muslim tradition.'" Writing in 2006, Lorimer reflected that the "theological transitions" of Charles R. Watson closely matched his own, even though by the time Lorimer joined the mission in 1952, Presbyterian missionaries "more or less held [AUC and Watson] at arms length."[25]

Addressing an audience of American Presbyterian missionaries, theologians, and seminarians in 1994, Lorimer tried to summarize some of the legacies of the American mission in Egypt, as well as its influences on Muslim society. He chose to pay tribute, not to converts like Kamil Mansur (whom Lorimer had known)[26] or to unnamed "secret believers," but rather to forthright Muslims who also expressed admiration for Christ and Christianity. Thus he cited "Sheikh Zaki who taught many of us our first Arabic, saying that he thought himself to be a Christian. He often attended church services because he appreciated the messages, and especially the excellent Arabic of the Egyptian preachers. But to be baptized and join the church, that he would not consider." He also recalled Miss Fatima Hamza, "a devout Muslima," who graduated from the ACG and dedicated her career to that institution. "I did not hear her say it," Lorimer wrote," but I can imagine her thinking to herself, 'I, as a faithful Muslima, can exemplify Christianity in my life and service quite as faithfully as any Christian.'" Lorimer concluded, "I know that the Christian message has been heard by many Muslims in the Middle East, and found an acceptance if not in the letter, certainly in the spirit."[27]

The idea that a person could be Christian in spirit without necessarily acknowledging a Christian identity, and that religious labels were of secondary importance, was one that Charles R. Watson had articulated in 1929. Contributing (along with S. A. Morrison, James K. Quay, and others) to the Inter-Mission Council report on the "General Political Situation [in Egypt] as Affecting Christ's Kingdom," Watson reflected on a recurring missionary concern—the paucity of converts from Islam and the social barriers to such conversion. He declared, "On restudying the life of Jesus I am amazed to discover the extent to which he dealt with human need as such and how infrequently he pressed the issue having to do with profession." Watson added, "I am perfectly ready to stand for courageous confession of Christ once the content is to be found within the life, but I think with the Moslem we must begin with transforming his life."[28]

A Muslim observing Watson's career in Egypt, and the history of the American missionary encounter at large, might point to the reciprocal process by which American Christians consciously or unconsciously embraced Islamic values as a result of their contact with Muslims. James K. Quay acknowledges this possibility in his memoir, called "A Missionary Journey," that he assembled from diary entries about his years in Egypt. In a diary entry from 1930 that he reproduced in this memoir, Quay described a conversation he had had with a Muslim student: "Ismail had just made a beautiful statement of his own concept of prayer when I said to him, 'Look out now, Ismail, we will make a Christian out of you if you keep traveling in that direction. In fact I think I would call you a Christian Moslem now.' He replied with a delightful twinkle in his eye, 'Do you know what I would call you? I would call you a Moslem Christian.'"[29] When Quay had first arrived in Egypt in 1919, he had been keen on the idea of evangelizing

Muslims and professed admiration for Samuel M. Zwemer.[30] But following heartfelt exchanges with Muslims, Quay's ideas substantially changed: while he continued to identify himself as a missionary, he was increasingly uncertain about who was giving witness to whom.

Quay's own mission was a mission transformed. Years later, after retiring from the vice presidency of Princeton Theological Seminary, Quay described an exchange that he had after a YMCA dinner lecture in Wilmington, Delaware. Asked how many converts from Islam he had made during his career, Quay responded none, but then changed his mind. "No. . . . Whenever you expose a man to the influence of Christ and as a result, some aspect of the man's character is changed for the better, you have converted that area of his life to the Gospel."[31]

The sons of R. S. McClenahan (1871–1949), who ran the mission's Assiut College before joining Charles R. Watson to start AUC, voiced a similar idea regarding their father's encounter with Islam and Muslims. The elder son, William McClenahan, grew up in Assiut where most people were friendly but where there were a few Muslim "haters in the streets"; these, he recalled, would sometimes shout "Khanzir! Khanzir!" ("Pig! Pig!") upon seeing Christian missionaries "and pitch a stone or tin can" at them. He also recalled the exchanges that his father had with "Sheikh Ahmed," his Muslim Arabic teacher.

> I can still see him in his daily afternoon sessions with Sheik Ahmed sitting in his study reading passages, alternately, of the Bible and the Koran in Arabic, with endless digressions into Commentaries— Father, in shirtsleeves, bent over a book; the sheik, curled up on a divan, enveloped in a cloud of cigarette smoke. Close friends, they bitterly debated every question of theology, disagreeing heatedly over the merits of Islam and Christianity. They would spend hours analyzing the characters of great men—Christ, Moses, Mohammed, Saladin, Harun El Rashid, St. Paul, and Richard the Lion Hearted. Forever afterwards, when they met they embraced each other with the warmest affection, each man firmly rooted in his own beliefs.[32]

Meanwhile, the younger son, John L. McClenahan, who grew up in cosmopolitan Cairo, recalled of his father, "He practiced his (semi) Calvinistic Christianity rather liberally ('I never shave with hot water because I don't want to become dependent on luxury'). We held family prayers on our knees in the drawing room. His intense studies of Islam and the Arabic culture touched him so deeply that I could imagine him converting to Islam, moved by the beauty, the poetry, and the precision of the language and the simplicity of its doctrine."[33]

John L. McClenahan took great pride in noting that the Egyptian government eventually bestowed on his father the "Order of Ismail," the highest tribute given to foreigners for service to Egypt.[34]

In 1980, the missionary Martha Roy told a story about a Muslim graduate of the ACG who had approached her sometime around 1956, when the Americans were deciding how to respond to the Egyptian government's demands about religious instruction. The former student chided her by saying, "You talk about love and you say you love us, but you can't really because our religion is part of us; if you reject that part of us, you reject the most important part of us."[35] Roy seemed to acknowledge that the "gospel of love" (as Charles R. Watson had called it) meant loving Muslims, and loving Muslims meant coming to terms with their Muslim identities.

During their century and more in Egypt, the American missionaries' attitudes toward Coptic Orthodoxy also underwent a transformation. Writing in 1897, Andrew Watson had compared the Coptic Orthodox Church to a mummy while John Hogg had called it "embalmed" and had accused it of "entombing" the Bible in a dead language (liturgical Coptic).[36] But Lorimer, in 1994, looked back on the missionaries' record and noted a different aspect of Hogg's encounter with Coptic Orthodoxy, by describing a meeting that occurred with the Coptic Orthodox patriarch some time during or shortly after the U.S. Civil War (1861–65). During this face-to-face encounter, Hogg reportedly said that Americans, unlike Orthodox priests, were preaching the "pure gospel." "Pure Gospel!" the pope was said to retort. "Have the Americans got the gospel? Why don't they teach it to their slaves if they have it? Why does brother go to war against brother? Why have they come to Egypt with their fine talk? We had the gospel before America was born. We don't need them to teach us. We know the gospel better than they do."[37]

A century later, in the mid-1960s, the American Presbyterians were much more inclined than their predecessors had been to take the patriarch's criticism to heart. The missionaries and mission executives were becoming involved in the civil rights movement—participating, for example, in voter registration drives in Mississippi—and were pressuring companies like Eastman Kodak in New York to increase its hiring of African Americans. The UPCUSA (as the UPCNA's successor was then known) was also beginning to use divestment as a strategy for challenging South African apartheid.[38] Bernard Quick, one of the missionaries uprooted by the Six-Day War in 1967 (and a man who later became inspired by Latin American liberation theology), recalled his career in Egypt and remarked in 1975, "The church in America is still basically a racist institution. The white churches are part of the de facto segregation that is a part of American society."[39] His comment reflected a vein of self-criticism that had been deepening among the American Presbyterians for some time.

By the 1960s, American missionaries were no longer seeking to draw Coptic Orthodox Christians into the Evangelical Church. The spirit of ecumenism, which was extending to Catholics as well, had ended the contest for Copts that had been so important in the late nineteenth century. The missionary Marjorie Dye, who spent her career working with CEOSS in literacy and social development projects, wrote along these lines in 1979: "We do not lure people from one church to another, but try to help them to become better Christians in their own churches."[40] Thus if the Evangelical Church did not expand in the second half of the twentieth century, this may have been partly because of the comity agreement that led churches to desist from growing at each other's expense.

In the second half of the twentieth century, and notwithstanding the growth of ecumenical relations, Evangelicals remained particularly sensitive to the condescension of Coptic Orthodox ecclesiastical leaders and on these grounds developed a closer relationship with Coptic Catholics who felt much the same. Amin Fahim, a Catholic active in the Christian Association of Upper Egypt, described the situation in 1987 by writing that "the Orthodox take their revenge on the Catholics who formerly treated them as heretics and schismatics; the Catholics and Protestants seek to affirm themselves by counterattacking and by cultivating their own identities; and that is without accounting for the internal struggles going on within each church." Fahim also noted that "If the Coptic Orthodox feel that they are second-class citizens, then the Catholics and Protestants feel that they are third-class citizens."[41] John G. Lorimer recalled, too, the remark that Shenouda III, the Coptic Orthodox patriarch, made to a visiting American Presbyterian church official in the mid-1980s: referring to the Evangelical Church, Shenouda reportedly said to the American, "Well, I see that you have come to visit one of your branches."[42] Presbyterians and Evangelicals appear to have interpreted Shenouda's comment as an aspersion upon the Evangelical Church's cultural (and perhaps also financial) independence, and by extension upon its Egyptian integrity.

Conversations with Evangelical pastors in 2005 suggest that relations between Evangelicals and Catholics are stronger and more cordial than ever, but that ambivalence and mistrust toward the Coptic Orthodox hierarchy continues.[43] Perhaps this explains why, in 2004, Evangelical leaders voted to change the church's official name from the Coptic Evangelical Church to the Evangelical Presbyterian Church of Egypt.[44] (By this time, the Evangelical community was still small, with its leaders estimating a quarter to half a million followers—though not all of them official church members—relative to Egypt's population of 77.5 million.)[45] The removal of the word "Coptic" (which the church had added in 1957, in the aftermath of the Suez Crisis, as a bid to establish its nationalist credentials) signaled a conscious distancing from Coptic Orthodoxy and a sense that Egyptian citizenship was more important than Copticity. Meanwhile, in 2005, leaders of CEOSS were supporting projects to benefit both Muslims and Christians and to improve the lot of Egyptians at large. CEOSS wanted to promote an Egyptian culture of citizenship, its director explained, not a culture in which Christians were *dhimmis*.[46]

In 1932, when *Re-Thinking Missions*, also known as the Hocking or Layman's Report appeared, several members of the American mission in Egypt expressed discomfort with the report's recognition of merit in non-Christian religions, as well as its advocacy of interfaith relations built on "a common search for truth."[47] Upon its debut, this report sharpened the line between liberal and conservative Protestants. But by the 1960s, Presbyterians were approaching missions in much the way that the report had suggested, that is, in a liberal ecumenical mode that emphasized social service and cooperation outside denominational boundaries.[48] Certainly in Egypt, the Presbyterians were engaging in rural literacy projects while embracing ideals of ecumenism (vis-à-vis other Christians) and respectful witness (vis-à-vis Muslims).

If the American Presbyterians in Egypt moved toward an increasingly liberal version of Protestantism, then this was not only because of developments in the home church (which had begun, for example, to ordain women as ministers in the late 1950s) but also because their experiences in Egypt convinced them that religious traditions could stifle and oppress and that departures from social conventions could lead to social progress. Charles R. Watson had been praising religious liberalism since the 1930s, when he was president of AUC. In a 1938 letter to his friend in the ecumenical movement, John R. Mott, Watson expressed concern lest the Protestant missionary movement shift "to the fundamentalist camp."[49] In other letters he worried about Muslim conservatives and was especially eager to see Muslim liberalism take hold.[50] Watson thought of liberalism as a move away from convention and a route to social change, and believed that social change in Egypt could foster the revision of everything from religious liberty (could a Muslim convert to Christianity?) to gender relations (could a woman sing on a public stage and retain her honor, or could young men and women socialize licitly?).[51] In the 1930s, Watson was ready to "welcome deviation and unorthodoxy as agencies of growth"—something that William Ernest Hocking, in a letter to the missionary S. A. Morrison, had identified as a feature of progressive modernity.[52] Watson anticipated, once again, some of the mission's later transitions.

By 1964, in a book that otherwise focused on the challenges facing postcolonial missions, a prominent missiologist lamented the ways in which a liberal-conservative divide was cleaving American missions abroad. He noted that this gap had begun to affect understandings of evangelicalism. Whereas the term "Evangelical" had once been synonymous with "Protestant," he wrote, "Today unfortunately some persons and organizations claim the word in a sectarian and partisan spirit, and in their exclusiveness they deny it to others who may disagree with them in some particular. They tend to call others 'liberals' and 'modernists' and to oppose the Ecumenical Movement and agencies associated with it."[53] Sectarianism among Protestants was destroying what this observer saw as the unity of the missionary movement.

When asked, "What has the term 'evangelical' meant to you?" Kenneth E. Nolin, who worked as a missionary in Egypt from 1952 to 1970 (with a hiatus following the evacuation of Americans in the Six-Day War), answered that he associated the term with the Arabic word al-Injil, meaning the New Testament or gospel. Referring to the fact that the Qur'an recognizes al-Injil as a sacred scripture that is part of Islam's heritage, he added, "I like the sense of contact with the people of Islam and their Qur'an that it [the word *injil*] gives, as is also true of the word *Allah* [God], used in the Arabic Bible."[54] Meanwhile, when asked whether American Presbyterians were still evangelicals, John G. Lorimer answered, "We are reluctant to surrender the title 'evangelical.' I am sure that most of my colleagues, and I myself, consider themselves 'evangelical' in the best sense of that word, as distinguished from 'fundamentalist.' The two words are sometimes mistakenly used as synonyms."[55]

By the time the Missionary Association disbanded in 1967, the American Presbyterian missionaries were liberals in important ways. They were "open-hearted" (in this case, toward the diverse Muslim and Christian populations of Egypt) and "open to the reception of new ideas or proposals of reform," in two dictionary senses of the term.[56] They were also open to the selection of women as church elders and to ordination of women as ministers in ways that most Egyptian Evangelicals were not.[57] The word "liberal" derives from the Latin term *liber*, meaning "free." A century of ruminating on the need for religious liberty and the freedom to profess beliefs that ran counter to tradition had transformed the missionaries into freethinkers of a kind.

AMERICA AND THE AMERICANS IN EGYPT

The American Presbyterians' relationship with the U.S. government changed significantly during the mission's history in Egypt. When the missionaries arrived in Egypt in 1854, they looked on the U.S. government as their ally and possible protector. Thus in 1861, through their intermediary the American consul, they were able to call on Abraham Lincoln to write to Said Pasha, the ruler of Egypt, when one of their protégés was imprisoned.[58] When former U.S. president Ulysses S. Grant and his wife, Julia, visited Cairo in 1878, the missionary Anna Young Thompson met them at their hotel and took Mrs. Grant to visit a mission girls' school.[59] In 1910, the missionary R. S. McClenahan (later dean of AUC) was appointed to escort Theodore Roosevelt from Khartoum to Assiut, following the former president's hunting expedition in the southern Sudan. William McClenahan later recalled, "Mr. Roosevelt had dinner in our home [in Assiut]. I saw him as he bit into a piece of Mother's mince pie, his whole face exploding into a grin. 'Bully!' he said. 'That's bully!' I loved him ever after."[60] These examples suggest how well positioned and socially at ease the American missionaries once were in relating to the American powerful.

The first big rupture in the missionaries' relationship with the U.S. government came when President Harry S. Truman recognized the state of Israel in 1948. This was also the first time that the American Presbyterians found themselves uncomfortable as Americans in Egypt, and the first time that they felt obliged to speak out against U.S. policy.[61] Their dissatisfaction with U.S. government policy toward the Arab-Israeli conflict had lasting effects on Presbyterian church policy toward the Middle East and has continued to influence the way that Presbyterians narrate the history of their Middle East missions.[62]

Charles R. Watson called AUC a "bridge of friendliness"[63] between the United States and Egypt but that metaphor applies equally to the American Presbyterian mission, as well as to the Cairo Central YMCA, which developed through American initiative. This bridge carried people and ideas. Indeed, the accounts of the American Presbyterians are full of scattered references to Egyptians who passed through American institutions and later went to the United States, some settling permanently, others staying for stints of work or study. Perhaps those who encountered the Americans in Egypt had a familiarity with the United States that made migration more conceivable or welcome. Egyptians who went to America included Warda Barakat, one of the first to take communion with the Presbyterians in the early 1860s. She settled in Illinois, as did Suweilim Sidhom, the

最號第二月十七民壹福漳集大記週三醫福章開來阿巴開醫大
二十年國將晉東在會念平十院晉州設華美任士學英

THIRTY·YEARS IN CHANGCHOW A Beloved Physician
BY C.G.SPARHAM

7.1. "Thirty Years in Changchow: A Beloved Physician," photograph taken at the retirement party of Ahmed Fahmy in Zhangzhou, south Fukien district, southern China, December 12, 1918. Reproduced from London Missionary Society/Council for World Mission Archives, School of Oriental and African Studies, University of London.

first Evangelical Church missionary to the southern Sudan, a century later.[64] Emigrants also included people like Eva Habib al-Misri, an ACG alumna (who won the Andrew Watson prize for academic excellence) and the first female graduate of AUC. Upon graduating from AUC, around 1930, she went to Smith College in Massachusetts on a full scholarship, but then returned to live in Egypt, where she worked with her mentor, Huda Sha'rawi, in the Egyptian feminist movement. In the early 1960s, Eva Habib al-Misri emigrated again and settled with her husband in New York City and later Princeton, New Jersey.[65] Another Egyptian who passed through Princeton was a Muslim identified in James K. Quay's memoir only as "Mustafa." Sometime in the early 1930s, the young Mustafa went on a YMCA camping trip to Sinai and declared that "he was a man of science and didn't believe in prayer." But as a result of watching some of the other boys praying on the sand, he began to perform his Muslim prayers regularly and then persuaded other Muslims to do likewise. ("I was glad to see it," Quay wrote, "because it indicated the outreach of the human heart for God no matter by what name it was called.") This Mustafa came to the United States for advanced study at Princeton (and visited Quay at Princeton Theological Seminary), but eventually returned to Egypt where he became a "high official in the diplomatic section of the government of Egypt" and later a professor at Cairo University.[66]

Even Ahmed Fahmy (1861–1933), the Muslim youth whom the Americans baptized in Cairo in 1877, found himself in the United States. After fleeing to Scotland in 1878 and then studying medicine in Edinburgh, Ahmed began a long career as a missionary in Zhangzhou, southern China, where he established the town's first hospital. (One of his successors later wrote that "Foreigners, then in the 1880s, were not welcomed generally [in Zhangzhou], and Dr. Fahmy was stoned on occasion.")[67] Ahmed eventually married an American missionary who was working in the same Chinese city. Denied the consular protection granted in China to British subjects (most egregiously, during the Boxer Uprising), Ahmed managed to secure U.S. citizenship through his marriage to an American.[68] Upon his retirement in 1919, Ahmed and his wife sailed from Hong Kong to Vancouver and then traveled across the continental United States so that they could visit relatives in New Jersey before crossing the Atlantic to Britain.[69]

The mission historian Kenneth S. Latourette wrote in 1944 that Christianity was "nearly nineteen and a half centuries" old but still "seemed to be only in its early stages. Not until the nineteenth and twentieth centuries did Christianity become really worldwide in its geographic extent."[70] As participants in a worldwide missionary movement, the American Presbyterians in Egypt were well aware that Christianity was becoming a globally diffuse religion. By the time they left Egypt in 1967, they were aware, too, that the United States was just one small part of this world and that it had no monopoly on "true gospel."

Notes

CHAPTER 1
THE AMERICAN MISSIONARY ENCOUNTER IN EGYPT

1. Philips, *Blessed Be Egypt My People*, 7; Jamison, *The United Presbyterian Story*, 198.

2. Russell, *Creating the New Egyptian Woman*, 114; Pollard, *Nurturing the Nation*, 106–14.

3. Ener, *Managing Egypt's Poor and the Politics of Benevolence*, 102–4; Hasan, *Christians versus Muslims in Modern Egypt*, 6, 71–78; Herrera, "'The Soul of a Nation,'" 275–94.

4. Rodgers, *Atlantic Crossings*, 1–2.

5. Makdisi, *Artillery of Heaven*.

6. Grabill, *Protestant Diplomacy and the Near East*.

7. Sharkey, "The American Mission in Egypt and the Arab-Israeli Conflict."

8. Sharkey, "Muslim Apostasy, Christian Conversion, and Religious Freedom in Egypt." More generally, Mayer, *Islam and Human Rights*, 132–33.

9. Little, *American Orientalism*; McAlister, *Epic Encounters*; Kuklick, *Puritans in Babylon*.

10. Lockman, *Contending Visions of the Middle East*, 96–97; Stanley, "Church, State, and the Hierarchy of 'Civilization,'" 61–62.

11. Beth Baron, "Women's Voluntary Social Welfare Organizations in Egypt," in *Gender, Religion, and Change in the Middle East*, ed. Okkenhaug and Flaskerud, 85–102; Tejirian, "Faith of Our Fathers."

12. Robert, *American Women in Mission*; Beaver, *American Protestant Women in World Mission*; Boyd and Brackenridge, *Presbyterian Women in America*, 159–73; Robert, "From Missions to Beyond Missions."

13. Presbyterian Historical Society (henceforth PHS) RG 209-2-30: Anna B. Criswell Papers, E. R. Balleny to Mary Young, Assiut, October 12, 1933; PHS RG 209-3-30: W. B. Jamison Papers, Jamison to Mills Taylor, Tanta, April 4, 1936.

14. Robert L. Tignor, conversation with the author, New York City, October 1, 2004.

15. B. Porter, *The Absent-Minded Imperialists*.

16. See Ben Jelloun, *French Hospitality*, 6.

17. Elder, *Vindicating a Vision*, 30.

18. John G. Lorimer, conversations with the author, Pasadena, California, August 27 and 29, 2004.

19. Noll, *American Evangelical Christianity*, 111–47; Waardenburg, "The Contemporary Period."

20. A. Watson, *The American Mission in Egypt*, 305–11; School of Oriental and African Studies, University of London, Archives and Manuscripts Library,

Papers of the Council for World Mission (henceforth SOAS CWM), "Annotated Register of L.M.S. Missionaries, 1796–1923," 176.

21. PHS, Proceedings of the Egyptian Association of the Missionaries of the UPCNA, Assiut, March 13–23, 1911, p. 6, item 6.

22. For example, on railway passes for clergymen and missionaries, see American University in Cairo, Charles R. Watson Papers (henceforth AUC Watson), Watson to the Ministry of Communications, January 3, 1927; *al-Balagh* (Cairo), July 3, 1933, p. 6.

23. A. Watson, *The American Mission in Egypt,* 50–51.

24. This issue is discussed more fully in chapter 3. See generally the chapter on apostasy in Friedmann, *Tolerance and Coercion in Islam,* 121–59. Regarding Muslim apostasy in modern Egypt, see Mayer, *Islam and Human Rights,* 154–55, 163, and passim; and Sharkey, "Muslim Apostasy, Christian Conversion, and Religious Freedom in Egypt."

25. AUC Watson, "Proposal for a Study of Religious Liberty," January 15, 1931, and related papers. Watson's papers at AUC show that he contributed to the following project: Davis, *Some Aspects of Religious Liberty of Nationals in the Near East.* See also PHS RG 209-20-17: W. B. Anderson Papers, Watson to Anderson, Avon-by-the-Sea, New Jersey, July 15, 1933.

26. See Saeed and Saeed, *Freedom of Religion, Apostasy, and Islam,* 116–17, 172.

27. Elder, "The Evangelical Church in Egypt," esp. p. 524; Donald Black to Heather J. Sharkey, Jenkintown, Pennsylvania, April 21, 2006. A British CMS missionary who worked closely with the American Presbyterians argued similarly: Morrison, "Egypt," 269.

28. PHS RG 209-21-24: Egypt mission, miscellaneous historical papers, "Should the American Mission Dissolve Its Organization and Merge Itself into the Evangelical Church and Its Organizations?" Assiut, March 24, 1939. A later and clearer articulation of this trend appeared in PHS RG 209-20-26: Donald Black Papers, "United Presbyterian Missions and the Church," Speech Delivered at Synod of Illinois, 1956, by Donald Black.

29. PHS RG 209-5-14: Harvey E. Philips Papers, Philips to R. W. Caldwell, Alexandria, September 25, 1937.

30. Lorimer, "Presbyterians in the Middle East," 43.

31. Galdas, *A Village Reborn.*

32. John G. Lorimer, e-mail message to Heather J. Sharkey, February 17, 2006.

33. Goddard, *A History of Christian-Muslim Relations,* 150–66, 182–86 and passim; Zebiri, *Muslims and Christians Face to Face,* 33–36.

34. Beinin, *The Dispersion of Egyptian Jewry;* Starr, "Remembering Cosmopolitan Egypt."

35. Wakin, *A Lonely Minority.*

36. References to Egyptian Muslims studying abroad recur, for example, in Egypt YMCA records. Kautz Family YMCA Archives, University of Minnesota (henceforth YMCA), Egypt, box #8, "Service in Egypt from 1919 to 1948" (a memoir), by James K. Quay, September 1975.

37. Wuthnow, *The Restructuring of American Religion,* esp. 87–88.

38. Bendroth, "An Understated Tale of Epic Social Change."

39. J. Smith, *From Colonialism to World Community*; Black, *Merging Mission and Unity*.

40. Presbyterian Historical Society, "Family Tree of Presbyterian Denomination."

41. Smylie, *A Brief History of the Presbyterians*.

42. Scouller, *A History of the United Presbyterian Church*, 148, 156, 177–78, 210–11, 228–31, 247–48.

43. McCulloch, *The United Presbyterian Church and Its Work in America*.

44. Jamison, *The United Presbyterian Story*, 5.

45. Presbyterian Church (U.S.A.), "Who We Are."

46. Hutchison, *Errand to the World*, 1.

47. Scouller, *A History of the United Presbyterian Church*, 241; Lorimer conversations.

48. Robinson, *Gilead*, 50.

49. On the Oil City, Pennsylvania, mission groups, see Lorimer, "Presbyterians in the Middle East," 21.

50. Jamison, *The United Presbyterian Story*, 5.

51. Garrett, "Sisters All," 222.

52. In 1901, the mission in Egypt had fifty-three foreign (American) workers of whom thirty-two were women, accounting for just over 60 percent. Glasgow, *Cyclopedic Manual of the United Presbyterian Church of North America*, 604–5. On women in the Protestant missionary movement, see Beaver, *American Protestant Women in World Mission*; Bowie, Kirkwood, and Ardener, *Women and Missions*; and Robert, *American Women in Mission*.

53. Jamison, *The United Presbyterian Story*, 5.

54. Robert, "The Origin of the Student Volunteer Watchword."

55. W. Hogg, *Ecumenical Foundations*. On the idea of the WCC as a Christian UN, see Wuthnow, *The Restructuring of American Religion*, 82; and Etherington, "Missions and Empire," 306.

56. Sanneh and Carpenter, *The Changing Face of Christianity*.

57. PHS, Minutes of the Thirty-Ninth Annual Meeting of the Egyptian Missionary Association, Cairo, February 23–March 3, 1910, and March 9 and 10, p. 5; PHS RG 209-4-07: R. S. McClenahan Papers, McClenahan to John D. Rockefeller, December 7, 1915.

58. Walls, "The American Dimension in the History of the Missionary Movement."

59. His father was R. C. Hutchison, and his father-in-law was James Quay, an ordained minister who served in the UPCNA mission in Egypt before becoming a director in the Cairo YMCA. Hutchison, *Errand to the World*, xi, and YMCA, Biographical Records, box 166, James K. Quay, file C: obituary of James K. Quay, *Princeton Packet*, November 17, 1981.

60. Hutchison, *Errand to the World*, xi, 1.

61. Ibid., 7, 204–8.

62. Harvard had the philosopher of religion and observer of missions William Ernest Hocking; Yale had the mission historian Kenneth S. Latourette; Chicago had R. Pierce Beaver. Robert, "From Missions to Beyond Missions," 363–64.

63. Black, *Merging Mission and Unity*; Sharkey, "Missionary Legacies"; Mallampalli, "British Missions and Indian Nationalism."

64. Wuthnow, *The Restructuring of American Religion*, 88; Coalter, Mulder, and Weeks, *The Re-Forming Tradition*, 52, 67–68.

65. F. Cooper, "Conflict and Connection."

66. Thorne, *Congregational Missions and the Making of an Imperial Culture in Nineteenth-Century England*, 3.

67. Gandhi, *Postcolonial Theory*; Loomba, *Colonialism/Postcolonialism*.

68. Camps, Hoedemaker, et al., *Missiology*, back cover and p. 2.

69. For example, Appadurai, "Disjuncture and Difference in the Global Cultural Economy."

70. "Secularism" and "secular," *Oxford English Dictionary*, 2nd ed., 1989, online version.

71. This argument is also made strongly in A. Porter, *Religion versus Empire*, 10–11, 13.

72. On the "failure" of Christian missionaries, see Makdisi, *Artillery of Heaven*, and Marten, *Attempting to Bring the Gospel Home*, 179, 184. I used to be more inclined to think about impact in terms of converts as well: see Sharkey, "Christians among Muslims."

73. Coleman, "Continuous Conversion." W.H.T. Gairdner made a similar point in *The Reproach of Islam*, 260–61, as did Cragg, almost fifty years later, in *The Call of the Minaret*, 304.

74. See chapter 5 regarding the ideas of Charles R. Watson and James K. Quay.

75. Hutchison, *Errand to the World*, 2, 203–4.

76. The work of American Presbyterians in Egypt, like that of LMS missionaries, was certainly characterized by authorship and textual production. Johnston, *Missionary Writing and Empire*, 3.

77. Exemplary works not yet cited include Makdisi, "Reclaiming the Land of the Bible"; Makdisi, *The Culture of Sectarianism*; Rogan, *Frontiers of the State in the Late Ottoman Empire*, 122–59; Okkenhaug, *"The Quality of Heroic Living, High Endeavor and Adventure"*; Doumato, *Getting God's Ear*; and Fleischmann, "The Impact of American Protestant Missions in Lebanon on the Construction of Female Identity." Collections of essays include Murre-van den Berg, *New Faiths in Ancient Lands*; Tejirian and Simon, *Altruism and Imperialism*; Marten, *Christian Witness between Continuity and New Beginnings*; and *Islam and Christian-Muslim Relations* 13:4 (2002) (special issue titled "Missionary Transformations: Gender, Culture, and Identity in the Middle East," ed. Eleanor Abdella Doumato). Consider also B. Cooper, *Evangelical Christians in the Muslim Sahel*; Shankar, "A Fifty-Year Muslim Conversion to Christianity"; and De Lorenzi, "Caught in the Storm of Progress."

78. One of the most influential books to acknowledge the cultural scope of missionary encounters has been Comaroff and Comaroff, *Of Revelation and Revolution*, though in their focus on colonial transformations, the Comaroffs elide issues of belief. Other ambitious works include Hall, *Civilising Subjects*; A. Porter, *Religion versus Empire*; Peel, *Religious Encounter and the Making of*

the Yoruba; Dunch, *Fuzhou Protestants and the Making of a Modern China*; and Viswanathan, *Outside the Fold*.

79. Gilley and Stanley, *World Christianities*.

CHAPTER 2
THE AMERICAN MISSION, COPTIC REFORM, AND THE MAKING
OF AN EGYPTIAN EVANGELICAL COMMUNITY, 1854–82

1. Finnie, *Pioneers East*, 137.
2. C. Watson, "Fifty Years of Foreign Missions in Egypt," 84.
3. A. Watson, *The American Mission in Egypt*, 3, 61–63, 406.
4. See Sheridan, "Coptic Christianity."
5. R. Hogg, *A Master-Builder on the Nile*, 96.
6. A. Watson, *The American Mission in Egypt*, 58.
7. Martin, "Statistiques chrétiennes d'Égypte."
8. PHS RG 209-1-23: J. R. Alexander, "Is the Mission Church in Egypt a 'Mature Church'?" [1935].
9. Harper, *The Church Memorial*, 330.
10. Jamison, *The United Presbyterian Story*, 78.
11. A. Watson, "Islam in Egypt," 34–35.
12. Stock, *The History of the Church Missionary Society*, 1:351, 3:514–15.
13. Lansing, *Egypt's Princes*, 12.
14. Wissa, *Assiout*, xi.
15. On news of the impending U.S. Civil War, see Lansing, *Egypt's Princes*, 212.
16. American Standard Version Bible.
17. Burke, "The Establishment of the American Presbyterian Mission in Egypt."
18. Lansing, *Egypt's Princes*, 8.
19. These charges recur in later accounts as well. See, for example, C. Watson, *In the Valley of the Nile*, 13, 53, 220, 224.
20. Lansing, *Egypt's Princes*, 32, 131, 220.
21. Scouller, *A History of the United Presbyterian Church*, 181; Jamison, *The United Presbyterian Story*, 98.
22. Sharkey, "American Missionaries, the Arabic Bible, and Coptic Reform in Late Nineteenth-Century Egypt."
23. Lansing, *Egypt's Princes*, 22–23.
24. Elliott, *Memoir of Lord Haddo*, 237–75, 406–13.
25. Lansing, *Egypt's Princes*, 242.
26. Cheapness was part of the strategy: see Howsam, *Cheap Bibles*.
27. Lansing, *Egypt's Princes*, 47–48, 88–90, 336–37.
28. The Rev. Emile Zaki of the Coptic Evangelical Presbyterian Church emphasized the importance of this curiosity vis-à-vis the Arabic Bible and oral folk epics in explaining his own family's nineteenth-century shift toward Protestantism. Rev. Emile Zaki, conversation with the author, Cairo, June 2, 2005.

29. Fahmy, *All the Pasha's Men*.

30. Lansing, *Egypt's Princes*, 150–51, 177.

31. Hamilton, *The Copts and the West*, 86–90.

32. For example, J. Salama, *Tarikh al-ta'lim al-ajnabi fi Misr*; Habib, *Tariq al-tahaddi*, 3–4, 11.

33. Lansing, *Egypt's Princes*, 38–39, 283, 286.

34. Hasan, *Christians versus Muslims in Modern Egypt*, 209–10; Oram, "Constructing Modern Copts," 70–71, 84, 135–40.

35. Lansing, *Egypt's Princes*, 35, 40, 186–87, 207, 309–10.

36. In *The American Mission in Egypt* (138, 287–91), A. Watson mentions that the Americans got the idea for consular prodding by seeing how Roman Catholics in Egypt got land.

37. Lansing, *Egypt's Princes*, 341–43; Elder, *Vindicating a Vision*, 31–34.

38. Skreslet, "The American Presbyterian Mission in Egypt."

39. Noll, "Evangelical Identity, Power, and Culture in the 'Great' Nineteenth Century," 31; Latourette, *A History of the Expansion of Christianity*, vols. 6 and 7.

40. Bebbington, *Evangelicalism in Modern Britain*, 3.

41. Noll, *The Old Religion in a New World*, 52–53.

42. United Presbyterian Church of North America, Board of Foreign Missions, *Rules and Recommendations for Foreign Missionaries and Candidates of the United Presbyterian Church*, 15.

43. Smylie, *A Brief History of the Presbyterians*. Regarding the UPCNA's Scottish antecedents, see Harper, *The Church Memorial*, 13, 38–39; Kerr, *The United Presbyterian Church of North America*, 1–5; Scouller, *A History of the United Presbyterian Church*, 145–56.

44. Scouller, *A History of the United Presbyterian Church*, 231.

45. McCulloch, *The United Presbyterian Church and Its Work in America*, 92–104; McGranahan, *Historical Sketch of the Freedmen's Missions of the United Presbyterian Church*.

46. Jamison, *The United Presbyterian Story*, 64–65.

47. W. Reid, *United Presbyterianism*, 14, 49.

48. Scouller, *A History of the United Presbyterian Church*, 240.

49. See Lansing, *Egypt's Princes*.

50. Goldsack, "How to Reach and Teach Illiterate Moslems," 32.

51. Cambridge University Library, Bible Society Archives (henceforth CUL BSA), *The Hundred and Eighteenth Report of the British and Foreign Bible Society for the Year Ending March MCMXXII* (London: The Bible House, 1922), 3; Roe, *A History of the British and Foreign Bible Society*, 174–206; and Bowen, *The Bible in Bible Lands*, 16–17, 37–38.

52. Rev. Menes Abdel Noor, conversation with the author, Cairo, May 23, 2005.

53. PHS RG 209-2-54: Davida M. Finney Papers, 1946–57, Papers on the mission literacy campaigns and the Laubach method; Dye et al., *Literacy—The Essential Skill*.

54. Robert, *Occupy Until I Come*, 75–81.

55. Jamison, *The United Presbyterian Story*, 128–29.

56. Geffen, "Industrial Development and Social Crisis," 356–57.

57. PHS, Minutes of the Twelfth General Assembly of the UPCNA at its meeting in Pittsburgh, May 25, 1870, fols. 550–52.

58. Jamison, *The United Presbyterian Story*, 128–29.

59. Ibid., 173; Abel, *Protestant Home Missions to Catholic Immigrants*.

60. J. Salama, *Tarikh al-ta'lim al-ajnabi fi Misr*, 45.

61. Hamilton, *The Copts and the West*.

62. A. Watson, *The American Mission in Egypt*, 55–58, 102; Jamison, *The United Presbyterian Story*, 79–80; Janin, *Les églises orientales et les rites orientaux*, 595; Fortescue, *The Uniate Eastern Churches*, 24.

63. [Rev. Père] Janin, *The Separated Eastern Churches*, 222; R. Hogg, *A Master-Builder on the Nile*, 95; Hamilton, *The Copts and the West*, 90. Disapproval persisted into the twentieth century. "[S]ad to say," noted a brochure for the American mission in 1927, raising funds for evangelization by railway travel, "the Coptic Christians in these Delta villages are very Moslem in their ideas." PHS, Minnehaha Finney, "Delta Car Glimpses" (Pittsburgh, 1927), 3.

64. Attwater, *The Christian Churches of the East*, vol. 1: *Churches in Communion with Rome*, 133; Fowler, *Christian Egypt*, 255; Lansing, *Egypt's Princes*, 34, 304.

65. Alexander, "A Great Adventure in the Valley of the Nile," 363.

66. Lansing, *Egypt's Princes*, 42.

67. Fortescue, *The Uniate Eastern Churches*, 37–38; Latourette, *A History of the Expansion of Christianity*, 6:7, 23–24.

68. Hajjar, *Les Chrétiens uniates du proche-orient*, 215.

69. Ibid., 258–60.

70. Latourette, *A History of the Expansion of Christianity*, 6:7, 23–24.

71. Hamilton, *The Copts and the West*, 88–89.

72. Hajjar, *Les Chrétiens uniates du proche-orient*, 259.

73. Attwater, *The Christian Churches of the East*, vol. 1: *Churches in Communion with Rome*, 132–41.

74. Guérin, *La France Catholique en Égypte*. Guérin gives many examples of consular mediation for the acquisition of mission property in Cairo, Alexandria, and other Delta towns, particularly during the eras of Muhammad Ali, Said Pasha, and Khedive Ismail: see pp. 41, 46, 158, 168, 179. Alas, Guérin's account does not cover Upper Egypt.

75. Lansing, *Egypt's Princes*, 38–41.

76. Janin, *Les églises orientales et les rites orientaux*; Guérin, *La France Catholique en Égypte*; Fortescue, *The Uniate Eastern Churches*; Attwater, *The Christian Churches of the East*, vol. 1: *Churches in Communion with Rome*.

77. Today some may regard the term "Uniate" as pejorative. See Melling, "Uniate." However, since the term has been used positively or neutrally in papal bulls and in scholarly works by Catholic writers, such as Fortescue, in *The Uniate Eastern Churches*, and Hajjar, in *Les Chrétiens uniates du proche-orient*, I use it here as well.

78. Lübeck, *Die Christlichen Kirchen des Orients*, 34–35; Attwater, *The Catholic Eastern Churches*, 138.

79. Barrett, Kurian, and Johnson, *World Christian Encyclopedia*, 1:250; Voile, *Les coptes d'Egypte sous Nasser*, 36.

80. J. Salama, *Tarikh al-ta'lim al-ajnabi fi Misr*, 43–44.

81. Guérin, *La France Catholique en Égypte*; J. Salama, *Tarikh al-ta'lim al-ajnabi fi Misr*, 43–46.

82. Railton, *No North Sea*; Leest, "Protestant Missionary Activities in Palestine."

83. Sedra, "John Lieder and His Mission in Egypt."

84. Meinardus, *Two Thousand Years of Coptic Christianity*, 70.

85. Butcher, *The Story of the Church of Egypt*, 2:395.

86. See also Richter, *A History of Protestant Missions in the Near East*, 67–69.

87. Hamilton, "The English Interest in the Arabic-Speaking Christians."

88. Stock, *The History of the Church Missionary Society*, 3:514.

89. Fowler, *Christian Egypt*, 250.

90. Rhodes, "Anglican Mission."

91. W. Reid, *United Presbyterianism*, 73.

92. Jamison, *The United Presbyterian Story*, 12.

93. Hatch, *The Democratization of American Christianity*, 9–10.

94. Jamison, *The United Presbyterian Story*, 18.

95. W. Reid, *United Presbyterianism*, 73, 90.

96. R. Hogg, *A Master-Builder on the Nile*, 104.

97. Jamison, *The United Presbyterian Story*, 80.

98. A. Watson, *The American Mission in Egypt*, 100–103.

99. CUL BSA Agent's Book, No. 133, Rev. A. Thomson (1871), "Book distribution in Egypt during 1870 by Mr. Schlotthauer, received August 14, 1871" (describing a Bible-selling trip that also involved Father Makhiel and Andrew Watson).

100. A. Watson, *The American Mission in Egypt*, 95, 98, 110, 116–19, 138–39, 152–54.

101. Ibid., 155, 163.

102. Elder, *Vindicating a Vision*, 38–40; Jamison, *The United Presbyterian Story*, 82–83; Mrs. Andrew Watson, "The Story of Bamba."

103. Interest in Dhulip Singh is more robust than ever, as evinced by the following three books, which also discuss Bamba: Campbell, *The Maharajah's Box*; Bance, *The Duleep Singhs*; and Ballantyne, *Between Colonialism and Diaspora*.

104. A. Watson, *The American Mission in Egypt*, 187–88, 237–38; C. Watson, "Fifty Years of Foreign Missions in Egypt," 89.

105. A. Watson, *The American Mission in Egypt*, 197.

106. C. Watson, "Fifty Years of Foreign Missions in Egypt," 87.

107. Sedra, "Ecclesiastical Warfare."

108. A. Watson, *The American Mission in Egypt*, 206. On the Van Dyck Bible from Beirut, see J. Thompson, *The Major Arabic Bibles*, 20–27.

109. This incident is also recounted in R. Hogg, *A Master-Builder on the Nile*, 223–24.

110. A. Watson, *The American Mission in Egypt*, 152–54, 197–206, 213–24, 225–38, 244–48, 251; see also R. Hogg, *A Master-Builder on the Nile*, 223–24.

111. A. Watson, *The American Mission in Egypt*, 290.

112. Noor conversation; Zaki conversation; Rev. Tharwat Wahba, conversation with the author, Philadelphia, November 9, 2005.

113. C. Watson, "Fifty Years of Foreign Missions in Egypt," 89; A. Watson, *The American Mission in Egypt,* 279.

114. See Beaver, *American Protestant Women in World Mission.*

115. Alexander, *A Sketch of the Story of the Evangelical Church of Egypt,* 14.

116. A. Watson, *The American Mission in Egypt,* 268–72.

117. Alexander, *A Sketch of the Story of the Evangelical Church of Egypt,* 15.

118. Elder, *Vindicating a Vision,* 59–61.

119. Wissa, *Assiout,* 111.

120. A. Watson, *The American Mission in Egypt,* 275.

121. Alexander, *A Sketch of the Story of the Evangelical Church of Egypt,* 24–25.

122. See Coad, *A History of the Brethren Movement.* Alas, Coad does not discuss the movement in Egypt.

123. Alexander, *A Sketch of the Story of the Evangelical Church of Egypt,* 26.

124. Wahba conversation.

125. R. Hogg, *A Master-Builder on the Nile,* 260. Another missionary's reaction to Pinkerton is discussed in Moffitt, "Anna Young Thompson," 102–3.

126. One source dates the entry of Pentecostal doctrines into Egypt to 1908, when an American missionary named George S. Brelsford arrived in Assiut. Nichol, *Pentecostalism,* 168.

127. Alexander, *A Sketch of the Story of the Evangelical Church of Egypt,* 18–22.

128. A. Watson, *The American Mission in Egypt,* 327.

129. The Evangelical Church's dominance in the Protestant sect has, in recent years, caused tensions with the tiny Egyptian Episcopal community. Noor conversation.

130. Butcher, *The Story of the Church of Egypt,* 2:395, 402.

131. Fowler, *Christian Egypt,* 274–79.

132. Guérin equates the propagation of Catholicism with the propagation of French culture, recording his thrill upon entering a classroom in Tanta, where students greeted him with a cry of "Vive la France!" Guérin, *La France Catholique en Égypte,* 98, 165–66.

133. Voile, *Les coptes d'Egypte sous Nasser,* 33–35.

134. Heyworth-Dunne, *An Introduction to the History of Education in Modern Egypt,* 415; Lia, *The Society of the Muslim Brothers in Egypt,* 3.

135. Meinardus, *Two Thousand Years of Coptic Christianity,* 60–61.

136. On Simeika, see D. M. Reid, *Whose Pharaohs,* 258–85; and Sedra, "Textbook Maneuvers," 8–11.

137. Meinardus, *Two Thousand Years of Coptic Christianity,* 69–72.

138. Hasan, *Christians versus Muslims in Modern Egypt,* 71–73, 76.

139. Ibid., 19, 92.

140. Ener, *Managing Egypt's Poor and the Politics of Benevolence,* 103.

141. Sedra, "Textbook Maneuvers."

142. Sedra, "Class Cleavages and Ethnic Conflict," 24–25.

143. Alexander, "A Great Adventure in the Valley of the Nile," 373, 375.

144. Lorimer, "Presbyterians in the Middle East," 6.

145. See Butcher, *The Story of the Church of Egypt,* 2:402; Fowler, *Christian Egypt,* 275–78.

146. Hasan, *Christians versus Muslims in Modern Egypt,* 202.

CHAPTER 3
THE COLONIAL MOMENT OF THE AMERICAN MISSION, 1882–1918

1. Gershoni and Jankowski, *Egypt, Islam, and the Arabs*; Ayalon, *Egypt's Quest for Cultural Orientation*.

2. Robinson and Gallagher, *Africa and the Victorians*.

3. A. Porter, *Religion versus Empire*, 222; Christensen and Hutchison, *Missionary Ideologies in the Imperialist Era*; Robert, *American Women in Mission*; Yates, *Christian Mission in the Twentieth Century*, 7–33.

4. Phillips, "Changing Attitudes in the Student Volunteer Movement of Great Britain and North America"; Robert, "The Origin of the Student Volunteer Watchword"; Mott, *The Evangelization of the World in This Generation*.

5. AUC Watson, Special Extracts from American Mission Minutes re: the plan for an American university in Cairo, 1904–17.

6. This point is made strongly in Stanley, *The Bible and the Flag*.

7. Sharkey, "Christians among Muslims," 56–57.

8. Colley, *Britons*, 8, 18, 53–54.

9. Anderson and Watson, *Far North in India*, 99–101.

10. Tibawi, *American Interests in Syria*, 19, 255.

11. C. Watson, *Egypt and the Christian Crusade*, 24, 180.

12. Werner, Anderson, and Wheeler, *Day of Devastation, Day of Contentment*, 230–41.

13. A. Porter, "Religion, Missionary Enthusiasm, and Empire," 244. Sanneh also discusses cultural reworking and indigenization in *Whose Religion Is Christianity*.

14. Peel, *Religious Encounter and the Making of the Yoruba*, 1.

15. Horton, "On the Rationality of Conversion."

16. Murre-van den Berg, *New Faiths in Ancient Lands*, 1; Sharkey, "A New Crusade or an Old One?"

17. Said, *Orientalism*, esp. p. 100.

18. Sharkey, "Arabic Antimissionary Treatises"; Sharkey, "Empire and Muslim Conversion."

19. Al-'Askar, *Al-Tansir wa-muhawalatuhu fi bilad al-khalij al-'arabi*, 13, 18–19, 21–22, 24.

20. Roberts, *The Colonial Moment in Africa*.

21. See also Makdisi, *Artillery of Heaven*.

22. A. Watson, *The American Mission in Egypt*, 36–37, 50–51.

23. Lewis, *The Jews of Islam*, 33.

24. The term "dhimmitude" came from the Lebanese politician, Beshir Gemayel, who used it in a speech in 1982, hours before his assassination. Bat Ye'or, *The Dhimmi*, 403–5; Bat Ye'or, *Islam and Dhimmitude*.

25. Ayoub, "Dhimmah in Qur'an and Hadith."

26. Lewis, *The Jews of Islam*, 24–25 and passim. A dated but still cited study, first published in 1930, is Tritton, *The Caliphs and Their Non-Muslim Subjects*.

27. Van Donzel, *Islamic Desk Reference*, 36; Friedmann, *Tolerance and Coercion in Islam*, 121–59; Cahen, "Dhimma."

28. For a sampling of this literature, see Lewis, *The Jews of Islam*; Beinin, *The Dispersion of Egyptian Jewry*; Levy, *Jews, Turks, Ottomans*; and Simon et al., *The Jews of the Middle East and North Africa in Modern Times*.

29. Masters, *Christians and Jews in the Ottoman Arab World*, 18, 38.

30. See, for example, Hourani and Shehadi, *The Lebanese in the World*, or on Coptic emigration, Khalil, *Aqbat al-Mahjar*.

31. A bleak assessment of the Coptic condition appears in Nisan, *Minorities in the Middle East*, 133–55. A rosier picture appears in Makari, "Christianity and Islam in Twentieth-Century Egypt."

32. Hasan, *Christians versus Muslims in Modern Egypt*, 29.

33. This theme of the Coptic Church as the successor to pharaonic Egypt is stressed in Rufayla, *Tarikh al-Umma al-Qibtiyya*, 3–15. Rufayla was a prominent late nineteenth-century Coptic intellectual who served as a teacher and then the director of the Great Coptic School in Cairo and later, during the reign of Khedive Ismail, as the director of the Egyptian government press. El Masri, *The Story of the Copts*, 525.

34. On the Coptic response to the Napoleonic invasion of 1798 and the British Occupation of 1882, see 'A. Ramadan, *Al-Dawr al-watani lil-kanisa al-misriyya 'abra al-'usur*, 247–60, 281–88. On twentieth-century events, see this work that focuses on the "national effort" of the Coptic Evangelical community: A. Salama, *Al-Injiliyyun wa-al-'amal al-qawmi*.

35. Shukri, *Al-Aqbat fi watan mutaghayyir*, 35; regarding Pope Shenouda III's publications on Israel, see 77–78.

36. Dr. Nabil Abadir, director of the Coptic Evangelical Organization for Social Services, conversation with the author, Cairo, May 26, 2005; Dr. Nabil Abadir, talk on the idea of the citizen and *dhimmi* in Egypt, delivered at the First Presbyterian Church of Haddonfield, New Jersey, November 1, 2004.

37. Hasanayn Muhammad Rabi', prefatory remarks, in 'A. Ramadan, *Al-Dawr al-watani lil-kanisa al-misriyya 'abra al-'usur*, 9. This volume apparently came out of a government-sponsored conference that sought to counteract an Egyptian Muslim Brother's public remark that the status of *dhimma* should be revived for Copts.

38. Hurewitz, *Diplomacy in the Near and Middle East*, 149–53.

39. Hourani, *Arabic Thought in the Liberal Age*; Lewis, *The Emergence of Modern Turkey*; Braude, "Foundation Myths of the *Millet* System."

40. Vander Werff, *Christian Mission to Muslims*, 111.

41. Stock, *The History of the Church Missionary Society*, 2:149–50.

42. Masters, *Christians and Jews in the Ottoman Arab World*, 137–39.

43. Viscount Stratford de Redcliffe to the Earl of Malmesbury, Constantinople, October 6, 1858, Document #10 in Bourne and Watt, *British Documents on Foreign Affairs*, Part 1: From the Mid-Nineteenth Century to the First World War, in Series B: The Near and Middle East, 1856–1914, ed. David Gillard, vol. 1: *The Ottoman Empire in the Balkans, 1856–1875*, 18–19.

44. Quataert, *The Ottoman Empire*, 65.

45. Masters makes this argument; so does Ma'oz in "Changing Relations between Jews, Muslims, and Christians during the Nineteenth Century."

46. Stock, *The History of the Church Missionary Society*, 2:151.

47. Elder, *Vindicating a Vision*, 31–34.

48. El Masri, *The Story of the Copts*, 455, 507. This work is an abridgement of al-Misri, *Qissat al-kanisa al-qibtiyya*.

49. See Renan, "What Is a Nation?"

50. Kepel, *Muslim Extremism in Egypt*.

51. Shukri, *Al-Aqbat fi watan mutaghayyir*, 176.

52. Meinardus, *Two Thousand Years of Coptic Christianity*, 66.

53. Hurewitz, *Diplomacy in the Near and Middle East*, 151.

54. Shukri, *Al-Aqbat fi watan mutaghayyir*, 175–88. Shukri's book includes a discussion of the issue in contemporary Egypt and also provides the Humayun decree in Arabic translation (183–86) and the "Ten Conditions" (187–88). Shukri claims that the Egyptian intellectual Faraj Fuda was the first person to raise the issue of the "Ten Conditions" with president Husni Mubarak, at a conference in 1990 (175). Note that in a well-publicized case, Islamic militants later assassinated Faraj Fuda, claiming that he was an apostate from Islam for advocating the separation of religion and state.

55. Ibrahim et al., *The Copts of Egypt*, 11.

56. A. Watson, *The American Mission in Egypt*, 105.

57. Ibid., 311.

58. Ibid., 351.

59. Dowling, *The Egyptian Church*, 11.

60. Ibid., 9.

61. Cole, *Colonialism and Revolution in the Middle East*; D. M. Reid, "The 'Urabi Revolution and the British Conquest." The latter study mentions Muslim-Christian violence briefly on p. 235. Strikingly, the issue of Muslim-Christian violence is more fully discussed in Buzpinar, "The Repercussions of the British Occupation of Egypt on Syria." Relying on British government records, Buzpinar comments on the prevalence of Muslim attacks on Christians in the small towns of Ottoman Syria and Palestine, such as Acre, Nazareth, and Homs, in the aftermath of the Urabi revolt.

62. For example, Toledano, *State and Society in Mid-Nineteenth-Century Egypt*; Baer, *Studies in the Social History of Modern Egypt*.

63. Masters, *Christians and Jews in the Ottoman Arab World*, 2.

64. O'Leary, *The Saints of Egypt*.

65. Masters, *Christians and Jews in the Ottoman Arab World*, 24.

66. Rufayla, *Tarikh al-Umma al-Qibtiyya*, 220–22; Meinardus, *Two Thousand Years of Coptic Christianity*, 65–66.

67. Hamilton, *The Copts and the West*, 11.

68. Hasan, *Christians versus Muslims in Modern Egypt*, 31–42; Voile, *Les coptes d'Egypte sous Nasser*, 33; Meinardus, *Two Thousand Years of Coptic Christianity*, 69; Shukri, *Al-Aqbat fi watan mutaghayyir*, 38; el Masri, *The Story of the Copts*, 507.

69. Carter, *The Copts in Egyptian Politics*; 'A. Ramadan, *Al-Dawr al-watani lil-kanisa al-misriyya 'abra al-'usur*; Hasan, *Christians versus Muslims in Modern Egypt*, 34–40; Wissa, *Assiout*.

70. D. M. Reid, "The 'Urabi Revolution and the British Conquest," 235.

71. A. Watson, "Islam in Egypt," 36; A. Watson, *The American Mission in Egypt*, passim.

72. R. Hogg, *A Master-Builder on the Nile*, 250.

73. The exact number was 1,036 members by 1881. Scouller, *A Manual of the United Presbyterian Church of North America*, 603.

74. R. Hogg, *A Master-Builder on the Nile*, 250.

75. Stanley, "Church, State, and the Hierarchy of 'Civilization,'" 74.

76. See, for example, Barnes, "'Evangelization Where It Is Not Wanted'"; Sharkey, "Christians among Muslims."

77. A. Porter, *Religion versus Empire*, 211. See also Prasch, "Which God for Africa?"; Walls, "Islam and the Sword"; Mott, *The Evangelization of the World in This Generation*, 115.

78. For example, Vander Werff, *Christian Mission to Muslims*, 145 (regarding Egypt); Sanneh, *Whose Religion Is Christianity*, 18–19; Sundkler and Steed, *A History of the Church in Africa*, 648.

79. A. Porter, "Religion, Missionary Enthusiasm, and Empire."

80. Leavitt, "Light in Egypt."

81. See Sharkey, *Living with Colonialism*, 67–70 and passim.

82. PHS, "The American Mission in Egypt," tourist brochure, n.d. [1922], p. 32.

83. Ranger, "The Invention of Tradition in Colonial Africa."

84. For example, on Nigeria, see Barnes, "'Evangelization Where It Is Not Wanted'"; on India, see Viswanathan, *Outside the Fold*.

85. Daly, *Empire on the Nile*; Warburg, *Islam, Sectarianism, and Politics in Sudan since the Mahdiyya*. Even Gordon himself had realized the sensitivity of Muslim public opinion, and during his period as the Turco-Egyptian governor-general in Khartoum (1877–80) had discouraged Christian missionaries from working in northern Sudan. Moore-Harell, *Gordon and the Sudan*.

86. Hefner, "Of Faith and Commitment," 99.

87. For example, Zwemer, *The Law of Apostasy in Islam*; Rice, *Crusaders of the Twentieth Century*, esp. 71–77; and Gairdner, *The Reproach of Islam*, esp. 260–307.

88. Cragg, *The Call of the Minaret*, 313–15. Gairdner, in *The Reproach of Islam*, 260–61, also addresses this concern over the financial worth of missions to Muslims, given the paucity of converts.

89. British missionaries noted the case, for example, of a seventeen- or eighteen-year-old Muslim youth named Muhammad ibn Ali, who wanted to be baptized. When he professed belief in Christ, they claimed, a Muslim crowd beat him and then strung him up in his house. He disappeared, but resurfaced two years later, having been apparently locked in the house. He asked the missionaries to take him away to be baptized. "When it was found out, he was forbidden to come, and no more has been heard of him since. His relations say that he is dead." Swan, *"Lacked Ye Anything,"* 22–24.

90. Zwemer, *The Law of Apostasy in Islam*, 18, 59.

91. Jessup, *The Setting of the Crescent and the Rising of the Cross*; see also Zwemer, *The Law of Apostasy in Islam*, 29.

92. See Friedmann, *Tolerance and Coercion in Islam*, 121–59.

93. See, for example, Kinnear, *She Sat Where They Sat*, 68.

94. A. Watson, "Islam in Egypt," 39.

95. Philips, *Blessed Be Egypt My People*: on Mikhail Mansour, 17–43; Shaikh Kamil Mansur, 44–64; and Nasrullah, 101–15.

96. "Is the Mission Church in Egypt a 'Mature Church'?" In the early 1930s (before big budget cuts occurred) the mission ran a home for converts and inquirers from Islam. PHS RG 209-2-48: W. T. Fairman Papers.

97. Hunt, "The Loneliness of the Convert."

98. Zwemer, *The Law of Apostasy in Islam*, 17.

99. PHS, Mansour, *A Visit to My Old Home*; Philips, *Blessed Be Egypt My People*: on Mikhail Mansour, 17–43, and on Kamil Mansur, 44–64.

100. Willis A. McGill, telephone conversation with the author, June 23, 2005.

101. James, *The Varieties of Religious Experience*.

102. Rambo, *Understanding Religious Conversion*, 1.

103. Hefner, "Of Faith and Commitment," 119.

104. *Annual Report of the United Presbyterian Mission in Egypt*, 1883–84, p. 25.

105. Kinnear, *She Sat Where They Sat*, 36.

106. Finney, *Tomorrow's Egypt*, 190. Finney's book contains the earliest reference to "secret believers" that I have seen in a publication of the American missionaries in Egypt. Zwemer uses the term "hidden disciples" in *The Law of Apostasy in Islam*, 105.

107. Philips, *Blessed Be Egypt My People*, 10.

108. The two people who expressed this idea most forcefully left the American Presbyterian mission to pursue other avenues of outreach in Egypt. These were Charles R. Watson and James K. Quay; see chapter 5.

109. United Presbyterian Church of North America, *Report of Commissioners* (1881), 7.

110. A. Watson, *The American Mission in Egypt*, 37.

111. Scouller, *A Manual of the United Presbyterian Church of North America*, 616–21.

112. Elder, *Vindicating a Vision*, 30.

113. Scouller, *A Manual of the United Presbyterian Church of North America*, 616–26.

114. Note that voluntary work remained important to the mission. In 1904, for example, fifteen young men from the mission's Assiut College volunteered as "evangelist colporteurs" during their summer vacations, visiting villages, selling Bibles and devotional books, and holding meetings in churches and streets. PHS, Minutes of the Thirty-Fifth Annual Meeting of the Egyptian Missionary Association, Assiut, February 8–17, 1905, p. 14.

115. Noor conversation.

116. Egypt, Census Department, *The Census of Egypt Taken in 1907*, 117–23, 408–9, 422–23.

117. Ibid., 462–63.

118. Ibid., 408–9.

119. Ibid., 430–33.

120. Elder, *Vindicating a Vision*, 97–98; Egypt, Census Department, *The Census of Egypt Taken in 1907*, 368–69.

121. Ibid., 462–63, 486–87.

122. By 1900 Coptic Orthodox schools were drawing many female teachers from the staff of American mission institutions, producing a shortage of teachers in the latter. Kinnear, *She Sat Where They Sat*, 53–54.

123. Philips, *Blessed Be Egypt My People*, 17–43.

124. Attwater, *The Catholic Eastern Churches*, 138.

125. Janin, *Les églises orientales et les rites orientaux*, 589.

126. PHS, *Annual Report of the United Presbyterian Mission in Egypt*, 1888, 5.

127. AUC Watson, Amir Boktor to R. S. McClenahan, Roucegno (Italy), August 11, 1937.

128. Wissa, *Assiout*, 105.

129. Philips, *Blessed Be Egypt My People*, 38.

130. The Rev. Emile Zaki told me in 2005 that his own church in the Qulali neighborhood of Cairo has sixty-eight official members but one hundred and fifty families who participate actively.

131. Elder, *Vindicating a Vision*, 107.

132. PHS, Forrest Scott Thompson, "The Present Crisis in the History of the American Mission in Egypt," typescript, c. 1912, 2–3.

133. Wissa, *Assiout*, 105.

134. Elder, *Vindicating a Vision*, 69–70; Scouller, *A Manual of the United Presbyterian Church of North America*, 622.

135. A. Watson, *The American Mission in Egypt*, 195.

136. PHS, *Annual Report of the United Presbyterian Mission in Egypt*, 1883–84, 9.

137. A. Thompson, "Mission Work in Egypt"; Kinnear, *She Sat Where They Sat*, 40–42. The slave trade had been abolished in Egypt during the reign of Said Pasha (1854–63), but traders coming from the Sudan still smuggled enslaved children into Egypt, where people were willing to buy them.

138. A. Watson, *The American Mission in Egypt*, 305.

139. Kinnear, *She Sat Where They Sat*, 38.

140. By 1880, three years after Ahmed's baptism, the American missionaries counted 500 Muslim children enrolled in their schools, and the numbers grew steadily into the twentieth century. By 1959, 67 percent of the students in the ACG were Muslim, while less than 4 percent were Protestants. J. Salama, *Tarikh al-ta'lim al-ajnabi fi Misr*, 123.

141. PHS RG 210-3-6: Andrew Watson, diaries, entries for December 22 and 24, 1877.

142. PHS RG 58-1-10: Anna Young Thompson Papers, diary, entry for November 19, 1877.

143. A. Watson, *The American Mission in Egypt*, 305–11; Kinnear, *She Sat Where They Sat*, 38–40 (note that Kinnear relies for her information on Thompson's diaries in PHS RG 58-1-10).

144. C. Watson, *Egypt and the Christian Crusade*, 177.

145. Kinnear, *She Sat Where They Sat*, 40; Philips, *Blessed Be Egypt My People*, 34–35.

146. Keddie, *An Islamic Response to Imperialism*.

147. Buruma, "Tariq Ramadan Has an Identity Issue"; T. Ramadan, *Western Muslims and the Future of Islam*.

148. A. Watson, *The American Mission in Egypt*, 308. See Kedourie, *Afghani and Abduh*, 45 and passim. Kedourie writes that Afghani practiced a "false but shadowy devotion."

149. PHS RG 58-1-10: Anna Young Thompson Papers, diary, entry for November 15, 1877.

150. Ibid., entry for November 17, 1877.

151. Elder, *Vindicating a Vision*, 30.

152. PHS, *Annual Report of the United Presbyterian Mission in Egypt*, 1883–84, 9.

153. Gordon and Gordon, "*We Twa*"; on Ahmed Fahmy, see 1:182–84, including details of the escape. Ahmed Fahmy apparently entertained hopes of returning, since he applied to the American missionaries in Egypt in 1895, seeking a medical appointment at their Tanta hospital. Nothing happened, however, and the paper trail on his application ran cold. Elder, *Vindicating a Vision*, 76–77.

154. Ibid., 1:183.

155. SOAS CWM, South China, Fukien, incoming correspondence files and reports, 1887–1920; SOAS, papers of Dr. Douglas Harman and Mrs. Gladys Harman, MS 380815, including "A History of Mission Medical Work in Changchow Fukien, China [by Jessie M. Platz]" and "File on Fahmy Family." Papers in the last files show that many years later, in 1947–49, a bequest from Ahmed's American widow enabled missionaries in China to rebuild the Chang Chew hospital, which Japanese bombing had destroyed during World War II. The hospital was still operating, in 1985, under Chinese government control.

156. A. Watson, *The American Mission in Egypt*, 361–63; C. Watson, *Egypt and the Christian Crusade*, 184–85.

157. Swan, "*Lacked Ye Anything*," esp. 20, 47, 53–54, 57–59; Yale Divinity School, Day Missions Library, Egypt General Mission Papers (henceforth YDS-EGM), Newsletter, Egypt General Mission, Ezbet el-Zeitoun, July 1914; and YDS-EGM, *Egypt General Mission: Its Origin and Work* (Belfast: Wm. Strain and Sons, 1902); see p. 25 on its policy toward the Evangelical Church.

158. A. Watson, *The American Mission in Egypt*, 360.

159. Charles R. Watson was born in 1873. In 1877, amid his father's diary entries noting the travails of Ahmed Fahmy, is one that reads, "This is Charley's birthday, he has been in great glee, with the toys & presents he received." PHS RG 210-3-6: Andrew Watson, diaries, entry for July 17, 1877.

160. Bays and Wacker, *The Foreign Missionary Enterprise at Home*, 1, 5. See also Hill, *The World Their Household*, 3 and passim; and Robert, *Gospel Bearers, Gender Barriers*, xi.

161. Robert, *American Women in Mission*, 1–80.

162. United Presbyterian Church of North America, Board of Foreign Missions, *Rules and Recommendations for Foreign Missionaries*, 9–10.

163. In *The World Their Household*, Hill attributes this phrase to Montgomery, *Western Women in Eastern Lands*.

164. Hunter, *The Gospel of Gentility*, xiii.

165. M. Reid, "Egypt."

166. PHS, *Zenana Workers: A Ladies' Missionary Magazine* 4:4 (April 1882).

167. *Zenana Workers* 4:5 (May 1882).

168. *Zenana Workers* 3:7 (July 1881); Robert, "The Origin of the Student Volunteer Watchword"; Phillips, "Changing Attitudes in the Student Volunteer Movement of Great Britain and North America."

169. See Robert, *Gospel Bearers, Gender Barriers*, 9–10; and Robert, *American Women in Mission*, 302–6.

170. Jamison, *The United Presbyterian Story*, 188.

171. McCulloch, *The United Presbyterian Church and Its Work in America*, 161–73.

172. *Women's Missionary Magazine of the United Presbyterian Church* 6 (1893), "Appendix: Statistics of Missionary Societies."

173. McCulloch, *The United Presbyterian Church and Its Work in America*, 166–67.

174. Donald Black, conversation with the author, Mission History Meeting, Presbyterian Historical Society, Philadelphia, April 4, 2006.

175. Mrs. J. P. White, Topeka, Kansas, "Women's Work for Women: Its Present," in United Presbyterian Church of North America, *Foreign Missionary Jubilee Convention*, 178–79, 181.

176. Harvard University Library, American Board of Commissioners for Foreign Missions, ABC 11.4, box 2, folder 3, letter from James Barton to J. H. Oldham re: Chap IV of the report of Commission VI on "Financial Support" (World Missionary Conference, Edinburgh, 1910). Thanks to Kaley Middlebrooks Carpenter for this reference. Its information is consonant with the pattern of giving that McCulloch reports for 1924: he claims that the UPCNA averaged $15.28 in per capita giving to foreign missions, leaving far behind the southern-stream Presbyterian Church U.S. ($9.11) and the northern-stream Presbyterian Church U.S.A. ($5.84) as well as all other Protestant denominations. McCulloch, *The United Presbyterian Church and Its Work in America*, 89.

177. Donald Black and Elisabeth Gelzer, conversations with the author, Mission History Meeting, Presbyterian Historical Society, Philadelphia, April 4, 2006. Donald Black made the point about tithing. Elisabeth Gelzer, who worked for the Presbyterian Church U.S.A. in Cameroon (before the 1958 merger with the UPCNA), made the point about correspondence and said that this emphasis on regular letter writing seemed to have been much stronger in the UPCNA than in the PCUSA.

178. Black conversation.

179. PHS RG 393: Skellie Family Papers, 1924–80. The collection was donated to the archive by the recipient church.

180. Kinnear, *She Sat Where They Sat*, 98.

181. Robert, *American Women in Mission*, 266, 294.

182. Murre-van den Berg, "Nineteenth-Century Protestant Missions and Middle Eastern Women," 106–7.

183. Heuser, "Culture, Feminism, and the Gospel," 165–66.

184. Kinnear, *She Sat Where They Sat*, passim and 38, 77–78.

185. Elder, *Vindicating a Vision*, 134–35; Lorimer, *The Presbyterian Experience in Egypt*, 256.

186. Kinnear, *She Sat Where They Sat*, 63, 81, 94–95.

187. Moffitt, "Anna Young Thompson," 6.

188. Ibid., 6, 180–82; Kinnear, *She Sat Where They Sat*, 86.

189. Kinnear, *She Sat Where They Sat*, 104–5.

190. A. Thompson, "The Woman Question in Egypt."

191. Robert, *American Women in Mission*, 263.

192. Montgomery, *Western Women in Eastern Lands*, 76. See also Robert, *Gospel Bearers, Gender Barriers*, 8–9.

193. Compare with Allison, *The Crescent Obscured*, xvii.

194. Barr, "Women's Work for Women—Its Past," 168.

195. Egypt, Census Department, *The Census of Egypt Taken in 1907*, 3.

196. Hutchison, *Errand to the World*, 90–91.

197. Abdul-Fady, *High Lights* [sic] *in the Near East.*

198. Wherry, *Methods of Mission Work among Moslems*; Zwemer, Wherry, and Barton, *The Mohammedan World of To-Day.*

199. On Watson's role in seeding the idea for the Edinburgh conference, see W. Hogg, *Ecumenical Foundations*, 102.

200. W. Hogg, *Ecumenical Foundations*, 98; Robert, *American Women in Mission*, 256.

201. Stanley, "Edinburgh 1910 and the Oikoumene," 97–99.

202. Kinnear, *She Sat Where They Sat*, 84.

203. Gairdner, *Echoes from Edinburgh.*

204. Ibid., 123.

205. World Missionary Conference, 1910, *Report of Commission III*, 214, 236–37.

206. Robert, *American Women in Mission*, 256.

207. Ibid., 256–58.

208. R. McClenahan, "The Training of Missionaries for Work among Muslims," 46.

209. Wherry, Mylrea, and Zwemer, *Lucknow*, 8; Weitbrecht, "The Lucknow Conference."

210. Zwemer, "Editorial."

211. AUC Archives and Special Collections, Samuel M. Zwemer scrapbook for Cairo Study Centre [1912–21].

212. Sharkey, "Christian Missionaries and Colloquial Arabic Printing."

213. PHS RG 81-27-19: COEMAR, American Christian Literature Society for Moslems (henceforth ACLSM), "Echoes from the Annual Meeting of the American Christian Literature Society for Moslems, Inc.: A Report of Progress with Extracts from Addresses by Robert E. Speer and Dr. Charles R. Watson," January 27, 1916.

214. PHS RG 81-27-19: COEMAR, ACLSM, Minutes of the Meeting of the Executive Committee of the A.C.L.S.M., Quogue, Long Island, New York, September 14, 1918.

215. Ibid., minutes for January 21, 1921, and February 18, 1921; PHS RG 81-28-2: COEMAR, Nile Mission Press papers, [Speer?] to Mr. John L. Oliver of Tunbridge Wells, England, November 12, 1920. The money for this NMP equipment came in 1921 from Mrs. Cyrus McCormick (i.e., Nettie Fowler McCormick), whose husband had made his fortune as the inventor of the mechanical grain harvester.

216. PHS, UPCNA RG 209-1-04: J. W. Acheson Papers, "A Summary of N.M.P. Annual Report for 1925," attached to a letter from Acheson to Edie, March 16, 1925.

217. A longstanding board member, for example, was the prominent PCUSA Presbyterian layman and mission activist Robert E. Speer. Speer's copies of ACLSM minutes are the ones now stored at the PHS in Philadelphia.

218. PHS UPCUSA RG 81-27-19: COEMAR, ACLSM, Minutes of the Meeting of the Executive Committee of the ACLSM, Quogue, Long Island, September 14, 1918, and Minutes of the Meeting of the Board of Directors of the ACLSM, April 18, 1919.

219. Zwemer, *The Disintegration of Islam*.

220. Sharkey, "Arabic Antimissionary Treatises"; Sharkey, "A New Crusade or an Old One?"; al-Shadhili, *Al-Wathiqa al-Islam al-khatar!* (consisting of a translation and commentary on one of Gairdner's speeches at the Edinburgh 1910 conference regarding "Christianization" of Muslims).

221. Nevertheless, some Christian evangelicals still praise Zwemer as "the Apostle to Islam." For example, see "About Samuel Zwemer," Zwemer Center for Muslim Studies, Columbia International University, http://www.ciu.edu/muslimstudies/samuelzwemer.html (accessed January 24, 2006).

222. At the ACLSM board meeting of April 1919, members listened to "a blasphemous comment on the death of Christ from a Moslem paper printed in Woking, England." At the meeting in January 1922, they heard that "The Moslems in America have a lively headquarters in Detroit where they have built a Mosque and from which place an attractive magazine 'The Moslem Sunrise' is published." At the January 1931 meeting, "Dr. Zwemer spoke briefly on Islam in America." The minutes for April 1931 note that a colporteur was distributing Christian literature to the Muslims of New York City. PHS UPCUSA RG 81-27-19: COEMAR, ACLSM, Minutes of the Meeting of the Board of Directors of the ACLSM, April 18, 1919, January 26, 1922, January 24, 1931, and April 17, 1931. Zwemer's journal, *The Moslem World*, also noted developments among Muslim communities in Europe and North America; see, for example, "The London Mosque Fund," *The Moslem World* 2:1 (1912): 98–99, and "Islamic Propaganda," *The Moslem World* 3:1 (1913): 86, about emerging Muslim missions to Christians.

223. Showalter, *The End of a Crusade*.

224. Robert, *American Women and Mission*, 272–73.

225. Zwemer, *The Disintegration of Islam*; Latourette, *A History of the Expansion of Christianity*, 7:8.

CHAPTER 4
EGYPTIAN NATIONALISM, RELIGIOUS LIBERTY, AND THE RETHINKING
OF THE AMERICAN MISSION, 1918–45

1. Mathews, *Roads to the City of God*, 8, 21–22, 28.

2. Latourette, *A History of the Expansion of Christianity*, 7:49.

3. Lorimer, "Presbyterians in the Middle East," 21; Kelsey, *The United Presbyterian Directory*, 34.

4. Gershoni and Jankowski, *Redefining the Egyptian Nation*, 5.

5. Ayalon, *Egypt's Quest for Cultural Orientation*; Ayalon, *The Press in the Arab Middle East*, 76.

6. C. Smith, *Islam and the Search for Social Order in Modern Egypt*, 1.

7. Carter, "On Spreading the Gospel to Egyptians Sitting in Darkness."

8. See, for example, this article from the Azhar journal: "Hawla hawadith al-tabshir," *Nur al-Islam*, Rabi' al-Awwal 1352 AH/June–July 1933, pp. 209–22.

9. PHS RG 209-5-13: Harvey Philips Papers, article from a Topeka, Kansas, newspaper [*The Capital*?], n.d. [1918]; Philips to W. B. Anderson, Topeka, November 5, 1918; Anderson to Friends, Philadelphia, September 13, 1918; Philips to Anderson, Topeka, November 15, 1918.

10. Gershoni and Jankowski, *Egypt, Islam, and the Arabs*, 73–74.

11. Ibid.

12. Gershoni and Jankowski, *Redefining the Egyptian Nation*, xiv.

13. Sonbol, *The New Mamluks*, xx, 214, 220–21.

14. Ayalon, *Egypt's Quest for Cultural Orientation*, 1, 7–12.

15. C. Smith, *Islam and the Search for Social Order in Modern Egypt*, 77.

16. Husayn, *Fi al-shi'r al-jahili*.

17. Ibid.

18. Davis, *Some Aspects of Religious Liberty of Nationals in the Near East*, 33–34; PHS, *Minutes of the Inter-Mission Council* (Cairo: Nile Mission Press, 1922), May 31, 1921, p. 6.

19. AUC Watson, memorandum [on religious liberty], n.d. [1926], and C. C. Adams to Watson, Cairo, December 3, 1925, including notes on 'Abd al-Raziq's book, *Al-Islam wa-usul al-hukm*.

20. PHS RG 209-5-18: James K. Quay Papers, Hassan A. M. Kadri to Mrs. Trowbridge, Governorate Prison, Cairo, July 19, 1920, and Quay to W. B. Anderson, Cairo, April 9, 1920.

21. Noll, *The Old Religion in a New World*, 142–47; Patterson, "The Loss of a Protestant Missionary Consensus"; Wuthnow, *The Restructuring of American Religion*, 132–48.

22. Hutchison, *The Modernist Impulse in American Protestantism*, 2.

23. Longfield, *The Presbyterian Controversy*; Weston, *Presbyterian Pluralism*; Scopes, *The World's Most Famous Court Trial*, 5.

24. Jamison, *The United Presbyterian Story*, 132–34; AUC Watson, Watson to John D. Rockefeller Jr., June 5, 1933; AUC Watson, Watson to John Mott, September 4, 1938.

25. AUC Watson, Charles C. Adams, Application for Appointment as a Missionary, the Board of Foreign Missions of the United Presbyterian Church of N.A., January 31, 1908, and letter describing Christian Experience, with application above, by Charles C. Adams, February 3, 1908.

26. Adams, *Islam and Modernism in Egypt*, 1.

27. PHS RG 209-1-19: C. C. Adams Papers, Adams to Dr. [W. B.] Anderson, Cairo, November 1, 1932.

28. C. Smith, *Islam and the Search for Social Order in Egypt*, viii, 185, 187–88.

29. Gershoni, "The Reader—'Another Production,'" 242.

30. Haykal, *Hayat Muhammad*, 3, 12, 14, 17. This was published in 1935 after having been serialized from 1932 to 1934.

31. Na'im, *Al-Judhur al-tarikhiyya*, 150; Ryad, "Muslim Responses to Missionary Activities in Egypt," 291.

32. Ener, *Managing Egypt's Poor and the Politics of Benevolence.*

33. A YMCA report noted in 1930, "The development of the YMCA [in Egypt] has been the prime cause of the organization of the Moslem Young Men's Association, with branches in different cities in Egypt, although the latter is generally considered to be a political religious movement aiming at the protection of Moslem youth who are in danger of contamination from Christian or foreign influences. We have offered our cooperation to this society, and its secretary has expressed the desire to study our organization." YMCA, Egypt, box #5, International Survey Committee, "Survey of the YMCA in Egypt," 3 vols., typescript, 1930, 1:96, 3:18.

34. The YMCA in Egypt was segregated by nationality. American Presbyterians started the first branch for Egyptian students at the mission's Assiut College in 1896. There was an Anglo-American branch in Cairo founded for expatriates in 1909–10; during World War I, this branch sponsored programs for British imperial troops. The major facility for Egyptians in Cairo opened in 1923, while other branches developed in Alexandria and Assiut city. "Survey of the YMCA in Egypt"; Barrett, *The War Work of the Y.M.C.A. in Egypt,* 30.

35. "Survey of the YMCA in Egypt," 1:iii–iv.

36. Kampffmeyer, "Egypt and Western Asia," 103–6, 134–35. Kampffmeyer visited the YMMA in Cairo when the organization was less than five years old; his account is remarkable for its freshness and detail.

37. Kampffmeyer, "Egypt and Western Asia," 153; Elder, *Vindicating a Vision,* 171–72.

38. Mallampalli, "British Missions and Indian Nationalism"; Oddie, "Anti-Missionary Feeling and Hindu Revivalism in Madras."

39. British missionaries were especially intrigued by al-Azhar. See Whately, *The Life and Work of Mary Louisa Whately,* appendix, "The Great College of Cairo," 153–59; Thornton, "Work among Educated Moslems in Cairo"; Morrison, *El Azhar Today and Tomorrow.*

40. Badeau, *The Middle East Remembered,* 70.

41. Lia, *The Society of the Muslim Brothers in Egypt,* 39, 59.

42. Ryad, "Rashid Rida and a Danish Missionary."

43. Lia, *The Society of the Muslim Brothers in Egypt,* 106.

44. Much of the impetus for the Vacation Bible Schools program came from Pressly Memorial Institute (PMI) in Assiut, which trained some of its students to run classes during their summer holidays. In 1933, the Vacation Bible Schools of the American mission enrolled nearly three thousand children, many of them Muslims. PHS RG 209-2-30: Anna B. Criswell Papers, miscellaneous correspondence with American donors regarding PMI programs, 1933. On the Vacation Bible School program of the American missionaries, see also J. Salama, *Tarikh al-ta'lim al-ajnabi fi Misr,* 201; and Hasan, *Christians versus Muslims in Modern Egypt,* 139. American Presbyterians also helped run Vacation Bible Schools under the aegis of the World's Sunday School Association (WSSA), an ecumenical organization that had its headquarters in Philadelphia, across the street from AUC's American offices. During his tenure as president of AUC, Charles R. Watson was in fact on the WSSA's Cairo board.

PHS RG 209-1-08: J. W. Acheson Papers: Stephen van R. Trowbridge, World's Sunday School Association [WSSA] Report for Egypt and the Sudan, 1929.

45. Annual reports of the BFBS, in Cambridge University Library, are full of café anecdotes from Egypt. For example, on page 71 of this society's 1920 report: "Colporteur George Kaoustos spends many of his evenings in Cairo visiting the *cafés*, bars, and other haunts of men, seeking to interest them in the Gospel. He is careful to avoid argument or discussion. His one great theme is the love of God in Christ Jesus, and on this he labours alike with Moslem and Jew."

46. Mitchell, *The Society of the Muslim Brothers*.

47. Al-Banna, *Mudhakkirat al-da'wa wa'l-da'iya*, 20.

48. PHS RG 360: file 6904, personnel file of Miss Florence Lillian White; Minutes of the Fifty-Third Annual Meeting of the Egyptian Missionary Association, Cairo, February 14–26, 1923, p. 294, item 353, no. 12, and p. 317, item 383, no. 2a; and Minutes of the Fifty-Fourth Annual Meeting of the Egyptian Missionary Association, Cairo, February 11–March 1, 1924, p. 437, item 483, no. 14. Lillian White was on furlough in 1924–25, so although her appointment to Egypt officially lasted until 1926, she may not have returned after her departure in 1924.

49. Elder, *Vindicating a Vision*, 171–72, 181, 192–93; Kelsey, *The United Presbyterian Directory*, 34; Lorimer, "Presbyterians in the Middle East," 21; Jamison, *The United Presbyterian Story*, 190–92.

50. Kampffmeyer, "Egypt and Western Asia," 105; Lia, *The Society of the Muslim Brothers in Egypt*, 97.

51. Ayalon, *Egypt's Quest for Cultural Orientation*, 10.

52. Wilson, *Apostle to Islam*, 19–22.

53. This is also evident from reviews of Dutch and German books that Zwemer wrote for *The Moslem World*.

54. PHS UPCUSA RG 81-27-19: COEMAR, ACLSM, Minutes, Reports, 1915–37.

55. PHS UPCUSA RG 81-27-20: COEMAR, ACLSM, Correspondence: "News Letter," a bulletin published by the ACLSM, No. 35, April 1937; and Membership Brochure for the ACLSM [1930s].

56. This volume was prepared for the Foreign Missions Conference of North America at the behest of the ACLSM, which entrusted Zwemer with the task in 1920. PHS UPCUSA RG 81-27-19: COEMAR, ACLSM, Minutes of the Meeting of the Board of Directors, New York City, June 3, 1920.

57. American Committee on Survey [sic] of Christian Literature for Moslems, *The Power of the Printed Page in the World of Islam*, 4.

58. PHS RG 209-2-58: Thomas J. Finney Papers, Finney to Charles R. Watson, Alexandria, August 21, 1910.

59. Tisdall, *The Religion of the Crescent, or Islam*, 72–73.

60. Minutes of the Egyptian Association of the Missionaries of the UPCNA, held in Cairo, October 18–26, 1910, 16–17.

61. PHS RG 209-2-58: Thomas J. Finney Papers, Finney to Charles R. Watson, Alexandria, n.d. [1910].

62. Elder, *Vindicating a Vision*, 197–98.

63. PHS UPCUSA RG 81-27-19: COEMAR, ACLSM, Minutes of the Meeting of the Board of Directors, February 24, 1937.

64. The NMP in Cairo received funds from the ACLSM to publish these tracts. PHS UPCUSA RG 81-27-19: COEMAR, ACLSM, Minutes of the Annual Meeting, New York City, January 24, 1918; Minutes of the Meeting of the Board of Directors, New York City, April 18, 1917; Minutes of the Meeting of the Board of Directors, New York City, January 29, 1927.

65. Kampffmeyer, "Egypt and Western Asia," 165.

66. Zwemer, *Islam*, viii, 173, 225–26.

67. Henry Martyn Centre for the Study of Mission and World Christianity, Westminster College, Cambridge University, correspondence files for the World Missionary Conference, 1910, *Report of Commission IV*: ECM 1/151, Rev. Samuel M. Zwemer, Dutch Reformed Church in America, Bahrein, No. 283.

68. Muhammad al-Husayni Raja, "Harakat al-tabshir al-masihi fi al-'alam al-islami," *Nur al-Islam*, Safar 1349AH/June–July 1930, pp. 71–73.

69. PHS RG 209-2-58: Thomas J. Finney Papers, Finney to Charles R. Watson, Alexandria, October 4, 1910.

70. Minutes of the Egyptian Association of the Missionaries of the UPCNA, held in Cairo, October 18–26, 1910, item #53, p. 19.

71. Wilson, *Apostle to Islam*, 77. By "Southern Presbyterian Church," Wilson is presumably referring to the southern-stream Presbyterian Church in the United States (PCUS), a denomination that merged with the successor to the UPCNA and PCUSA in 1983.

72. Minutes of the Forty-Second Annual Meeting of the Egyptian Missionary Association, Cairo, February 20–28 and March 12, 1912, item #32, pp. 13–14; PHS RG 209-19-01: Board of Foreign Missions, Series II: Minutes and Reports, Minutes of the Egypt Mission (Cairo Evangelistic Committee), 1917–27; PHS RG 209-6-35: S. M. Zwemer Papers, 1913–18; PHS UPCUSA RG 81-27-19: COEMAR, ACLSM, Minutes of the Meeting of the Board of Directors, New York, October 8, 1921; AUC Watson, World's Sunday School Association, "Report for Egypt and the Sudan: 1929," by Stephen van R. Trowbridge, typescript copy.

73. Abdul-Fady, *High Lights* [sic] *in the Near East*, 57; PHS UPCUSA RG 81-27-19: COEMAR, ACLSM, Minutes of the Meeting of the Board of Directors, New York, November 23, 1921; ACLSM, Minutes of the Meeting of the Board of Directors, New York, January 28, 1928.

74. Wilson, *Apostle to Islam*, 80.

75. PHS RG 209-2-21: Rev. Dr. James Howard Boyd Papers, Boyd to Charles R. Watson, Tanta, May 13, 1914.

76. Kinnear, *She Sat Where They Sat*, 73.

77. PHS RG 209-5-18: James K. Quay Papers, Quay to [W. B. Anderson], Cairo, April 9, 1920.

78. PHS RG 209-3-05: Russell Galt Papers, Galt to "W. B." [Anderson], Cairo, November 6, 1921.

79. PHS RG 209-1-02: Papers of J. W. Acheson, [Anderson?] to Acheson, November 21, 1924; RG 209-1-03: Papers of J. W. Acheson, 1925, Acheson to W. B. Anderson, December 17, 1924; Acheson to Anderson, February 10, 1925;

Anderson to Acheson, February 28, 1925; RG 209-5-13: Harvey Philips Papers, Philips to Anderson, Cairo, May 22, 1922.

80. AUC Watson, Watson to Speer, June 21, 1928.

81. Mathews, *Roads to the City of God*, viii.

82. AUC Watson, Watson to Speer, June 21, 1928.

83. Na'im, *Al-Judhur al-tarikhiyya*, 201–5.

84. PHS RG 209-5-13: Harvey E. Philips Papers, Philips to W. B. Anderson, Cairo, May 22, 1922.

85. Wilson, *Apostle to Islam*, 89–90.

86. For example, al-Bisati, *Al-Tabshir wa-athruhu*, 126; al-Jundi, *Al-Islam fi wajh al-taghrib*, 46. One source calls Zwemer "the most dangerous evangelist in the Middle East": al-Dahhan, *Quwa al-sharr al-mutahalifa*, 112. References to Zwemer pepper the books surveyed in Sharkey, "Arabic Antimissionary Treatises."

87. Wilson Jr., "The Legacy of Samuel Zwemer."

88. In "Muslim Responses to Missionary Activities in Egypt," Ryad also describes Zwemer's distribution of tracts in al-Azhar as a two-time affair, drawing information from the newspaper *al-Balagh* (April 19 and 22, 1928).

89. CUL BSA, *The Hundred and Eleventh Report of the British and Foreign Bible Society for the Year Ending March MCMXV*, 147, and *The Hundred and Twelfth Report of the British and Foreign Bible Society for the Year Ending March MCMXVI*, 122.

90. Wilson, *The Apostle to Islam*, 88.

91. PHS RG 209-21-16: "Deputation Tour of Egypt [1923–24]," report by W. B. Anderson, typescript, 1924.

92. *Al-Balagh*, June 13, 1933, p. 9.

93. AUC Watson, papers pertaining to the Conference on Extension Work, American University in Cairo, May 29, 1925; and "The Work of the Division of Extension," 1925–26.

94. AUC Ewart Memorial Hall Papers, Memorandum concerning the Address by Dr. Fakhry M. Farag in Ewart Memorial Hall of the American University on the evening of February 4, 1930, Title of Address: "Shall Women and Men Be Equal in Their Rights and Duties?"

95. AUC Ewart Memorial Hall Papers, translations from *Kawkab al-Sharq*, February 12, 1930, article by Abbas Hafez, titled "Chastity with Violence? A Glance at a Crazy Lecture," and *al-Ahram*, February 16, 1930, article by Miss Azza Fozy.

96. *Al-Siyasa*, April 17, 1930, p. 5, and May 26, 1930, p. 4; *al-Fath*, 7 Safar 1349/ July 4, 1930, p. 4; and AUC Watson, R. S. McClenahan to Watson, Cairo, May 26, 1930.

97. Murphy, *The American University in Cairo*, 57–58; PHS RG 209-1-08: J. W. Acheson Papers, letter to William Paton [of the IMC in London], April 16, 1930.

98. AUC Watson, Watson to Gunther, the American minister in Cairo, February 18, 1932, and R. S. McClenahan to Watson, Cortina D'Ampezzo, Italy, June 27, 1930.

99. AUC Watson, Division of Extension, AUC, Report to the President, 1929–30, by R. S. McClenahan.

100. AUC Watson, R. S. McClenahan to Watson, Cortina D'Ampezzo, Italy, June 27, 1930; Murphy, *The American University in Cairo*, 57–58.

101. In April 1930, *al-Siyasa* covered much of the news relating to Fakhry Farag, Kamil Mansur, and Christian missionaries under the same headlines, "The Assault on the Islamic Religion" or "The Defamation of the Islamic Religion." See, for example, *al-Siyasa*, April 14, 1930, p. 1; April 15, 1930, p. 4; April 17, 1930, p. 4. On April 24, 1930 (pp. 4–5), *al-Fath* published an article titled "The Assault on the Islamic Religion" that included a reference to Zwemer, followed by an article titled "Defamation of Islam in the American Schools in Egypt" about the Fakhry Farag and Kamil Mansur affairs.

102. Philips, *Blessed Be Egypt My People*, 7, 44–64.

103. A detailed account, written by the secretary of the American Presbyterian mission to the Pennsylvania woman who provided Kamil Mansur's salary, appears in PHS RG 209-1-08: J. W. Acheson Papers, [Acheson] to Mrs. Louis McCalmont of West View, Pennsylvania, n.d. [May 1930]. Coverage of the Kamil Mansur and Fakhry Farag affairs, and of related discussion in the Egyptian parliament, appeared in *al-Fath,* 25 Dhu al-Qa'da 1348/April 24, 1930, p. 5.

104. *Al-Siyasa*, April 14, 1930, p. 3.

105. *Al-Siyasa*, April 14, 1930; *al-Fath,* 25 Dhu al-Qa'da 1348/April 24, 1930; *al-Siyasa*, April 15, 1930; *al-Fath,* 25 Dhu al-Qa'da 1348/April 24, 1930.

106. *Al-Fath,* 25 Dhu al-Qa'da 1348/April 24, 1930, p. 4.

107. An article specifically on evangelism in American schools appeared in ibid., 8.

108. *Al-Siyasa*, April 14, 1930, p. 1.

109. Na'im, *Tarikh jami'at muqawamat al-tansir al-misriyya*, 7–9.

110. *Al-Fath,* 14 Safar 1349/July 11, 1930, p. 15.

111. PHS RG 209-1-08: J. W. Acheson Papers, Acheson to Taylor, Cairo, December 2, 1930.

112. Elder, *Vindicating a Vision*, 334; Philips, *Blessed Be Egypt My People*, frontispiece photograph of Kamil Mansur as an elderly man.

113. PHS RG 209-1-08: J. W. Acheson Papers, translation of an article, "An Explicit Statement by the Shaykh of al-Azhar," that appeared in *Kawkab al-Sharq*, Cairo, April 19, 1930, with annotation added by Acheson; and [unsigned] letter to Paton, April 16, 1930.

114. PHS RG 209-1-08: J. W. Acheson Papers, Minutes of the Meeting of the Subcommittee of the Inter-Mission Council on "Missions and Government," held Wednesday, April 16, 1930 (marked "Strictly Confidential").

115. Carter, "On Spreading the Gospel to Egyptians Sitting in Darkness," 18, 29.

116. Ibid., 21, 26–27.

117. Na'im, *Tarikh jami'at al-muqawamat al-tansir al-misriyya*, 10.

118. PHS RG 209-1-08: J. W. Acheson Papers, Acheson to W. B. Anderson, Cairo, May 14, 1930; and Acheson to Anderson, Cairo, April 18, 1930.

119. PHS RG 209-1-08: J. W. Acheson Papers, translated excerpt from *al-Siyasa*, April 16, 1930, p. 5.

120. See, for example, *al-Siyasa*, April 14, 1930.

121. See, for example, *al-Fath,* 2 Sha'ban 1348/January 2, 1930, pp. 8–10, and 6 Rajab 1349/November 27, 1930, p. 8. Hasan al-Banna wrote to *al-Fath* to report the activities of the fledgling Muslim Brotherhood in stimulating Muslims to faith: 21 Dhu al-Qa'da 1349/April 9, 1931, p. 8.

122. *Al-Fath,* 29 Muharram 1349/June 26, 1930, p. 15.

123. PHS RG 209-1-10: J. W. Acheson Papers, Quotations from the Cairo Press: Discussions Arising Out of the Incident of the Young Man Youssef Abdel Samad and Later on the Problems of Evangelization in Egypt [1932].

124. PHS RG 209-1-10: J. W. Acheson Papers, translation, "Preachers and Christians in an Islamic Country," *al-Kashkul,* January 29, 1932; AUC Watson, file of papers pertaining to controversies over AUC's Religious Mission, 1924–32, including translated typescript of an article titled "Teachers or Preachers?"

125. AUC Watson, W. B. Anderson to Watson, Philadelphia, January 6, 1928.

126. Watson referred to their institution as the Gospel Center in 1933, when he noted that the Inter-Mission Council had rejected Erian Butros's application for membership. AUC Watson, Watson to Philips, June 9, 1933.

127. PHS RG 209-1-10: J. W. Acheson Papers, "Memorandum Re: The Case of Youssef [Abdel Samad]" by Mrs. Erian Butros, January 24, 1932.

128. PHS RG 209-1-10: J. W. Acheson Papers, résumé of an interview between R. S. McClenahan and S. A. Morrison of the Inter-Mission Council and H. E. Ismail Sidky Pasha, prime minister of the Egyptian government, February 20, 1932.

129. PHS RG 209-3-41: Lucy Lightowler Papers, Lightowler to Miss Grier, Mansura, March 30, 1932.

130. PHS RG 209-1-10: J. W. Acheson Papers, Acheson to W. B. Anderson, March 15, 1932.

131. Na'im, *Tarikh jami'at muqawamat al-tansir al-misriyya,* 10–11, 14–15.

132. PHS RG 209-1-10: J. W. Acheson Papers, A. W. Keown-Boyd to Morrison, [Ministry of the Interior, European Department, Office of the Director-General], Cairo, April 26, 1932; typescript copy marked "Not for News."

133. PHS RG 209-4-07: R. S. McClenahan Papers, W. L. McClenahan to Drs. Watson and Anderson, Heliopolis, March 18, 1915. EGM missionaries were even fonder of tent shows. YDS-EGM, "The Tent Mission, Cairo," undated brochure [c. 1912].

134. PHS RG 209-1-10: J. W. Acheson Papers, Acheson to W. B. Anderson, March 15, 1932.

135. *Nur al-Islam,* Rabi' al-Awwal 1352/June–July 1933, pp. 209–11.

136. Baron, "Summer of '33."

137. Yale Divinity School, Papers of the Salaam Mission to Mohammedans (henceforth YDS-Salaam), Maria Ericsson, *The Swedish Mission Story: Egypt* (n.p., [1924]), 23.

138. *Al-Balagh,* June 13, 1933, p. 1. Drawing on different sources, Umar Ryad calls her "Turkiyya Hasan al-Sayyid Yusuf" so that even her extended name is up for debate. Ryad, "Muslim Responses to Missionary Activities in Egypt," 291. Regarding the social ambiguity of orphans and of Turkiyya Hasan in particular, see Baron, "Summer of '33."

139. *Al-Balagh,* June 14, 1933, p. 14, and June 18, 1933, p. 5.

140. PHS RG 209-5-13: Harvey Philips Papers, Maria Ericsson to Turkiyya Hasan [Flint, Michigan, September 8, 1932], typescript copy based on a photograph submitted by A. W. Keown-Boyd to the Inter-Mission Council.

141. Maria Ericsson apparently had contacts with Harry Bultema, a Dutch American pastor from Michigan who became strongly associated with premillennial doctrines and who split off from the Christian Reformed Church to found a new church, the Berean Reformed Church, in 1920. On a promotional brochure from the mid-1920s, the Salaam mission identified Bultema as the president of its "Council of Referees." YDS-Salaam, brochure, Salaam Mission Interdenominational, n.d. [1920s]. On the growth of premillennialist evangelical "faith missions," see Robert, "'The Crisis of Missions.'"

142. YDS-Salaam, brochure, Salaam Mission Interdenominational, n.d. [1920s].

143. PHS RG 209-5-13: Harvey Philips Papers, A. W. Keown-Boyd, Ministry of the Interior, European Department, to Mr. George Swann [sic], chairman of the Inter-Mission Council of Egypt, June 14, 1933.

144. PHS, Minutes of the Summer Meeting of the Egyptian Missionary Association, Ramleh, July 1920, item 23, pp. 14–17, including list of founding members.

145. Ibid.

146. Beach and Fahs, World Missionary Atlas, 87. On the Pentecostal missions in Egypt, see Nichol, Pentecostalism, 167–68.

147. Al-Balagh, July 1, 1933, p. 6.

148. Al-Balagh, June 29, 1933, p. 7. The front-page headline for al-Balagh on June 19, 1933, had read: "Balagh Investigation into Missionary Activities in Tanta; Conversation with Sheikh of the Ahmadi Mosque: Missionaries Lure Children by Giving Them Sweets."

149. YMCA, Egypt, box #8, Pont Limoun Club for Underprivileged Boys, Report for 1937–38 (including history of the club).

150. PHS RG 209-5-38: Jane C. Smith Papers, Smith to Anna Milligan, June 18, 1933.

151. Al-Balagh, June 15, 1933, p. 1 (headline: "How Missionaries Christianized [nassaru] a Muslim Girl and Married Her to a Christian; The Shari'a Court Issues a Judgment of Separation and the Missionaries Obstruct the Execution of the Judgment; a Letter from New York to the Woman"). On the order placing Nazla Ibrahim Ghunaym under her grandfather's guardianship, see al-Balagh, July 1, 1933, p. 7. Many of the details of Nazla Ibrahim Ghunaym, including the name of her husband, come from the al-Balagh reports. The newspaper does not identify her school as part of the EGM mission but only names its location in Zeitoun. This was a major center for the EGM, which ran a home there for Muslim women converts. Swan, "Lacked Ye Anything," 51–52.

152. Nur al-Islam, Rabi' al-Awwal 1352AH/June–July 1933, pp. 209–11; al-Balagh, June 17, 1933, pp. 1, 7. The latter article declared, "Readers of al-Balagh know that the Salaam School in Port Said is a nest (wakr) of evangelization but they may not know that it is also a nest of love and that the missionaries use this ardent desire as a tool of Christianization."

153. PHS RG 209-1-11: J. W. Acheson Papers, C. C. Adams to W. B. Anderson, Sidi Bishr, July 25, 1933; Cairene, "Egypt and Religious Liberty." "Cairene" was clearly C. C. Adams. PHS RG 209-1-19: C. C. Adams Papers, Adams to Anderson, Cairo, June 26, 1933.

154. PHS RG 209-1-11: J. W. Acheson Papers, C. C. Adams to W. B. Anderson (with translations of articles attached, and including a discussion of the Society for the Defense of Islam), Sidi Bishr, July 25, 1933.

155. It is called Society for Defense of Islam, for example, in Carter, "On Spreading the Gospel."

156. Na'im, *Tarikh jami'at muqawamat al-tansir al-misriyya*, 20.

157. Al-Bisati, *Al-Tabshir wa-athruhu*, 45.

158. Sudan Archive, University of Durham, SAD G//S 1118, Unity High School, Khartoum, Sudan, Log Book No. 1, 1903–42, entry for May 1916.

159. PHS RG 209-1-19: C. C. Adams Papers, Adams to Dr. Anderson, Cairo, June 26, 1933.

160. Baron, "Summer of '33." On June 20, 1933, for example, the newspaper *al-Balagh* enjoined the government to do its duty by acting "for the sake of the honor of the state religion, of the Muslim nation (*umma*), and of public order" (p. 1).

161. Na'im, *Tarikh jami'at muqawamat al-tansir al-misriyya*, 31–32; Carter, "On Spreading the Gospel," 28.

162. Baron, "Summer of '33"; Baron, "Revival on the Nile."

163. Lia, *The Society of the Muslim Brothers in Egypt*, 94, 112–13. Solihin, in *Copts and Muslims*, 48–52, praises the Muslim Brotherhood for leading the efforts "to rescue the people from being Christianized" in this period.

164. Ryad, "Muslim Responses to Missionary Activities in Egypt," 306. On al-Azhar's adversarial relationship with the Muslim Brotherhood, see Hatina, "Historical Legacy and the Challenge of Modernity in the Middle East," 57–58.

165. Baron, "Summer of '33."

166. AUC Watson, Minutes of the Egypt Inter-Mission Council, held at Central YMCA, Cairo, March 20, 1941.

167. American immigration records show that Maria Ericsson of "Port-Said Egypt" was sixty years old when she arrived at Ellis Island in New York in 1924. Passenger record for Maria Ericsson, Statue of Liberty–Ellis Island Foundation, Inc., http://www.ellisisland.org (accessed July 26, 2006). The last reference I have found to Ericsson comes from a Finnish-language source discussing Maria Ericsson and her Salaam mission cofounder, Anna Eklund: Pekkola, *Jumalan poluilla islamin erämaassa*.

168. Ghazal, *Al-Hiyal wa'l-Asalib al-Munharifa fi al-da'wa ila al-tabshir*, 28–29; see also Sharkey, "Arabic Antimissionary Treatises."

169. PHS RG 209-5-13: Harvey Philips Papers, A. W. Keown-Boyd to George Swan, July 1, 1933.

170. PHS RG 209-6-06: F. Scott Thompson Papers, Thompson to R. W. Caldwell, Schutz, Alexandria, August 24, 1933.

171. *Al-Balagh*, June 13, 1933, p. 9.

172. Gershoni and Jankowski, *Redefining the Egyptian Nation*, 55.

173. J. Salama, *Tarikh al-ta'lim al-ajnabi fi Misr*, 23.

174. *Al-Siyasa*, April 9, 1934, p. 1.

175. The missionaries apparently anticipated passage of this law. PHS RG 209-1-10: J. W. Acheson Papers, Acheson to W. B. Anderson, Cairo, April 18, 1932.

176. PHS RG 209-5-12: Frances M. Patton Papers, Patton to Friends, July 21, 1933.

177. J. Salama, *Tarikh al-ta'lim al-ajnabi fi Misr*, 197.

178. Ibid., 280.

179. PHS RG 209-1-12: J. W. Acheson Papers, Acheson to W. B. Anderson, September 29, 1934, with text of "Law No. 40, 1934, re: Free Schools Regulation" attached; and George Swan (chair, Egypt Inter-Mission Council) and E. E. Elder (secretary) to A. W. Keown-Boyd (Ministry of Interior, Cairo), Cairo, September 3, 1934; Elder, *Vindicating a Vision*, 243–44.

180. PHS RG 209-3-40: Charles A. Laughead Papers, Laughead to Taylor, Tanta, June 18, 1936, and Taylor to Laughead, February 27, 1936.

181. PHS RG 209-1-21: C. C. Adams Papers, Adams to R. W. Caldwell, Cairo, October 3, 1938.

182. PHS RG 209-1-22: C. C. Adams Papers, Adams to R. W. Caldwell, Cairo, May 30, 1939; Adams to Caldwell, Cairo, August 3, 1939; Adams to Caldwell, Sidi Bishr, August 11, 1939.

183. AUC Watson, Extracts from Minutes of Montreux Conference Proceedings, Based on notes taken by Dr. Watson [1937]; His Excellency Moustapha Nahas Pasha to Euan Wallace, Head of the Delegation for the United Kingdom, Capitulations Conference, Montreux, May 8, 1937 [copy amid the papers of the Egypt Inter-Mission Council].

184. AUC Watson, "The Next Ten Years of Missions and Government Relations" by Dr. Charles R. Watson, talk presented at the meeting of the Egypt Inter-Mission Council, Central YCMA, Cairo, February 10, 1944. On how the Montreux Convention applied to Americans, see AUC Watson, Wallace Murray to A. L. Warnhuis, Washington, DC, July 21, 1938, copy; and PHS RG 209-21-25: Egypt Mission, Miscellaneous Papers, "International Convention Regarding the Abolition of the Capitulations in Egypt," from U.S. State Department, "Press Releases," Saturday, September 24, 1938.

185. AUC Watson, Watson to R. S. McClenahan, October 28, 1937.

186. AUC Watson, Strictly Confidential, Minutes of the Meeting of the "Missions and Government" Committee of the Egypt Inter-Mission Council, held at AUC, December 1, 1937.

187. PHS RG 209-5-14: Harvey E. Philips Papers, Philips to R. W. Caldwell, Alexandria, May 13, 1937.

188. PHS RG 209-3-17: F. D. Henderson Papers, Henderson to Glenn Reed, Assiut, April 8, 1939.

189. PHS RG 209-6-04: F. Scott Thompson Papers, Thompson (chairman, Committee on Education) to the superintendents of the schools of the American Mission in Egypt, October 30, 1940.

190. PHS RG 209-2-30: Anna B. Criswell Papers, file of papers containing correspondence with American donors for programs and scholarships at PMI, 1933.

191. Wuthnow, *The Restructuring of American Religion*, 25–26.

192. PHS RG 209-3-32: Hugh Espy Kelsey Papers, Kelsey to W. B. Anderson, Hartford, February 10, 1934; PHS RG 209-3-17: F. D. Henderson Papers, "Report of Committee on Evangelism Made to the Egyptian Mission Association," January 1937.

193. PHS RG 209-3-28: Earl R. Jamieson Papers, Jamieson to W. B. Anderson, Fayoum, October 15, 1932.

194. PHS RG 209-1-10: J. W. Acheson Papers, Acheson to Mrs. Sands [of Women's Board?], July 5, 1932; RG 209-2-41: E. E. Elder Papers, Elder to Glenn Reed, Cairo, December 29, 1942.

195. PHS RG 209-3-17: F. D. Henderson Papers, "Report of Committee on Evangelism made to the Egyptian Mission Association," January 1937.

196. Philips, *The Question Box*, 25.

197. PHS RG 209-1-10: J. W. Acheson Papers, Acheson to W. B. Anderson, Ramleh, June 30, 1932.

198. Walls, "The American Dimension in the History of the Missionary Movement," 12–13; Dawson, "Funding Mission in the Early Twentieth Century."

199. PHS RG 209-1-10: J. W. Acheson Papers, Acheson to W. B. Anderson, September 2, 1932.

200. Elder, "The Evangelical Church in Egypt," 522.

201. "Is the Mission Church in Egypt a 'Mature Church'?"; PHS RG 209-5-14: Harvey E. Philips Papers, extracts from minutes of American Mission Association referring to self-support of the Synod of the Nile, 1909–36. On the relationship between mission and church, see Sharkey, "American Mission, Egyptian Church"; and Sharkey, "American Presbyterian Missionaries and the Egyptian Evangelical Church."

202. PHS RG 209-2-48: W. T. Fairman Papers, Fairman to W. B. Anderson, March 15, 1937; "Should the American Mission Dissolve Its Organization and Merge Itself into the Evangelical Church and Its Organizations?"; RG 209-4-02: Neal McClanahan Papers, McClanahan to Gilmore, Assiut, April 4, 1940; RG 209-2-41: E. E. Elder Papers, Elder to Glenn Reed, Cairo, August 13, 1941.

203. PHS RG 209-1-13: J. W. Acheson Papers, "Report of the Committee on Evangelism" [1934].

204. PHS RG 209-5-14: Harvey E. Philips Papers, Philips to W. B. Anderson and Members of the Board, Alexandria, July 29, 1938; Philips to R. W. Caldwell, Alexandria, September 25, 1937.

205. PHS RG 209-5-14: Harvey E. Philips Papers, Philips to Dr. Reid and Members of the Foreign Board, Alexandria, August 2, 1939.

206. PHS RG 209-2-48: W. T. Fairman Papers, Fairman to W. B. Anderson, Heliopolis, February 20, 1933.

207. PHS RG 209-5-14: Harvey E. Philips Papers, Philips to R. W. Caldwell, Alexandria, July 31, 1937.

208. *Al-Siyasa*, May 4, 1930, p. 1, and May 7, 1930, p. 1.

209. *Al-Siyasa Mulhaq*, Literary Supplement No. 2733, Cairo, Friday, 24 Shawal 1350/February 26, 1932, p. 12.

210. *Al-Balagh*, July 3, 1933, p. 12, and June 21, 1933, p. 12.

211. See Buruma and Margalit, *Occidentalism*.

212. Hasan al-Banna, "Hawla Jami'at al-Ikhwan al-Muslimin," *al-Fath,* 21 Dhu'l-Qa'da 1349/April 9, 1931, p. 8.

213. For example, *al-Fath,* 6 Rabi' al-Awwal 1352/June 29, 1933, pp. 13–14, and 13 Rabi' al-Awwal 1352/July 6, 1933, pp. 6–7, on Muslims taking French citizenship; *al-Fath,* 24 Rabi' al-Awwal 1356/June 4, 1937, p. 13, on the new mosque in London; and *al-Fath,* 11 Dhu'l-Qa'da 1348/April 10, 1930, p. 13, on a meeting of five hundred Muslims in South Shields.

214. "Islam in the Land of the English," *Nur al-Islam,* Jumada al-Ula 1349AH/ September–October 1930, pp. 380–82; "Muslims in Western Europe," *Nur al-Islam,* Jumada al-Ula 1350/September–October 1931, pp. 452–56.

215. *Al-Fath,* 12 Rabi' al-Awwal 1349/August 7, 1930, pp. 3, 13, 15. On the "Judaization of Palestine," see, for example, *al-Fath,* 1 Jumada al-Akhira 1352/ September 21, 1933, p. 2.

216. J. McClenahan, *On Going a Journey,* 7–8.

217. "Should the American Mission Dissolve Its Organization and Merge Itself into the Evangelical Church and Its Organizations?"; PHS RG 209-5-14: Harvey E. Philips Papers, Philips to Glenn Reed, Alexandria, January 22, 1940.

218. A. Watson, *The American Mission in Egypt,* 58; PHS RG 209-6-24: Charles R. Watson Papers, Watson to W. B. Anderson, October 13, 1936.

219. Hasan, *Christians versus Muslims in Modern Egypt,* 73.

220. PHS RG 209-3-14: E. E. Grice Papers, Grice to W. B. Anderson, Mansura, Egypt, January 19, 1937.

221. Latourette, *A History of the Expansion of Christianity,* 7:51.

222. Dunch, *Fuzhou Protestants and the Making of a Modern China;* Mallampali, *Christians and Public Life in Colonial South India.*

223. AUC Watson, John D. Rockefeller Jr. to Watson, New York City, February 3, 1933; and Watson to John D. Rockefeller Jr., June 5, 1933.

224. C. Watson, "Rethinking Missions."

225. Hocking, *Re-Thinking Missions,* ix, 28, 37, 40, 82, 92–93.

226. Hutchison, *Errand to the World,* 157, 162, 170.

227. PHS RG 209-5-08: C. A. Owen Papers, Owen to W. B. Anderson, Assiut, January 20, 1933, describing the Missionary Association's chapter-by-chapter discussion of the book.

228. PHS RG 209-1-11: J. W. Acheson Papers, Acheson to W. B. Anderson, January 28, 1933.

229. PHS RG 209-2-16: Ella M. Barnes Papers, Ella M. Barnes to Mrs. Giffen, Fowler Orphanage, Cairo, February 24, 1933.

230. PHS RG 209-5-08: C. A. Owen Papers, W. B. Anderson to Owen, Philadelphia, February 8, 1933.

231. PHS RG 209-6-05: F. Scott Thompson Papers, "Mission Association's Replies to the Board's Questions on the Laymen's [*sic*] Report" [January 1934].

232. AUC Watson, Watson to John R. Mott, off Crete, September 4, 1938.

233. Patterson, "The Loss of a Protestant Missionary Consensus."

234. Wacker, "The Waning of the Missionary Impulse," 191.

235. Coalter, Mulder, and Weeks, *The Re-Forming Tradition,* 45–47, 167–71.

236. PHS RG 209-1-23: J. R. Alexander Papers, J. R. Alexander, "Mission Education in Egypt: A Retrospect, a Survey, an Argument, a Suggestion," Cairo, December 14, 1932.

237. PHS RG 209-5-14: Harvey E. Philips Papers, Philips to W. B. Anderson, Alexandria, January 20, 1937; Philips to Dr. Taylor, Alexandria, May 8, 1939; and extracts from minutes of American Mission Association referring to self-support of the Synod of the Nile, 1909–36. A similar tone of frustration toward Egyptian pastors pervades "Should the American Mission Dissolve Its Organization and Merge Itself into the Evangelical Church and Its Organizations?"

238. Carson, *Agricultural Missions*, 4; C. Watson, *What Is This Moslem World*, x.

239. PHS RG 209-2-51: Davida Finney Papers, Finney to W. B. Anderson, Assiut, February 6, 1933; Finney, *Tomorrow's Egypt*.

240. PHS RG 209-4-13: Milo C. McFeeters Papers, reprint from the *Egyptian Gazette*, "Dairying Possibilities from Egypt," three-part article by M. C. McFeeters, n.d. [c. 1933]; RG 209-4-14: Milo C. and Elma McFeeters Papers, Milo and Elma McFeeters to Friends, Assiut, December 3, 1949; RG 209-21-43: El Afadra Livestock Project, 1952–56.

241. Fitzmier and Balmer, "A Poultice for the Bite of the Cobra," 113.

242. Lachs and Hester, *A William Ernest Hocking Reader*, xi.

243. G. Anderson, "American Protestants in Pursuit of Mission," 396–99.

244. Davis, *Some Aspects of Religious Liberty of Nationals in the Near East*, vii, 9, 11, 15–16, 33–34.

245. AUC Watson, copy of letter from William Ernest Hocking to S. A. Morrison, June 10, 1930.

246. The papers of J. W. Acheson, stored in PHS (RG 209-1-08 to RG 209-1-11), give insights into this mission policy of silent diplomacy.

247. PHS RG 209-1-11: J. W. Acheson Papers, Strictly Confidential, Subject to Ratification, "The Policy of the Foreign Missionary Societies of the Egypt Inter-Mission Council, and certain other missionary bodies with regard to their Work in Egypt, as formulated by them on October 18, 1932." A final printed copy of the statement is found in RG 209-1-13, the file of J. W. Acheson's papers for 1934.

248. On the missionary tendency to promote autonomous individualism as a modern "global universal," see Dunch, "Beyond Cultural Imperialism," 321.

249. PHS RG 209-1-13: J. W. Acheson Papers, "The Policy of the Foreign Missionary Societies of the Egypt Inter-Mission Council, and certain other missionary bodies with regard to their Work in Egypt, as formulated by them on October 18, 1932."

250. *Al-Balagh*, June 23, 1933, p. 1.

251. PHS RG 209-2-02: E. M. Bailey Papers, newspaper clipping, [*Egyptian Gazette*?], April 16, 1940.

252. PHS RG 209-2-41: E. E. Elder Papers, Elder to Glenn Reed, Cairo, July 11, 1940; résumé of the Discussion of the Draft Law forbidding religious propaganda, from the Senate's record of May 27, 1940; and Elder to Reed, Cairo, December 29, 1942.

253. PHS RG 209-1-11: J. W. Acheson Papers, "Report of a Conference on Methods of Work Held by Members of the American Mission," August 2, 1932, remarks by Dr. E. E. Elder.

254. Elder, *Vindicating a Vision*, 238–41, 248.

255. Ibid., 171.

256. PHS RG 209-5-20: Henry Rankin Papers, Rankin to Friends, Cairo, April 12, 1920.

257. Elder, *Vindicating a Vision*, 288; PHS RG 209-3-17: F. D. Henderson Papers, Henderson to Glenn Reed, July 29, 1944. John G. Lorimer recalled that *The Witness* was leased, not technically sold, to the alumnae association and that in the 1950s American missionaries and CEOSS administrators asked to have it returned for visiting Upper Egyptian villages where CEOSS had projects. John G. Lorimer to Heather J. Sharkey, e-mail communication, May 3, 2007.

258. Philips, *The Question Box*, 25; PHS RG 209-5-10: Venna R. Patterson Papers, "Statistics for the Egyptian Mission," 1944.

259. "Statistics for the Egyptian Mission," 1944.

260. Beach and Fahs, *World Missionary Atlas*, 132.

261. Philips, *The Question Box*, 27.

262. "Statistics for the Egyptian Mission," 1944.

263. PHS RG 209-5-14: Harvey E. Philips Papers, Philips to Mills Taylor, Alexandria, May 8, 1939.

264. PHS RG 209-5-37: Walter J. Skellie Papers, Skellie to Glenn Reed, Luxor, April 19, 1939.

265. Elder, *Vindicating a Vision*, 322; AUC Watson, Charles R. Watson to Rev. J. H. Nicol of the American Mission in Beirut, Syria, May 9, 1933. Correspondence relating to the NECC is scattered throughout Watson's papers at AUC.

266. J. Salama, *Tarikh al-ta'lim al-ajnabi fi Misr*, 45, 105 (on the national and ethnic profile of Catholic missions).

267. PHS RG 209-1-11: J. W. Acheson Papers, "Minutes of the Meeting of the Egypt Inter-Mission Council, Held at the Central YMCA," Cairo, Egypt, October 18, 1933.

268. AUC Watson, World's Sunday School Association, "Report for Egypt and the Sudan: 1929."

269. Kraemer, *The Christian Message in a Non-Christian World*.

270. Altizer, "Mission and Dialogue."

271. Tignor, *Capitalism and Nationalism at the End of Empire*, 29.

CHAPTER 5
THE MISSION OF THE AMERICAN UNIVERSITY IN CAIRO

1. AUC Watson, Watson to the Board of Foreign Missions of the UPCNA, Philadelphia, April 24, 1916; and other papers about the inception of the AUC idea, 1903–15.

2. "Report for Egypt and the Sudan: 1929."

3. W. Hogg, *Ecumenical Foundations*, 183.

4. This assertion is based on conversations with retired missionaries, including Willis A. McGill Jr., John G. Lorimer, and Martha Roy, and Egyptian pastors, including Menes Abdel Noor, Emil Zaki, and Tharwat Wahba.

5. PHS Manuscript, call no. V H Un31b, "Lives on [*sic*] Missionaries of the United Presbyterian Church of North America," vol. 5.

6. A. Watson, *The American Mission in Egypt*; C. Watson, *The Sorrow and Hope of the Egyptian Sudan*, 137.

7. Dodge, "Princeton and the Near East"; Kaplan, *The Arabists*.

8. "Princeton Student Debaters" and "Princeton News of Interest: Men Who Will Take Part in the Junior Oratorical Contest," *New York Times*, April 27, 1894, p. 9, and June 11, 1894, p. 12.

9. C. Watson, "Fifty Years of Foreign Missions in Egypt," 84.

10. PHS H5: Charles Roger Watson (personnel file), personal information written by Charles R. Watson, December 14, 1909.

11. W. Hogg, *Ecumenical Foundations*, 102.

12. Mott, *The Evangelization of the World in This Generation*, 115.

13. C. Watson, *In the Valley of the Nile*, 172–73; C. Watson, *Egypt and the Christian Crusade*, 95.

14. C. Watson, *Egypt and the Christian Crusade*, 265.

15. Evangelical Church, Synod of the Nile (henceforth EC-Synod), "A Statement: The University in Cairo and the American Mission in Egypt," n.d. [c. 1921]. Thanks to Stanley H. Skreslet for sharing copies of these records.

16. PHS RG 209-1-23: J. R. Alexander Papers, letters from Alexander to Watson, 1913–15, regarding plans for the university in Cairo; and EC-Synod, excerpts of mission correspondence and minutes regarding plans for the university in Cairo, 1899–1917, fourteen-page typescript. See also Murphy, *The American University in Cairo*, 1–18.

17. Thornton, "Work among Educated Moslems in Cairo," 76; Gairdner, *D. M. Thornton*.

18. World Missionary Conference, *Report of Commission III*, 236–37; Wherry, Mylrea, and Zwemer, *Lucknow, 1911*.

19. AUC, Samuel M. Zwemer scrapbook for the Cairo Study Centre, 1912–21: Prospectus of the Study Centre for Arabic and Islam in Cairo [1912]; and "Cairo Study-Centre for Arabic, Islam, and Moslem Evangelisation," Report of First Session, 1912–13.

20. AUC, SOS, First Record Book, 1911–56.

21. AUC Watson Papers on the School of Oriental Studies, 1921–44; AUC, SOS, First Record Book, 1911–56; Gairdner, *Egyptian Colloquial Arabic* (later editions appeared in 1926, 1944, and 1953); Sharkey, "Christian Missionaries and Colloquial Arabic Printing."

22. AUC, Archives and Special Collections, Dean Richard F. Crabbs Papers, Center for Arabic Studies and Center for Arabic Studies Abroad, c. 1965–73.

23. Murphy, *The American University in Cairo*, 1–18, esp. p. 16. Watson invited the PCUSA to join the effort, but its leaders declined, citing budgetary deficits. AUC Watson, Stanley White, secretary, Board of Foreign Missions of the PCUSA, to Watson, New York, April 22, 1924.

24. Walls, "The American Dimension in the History of the Missionary Movement," 12–14. Watson felt comfortable in the world of big-business fund-raising. The report on the 1904 jubilee celebration for UPCNA missions credited Watson for organizing a meeting for "business men" on issues of mission financing. United Presbyterian Church of North America, *Missionary Jubilee Convention*, 150.

25. American Presbyterian missionaries who joined the AUC faculty included R. S. McClenahan, E. E. Elder, and C. C. Adams.

26. EC-Synod, excerpts of mission correspondence and minutes regarding plans for the university in Cairo, 1899–1917; and EC-Synod, "A Statement: The University in Cairo and the American Mission in Egypt," n.d. [c. 1921].

27. PHS RG 209-1-23: J. R. Alexander Papers, Alexander to Dr. [W. B.] Anderson, Cairo, September 14, 1915. On the parallel history of the American University in Beirut (AUB), see B. Anderson, "Liberal Education at the American University of Beirut."

28. PHS RG 209-6-24: C. R. Watson Papers, Watson to [W. B.] Anderson, Cairo, November 22, 1922.

29. Jamison, *The United Presbyterian Story*, 98–99.

30. PHS RG 209-21-16: W. B. Anderson Papers, report on Anderson's tour of Egypt, 1923–24.

31. EC-Synod, "University and Mission Relations," n.d. [c. 1926].

32. PHS RG 209-6-24: C. R. Watson Papers, Watson to [W. B.] Anderson, Cairo, October 5, 1922. An incident two years later proved how sensitive Christian teaching could be. Responding to a report (which was later retracted) about an Iraqi Muslim student's conversion to Christianity, the Arabic newspaper *al-Liwa'* published an article about AUC titled "Teachers or Preachers?" It called the university's ethics classes an attack on Islam and Muhammad, and demanded that the government curb religious instruction in foreign schools. *Al-Liwa'* (Cairo), May 27, 1924, translated article in AUC Watson, Controversies over AUC's Religious Mission, 1924–32.

33. Badeau, *The Middle East Remembered*, 49.

34. Robert, "The First Globalization."

35. AUC Watson, Watson to Robert E. Speer, June 21, 1928.

36. C. Watson, *In the Valley of the Nile*, 235–36; C. Watson, "Fifty Years of Foreign Missions," 85.

37. C. Watson, *Egypt and the Christian Crusade*; compare with other works of the period, such as Zwemer, Wherry, and Barton, *The Mohammedan World of To-Day*; Gairdner, *The Reproach of Islam*; and Mott, *The Decisive Hour of Christian Missions*, 57.

38. See, for example, Pierard, "Pax Americana and the Evangelical Missionary Advance."

39. Said, *Orientalism*.

40. Watson et al., *The Presentation of Christianity to Moslems*, 11, 77, 82–87, 104–5.

41. Hutchison, *The Modernist Impulse in American Protestantism*, 4.

42. A. Watson, "Islam in Egypt."

43. Marsden, *The Soul of the University*.

44. AUC Watson, Watson to J. H. Oldham, London, July 10, 1932.

45. On the anti-missionary agitation, see chapter 4.

46. AUC Watson, Watson to Robert E. Speer, June 21, 1928.

47. *Al-Siyasa* (Cairo), January 26, 1932, cited in PHS RG 209-1-10: J. A. Acheson Papers, "Quotations from the Cairo Press: Discussions Arising Out of the Incident of the Young Man Youssef Abdel Samad and Later on the Problems of Evangelization in Egypt" (1932).

48. AUC Watson, file of papers labeled "Controversies over AUC's Religious Mission," including translations of Arabic newspaper articles regarding the case of Abdel Kader Al Husseini, May 28–June 22, 1932 (from *al-Balagh*, *al-Muqattam*, *Kawkab al-Sharq*, and *al-Siyasa*).

49. Badeau, *The Middle East Remembered*, 58–59; see also Murphy, *The American University in Cairo*, 76–78.

50. Lia, *The Society of the Muslim Brothers in Egypt*, 78.

51. On the efforts of the Egypt Inter-Mission Council in this period, see Sharkey, "Muslim Apostasy, Christian Conversion, and Religious Freedom in Egypt."

52. W. Hogg, *Ecumenical Foundations*, 189.

53. AUC Watson, Watson to H. E. Ismail Sidky Pasha, November 4, 1932; Ismail Sidky Pasha to Watson, invitation to a soirée at the Semiramis Hotel, January 26, 1933.

54. AUC Watson, Watson to T.H.P. Sailer of the Missionary Education Movement, February 22, 1933.

55. AUC Watson, "General Circular to American Staff, Subject: Our American Attitude toward the Egyptian Government Course," n.d.

56. AUC Watson, Watson to W. B. Smith of the Cairo YMCA, September 19, 1928.

57. YMCA, Biographical Records, box 166, file for James K. Quay, biographical sketch, n.d. [1930].

58. PHS RG 209-6-24: Charles R. Watson Papers, Watson to Quay, Cairo, July 17, 1925. The report was American Committee on Survey [*sic*] of Christian Literature for Moslems, *The Power of the Printed Page in the World of Islam*.

59. On the social convergence of Watson and Quay within mission, church, and YMCA circles, see, for example, PHS RG 209-20-15: The American Church of Cairo, Historical Sketch, including programs for services, 1929; PHS RG 209-1-08: J. W. Acheson Papers, Strictly Confidential, Minutes, Meeting of the Sub-Committee of the Inter-Mission Council on "Missions and Government," held on Tuesday, April 22, 1930; AUC Watson, Watson to Quay, Cairo, November 29, 1944. Reports in the YMCA archives in Minnesota also show that Watson donated annually to the Cairo YMCA.

60. Attached to these diary excerpts was a note that Quay wrote in 1960, explaining, "I had completely forgotten its existence and I don't even know why it was written unless to help me marshal my ideas for speeches in America." YMCA, Biographical Records, box 166, file for James K. Quay, Quay to Virginia Downs, Princeton, March 9, 1960.

61. Quay, "Service in Egypt from 1919 to 1948."

62. YMCA, Biographical Records, box 166, file for James K. Quay, "A Missionary Journey" (some items from a five-year diary of James K. Quay [1928–33]),

typescript, n.d. [compiled March 5, 1960, from diary notes compiled c. 1933], entries for December 25, 1928, and January 13 and May 7, 1929.

63. AUC Watson, George Swan, compiler [on behalf of Inter-Mission Council], "The Report from Egypt," Council for Western Asia and North Africa, n.d. [1929], Re: "General Political Situation as Affecting Christ's Kingdom."

64. "Survey of the YMCA in Egypt," 2:152, 163.

65. PHS RG 209-5-18: James K. Quay Papers, Quay to W. B. Anderson, on-board the *Ibis*, March 27, 1920, and Quay to Anderson, Cairo, May 16, 1919, and September 6, 1919.

66. PHS RG 209-3-05: Russell Galt Papers, Galt to W. B. Anderson, Cairo, November 6, 1921.

67. YMCA, Biographical Records, box 166, file for James K. Quay, "A Missionary Journey," entry for March 27, 1930.

68. YMCA, Biographical Records, box 166, file for James K. Quay, Quay to Virginia Downs, Princeton, March 9, 1960, and postscript to "A Missionary Journey," Princeton, March 4, 1960.

69. AUC Watson, Watson to T.H.P Sailer, September 17, 1927.

70. AUC Watson, Watson to Robert E. Speer, May 26, 1930.

71. AUC Watson, Watson to John D. Rockefeller Jr., June 5, 1933, and Rockefeller to Watson, telegram, July 26, 1932; C. Watson, "Rethinking Missions."

72. Wacker, "The Waning of the Missionary Impulse"; Fitzmier and Balmer, "A Poultice for the Bite of the Cobra." Watson knew about Buck's support for the Hocking Report because Rockefeller sent him her review of it. AUC Watson, John D. Rockefeller Jr. to Watson, New York, February 3, 1933.

73. Hocking, *Re-Thinking Missions*, 9, 28, 40, 46, 47, 82, 85, 92.

74. Fitzmier and Balmer, "A Poultice for the Bite of the Cobra," 116, 122–23.

75. AUC Watson, Watson to John D. Rockefeller Jr., June 5, 1933.

76. C. Watson, *Do New World Conditions Challenge Changes in Missionary Method and Policy?* [marked "Printed Only for Private Circulation"], 8.

77. This condensed version appeared as C. Watson, "The Challenge of the Present Crisis"; this quotation comes from an editorial blurb on p. 123.

78. C. Watson, "Our Religious Policies," 3–4.

79. Ibid., 10–11.

80. C. Watson, *What Is This Moslem World*, ix–x.

81. "Finds Our Ideals Growing in Islam: Dr. Watson Calls Auto and Movie Chiefs Agents in Spreading Knowledge of the West," *New York Times*, November 22, 1926, p. 26.

82. C. Watson, *What Is This Moslem World*, 140–41, 144, 180–81, 189.

83. "Dr. Watson Urges Social Integration: He Says in Baccalaureate at Vassar That Americans Are Lacking in Cohesion," *New York Times*, June 13, 1932, p. 8.

84. C. Watson, "Egypt—What Price Progress?"

85. AUC Watson, papers pertaining to the Extension Division, including R. S. McClenahan's "Report to the President on the Division of Extension," 1929–30; Minutes on Arabic Extension Lectures, 1932–33; and Watson to Taha Hussein Bey, February 5, 1944.

86. Murphy, *The American University in Cairo*, 114.

87. Danielson, *The Voice of Egypt*, 86–87, 147.

88. PHS RG 209-1-22: C. C. Adams Papers, Adams to Glenn Reed, March 17, 1939.

89. AUC Watson, files on the Umm Kulthum concerts; PHS RG 209-4-01: Neal McClanahan Papers, Charles R. Watson to Moawad Hanna, May 28, 1938, and McClanahan to Reid [*sic*], "In Explanation of the Accompanying Paper," Assiut College [1938]. This controversy is discussed at length in Sharkey, "Umm Kulthum at the American University in Cairo."

90. AUC Watson, papers pertaining to the conference on Extension Work, AUC, May 29, 1925; and "The Work of the Division of Extension, Report for 1925–26." Dr. Fakhry Farag stopped lecturing in 1930, when he became embroiled in a lawsuit on charges of defaming Islam, but screenings of *The Gift of Life* continued.

91. AUC Watson, Division of Extension, "Report on Administration and Research," n.d. [1935].

92. A harrowing description of these wartime brothels appears in Upson's memoirs: Abdul-Fady, *High Lights [sic] in the Near East*, 68–77.

93. "Survey of the YMCA in Egypt," 2:77.

94. AUC Watson, Watson to H. E. Shahin Pasha, October 21, 1932.

95. T. R. Ybarra, "Americans' University Growing Up in Cairo," *New York Times*, June 17, 1928, p. 128.

96. C. Watson, *What Is This Moslem World*, 165.

97. C. Watson, "Egypt—What Price Progress," 72.

98. AUC Watson, memorandum on University Extension Program, n.d. [c. 1929].

99. YMCA, Egypt, box #8, Central Branch Cairo, "Summary Report," 1938.

100. AUC Watson, Division of Extension, "Report on Administration and Research."

101. AUC Watson, "Memorandum on University Extension Program," n.d. [c. 1929].

102. AUC Watson, "The University and Community Service," text of a speech delivered at the dedication of Ewart Memorial Hall, April 11, 1928.

103. C. Watson, *What Is This Moslem World*, ix–x.

104. Amir Boktor's English publications include *School and Society in the Valley of the Nile* and *The Development and Expansion of Education in the United Arab Emirates*. The Arabic publications of Amir Buqtur include *Al-Dunya fi Amrika*; *Al-Danimarkah*; *Fann al-zawaj*; and *Anta . . . wa ana, min ja'na?*

105. Boktor cites credentials as "AUC Secretary" in an article he published in the Arabic paper *al-Muqattam* on the Scopes trial. Watson expressed concern lest this article draw AUC into "public controversy" over the theory of evolution. AUC Watson, Arthur T. Upson to Watson, October 6, 1925; and Watson to Upson, October 8, 1932.

106. AUC Watson, extracts from "Outlines of Philosophy" by Vinet, personal notes, n.d. Watson engaged with the ideas of the Swiss theologian and advocate of religious liberty Alexandre-Rodolphe Vinet (1797–1847).

107. AUC Watson, Amir Boktor to R. S. McClenahan, Roucegno, Italy, August 11, 1937.

108. AUC Watson, R. S. McClenahan to Watson, Dresden, August 20, 1937.

109. AUC Watson, Watson to John R. Mott, January 10, 1940.

110. AUC Watson, "The Next Ten Years of Missions and Government Relations," talk delivered by Charles R. Watson at the meeting of the Egypt Inter-Mission Council, February 10, 1944.

111. "Mainline Churches," in *Dictionary of Christianity in America*, ed. D. G. Reid, 700–701.

112. C. Watson, *The Big Idea*, 21.

113. "Egypt Taking Place among the Nations," *New York Times*, February 19, 1928, p. 51.

114. "Christian Opportunity in the Near East Seen by Head of Cairo University," *New York Times*, October 29, 1934, p. 13.

115. AUC Watson, John S. Badeau to Dr. C. H. Foster, of the Division of Cultural Relations, U.S. Department of State, April 28, 1943.

116. AUC Watson, Service Contract of the U.S. War Department with the Council of the American University at Cairo, July 1, 1943.

117. AUC Watson, Watson to the Middle East Division of the Federal Economic Administration (FEA), via Mr. Stranger of the American Legation of Cairo, January 20, 1945.

118. Badeau, *The Middle East Remembered*.

119. AUC Watson, Watson to C. C. Adams of the SOS, January 11, 1945; and C. C. Adams, "Memorandum to the Members of the SOS Faculty," July 20, 1944.

120. C. Watson, *The Big Idea*, 20–21.

121. Watson to the Middle East Division of the Federal Economic Administration (FEA), January 20, 1945.

122. Murphy, *The American University in Cairo*, 131.

123. Ibid., 99; Lamont, *The American University in Cairo*, 12.

124. "Survey of the YMCA in Egypt," 1:vi.

125. This development may have also reflected the natural progression of Watson's brand of Christian activism, for as Dana L. Robert notes, "It can be argued that the embrace of internationalism by some missionaries within Protestant liberalism after World War I set in motion a secularizing trend that ultimately rejected its missionary origins." Robert, "The First Globalization," 54.

126. B. Anderson, "Liberal Education at the American University of Beirut"; Goffman, "Masking the Mission."

127. Hart, *Dictionary of the Presbyterian and Reformed Tradition in America*.

128. McGill telephone conversation.

129. For a recent analysis of AUC's American character in the Egyptian social context, see Lash, "Exporting Education."

130. For a list of NGOs that have worked with CEOSS, see Lorimer, *The Presbyterian Experience in Egypt*, 95.

131. Tejirian and Simon, *Altruism and Imperialism*.

CHAPTER 6
TURNING TO THE LIFE OF THE CHURCH: AMERICAN MISSION IN AN AGE
OF EGYPTIAN DECOLONIZATION AND ARAB-ISRAELI POLITICS, 1945–67

1. PHS RG 209-2-10: Ewing M. Bailey Papers, Confidential, "Memorandum on Remarks Made by Glenn Reed before the Association of the American Mission in Egypt Concerning Compliance with the Law Requiring Schools to Teach Islam to Muslim pupils (July 2, 1956)."

2. Lamb, *The Call to Retrieval*, 4.

3. Lorimer conversation, August 29, 2004; John G. Lorimer to Heather J. Sharkey, Pasadena, January 7, 2005.

4. Monroe, *Britain's Moment in the Middle East*.

5. Cragg, *The Call of the Minaret*, 304.

6. Ibid., 305.

7. PHS, Martha A. Roy and Willis A. McGill, "Report on the Middle East Crisis and the Egypt Mission," typescript, New York City, June 21, 1967.

8. Lorimer, "Presbyterians in the Middle East," 43.

9. Galdas, *A Village Reborn*; Dye, *The CEOSS Story*, 59.

10. Tignor, *State, Private Enterprise, and Economic Change in Egypt*, 175–80.

11. Vitalis, *When Capitalists Collide*, 48–50.

12. Morrison, *Religious Liberty in the Near East*, 21. See Wakin, *A Lonely Minority*, 49, for a similar argument.

13. J. Salama, *Tarikh al-ta'lim al-ajnabi fi Misr*, 20, 126–27, 131.

14. Ahmad, *Al-Ajanib wa-athruhum fi al-mujtama' al-misri*, 2:5, 109–11.

15. J. Salama, *Tarikh al-ta'lim al-ajnabi fi Misr*, 20, 126–27; Ahmad, *Al-Ajanib wa-athruhum fi al-mujtama' al-misri*, 168–70.

16. PHS RG 209-6-22: Bradley Watkins Papers, Watkins to Members of the Committee on Education, the American Mission in Egypt, Luxor, March 17, 1947.

17. J. Salama, *Tarikh al-ta'lim al-ajnabi fi Misr*, 23, 280; PHS RG 209-2-42: E. E. Elder Papers, typescript copy of article about Law 38 from the *Egyptian Gazette*, Sunday, May 2, 1948.

18. Gershoni and Jankowski, *Redefining the Egyptian Nation*, xiv, 14, 54–78; Sonbol, *The New Mamluks*.

19. PHS RG 209-2-05: E. M. Bailey Papers, Bailey to Glenn Reed, Assiut, January 20, 1947, and Bailey to Reed, Assiut, January 31, 1947.

20. See also Wakin, *A Lonely Minority*, 67, on Christians and Arabic policy.

21. PHS RG 209-6-23: Bradley Watkins Papers, Watkins to Glenn Reed, Luxor, October 3, 1947, and RG 209-6-22: Bradley Watkins Papers, Watkins to Members of the Committee on Education, the American Mission in Egypt, Luxor, March 17, 1947. Further discussion of mounting government regulations and pressures at this time appears in PHS RG 209-2-05: E. M. Bailey Papers, Bailey to Reed, Assiut, January 20, 1947.

22. PHS RG 209-1-15: J. W. Acheson Papers, Acheson to Reed, Cairo, January 15, 1947; Acheson to Caldwell, Schutz, Alexandria, August 6, 1947; Acheson to Hugh Kelsey, Schutz, Alexandria, August 6, 1937; Acheson to Kelsey, Cairo, November 7, 1947.

23. PHS RG 209-2-43: E. E. Elder Papers, letter from the leaders of the Anglican Church in Egypt and the American Mission in Egypt [Bishop Allen and Elder], to His Excellency the Minister of Public Instruction, Cairo, October 5, 1949.

24. PHS RG 209-2-43: E. E. Elder Papers, "Summary of Interview with His Excellency Ahmad Moursi Badr Bey, Minister of Education," October 12, 1949.

25. PHS RG 209-2-05: E. M. Bailey Papers, Bailey to Glenn Reed, Minya, November 1948.

26. Dye, *The CEOSS Story*; Hasan, *Christians versus Muslims in Modern Egypt*, 92 and passim.

27. PHS UPCUSA RG 115-13-7: NECC, Minutes of the Meeting of the Committee on Work among Moslems, New York City, January 14, 1948. The UPCNA representative was Hugh Kelsey, a former missionary to Egypt.

28. PHS RG 209-2-42: E. E. Elder Papers, Elder to Glenn Reed, May 18, 1948; Elder on behalf of the American Mission to Truman, Cairo, May 17, 1948; and Elder on behalf of the American Mission to Whom It May Concern, n.d.

29. PHS RG 209-4-30: Helen J. Martin Papers, Martin to Glenn Reed, Cairo, May 22, 1948.

30. PHS RG 209-2-53: Davida Finney Papers, Finney to Friend of the Laubach Campaign, Cairo, December 12, 1950; Garraud of UNRWA to Finney, Beirut, August 17, 1951; and Finney to Glenn [Reed], Cairo, June 15, 1951.

31. PHS RG 209-2-55: Davida Finney Papers, Finney to Mrs. Arthur B. McBride, Sterling, Kansas, July 24, 1950.

32. PHS RG 209-2-53: Davida Finney Papers, 1946–50, Finney to Rev. A. R. Stevenson, Cairo, February 23, 1952.

33. PHS RG 209-6-07: F. Scott Thompson Papers, "With the Quaker Relief Unit in Gaza," undated memoir by John A. Thompson (son of F. Scott Thompson).

34. AUC Watson, letter to the editor, *New York Times*, December 5, 1947, p. 24. One of Watson's articles, "The Partition of Palestine," appeared posthumously in the church journal *United Presbyterian* (February 16, 1948).

35. Quoted in Grabill, "Protestant Diplomacy and Arab Nationalism," 122.

36. Badeau, *The Middle East Remembered*, 115.

37. Lorimer, "Presbyterians in the Middle East."

38. Lorimer conversation, August 27, 2004; Lorimer, *The Presbyterian Experience in Egypt*, 186–87.

39. Murphy, *The American University in Cairo*, 108–10, 132–34, 172–75.

40. Kaplan, *The Arabists*, 9.

41. Grabill, "Protestant Diplomacy and Arab Nationalism," 113.

42. Morrison, "Egypt: Land of Paradox."

43. United Nations General Assembly, "Universal Declaration of Human Rights."

44. "The Policy of the Foreign Missionary Societies of the Egypt Inter-Mission Council, and certain other missionary bodies with regard to their Work in Egypt, as formulated by them on October 18, 1932."

45. PHS UPCUSA RG 115-13-7: NECC, Foreign Missions Conference of North America, Committee on Work among Moslems, Digests of Reports

presented to the Committee for the Restudy of Christian-Moslem Relations, 1947–48.

46. M. Glen Johnson, "Magna Carta for Mankind: Writing the Universal Declaration of Human Rights," in *The Universal Declaration of Human Rights*, ed. Johnson and Symonides, 19–75, esp. 22–23.

47. Quay, "Service in Egypt from 1919 to 1948." In this same collection, see also YMCA, Biographical Records, box #166, file for James K. Quay, including "A Missionary Journey."

48. Arzt, "The Application of International Human Rights Law in Islamic States," esp. p. 216; Morsink, *The Universal Declaration of Human Rights*, 24–25.

49. Morrison, *Middle East Survey*, 112–15.

50. Ibid., 114–16.

51. Ibid., 170–71.

52. Ibid., 173, 175.

53. PHS RG 209-2-06: E. M. Bailey Papers, "Egypt News Letter," by E. M. Bailey, May 31, 1951 [typescript draft].

54. Ahlstrom, *A Religious History of the American People*, 785–804.

55. PHS RG 209-2-45: Earl E. Elder Papers, E. E. Elder, description of recent events, marked "Confidential, do not quote in papers," n.d. [February 8, 1952].

56. PHS RG 209-4-31: Helen J. Martin Papers, mimeographed letter from Helen J. Martin, Cairo, February 1, 1952, marked "Strictly not for publication."

57. PHS RG 209-10-03: Reports, Egypt Mission Stations, 1951–52, "Report on Recent Events," marked "Strictly not for publication, copies sent by pouch by permission of Mr. Buffalo," February 1, 1952; Oliver, "Lest We Forget," 269.

58. Tignor, *State, Private Enterprise, and Economic Change in Egypt*, 251.

59. Oliver, "Lest We Forget," 273.

60. Goldschmidt, *Modern Egypt*, 96.

61. Woodward, *Nasser*, 19.

62. Alterman, "American Aid to Egypt in the 1950s," esp. 52–55.

63. PHS RG 209-21-43: The El Afadra Livestock Project, 1952–56, Report by Earl M. Kroth, "The El Afadra Livestock Project—An Experiment in Helping Egyptian Villages, the Ford Foundation and Assiut College, 1952–1956," June 15, 1957; Lorimer, *The Presbyterian Experience in Egypt*, 97–102.

64. Dye, *The CEOSS Story*, 62–63, 81; Dye et al., *Literacy—The Essential Skill*, 113.

65. PHS RG 209-21-55: Ford Foundation, "Proposed Projects for Egypt under Cooperation of the American College for Girls, Cairo, Egypt, and the Ford Foundation, June 1952," under the direction of the Board of Foreign Missions of the UPCNA, Philadelphia.

66. Badeau, *The Middle East Remembered*, 139–41.

67. Wakin, *A Lonely Minority*, 48; Badeau, *The Middle East Remembered*, 139.

68. I will not identify the pastor because he was clearly nervous discussing the subject. See also Wissa, *Assiout*, 121.

69. See, for example, Morrison, "Egypt: Land of Paradox," 267–68 (written in 1946).

70. Ayrout, *The Egyptian Peasant*, 16. Upon its initial debut in 1938, the book was titled *Moeurs et coutoumes des fellahs*.

71. John Alden Williams, foreword to Ayrout, *The Egyptian Peasant*, x–xi.

72. Lorimer e-mail, February 17, 2006.

73. Virtue, *A Vision of Hope*, 24–26.

74. Ibid., 42–49; Habib, *Tariq al-tahaddi*, 15–16, 21, and passim; Dye, *The CEOSS Story*, 72–73. On Samuel Habib's call for gender reforms, see also A. Salama, *Al-Injiliyyun wa-al-'amal al-qawmi*, 136–38.

75. PHS RG 209-21-39: Egypt Mission Newsletters, "Egyptian News Letter," Cairo, June 2, 1953.

76. A. Salama, *Al-Injiliyyun wa-al-'amal al-qawmi*, 200.

77. Morrison, *Middle East Survey*, 117.

78. Wakin, *A Lonely Minority*, 70.

79. Egypt Mission Newsletters, "Egyptian News Letter."

80. Wakin, *A Lonely Minority*, 43–47, 54–55, 59–60.

81. PHS RG 209-10-05: Egypt Minutes 1955, Minutes of the Association of the American Mission in Egypt, Sidi Bishr, June 28–30, 1955, p. 275; RG 209-2-09: Ewing M. Bailey Papers, Bailey to Donald Black, Cairo, March 30, 1955.

82. Quoted in Lorimer, *The Presbyterian Experience in Egypt*, 159.

83. For example, al-Shalabi, *Afiqu ayyuha al-muslimun qabla 'an tadfa'u al-jizya*; al-'Askar, *Al-Tansir wa-muhawalatuhu fi bilad al-khalij al-'arabi*; al-Hasin, *Al-Khatar al-tabshiri al-salibi fi al-Kuwayt*. Hasin's book is about Kuwait, and yet he specifically mentions the Copts of Egypt as a Christian people who have exceeded their bounds (see pp. 12, 15).

84. Sharkey, "Arabic Antimissionary Treatises."

85. Khalidi and Farrukh, *Al-Tabshir wa'l-isti'mar fi al-bilad al-'arabiyya*, 36. Regarding this book, see also Goddard, *A History of Christian-Muslim Relations*, 134.

86. Khalidi and Farrukh, *Al-Tabshir wa'l-isti'mar fi al-bilad al-'arabiyya*, 34.

87. Ibid., 233.

88. Milligan, *Facts and Folks in Our Fields Abroad*, 20–21.

89. PHS RG 209-2-45: Earl E. Elder Papers, Elder to Glenn Reed, Cairo, May 15, 1954.

99. Morrison, *Middle East Survey*, 119.

91. Lorimer, "Presbyterians in the Middle East," 38.

92. See also PHS RG 209-19-07: Egypt Reports, 1956, "The American Mission in Egypt, Narrative Report of the Secretary for the Year 1956, by E. M. Bailey."

93. J. Salama, *Tarikh al-ta'lim al-ajnabi fi Misr*, 177–78, 280–81.

94. PHS RG 209-2-10: Ewing M. Bailey Papers, excerpt from text of Article 17 of Law 583, 1955.

95. PHS RG 209-2-10: Ewing M. Bailey Papers, Egypt, Statistics, 1954–55, "The American Mission in Egypt, Narrative Report of the Secretary for the Year 1956, by E. M. Bailey." By the time Bailey wrote in 1957, the mission's schools were reduced to fourteen.

96. Monroe, *Britain's Moment in the Middle East*; Vitalis, "The 'New Deal' in Egypt," esp. 212.

97. Tignor, *Capitalism and Nationalism at the End of Empire*, 114, 128.

98. Ibid., 130–35; Beinin, *The Dispersion of Egyptian Jewry*.

99. PHS RG 209-2-10: Ewing M. Bailey Papers, Bailey to Donald Black, January 17, 1956.

100. "The American Mission in Egypt, Narrative Report of the Secretary for the Year 1956, by E. M. Bailey."

101. PHS RG 209-2-10: Ewing M. Bailey Papers, Confidential, "The Report on Field Deputation by Dr. Reed and Dr. Black Concerning Teaching of Islam in Schools in Egypt, June 23–July 8, 1956."

102. PHS RG 209-2-10: Ewing M. Bailey Papers, American Mission in Egypt, "Notice Now Being Sent to Muslim Parents," 1956.

103. PHS RG 209-2-10: Ewing M. Bailey Papers, article from *Egyptian Gazette*, May 21, 1956, typescript copy: "Govt. to Exercise Control over All Private Schools: Yussef Explains Purpose of New Law."

104. "The Report on Field Deputation by Dr. Reed and Dr. Black Concerning Teaching of Islam in Schools in Egypt, June 23–July 8, 1956."

105. Ibid.

106. Ibid.

107. "The American Mission in Egypt, Narrative Report of the Secretary for the Year 1956, by E. M. Bailey."

108. "The Report on Field Deputation by Dr. Reed and Dr. Black Concerning Teaching of Islam in Schools in Egypt, June 23–July 8, 1956."

109. PHS RG 209-2-10: Ewing M. Bailey Papers, Donald Black to [all] the [active] Pastors of the United Presbyterian Church, Philadelphia, July 12, 1956; and Confidential for Pastors, "STATEMENT Concerning the Teaching of Islam to Muslim Pupils Enrolled in Schools of the American Mission in Egypt."

110. "The American Mission in Egypt, Narrative Report of the Secretary for the Year 1956, by E. M. Bailey"; RG 209-2-11: Ewing M. Bailey Papers, the American Mission, Minutes of the Executive Committee Meeting, November 29, 1956.

111. See A. Watson, *The American Mission in Egypt*, 328; C. Watson, *Egypt and the Christian Crusade*, 179; Morrison, "Egypt: Land of Paradox," 269; Morrison, *Middle East Survey*, 112; Elder, *Vindicating a Vision*, 72–73; Ibrahim et al., *The Copts of Egypt*, 11; Shukri, *Al-Aqbat fi watan mutaghayyir*, 187-88, 200–202; Hasan, *Christians versus Muslims in Modern Egypt*, 209–10; Oram, "Constructing Modern Copts," 70–71, 84, 135–40; Hamilton, *The Copts and the West*, 31–32.

112. PHS RG 209-2-10: Ewing M. Bailey Papers, Bailey to Donald Black, Cairo, August 23, 1956, and September 20, 1956.

113. J. Salama, *Tarikh al-ta'lim al-ajnabi fi Misr*, 24.

114. CUL BSA, *One Hundred and Fifty-Third and Fifty-Fourth Reports of the British and Foreign Bible Society for the Years Ending December 31st 1957 and 1958*, 83–85.

115. PHS RG 209-2-10: Ewing M. Bailey Papers, Bailey to Donald Black, Cairo, November 19, 1956; Sharkey, "Empire and Muslim Conversion"; Rhodes, "Anglican Mission." The NMP moved to Beirut and years later merged into a Christian media enterprise in Cyprus. See PHS UPCUSA RG 115-14-9: Nile Mission Press, Announcement, Beirut, September 19, 1957.

116. PHS RG 209-2-10: Ewing M. Bailey Papers, Bailey to Donald Black, Cairo, December 3, 1956.

117. PHS RG 209-20-02: Annual Reports, Various Stations, 1957, "Mission Stations, Egypt, American staff list" [1957, typescript].

118. Lorimer, "Presbyterians in the Middle East," 40.

119. PHS RG 209-2-11: Ewing M. Bailey Papers, Donald Black to Bailey and Lorimer, February 20, 1957; Bailey to Black, Cairo, February 18, 1957.

120. Black, "Board of Foreign Missions of the United Presbyterian Church of North America."

121. PHS RG 209-2-11: Ewing M. Bailey Papers, Lowrie [Anderson] to Black, Khartoum, February 14, 1957.

122. Sharkey, "Missionary Legacies," 84–85.

123. Abadir conversation.

124. Sheridan, "Coptic Christianity," 135.

125. Smylie, A Brief History of the Presbyterians, 124; Bendroth, "An Understated Tale of Epic Social Change."

126. Black, Merging Mission and Unity, 37–38.

127. PHS RG 209-20-26: Donald Black Papers, "Looking Ahead in Policy," mimeograph from the Foreign Board [1955].

128. PHS RG 209-2-11: Ewing M. Bailey Papers, Bailey to Donald Black, Cairo, May 16, 1957.

129. Jamison, The United Presbyterian Story, 198.

130. J. Smith, From Colonialism to World Community, 184.

131. Quick, "He Who Pays the Piper," 13–15, 71–72, 82, 96.

132. Bonk, Missions and Money, 4, 38.

133. See Jamison, The United Presbyterian Story, 198–99.

134. Black, "Board of Foreign Missions of the United Presbyterian Church of North America."

135. Lorimer, "Presbyterians in the Middle East," 38.

136. Sproul, "The American College for Girls, Cairo, Egypt," 82–86.

137. Lorimer conversations; Dye, The CEOSS Story. Lorimer's Presbyterian Experience in Egypt, published in 2007, attempts to restore that elision.

138. PHS UPCUSA RG 115-13-8: NECC, Donald Black to John C. Smith and Margaret Shannon, COEMAR, UPCUSA, December 7, 1962.

139. Skreslet, "Presbyterians and the Middle East."

140. Lorimer e-mail, February 17, 2006.

141. A. Salama, Al-Injiliyyun wa-al-'amal al-qawmi, 9; Dye, The CEOSS Story, 59.

142. Greeley, The Catholic Revolution, 54; Noll, The Old Religion in a New World, 173; Wuthnow, The Restructuring of American Religion, 94; Sundkler and Steed, A History of the Church in Africa, 4–5.

143. Lorimer e-mail, February 17, 2006.

144. Black, Merging Mission and Unity, 55–56.

145. Noor conversation; see also Lorimer, "Presbyterians in the Middle East," 43–44. For a Catholic source, see Fahim, "Modestes recherches d'une communauté de laïcs," 174.

146. Atiya, A History of Eastern Christianity, 120–21.

147. Voile, Les coptes d'Egypte sous Nasser, 44, 54, 58, 63–64; Oram, "Constructing Modern Copts."

148. Hasan, *Christians versus Muslims in Modern Egypt*, 3.

149. Lorimer, "Presbyterians in the Middle East," 43.

150. Quick, "He Who Pays the Piper," 65.

151. Black, *Merging Mission and Unity*, 120–22, 125; J. Smith, *From Colonialism to World Community*, 262–81; Flipse, "To Save 'Free Vietnam' and Lose Our Souls."

152. YMCA, Egypt UAR Reports and Correspondence, 1959–62: Report of Visit to United Arab Republic, November 8–11, 1959, by Paul M. Limbert, marked "For Limited Circulation."

153. Black, *Merging Mission and Unity*, 71–72. This effort paid big dividends after 1974, when President Anwar Sadat launched an "opening up" (*infitah*) policy of attracting foreign investment in Egypt. With the help of the U.S. State Department, the UPCUSA was able to claim two million dollars from the Egyptian government for "land and buildings expropriated by various means in the two decades after the revolution in 1952." Lorimer, *The Presbyterian Experience in Egypt*, 210–15; Skreslet, "Presbyterians and the Middle East."

154. Paul VI, *Nostra Aetate*.

155. Quoted in A. Salama, *Al-Injiliyyun wa-al-'amal al-qawmi*, 320.

156. Lorimer, *The Presbyterian Experience in Egypt*, 171–72. This story gives credence to the claim that Arab states pressured Arab churches to reject or mitigate this "exculpation" among their followers. Bat Ye'or, *Islam and Dhimmitude*, 272–73.

157. Donald Black to Heather J. Sharkey, Jenkintown, Pennsylvania, April 28, 2006.

158. J. McClenahan, *On Going a Journey*, 16.

159. Quick, "He Who Pays the Piper," 66.

160. Kenneth E. Nolin to Heather J. Sharkey, Claysville, Pennsylvania, September 13, 2006. See also Lorimer, *The Presbyterian Experience in Egypt*, 170, 244.

161. Lorimer telephone conversation, August 23, 2004.

162. Alexander, *A Sketch of the Story of the Evangelical Church of Egypt*, 18; Lorimer, "Presbyterians in the Middle East," 42.

163. Sproul, "The American College for Girls, Cairo, Egypt," 86–87.

164. Ibid., 86–87.

165. Regarding the Van Dyck Bible, see J. Thompson, *The Major Arabic Bibles*, 20–27.

166. Roy and McGill, "Report on the Middle East Crisis and the Egypt Mission."

167. Dye, *The CEOSS Story*, 18–19.

168. Abdel-Malek, "Martha Roy."

169. Moftah, Toth, and Roy, *The Coptic Orthodox Liturgy of St. Basil*; Martha Roy, conversation with the author, Cairo, June 2, 2005.

170. A. Salama, *Al-Injiliyyun wa-al-'amal al-qawmi*, 221–76, esp. 230–33. Standing outside this alliance of Christians, however, were small Egyptian Pentecostal communities whose members regarded the establishment of Israel as a precursor to the second coming of Christ. Wahba conversation.

171. A. Salama, *Al-Injiliyyun wa-al-'amal al-qawmi*, 301–11.

172. J. Smith, *From Colonialism to World Community*, 285.

173. Skreslet, "Presbyterians and the Middle East"; Sharkey, "The American Mission in Egypt and the Arab-Israeli Conflict."

174. Lorimer, "Presbyterians in the Middle East," 30–31.

175. Baron, "The Origins of Family Planning in Egypt"; Alterman, "American Aid to Egypt in the 1950s."

176. Robert, "From Missions to Beyond Missions," 363. At the biannual meeting of the Mission History Group, held at the PHS in Philadelphia on April 4, 2006, David Gelzer, a former missionary to Cameroon, remarked that his church in Swarthmore, Pennsylvania, had not been involved in foreign mission activities since the mid-1960s; he was trying to revive interest by initiating a project to counteract the spread of HIV in Ghana.

177. Hutchison, *Errand to the World*; Coalter, Mulder, and Weeks, *The Re-Forming Tradition*.

CONCLUSION: CONVERSIONS AND TRANSFORMATIONS

1. Sheridan Gilley, introduction to *The Cambridge History of Christianity*, vol. 8: *World Christianities*, ed. Gilley and Stanley, 9.

2. Cragg, *The Call of the Minaret*, 313.

3. Jamison, *The United Presbyterian Story*, 198.

4. Martin, "Statistiques chrétiennes d'Égypte," 66.

5. Wakin, *A Lonely Minority*, 135–36; Zaki conversation.

6. Wissa, *Assiout*, 179.

7. PHS RG 209-20-13: "The American Mission in Egypt, 1854–1954: Program for the Centennial Celebration, November 15–16, 1954."

8. PHS RG 209-2-06: E. M. Bailey Papers, Egyptian Newsletter, Heliopolis, January 7, 1951.

9. PHS RG 209-1-23: J. R. Alexander Papers, Alexander to Taylor, Assiut, September 27, 1935, and "Is the Mission Church in Egypt a 'Mature Church'?"

10. Philips, *Blessed Be Egypt My People*, 9; on the Mansur brothers, see 17–43 and 44–64.

11. Philips, *Blessed Be Egypt My People*, 10.

12. Morrison, *Middle East Survey*, 181.

13. Cragg, *The Call of the Minaret*, 306, 318.

14. Beaver, *From Missions to Mission*, 12–14.

15. Goddard, *A History of Christian-Muslim Relations*, 181–86.

16. Lorimer conversations; Kenneth E. Nolin to Heather J. Sharkey, Claysville, Pennsylvania, October 18, 2006.

17. Pierce, "Secret Missionaries Draw New Scrutiny."

18. Steele, *Not in Vain*, 75–76.

19. See, for example, "Is the Mission Church in Egypt a 'Mature Church'?"; "Should the American Mission Dissolve Its Organization and Merge Itself into the Evangelical Church and Its Organizations?"; and PHS RG 209-5-14:

Harvey E. Philips Papers, memorandum on relations between the American Mission and the Synod of the Nile, 1939 (Strictly Confidential).

20. Bat Ye'or, *The Dhimmi*.

21. Rev. Donald Black, "Board of Foreign Missions, United Presbyterian Church of North America, 1954–58: Reflections," unpublished typescript, n.d.

22. C. Watson, *Do New World Conditions Challenge Changes in Missionary Method and Policy*, 8.

23. C. Watson, *What Is This Moslem World*, ix–x.

24. AUC Watson, Watson to W. B. Anderson, August 6, 1937.

25. Lorimer e-mail, February 17, 2006.

26. Lorimer conversations. During Lorimer's childhood in Egypt, Kamil Mansur was an occasional guest in the family home.

27. Lorimer, "Presbyterians in the Middle East," 33.

28. AUC Watson, George Swan, compiler [on behalf of Inter-Mission Council], "The Report from Egypt," Council for Western Asia and North Africa, n.d. [1929].

29. YMCA, Biographical Records, box 166, file for James K. Quay, "A Missionary Journey," entry for March 27, 1930.

30. PHS RG 209-5-18: James K. Quay Papers, Quay to [Anderson], Cairo, April 9, 1920.

31. YMCA, Biographical Records, box 166, file for James K. Quay, "A Missionary Journey," postscript, Princeton, New Jersey, March 5, 1960.

32. W. McClenahan, *G.P.*, 16–17.

33. J. McClenahan, *A Sample of Ancestors*, 4.

34. John L. McClenahan, telephone conversation with the author, Richmond, Virginia, February 17, 2006.

35. Sproul, "The American College for Girls, Cairo, Egypt," 81.

36. A. Watson, *The American Mission in Egypt*, 58; R. Hogg, *A Master-Builder on the Nile*, 95–96.

37. Lorimer, "Presbyterians in the Middle East," 6.

38. J. Smith, *From Colonialism to World Community*, 262; Black, *Merging Mission and Unity*, 132–33, 145.

39. Quick, "He Who Pays the Piper," 44, 132, 163.

40. Dye, *The CEOSS Story*, 36.

41. Fahim, "Modestes recherches d'une communauté de laïcs," 174.

42. Lorimer, "Presbyterians in the Middle East," 43.

43. Noor conversation; Zaki conversation.

44. Skreslet, "Presbyterians and the Middle East."

45. Abadir conversation; Zaki conversation; Noor conversation; Wahba conversation. The 2005 population estimate for Egypt appeared in U.S. Government, Central Intelligence Agency, *The World Factbook*, 2005 edition, Egypt country study, http://www.cia.gov/cia/publications/factbook/geos/eg.html (accessed July 5, 2005).

46. Abadir conversation; videocassette recording, Coptic Evangelical Organization for Social Services, "CEOSS Development Strategies in Egypt," 1999; and CEOSS, "From Mission to Practice," *Annual Review 2004*, 2.

47. Hocking, *Re-Thinking Missions*, 47.

48. Fitzmier and Balmer, "A Poultice for the Bite of the Cobra."

49. AUC Watson, Watson to John R. Mott, written [on boat] off Crete, September 4, 1938; Watson also expressed concerns about American Christian fundamentalists in Watson to John D. Rockefeller Jr., June 5, 1933.

50. AUC Watson, Watson to William Ernest Hocking, December 16, 1938; "The Next Ten Years of Missions and Government Relations" by Dr. Charles R. Watson, outline of talk delivered at the meeting of the Egypt Inter-Mission Council, Central YCMA, Cairo, February 10, 1944.

51. Watson also connected critical thinking about religion to the achievement of greater liberty. AUC Watson, Syllabus for Second Year Bible [1925].

52. AUC Watson, copy of letter from William Ernest Hocking to S. A. Morrison, June 10, 1930.

53. Beaver, *From Missions to Mission*, 97–98.

54. Nolin to Sharkey, October 18, 2006.

55. John G. Lorimer to Heather J. Sharkey, e-mail communication, May 3, 2007.

56. "Liberal" (adjective), *Oxford English Dictionary*, 2nd online ed., 1989.

57. Lorimer, *The Presbyterian Experience in Egypt*, 253–54.

58. Elder, *Vindicating a Vision*, 31–34.

59. Kinnear, *She Sat Where They Sat*, 44.

60. W. McClenahan, *G.P.*, 19.

61. Lorimer, "Presbyterians in the Middle East," 30.

62. Skreslet, "Presbyterians and the Middle East."

63. C. Watson, *The Big Idea*, 20–21.

64. Elder, *Vindicating a Vision*, 30; Virtue, *A Vision of Hope*, 15.

65. Sproul, "The American College for Girls, Cairo, Egypt," 111–13; Murphy, *The American University in Cairo*, 42.

66. YMCA, Biographical Records, box 166, file for James K. Quay, "A Missionary Journey," including the postscript, Princeton, New Jersey, March 5, 1960; and Quay, "Service in Egypt from 1919 to 1948." For more references to Egyptians going to America, see Lorimer, *The Presbyterian Experience in Egypt*, 20, 45; and Wissa, *Assiout*, 119, 350–51, 361.

67. SOAS, Papers of Dr. Douglas Harman and Mrs. Gladys Harman, MS 380815/1/1: "A History of Mission Medical Work in Changchow Fukien, China II: A Letter from Gladys Busby," February 18, 1987.

68. Gordon and Gordon, "*We Twa*," 182–84.

69. SOAS CWM, South China-Fukien, Incoming Correspondence, box 12, File 4, 1919: Ahmed Fahmy to F. H. Hawkins, Summit, New Jersey, October 1, 1919. His wife was the former Susan Rankin Duryee, a missionary of the Reformed Church in America mission in Amoy. See SOAS, Annotated Register of L.M.S. Missionaries, 1796–1923, appendix A, p. 176, #854.

70. Latourette, *A History of the Expansion of Christianity*, 7:1.

Bibliography

ARCHIVES AND SPECIAL COLLECTIONS

American University in Cairo, Manuscripts and Special Collections
Cambridge University Library, Bible Society Archives
Dar al-Kutub, Periodicals Section, Cairo
Durham University Library, Sudan Archive
Henry Martyn Centre for the Study of Mission and World Christianity, Westminster College, Cambridge University
Kautz Family YMCA Archives, University of Minnesota
Presbyterian Historical Society
Princeton University Library
School of Oriental and African Studies, University of London, Manuscripts and Special Collections (including the Council for World Mission archives)
University of Pennsylvania Libraries (including Manuscripts and Special Collections)
Yale Divinity School, Day Missions Library

JOURNALS

Al-Balagh
Al-Fath
Kawkab al-Sharq
The Moslem World
New York Times
Nur al-Islam: Majallat al-Azhar
Al-Siyasa
Al-Siyasa, Mulhaq (literary supplement)
United Presbyterian
Women's Missionary Magazine of the United Presbyterian Church Zenana Workers: A Ladies' Missionary Magazine

PHD DISSERTATIONS

Burke, Jeffrey C. "The Establishment of the American Presbyterian Mission in Egypt, 1854–1940: An Overview." PhD diss., McGill University, 2000.
Heuser, Frederick J., Jr. "Culture, Feminism, and the Gospel: American Presbyterian Women and Foreign Missions, 1870–1923." PhD diss., Temple University, 1991.

Lash, Jeffrey William. "Exporting Education: The Case of the American University in Cairo." PhD diss., Texas State University–San Marcos, 2001.

Moffitt, Louisa Bond. "Anna Young Thompson: American Missionary, Cultural Ambassador, and Reluctant Feminist in Egypt, 1872–1932." PhD diss., Georgia State University, 2003.

Oram, Elizabeth E. "Constructing Modern Copts: The Production of Coptic Christian Identity in Contemporary Egypt." PhD diss., Princeton University, 2004.

Sedra, Paul. "Textbook Maneuvers: Evangelicals and Educational Reform in Nineteenth-Century Egypt." PhD diss., New York University, 2006.

Sproul, Christine. "The American College for Girls, Cairo, Egypt: Its History and Influence on Egyptian Women—A Study of Selected Graduates." PhD diss., University of Utah, 1982.

UNPUBLISHED WORKS

Baron, Beth. "The Origins of Family Planning in Egypt." Paper presented at the University of Pennsylvania, Philadelphia, April 21, 2005.

———. "Revival on the Nile: Mama Trasher and the Assiout Orphanage." Paper presented at the conference "Competing Kingdoms: Women, Mission, Nation, and American Empire, 1812–1930." Rothermere American Institute, University of Oxford, April 27–29, 2006.

———. "Summer of '33: Orphans, Missionaries, Muslim Brothers, and Others." Paper presented at the conference of the American Historical Association, Philadelphia, January 6, 2006.

Black, Donald. "Board of Foreign Missions of the United Presbyterian Church of North America, 1954–58: Reflections of the Executive Secretary." Unpublished typescript, Presbyterian Historical Society, n.d.

Leest, Charlotte van der. "Protestant Missionary Activities in Palestine (1846–1879): A Source of Rivalry between Protestants and Roman Catholics." Paper presented at the Middle East Studies Association Conference, Washington, DC, November 19, 2005.

Lorimer, John G. "Presbyterians in the Middle East: A Retrospective." W. Don McClure Lectures on World Mission and Evangelism, Pittsburgh Theological Seminary, 1994. Held at Presbyterian Historical Society and at Pittsburgh Theological Seminary Library.

Oliver, Jay C. "Lest We Forget: Memoirs." Typescript, Texas Christian University, Forth Worth, n.d. [1973].

Quick, Bernard E. "He Who Pays the Piper . . . : A Study of Economic Power and Mission in a Revolutionary World." Foreword by M. Richard Shaull. Unpublished mimeograph typescript, held at Union Theological Seminary, Columbia University, 1975.

Rhodes, Matthew. "Anglican Mission: Egypt, a Case Study." Paper delivered at the Henry Martyn Centre, Westminster College, Cambridge University, May 2003. Available at http://www.martynmission.cam.ac.uk/CMRhodes.htm.

Sharkey, Heather J. "American Missionaries, the Arabic Bible, and Coptic Reform in Late Nineteenth-Century Egypt." Paper presented at the annual meeting of the Middle East Studies Association (MESA), Boston, November 18, 2006.

―――. "The American Mission in Egypt and the Arab-Israeli Conflict: A Study of Church Politics in the Middle East, 1948–2005." Paper presented at a symposium on "Mission in the Middle East: NGOs and the New Evangelism," Middle East Institute, Columbia University, December 5, 2005.

Starr, Deborah. "Remembering Cosmopolitan Egypt." Paper presented at the Middle East Center Symposium "Cosmopolitan Egypt," University of Pennsylvania, February 9, 2007.

BOOKS, ARTICLES, AND OTHER MATERIALS

'Abd al-Raziq, 'Ali. *Al-Islam wa-usul al-hukm*. Cairo, 1925.

Abdel-Malek, Moushira. "Martha Roy: A Hymn on the Nile." *Al-Ahram Weekly Online*, 30 March–5 April 2000, no. 475, http://weekly.ahram.org .eg/2000/475/profile.htm (accessed July 27, 2007).

Abdul-Fady [Arthur T. Upson]. *High Lights [sic] in the Near East: Reminiscences of Nearly 40 Years' Service*. London: Marshall, Morgan and Scott, 1936.

Abel, Theodore. *Protestant Home Missions to Catholic Immigrants*. New York: Institute of Social and Religious Research, 1933.

Adams, C. C. *Islam and Modernism in Egypt: A Study of the Modern Reform Movement Inaugurated by Muhammad 'Abduh*. London: Oxford University Press, 1933.

Ahlstrom, Sydney E. *A Religious History of the American People*. New Haven: Yale University Press, 1972.

Ahmad, Nabil 'Abd al-Hamid Sayyid. *Al-Ajanib wa-athruhum fi al-mujtama' al-misri, min sanat 1882 ila sanat 1992*. 2 vols. Damietta: Maktabat Nansi, n.d. [2004].

Alexander, J. R. "A Great Adventure in the Valley of the Nile." *Biblical Review* 10:3 (1925): 354–82.

―――. *A Sketch of the Story of the Evangelical Church of Egypt*. Alexandria: Whitehead Morris Limited, 1930.

Allison, Robert J. *The Crescent Obscured: The United States and the Muslim World, 1776–1815*. Chicago: University of Chicago Press, 1995.

Alterman, Jon B. "American Aid to Egypt in the 1950s: From Hope to Hostility." *Middle East Journal* 52:1 (1998): 51–69.

Altizer, Thomas J. J. "Mission and Dialogue: 50 Years after Tambaram." *The Christian Century*, April 6, 1988, p. 340.

American Committee on Survey [sic] of Christian Literature for Moslems. *The Power of the Printed Page in the World of Islam*. Cairo, 1922.

Anderson, Betty S. "Liberal Education at the American University of Beirut." In *The Roots of Liberal Thought in the Eastern Mediterranean*, ed. Thomas Philipp and Christoph Schumann, forthcoming.

Anderson, Gerald H. "American Protestants in Pursuit of Mission: 1886–1986." In *Missiology*, ed. Camps, Hoedemaker, et al., pp. 374–420.

Anderson, William B., and Charles R. Watson. *Far North in India: A Survey of the Mission Field and Work of the United Presbyterian Church in the Punjab*.

Philadelphia: Board of Foreign Missions of the United Presbyterian Church of North America, 1909.

Appadurai, Arjun. "Disjuncture and Difference in the Global Cultural Economy." In *Global Culture: Nationalism, Globalization and Modernity*, ed. Mike Featherstone. London: Sage Publications, 1990, pp. 295–310.

Arzt, Donna E. "The Application of International Human Rights Law in Islamic States." *Human Rights Quarterly* 12:2 (1990): 202–30.

'Askar, 'Abd al-'Aziz ibn Ibrahim al-. *Al-Tansir wa-muhawalatuhu fi bilad al-khalij al-'arabi*. Riyadh: Maktabat al-'Abikan, 1993.

Atiya, Aziz S. *A History of Eastern Christianity*. London: Methuen, 1968.

Attwater, Donald. *The Catholic Eastern Churches*. Milwaukee: Bruce Publishing Company, 1937.

———. *The Christian Churches of the East*. Vol. 1: *Churches in Communion with Rome*. Milwaukee: Bruce Publishing Company, 1946.

Ayalon, Ami. *Egypt's Quest for Cultural Orientation*. Tel Aviv: Moshe Dayan Center for Middle Eastern and African Studies, 1999.

———. *The Press in the Arab Middle East: A History*. New York: Oxford University Press, 1995.

Ayoub, Mahmoud. "Dhimmah in Qur'an and Hadith." In *Muslims and Others in Early Islamic Society*, ed. Robert Hoyland. Aldershot, UK: Ashgate, 2004, pp. 25–35.

Ayrout, Henry Habib. *The Egyptian Peasant*. Trans. and intro. John Alden Williams. Cairo: American University in Cairo Press, 2005.

Badeau, John S. *The Middle East Remembered*. Washington, DC: Middle East Institute, 1983.

Baer, Gabriel. *Studies in the Social History of Modern Egypt*. Chicago: University of Chicago Press, 1969.

Ballantyne, Tony. *Between Colonialism and Diaspora: Sikh Cultural Formations in an Imperial World*. Durham: Duke University Press, 2006.

Bance, Peter. *The Duleep Singhs: The Photograph Album of Queen Victoria's Maharajah*. Stroud, UK: Sutton Publishing, 2004.

Banna, Hasan al-. *Mudhakkirat al-da'wa wa'l-da'iya*. Damascus: Al-Maktab al-Islami, 1978.

Barnes, Andrew E. "'Evangelization Where It Is Not Wanted': Colonial Administrators and Missionaries in Northern Nigeria during the First Third of the Twentieth Century." *Journal of Religion in Africa* 25:4 (1995): 412–41.

Baron, Beth. "Women's Voluntary Social Welfare Organizations in Egypt." In *Gender, Religion, and Change in the Middle East: Two Hundred Years of History*, ed. Okkenhaug and Flaskerud, 85–102.

Barr, Mrs. W. W. "Women's Work for Women—Its Past." In *Foreign Missionary Jubilee Convention of the United Presbyterian Church of N.A.* Philadelphia: Board of Foreign Missions of the UPCNA, 1905, pp. 163–69.

Barrett, David B., George T. Kurian, and Todd M. Johnson. *World Christian Encyclopedia: A Comparative Survey of Churches and Religions in the Modern World*. 2nd ed. 2 vols. Oxford: Oxford University Press, 2001.

Barrett, James W. *The War Work of the Y.M.C.A. in Egypt*. Preface by Edmund H. H. Allenby. London: H. K. Lewis and Company, 1919.

Bat Ye'or. *The Dhimmi: Jews and Christians under Islam*. Trans. David Maisel, Paul Fenton, and David Littman. Rev. ed. Rutherford, NJ: Fairleigh Dickinson University Press, 1985.

———. *Islam and Dhimmitude*. Trans. Miriam Kochan and David Littman. Madison, NJ: Fairleigh Dickinson Press, 2002.

Bays, Daniel H., and Grant Wacker, eds. *The Foreign Missionary Enterprise at Home: Explorations in North American Cultural History*. Tuscaloosa: University of Alabama Press, 2003.

Beach, Harlan P., and Charles H. Fahs, eds. *World Missionary Atlas*. New York: Institute of Social and Religious Research, 1925.

Beaver, R. Pierce. *American Protestant Women in World Mission: History of the First Feminist Movement in North America*. Rev. ed. Grand Rapids, MI: William B. Eerdmans, 1980.

———. *From Missions to Mission: Protestant World Mission Today and Tomorrow*. New York: Association Press, 1964.

Bebbington, David. *Evangelicalism in Modern Britain: A History from the 1730s to the 1980s*. London: Routledge, 1989.

Beinin, Joel. *The Dispersion of Egyptian Jewry*. Berkeley: University of California Press, 1998.

Ben Jelloun, Tahar. *French Hospitality: Racism and North African Immigrants*. Trans. Barbara Bray. New York: Columbia University Press, 1999.

Bendroth, Margaret Lamberts. "An Understated Tale of Epic Social Change: Women's Ordination 50 Years Ago and Now." *Journal of Presbyterian History* 83:2 (2005): 105–17.

Bisati, Ahmad Sa'd al-Din al-. *Al-Tabshir wa-athruhu fi al-bilad al-'arabiyya al-islamiyya*. Cairo: Dar Abu'l-Majd lil-Tiba'a, 1409AH/1989.

Black, Donald. *Merging Mission and Unity*. Philadelphia: Geneva Press, 1986.

Boktor, Amir. *The Development and Expansion of Education in the United Arab Emirates*. Cairo: American University at Cairo Press, 1963.

———. *School and Society in the Valley of the Nile*. Cairo: Elias' Modern Press, 1936.

———. *See also* Buqtur, Amir.

Bonk, Jonathan J. *Missions and Money: Affluence as a Western Missionary Problem*. Maryknoll, NY: Orbis Books, 1991.

Bourne, Kenneth, and D. Cameron Watt, gen. eds. *British Documents on Foreign Affairs: Reports and Papers from the Foreign Office Confidential Print*. Part 1: From the Mid-Nineteenth Century to the First World War. In Series B: The Near and Middle East, 1856–1914, ed. David Gillard. Vol. 1: *The Ottoman Empire in the Balkans, 1856–1875*. Lanham, MD: University Publications of America, 1984.

Bowen, Marcellus. *The Bible in Bible Lands: History of the Levant Agency*. New York: American Bible Society, 1917.

Bowie, Fiona, Deborah Kirkwood, and Shirley Ardener, eds. *Women and Missions: Past and Present, Anthropological and Historical Perceptions*. Providence, RI: Berg, 1993.

Boyd, Lois A., and R. Douglas Brackenridge. *Presbyterian Women in America: Two Centuries of a Quest for Status*. Westport, CT: Greenwood Press, 1983.

Braude, Benjamin. "Foundation Myths of the *Millet* System." In *Christians and Jews in the Ottoman Empire*, ed. Benjamin Braude and Bernard Lewis. Vol. 1. New York: Holmes and Meier, 1982, pp. 69–88.

Buckser, Andrew, and Stephen D. Glazier, eds. *The Anthropology of Religious Conversion*. Lanham, MD: Rowman and Littlefield, 2003.

Buqtur, Amir. *Anta . . . wa ana, min ja'na? Wa-kayfa nasha'na*. Cairo: Dar al-Hilal, 1966.

———. *Al-Danimarkah: Munsha'atuha al-l-ijtima'iyya wa-madarisuha al-sha'biyya*. Cairo: Qism al-Tarbiya bil-Jami'a al-Amrikiyya, 1941.

———. *Al-Dunya fi Amrika*. Cairo: Al-Matba'a al-'Asriyya, 1926.

———. *Fann al-zawaj*. N.p., 1961.

———. *See also* Boktor, Amir.

Buruma, Ian. "Tariq Ramadan Has an Identity Issue." *New York Times Magazine*, February 4, 2007.

Buruma, Ian, and Avishai Margalit. *Occidentalism: The West in the Eyes of Its Enemies*. New York: Penguin, 2004.

Butcher, E. L. *The Story of the Church of Egypt*. 2 vols. London: Smith, Elder and Company, 1897.

Buzpinar, S. Tufan. "The Repercussions of the British Occupation of Egypt on Syria, 1882–83." *Middle Eastern Studies* 36:1 (2000): 82–91.

Cahen, C. "Dhimma." *Encyclopaedia of Islam*. New ed. Vol. 2. Leiden: Brill, 1983, pp. 227–31.

Cairene [*sic*]. "Egypt and Religious Liberty." *International Review of Missions* 22 (October 1933): 530–48.

Campbell, Christy. *The Maharajah's Box: An Imperial Story of Conspiracy, Love, and a Guru's Prophecy*. London: HarperCollins, 2000.

Camps, A., L. A. Hoedemaker, et al., eds. *Missiology: An Ecumenical Introduction: Texts and Contexts of Global Christianity*. Grand Rapids, MI: William B. Eerdmans, 1995.

Carpenter, Joel A., and Wilbert R. Shenk, eds. *Earthen Vessels: American Evangelicals and Foreign Missions, 1880–1980*. Grand Rapids, MI: William B. Eerdmans, 1990.

Carson, Arthur L. *Agricultural Missions: A Study Based upon the Experience of 236 Missionaries and Other Rural Workers*. New York: n.p., 1933.

Carter, B. L. *The Copts in Egyptian Politics*. London: Croom Helm, 1986.

———. "On Spreading the Gospel to Egyptians Sitting in Darkness: The Political Problem of Missionaries in Egypt in the 1930s." *Middle Eastern Studies* 20 (1984): 18–36.

Christensen, Torben, and William R. Hutchison, eds. *Missionary Ideologies in the Imperialist Era: 1880–1920*. Århus, Denmark: Aros, 1982.

Coad, F. Roy. *A History of the Brethren Movement: Its Origins, Its Worldwide Development, and Its Significance for the Present Day*. Grand Rapids, MI: William B. Eerdmans, 1968.

Coalter, Milton J., John M. Mulder, and Louis B. Weeks, eds. *The Diversity of Discipleship: The Presbyterians and Twentieth-Century Christian Witness*. Louisville: Westminster/John Knox Press, 1991.

———. *The Re-Forming Tradition: Presbyterians and Mainstream Protestantism*. Louisville: Westminster/John Knox Press, 1992.

Cole, Juan R. I. *Colonialism and Revolution in the Middle East: Social and Cultural Origins of Egypt's 'Urabi Movement*. Princeton: Princeton University Press, 1993.

Coleman, Simon. "Continuous Conversion? The Rhetoric, Practice, and Rhetorical Practice of Charismatic Protestant Conversion." In *The Anthropology of Religious Conversion*, ed. Buckser and Glazier, 15–27.

Colley, Linda. *Britons: Forging the Nation, 1707–1837*. 2nd ed. New Haven: Yale University Press, 2005.

Comaroff, John L., and Jean Comaroff. *Of Revelation and Revolution*. 2 vols. Chicago: University of Chicago Press, 1991, 1997.

Cooper, Barbara M. *Evangelical Christians in the Muslim Sahel*. Bloomington: Indiana University Press, 2006.

Cooper, Frederick. "Conflict and Connection: Re-Thinking African Colonial History." *American Historical Review* 99:5 (1999): 1516–45.

Coptic Evangelical Organization for Social Services. "CEOSS Development Strategies in Egypt."Videocassette recording, 1999.

———. "From Mission to Practice." *CEOSS Annual Review* (2004): 2.

Cragg, Kenneth. *The Call of the Minaret*. 2nd rev. ed. Maryknoll, NY: Orbis Books, 1985.

Dahhan, Muhammad Muhammad al-. *Quwa al-sharr al-mutahalifa: Al-ishtiraq, al-tabshir, al-isti'mar, wa mawqifha min al-islam wa'l-muslimin*. Mansura: Dar al-Wafi', 1406AH/1986.

Daly, M. W. *Empire on the Nile: The Anglo-Egyptian Sudan, 1898–1934*. Cambridge: Cambridge University Press, 1986.

Danielson, Virginia. *The Voice of Egypt: Umm Kulthum, Arabic Song, and Egyptian Society in the Twentieth Century*. Chicago: University of Chicago Press, 1997.

Davis, Helen Clarkson Miller, comp. *Some Aspects of Religious Liberty of Nationals in the Near East: A Collection of Documents*. New York: Harper and Brothers, 1938.

Dawson, David G. "Funding Mission in the Early Twentieth Century." *International Bulletin of Missionary Research* 24 (October 2000): 155–58.

De Lorenzi, James. "Caught in the Storm of Progress: Timoteos Saprichian, Ethiopia, and the Modernity of Christianity." *Journal of World History*, forthcoming.

Dodge, Bayard. "Princeton and the Near East." *Princeton Alumni Weekly* 39:8 (1938): 159–66.

Donzel, E. J. van. *Islamic Desk Reference*. Leiden: Brill, 1994.

Doumato, Eleanor Abdella. *Getting God's Ear: Women, Islam, and Healing in Saudi Arabia and the Gulf*. New York: Columbia University Press, 2000.

Dowling [Archdeacon Theodore Edward]. *The Egyptian Church*. London: Cope and Fenwick, 1909.

Dunch, Ryan. "Beyond Cultural Imperialism: Cultural Theory, Christian Missions, and Global Modernity." *History and Theory* 41 (2002): 301–25.

———. *Fuzhou Protestants and the Making of a Modern China, 1857–1927*. New Haven: Yale University Press, 2001.

Dye, Marjorie. *The CEOSS Story*. Cairo: Dar al-Thaqafah, 1979.

Dye, Marjorie, Davida Finney, Adib Galdas, and Samuel Habib. *Literacy—The Essential Skill: A Handbook for Literacy Workers*. New York: Committee on World Literacy and Christian Literature, 1964.

Egypt, Census Department. *The Census of Egypt Taken in 1907, under the Direction of C. C. Lowis.* Cairo: National Printing Department, 1909.

Egypt General Mission. *Egypt General Mission: Its Origin and Work.* Belfast: Wm. Strain and Sons, 1902.

Elder, Earl E. "The Evangelical Church in Egypt: A Study in the Development of a 'Younger Church.'" *International Review of Missions* (October 1937): 514–25.

———. *Vindicating a Vision: The Story of the American Mission in Egypt, 1854–1954.* Philadelphia: United Presbyterian Board of Foreign Missions, 1958.

Elliott, E. B., ed. *Memoir of Lord Haddo, in His Latter Years, Fifth Earl of Aberdeen.* 5th rev. ed. London: Seeley, Jackson and Halliday, 1869.

Ener, Mine. *Managing Egypt's Poor and the Politics of Benevolence, 1800–1952.* Princeton: Princeton University Press, 2003.

Ericsson, Maria. *The Swedish Mission Story: Egypt.* N.p. [1924].

Etherington, Norman. "Missions and Empire." In *The Oxford History of the British Empire*, gen. ed. Wm. Roger Louis. Vol. 5: *Historiography*, ed. Robin W. Winks. Oxford: Oxford University Press, 1999, pp. 303–14.

Fahim, Amin. "Modestes recherches d'une communauté de laïcs du tiers-monde et des congrégations religieuses." *SEDOS Bulletin* 19:5 (1987): 173–83.

Fahmy, Khaled. *All the Pasha's Men: Mehmed Ali, His Army, and the Making of Modern Egypt.* Cambridge: Cambridge University Press, 1997.

Finney, Davida. *Tomorrow's Egypt.* Pittsburgh: Women's General Missionary Society, 1939.

Finney, Minnehaha. "Delta Car Glimpses." Pittsburgh: Women's General Missionary Society of the United Presbyterian Church of North America, 1927.

Finnie, David H. *Pioneers East: The Early American Experience in the Middle East.* Cambridge, MA: Harvard University Press, 1967.

Fitzmier, John R., and Randall Balmer. "A Poultice for the Bite of the Cobra: The Hocking Report and Presbyterian Missions in the Middle Decades of the Twentieth Century." In *The Diversity of Discipleship*, ed. Coalter, Mulder, and Weeks, 105–25.

Fleischmann, Ellen. "The Impact of American Protestant Missions in Lebanon on the Construction of Female Identity." *Islam and Christian-Muslim Relations* 13:4 (2002): 411–26.

Flipse, Scott. "To Save 'Free Vietnam' and Lose Our Souls: The Missionary Impulse, Voluntary Agencies, and Protestant Dissent against the War, 1965–71." In *The Foreign Missionary Enterprise at Home*, ed. Bays and Wacker, 206–22.

Fortescue, Adrian. *The Uniate Eastern Churches*, ed. George D. Smith. 1923. Reprint, New York: Frederick Ungar Publishing, 1957.

Fowler, Montague. *Christian Egypt: Past, Present, and Future.* 2nd ed. London: Church Newspaper Company, 1902.

Friedmann, Yohanan. *Tolerance and Coercion in Islam: Interfaith Relations in the Muslim Tradition.* Cambridge: Cambridge University Press, 2003.

Gairdner, W.H.T. *D. M. Thornton: A Study in Missionary Ideals and Methods.* New York: Fleming H. Revell Company, 1909.

———. *Echoes from Edinburgh, 1910: An Account and Interpretation of the World Missionary Conference.* Intro. John R. Mott. New York: Laymen's Missionary Movement, 1910.

———. *Egyptian Colloquial Arabic: A Conversation Grammar and Reader.* Cambridge: W. Heffer and Sons, 1917.

———. *The Reproach of Islam.* London: London Missionary Society, 1909.

Galdas, Adib. *A Village Reborn: The Transformation of the People of a Village in Central Egypt after They Had Learned to Read in an All-Village Literacy Campaign: Told by Adib Galdas of Deir Abu Hinnis to Davida Finney.* New York: Committee on World Literacy and Christian Literature, 1958.

Gandhi, Leela. *Postcolonial Theory: A Critical Introduction.* New York: Columbia University Press, 1998.

Garrett, Shirley S. "Sisters All: Feminism and the American Women's Missionary Movement." In *Missionary Ideologies in the Imperialist Era*, ed. Christensen and Hutchison, pp. 221–30.

Geffen, Elizabeth M. "Industrial Development and Social Crisis, 1841–1854." In *Philadelphia: A 300-Year History*, ed. Russell F. Weigley. New York: W. W. Norton, 1982, pp. 307–62.

Gershoni, Israel. "The Reader—'Another Production': The Reception of Haykal's Biography of Muhammad and the Shift of Egyptian Intellectuals to Islamic Subjects in the 1930s." *Poetics Today* 15:2 (1994): 241–77.

Gershoni, Israel, and James P. Jankowski. *Egypt, Islam, and the Arabs: The Search for Egyptian Nationhood, 1900–1930.* New York: Oxford University Press, 1986.

———. *Redefining the Egyptian Nation, 1930–1945.* Cambridge: Cambridge University Press, 1995.

Ghazal, Mustafa Fawzi 'Abd al-Latif. *Al-Hiyal wa'l-Asalib al-Munharifa fi al-da'wa ila al-tabshir.* N.p.: Matabi' al-Majmu'a al-I'lamiyya, n.d. [late 1990s].

Gilley, Sheridan, and Brian Stanley, eds. *The Cambridge History of Christianity.* Vol. 8: *World Christianities, c. 1815–1914.* Cambridge: Cambridge University Press, 2006.

Glasgow, William Melanchthon. *Cyclopedic Manual of the United Presbyterian Church of North America.* Pittsburgh: United Presbyterian Board of Publication, 1903.

Goddard, Hugh. *A History of Christian-Muslim Relations.* Chicago: New Amsterdam Books, 2000.

Goffman, Caroline. "Masking the Mission: Cultural Conversion at the American College for Girls." In *Altruism and Imperialism*, ed. Tejirian and Simon, pp. 88–119.

Goldsack, W. "How to Reach and Teach Illiterate Moslems." In *Methods of Mission Work among Moslems*, ed. Wherry, 29–40.

Goldschmidt, Arthur, Jr. *Modern Egypt: The Formation of a Nation-State.* 2nd ed. Boulder, CO: Westview Press, 2004.

Gordon, John Campbell (Marquess of Aberdeen and Temair) and Ishbel Gordon (Marchioness of Aberdeen and Temair). *"We Twa": Reminiscences of Lord and Lady Aberdeen.* 2 vols. London: W. Collins Sons and Company, 1925.

Grabill, Joseph L. "Protestant Diplomacy and Arab Nationalism, 1914–1948." *American Presbyterians: Journal of Presbyterian History* 64:2 (1986): 113–24.

———. *Protestant Diplomacy and the Near East: Missionary Influence on American Policy, 1810–1927.* Minneapolis: University of Minnesota Press, 1971.

Greeley, Andrew. *The Catholic Revolution: New Wine, Old Wineskins, and the Second Vatican Council.* Berkeley: University of California Press, 2004.

Guérin, Victor. *La France Catholique en Égypte.* Tours: Alfred Mame et Fils, 1894.

Habib, Samwa'il. *Tariq al-tahaddi: Qissat hayat al-Duktur al-Qiss Samwa'il Habib kama rawaha.* Cairo: Dar al-Thaqafa, 1999.

Hackett, Rosalind I. J., ed. *Proselytization Revisited: Rights, Free Markets, and Culture Wars.* London: Equinox, forthcoming.

Hajjar, Joseph. *Les Chrétiens uniates du proche-orient.* Paris: Éditions du Seuil, 1962.

Hall, Catherine. *Civilising Subjects: Metropole and Colony in the English Imagination, 1830–1867.* Chicago: University of Chicago Press, 2002.

Hamilton, Alastair. *The Copts and the West, 1439–1822: The European Discovery of the Egyptian Church.* Oxford: Oxford University Press, 2006.

———. "The English Interest in the Arabic-Speaking Christians." In *The "Arabik" Interest of the Natural Philosophers in Seventeenth-Century England,* ed. G. A. Russell. Leiden: E. J. Brill, 1994, pp. 30–53.

Harper, R. D. *The Church Memorial: Containing Important Historical Facts and Reminiscences Connected with the Associate and Associate Reformed Churches Previous to Their Union as the United Presbyterian Church of North America.* Columbus, OH: Follett, Foster, and Company, 1858.

Hart, D. G., ed. *Dictionary of the Presbyterian and Reformed Tradition in America.* Downers Grove, IL: InterVarsity Press, 1999.

Hasan, S. S. *Christians versus Muslims in Modern Egypt: The Century-Long Struggle for Coptic Equality.* Oxford: Oxford University Press, 2003.

Hasin, Ahmad ibn Abd al-'Aziz al-. *Al-Khatar al-tabshiri al-salibi fi al-Kuwayt.* 8th ed. N.p., 1416AH/1996.

Hatch, Nathan O. *The Democratization of American Christianity.* New Haven: Yale University Press, 1989.

Hatina, Meir. "Historical Legacy and the Challenge of Modernity in the Middle East: The Case of al-Azhar in Egypt." *Muslim World* 93 (2003): 51–68.

Haykal, Muhammad Husayn. *Hayat Muhammad.* 9th ed. Cairo: Maktabat al-Nahda al-Misriyya, 1965.

———. *Zaynab.* Cairo: Maktabat al-Nahda al-Misriyya, 1963.

Hefner, Robert W. "Of Faith and Commitment: Christian Conversion in Muslim Java." In *Conversion to Christianity: Historical and Anthropological Perspectives on a Great Transformation,* ed. Robert W. Hefner. Berkeley: University of California Press, 1993, pp. 99–125.

Herrera, Linda. "'The Soul of a Nation': 'Abdallah Nadim and Educational Reform in Egypt (1845–1896)." In *Altruism and Imperialism,* ed. Tejirian and Simon, pp. 275–94.

Heyworth-Dunne, J. *An Introduction to the History of Education in Modern Egypt.* London: Luzac and Company, 1938.

Hill, Patricia R. *The World Their Household: The American Woman's Foreign Mission Movement and Cultural Transformation, 1870–1920.* Ann Arbor: University of Michigan Press, 1985.

Hocking, William Ernest, ed. *Re-Thinking Missions: A Laymen's Inquiry after One Hundred Years*. New York: Harper and Brothers, 1932.

Hogg, Rena L. *A Master-Builder on the Nile, being a record of the life and aims of John Hogg, D.D., Christian Missionary*. Pittsburgh: United Presbyterian Board of Publication, 1914.

Hogg, William Richey. *Ecumenical Foundations: A History of the International Missionary Council and Its Nineteenth-Century Background*. New York: Harper and Brothers, 1952.

Horton, Robin. "On the Rationality of Conversion: Parts I and II." *Africa* 45:3–4 (1975): 219–35, 373–99.

Hourani, Albert. *Arabic Thought in the Liberal Age, 1798–1939*. London: Oxford University Press, 1962.

Hourani, Albert, and Nadim Shehadi, eds. *The Lebanese in the World: A Century of Emigration*. London: I. B. Tauris, 1992.

Howsam, Leslie. *Cheap Bibles: Nineteenth-Century Publishing and the British and Foreign Bible Society*. Cambridge: Cambridge University Press, 1991.

Hunt, James G. "The Loneliness of the Convert." *The Moslem World* 8:2 (1918): 158–61.

Hunter, Jane. *The Gospel of Gentility: American Woman Missionaries in Turn-of-the-Century China*. New Haven: Yale University Press, 1984.

Hurewitz, J. C. *Diplomacy in the Near and Middle East: A Documentary Record, 1535–1914*. Princeton: D. Van Nostrand Company, 1956.

Husayn, Taha. *Fi al-shi'r al-jahili*. Cairo, 1926.

Hutchison, William R. *Errand to the World: American Protestant Thought and Foreign Missions*. Chicago: University of Chicago Press, 1987.

———. *The Modernist Impulse in American Protestantism*. Cambridge, MA: Harvard University Press, 1976.

Ibrahim, Saad Eddin, et al. *The Copts of Egypt*. London: Minority Rights Group, 1996.

James, William. *The Varieties of Religious Experience: A Study in Human Nature*. London: Longmans, Green, 1902.

Jamison, Wallace N. *The United Presbyterian Story: A Centennial Study, 1858–1958*. Pittsburgh: Geneva Press, 1958.

Janin, Raymond. *Les églises orientales et les rites orientaux*. 2nd ed. Paris: Imprimerie Paul Feron-Vrau, 1926.

Janin [Rev. Père]. *The Separated Eastern Churches*. Trans. the Very Revd. Canon P. Boylan. London: Sands and Company, 1933.

Jessup, Henry Harris. *The Setting of the Crescent and the Rising of the Cross, or Kamil Abdul Messiah, a Syrian Convert from Islam to Christianity*. Philadelphia: Westminster Press, 1899.

Johnson, M. Glen, and Janusz Symonides, eds. *The Universal Declaration of Human Rights: A History of Its Creation and Implementation, 1948–1998*. Preface by Federico Mayor. Paris: UNESCO, 1998.

Johnston, Anna. *Missionary Writing and Empire, 1800–1860*. Cambridge: Cambridge University Press, 2003.

Jundi, Anwar al-. *Al-Islam fi wajh al-taghrib: Mukhattat al-tabshir wa'l-ishtiraq*. Cairo: Dar al-I'tisam, 1986.

Kampffmeyer, Georg. "Egypt and Western Asia." In *Whither Islam? A Survey of Modern Movements in the Moslem World*, ed. H.A.R. Gibb. London: Victor Gollancz, 1932, pp. 101–70.

Kaplan, Robert D. *The Arabists: The Romance of an Arab Elite*. New York: The Free Press, 1993.

Keddie, Nikki R. *An Islamic Response to Imperialism: Political and Religious Writings of Sayyid Jamal al-Din al-Afghani*. Berkeley: University of California Press, 1983.

Kedourie, Elie. *Afghani and Abduh: An Essay on Religious Unbelief and Political Activism in Modern Islam*. New York: Humanities Press, 1966.

Kepel, Gilles. *Muslim Extremism in Egypt: The Prophet and Pharaoh*. Trans. Jon Rothschild. Berkeley: University of California Press, 1986.

Kelsey, Hugh Alexander. *The United Presbyterian Directory: A Half-Century Survey, 1903–1958*. Pittsburgh: Pickwick Press, 1958.

Kerr, D. R. *The United Presbyterian Church of North America*. Pittsburgh: United Presbyterian Board of Publication, 1860.

Khalidi, Mustafa, and 'Umar Farrukh. *Al-Tabshir wa'l-isti'mar fi al-bilad al-'arabiyya*. 2nd ed. Beirut: n.p., 1957.

Khalil, Majdi. *Aqbat al-Mahjar*. Cairo: Matbu'at Dar al-Khayyal, 1999.

Kinnear, Elizabeth Kelsey. *She Sat Where They Sat: A Memoir of Anna Young Thompson of Egypt*. Grand Rapids, MI: William B. Eerdmans, 1971.

Kraemer, Hendrik. *The Christian Message in a Non-Christian World*. New York: Harper, 1938.

Kuklick, Bruce. *Puritans in Babylon: The Ancient Near East and American Intellectual Life, 1880–1930*. Princeton: Princeton University Press, 1996.

Lachs, John, and D. Micah Hester, eds. *A William Ernest Hocking Reader*. Nashville: Vanderbilt University Press, 2004.

Lamb, Christopher. *The Call to Retrieval: Kenneth Cragg's Christian Vocation to Islam*. London: Grey Seal, 1997.

Lamont, Thomas A. *The American University in Cairo, 1987–1995*. Cairo: American University in Cairo, 1997.

Lansing, Gulian. *Egypt's Princes: A Narrative of Missionary Labor in the Valley of the Nile*. 2nd ed. Philadelphia: William S. Rentoul, 1864.

Latourette, Kenneth Scott. *A History of the Expansion of Christianity*, Vol. 6: *The Great Century in Northern Africa and Asia, A.D. 1800–A.D. 1914*. New York: Harper and Brothers, 1944.

———. *A History of the Expansion of Christianity*, Vol. 7: *Advance through the Storm, A.D. 1914 and After, with Concluding Generalizations*. New York: Harper and Brothers, 1945.

Leavitt, George R. "Light in Egypt." *Women's Missionary Magazine of the United Presbyterian Church* 8:12 (1895): 314–16.

Levy, Avigdor, ed. *Jews, Turks, Ottomans: A Shared History, Fifteenth through the Twentieth Century*. Syracuse: Syracuse University Press, 2002.

Lewis, Bernard. *The Emergence of Modern Turkey*. London: Oxford University Press, 1961.

———. *The Jews of Islam*. Princeton: Princeton University Press, 1984.

Lia, Brynjar. *The Society of the Muslim Brothers in Egypt: The Rise of an Islamic Mass Movement, 1928–1942*. Foreword by Jamal al-Banna. Reading, UK: Ithaca Press, 1998.

Little, Douglas. *American Orientalism: The United States and the Middle East since 1945*. Chapel Hill: University of North Carolina Press, 2002.

Lockman, Zachary. *Contending Visions of the Middle East: The History and Politics of Orientalism*. Cambridge: Cambridge University Press, 2004.

Longfield, Bradley J. *The Presbyterian Controversy: Fundamentalists, Modernists, and Moderates*. New York: Oxford University Press, 1991.

Loomba, Ania. *Colonialism/Postcolonialism*. New York: Routledge, 1998.

Lorimer, Jack. *The Presbyterian Experience in Egypt, 1950–2000*. Denver: Outskirts Press, 2007.

Lübeck, Konrad. *Die Christlichen Kirchen des Orients*. Kempten und München: Verlag der Jos. Kösel'schen [sic] Buchhandlung, 1911.

Makari, Peter E. "Christianity and Islam in Twentieth-Century Egypt: Conflict and Cooperation." *International Review of Mission* 89:352 (2000): 88–98.

Makdisi, Ussama. *Artillery of Heaven: American Missionaries and the Failed Conversion of the Middle East*. Ithaca: Cornell University Press, 2007.

———. *The Culture of Sectarianism: Community, History, and Violence in Nineteenth-Century Ottoman Lebanon*. Berkeley: University of California Press, 2000.

———. "Reclaiming the Land of the Bible: Missionaries, Secularism, and Evangelical Modernity." *American Historical Review* 102:3 (1997): 680–713.

Mallampalli, Chandra. "British Missions and Indian Nationalism, 1880–1908: Imitation and Autonomy in Calcutta and Madras." In *The Imperial Horizons of British Protestant Missions*, ed. Porter, 158–82.

———. *Christians and Public Life in Colonial South India, 1863–1937: Contending with Marginality*. London: RoutledgeCurzon, 2004.

Mansour, Kamil Effendi. *A Visit to My Old Home*. Trans. W. T. Fairman. Pittsburgh: Women's General Missionary Society of the United Presbyterian Church of North America, n.d. [1925].

Mansur, Malik. *Wasa'il imbiriliyya fi al-takhrib al-thaqafi*. Baghdad: Dar al-Thawra, 1977.

Ma'oz, Moshe. "Changing Relations between Jews, Muslims, and Christians during the Nineteenth Century, with Special Reference to Ottoman Syria and Palestine. In *Jews, Turks, Ottomans*, ed. Levy, 108–18.

Marsden, George M. *The Soul of the University: From Protestant Establishment to Established Nonbelief*. New York: Oxford University Press, 1994.

Marten, Michael. *Attempting to Bring the Gospel Home: Scottish Missions to Palestine, 1839–1917*. London: Tauris Academic Studies, 2006.

———, ed. *Christian Witness between Continuity and New Beginnings: Modern Historical Missions in the Middle East*. Munster: LIT-Verlag, 2007.

Martin, Maurice. "Statistiques chrétiennes d'Égypte." *Travaux et Jours* (Beirut), 24 (1967): 65–75.

el Masri, Iris Habib. *The Story of the Copts*. [Cairo?]: Middle East Council of Churches, 1978.

———. *See also* Misri, Iris Habib al-.

Masters, Bruce. *Christians and Jews in the Ottoman Arab World: The Roots of Sectarianism*. Cambridge: Cambridge University Press, 2001.

Mathews, Basil. *Roads to the City of God: A World Outlook from Jerusalem*. Garden City, NY: Doubleday, Doran and Company, 1928.

Mayer, Ann Elizabeth. *Islam and Human Rights: Tradition and Politics*. 3rd ed. Boulder, CO: Westview Press, 1999.

McAlister, Melani. *Epic Encounters: Culture, Media, and U.S. Interests in the Middle East, 1945–2000*. Berkeley: University of California Press, 2001.

McClenahan, John L. *On Going a Journey: A Doctor's Logbook*. Privately published by the author, 2001.

———. *A Sample of Ancestors*. Richmond, VA: Dietz Press, 2000.

McClenahan, R. S. "The Training of Missionaries for Work among Muslims: Their Intellectual and Spiritual Qualifications." In *Lucknow*, ed. Wherry, Mylrea, and Zwemer, 45–72.

McClenahan, William U. *G.P.* Ed. John L. McClenahan. Philadelphia: Dorrance and Company, 1974.

McCulloch, W. E. *The United Presbyterian Church and Its Work in America*. Pittsburgh: Board of Home Missions of the United Presbyterian Church of North America, 1925.

McGranahan, Ralph Wilson. *Historical Sketch of the Freedmen's Missions of the United Presbyterian Church, 1862–1904*. Knoxville: Knoxville College Printing Department, 1905.

M'Clurkin, J. K. "Fifty Years of Mission Work in India." In *Foreign Missionary Jubilee Convention of the United Presbyterian Church of N.A.* Philadelphia: Board of Foreign Missions of the UPCNA, 1905, pp. 202–16.

Meinardus, Otto F. A. *Two Thousand Years of Coptic Christianity*. Cairo: American University in Cairo Press, 1999.

Melling, David J. "Uniate." In *The Blackwell Dictionary of Eastern Christianity*, ed. Ken Parry et al. Oxford: Blackwell, 1999, p. 505.

Milligan, Anna A. *Facts and Folks in Our Fields Abroad*. 2nd ed. Philadelphia: United Presbyterian Board of Foreign Missions, 1921.

Misri, Iris Habib al-. *Qissat al-kanisa al-qibtiyya*. 7 vols. Cairo: n.p., 1960–75.

———. *See also* el Masri, Iris Habib.

Mitchell, Richard P. *The Society of the Muslim Brothers*. Foreword by John O. Voll. Oxford: Oxford University Press, 1993.

Moftah, Ragheb, Margit Toth, and Martha Roy, comps. and eds. *The Coptic Orthodox Liturgy of St. Basil*. Cairo: American University in Cairo Press, 1998.

Monroe, Elizabeth. *Britain's Moment in the Middle East, 1914–1956*. London: Methuen, 1965.

Montgomery, Helen Barrett. *Western Women in Eastern Lands: An Outline Study of Fifty Years of Women's Work in Foreign Missions*. New York: Macmillan, 1910.

Moore-Harell, Alice. *Gordon and the Sudan: Prologue to the Mahdiyya, 1877–1880*. Foreword by Gabriel Warburg. London: Frank Cass, 2001.

Morrison, S. A. *El Azhar Today and Tomorrow*. Cairo, n.d.

———. "Egypt: Land of Paradox." *World Dominion*, September 1946, pp. 267–71.

———. *Middle East Survey: The Political, Social, and Religious Problems*. London: SCM Press, 1954.

———. *Religious Liberty in the Near East*. Post War Survey Series No. 1. London: World Dominion Press, 1948.

Morsink, Johannes. *The Universal Declaration of Human Rights: Origin, Drafting, and Intent*. Philadelphia: University of Pennsylvania Press, 1999.

Mott, John R. *The Decisive Hour of Christian Missions*. New York: Student Volunteer Movement for Foreign Missions, 1911.

———. *The Evangelization of the World in This Generation*. New York: Student Volunteer Movement for Foreign Missions, 1900.

Murphy, Lawrence R. *The American University in Cairo: 1919–1987*. Cairo: American University in Cairo Press, 1987.

Murre-van den Berg, Heleen, ed. *New Faiths in Ancient Lands: Western Missions in the Middle East in the Nineteenth and Early Twentieth Centuries*. Leiden: Brill, 2006.

———. "Nineteenth-Century Protestant Missions and Middle Eastern Women: An Overview." In *Gender, Religion and Change in the Middle East*, ed. Okkenhaug and Flaskerud, 103–22.

Na'im, Khalid Muhammad. *Al-Judhur al-tarikhiyya lil-irsaliyyat al-tansir al-ajnabiyya fi Misr, 1856–1986: Dirasa watha'iqiyya*. Cairo: Kitab al-Mukhtar, 1988.

———. *Tarikh jami'at muqawamat al-tansir al-misriyya (1927–33)*. Cairo: Kitab al-Mukhtar, n.d. [1987?].

Nichol, John Thomas. *Pentecostalism*. New York: Harper and Row, 1966.

Nisan, Mordechai. *Minorities in the Middle East*. 2nd ed. Jefferson, NC: McFarland and Company, 2002.

Noll, Mark A. *American Evangelical Christianity: An Introduction*. Oxford: Blackwell, 2001.

———. "Evangelical Identity, Power, and Culture in the 'Great' Nineteenth Century." In *Christianity Reborn: The Global Expansion of Evangelicalism in the Twentieth Century*, ed. Donald M. Lewis. Grand Rapids, MI: William B. Eerdmans, 2004, pp. 31–51.

———. *The Old Religion in a New World: The History of North American Christianity*. Grand Rapids, MI: William B. Eerdmans, 2002.

Oddie, Geoffrey. "Anti-Missionary Feeling and Hindu Revivalism in Madras: The Hindu Preaching and Tract Societies, 1886–1891." In *Images of Man: Religious and Historical Process in South Asia*, ed. Fred W. Clothey. Madras: New Era Publications, 1982, pp. 217–42.

Okkenhaug, Inger Marie. *"The Quality of Heroic Living, High Endeavor and Adventure": Anglican Mission, Women, and Education in Palestine, 1888–1948*. Leiden: Brill, 2002.

Okkenhaug, Inger Marie, and Ingvild Flaskerud, eds. *Gender, Religion, and Change in the Middle East: Two Hundred Years of History*. Oxford: Berg, 2005.

O'Leary, De Lacy. *The Saints of Egypt*. London: Society for Promoting Christian Knowledge, 1937.

Patterson, James Alan. "The Loss of a Protestant Missionary Consensus: Foreign Missions and the Fundamentalist-Modernist Conflict." In *Earthen Vessels*, ed. Carpenter and Shenk, 73–91.

Paul VI. *Nostra Aetate: Declaration on the Relation of the Church to Non-Christian Religions.* October 28, 1965. http://www.vatican.va/archive/hist_councils/ii_vatican_council/documents/vat-ii_decl_19651028_nostra-aetate_en.html (accessed August 6, 2007).

Peel, J.D.Y. *Religious Encounter and the Making of the Yoruba.* Bloomington: Indiana University Press, 2000.

Pekkola, Helmi. *Jumalan poluilla islamin erämaassa.* Porvoo, Finland: Werner Söderström osakeyhtiö, 1934.

Philips, H. E. *Blessed Be Egypt My People [Isaiah 19:25]: Life Studies from the Land of the Nile.* Philadelphia: Judson Press, 1953.

———. *The Question Box: A Catechism on Missions in Egypt.* [Pittsburgh?:] Publicity Committee of the Egyptian Mission of the United Presbyterian Church of North America, 1939.

Phillips, Clifton J. "Changing Attitudes in the Student Volunteer Movement of Great Britain and North America, 1886–1928." In *Missionary Ideologies in the Imperialist Era*, ed. Christensen and Hutchison, 131–45.

Pierard, Richard V. "Pax Americana and the Evangelical Missionary Advance." In *Earthen Vessels*, ed. Carpenter and Shenk, 155–79.

Pierce, John. "Secret Missionaries Draw New Scrutiny." *Christian Century*, May 17, 2003, pp. 12–13.

Pollard, Lisa. *Nurturing the Nation: The Family Politics of Modernizing, Colonizing, and Liberating Egypt, 1805–1923.* Berkeley: University of California Press, 2005.

Porter, Andrew, ed. *The Imperial Horizons of British Protestant Missions, 1880–1914.* Grand Rapids, MI: William B. Eerdmans, 2003.

———. "Religion, Missionary Enthusiasm, and Empire." In *The Oxford History of the British Empire*, gen. ed. Wm. Roger Louis. Vol. 3: *The Nineteenth Century*, ed. Andrew Porter. Oxford: Oxford University Press, 1999, pp. 222–46.

———. *Religion versus Empire? British Protestant Missionaries and Overseas Expansion, 1700–1914.* New York: Manchester University Press, 2004.

Porter, Bernard. *The Absent-Minded Imperialists: Empire, Society, and Culture in Britain.* Oxford: Oxford University Press, 2004.

Prasch, Thomas. "Which God for Africa? The Islamic-Christian Missionary Debate in Late Victorian England." *Victorian Studies* 33 (1989): 51–73.

Presbyterian Church (U.S.A.). "Who We Are." http://www.pcusa.org/navigation/whoweare.htm (accessed January 10, 2008).

Presbyterian Historical Society. "Family Tree of Presbyterian Denomination." http://www.history.pcusa.org/pres_hist/family_connections.html (accessed September 5, 2005).

Quataert, Donald. *The Ottoman Empire, 1700–1922.* Cambridge: Cambridge University Press, 2000.

Railton, N. M. *No North Sea: The Anglo-German Evangelical Network in the Middle of the Nineteenth Century.* Leiden: Brill, 2000.

Ramadan, 'Abd al-'Azim, ed. *Al-Dawr al-watani lil-kanisa al-misriyya 'abra al-'usur.* Cairo: Al-Hay'a al-Misriyya al-'Amma lil-Kitab, 2002.

Ramadan, Tariq. *Western Muslims and the Future of Islam.* Oxford: Oxford University Press, 2004.

Rambo, Lewis R. *Understanding Religious Conversion.* New Haven: Yale University Press, 1993.

Ranger, Terence. "The Invention of Tradition in Colonial Africa." In *The Invention of Tradition,* ed. Eric Hobsbawm and Terence Ranger. Cambridge: Cambridge University Press, 1983, pp. 211–62.

Reid, Daniel G., ed. *Dictionary of Christianity in America.* Downers Grove, IL: InterVarsity Press, 1990.

Reid, Donald Malcolm. "The 'Urabi Revolution and the British Conquest, 1879–1882." In *The Cambridge History of Egypt,* ed. M. W. Daly. Vol. 2. Cambridge: Cambridge University Press, 1998, pp. 217–38.

———. *Whose Pharaohs? Archaeology, Museums, and Egyptian National Identity from Napoleon to World War I.* Berkeley: University of California Press, 2002.

Reid, Mary B. "Egypt." *Women's Missionary Magazine of the United Presbyterian Church* 8:9 (April 1895): 246–48.

Reid, William J. *United Presbyterianism.* 8th ed. Pittsburgh: United Presbyterian Board of Publication, 1900.

Renan, Ernest. "What Is a Nation?" In *Becoming National: A Reader,* ed. Geoff Eley and Ronald Gregor Suny. New York: Oxford University Press, 1996, pp. 41–55.

Rice, W. A. *Crusaders of the Twentieth Century, or the Christian Missionary and the Muslim: An Introduction to Work among Muhammadans.* London: Church Missionary Society, 1910.

Richter, Julius. *A History of Protestant Missions in the Near East.* 1910. Reprint, New York: AMS Press, 1970.

Robert, Dana L. *American Women in Mission: A Social History of Their Thought and Practice.* Macon, GA: Mercer University Press, 1996.

———. "'The Crisis of Missions': Premillennial Mission Theory and the Origin of the Independent Evangelical Missions." In *Earthen Vessels,* ed. Carpenter and Shenk, 29–46.

———. "The First Globalization: The Internationalization of the Protestant Missionary Movement between the World Wars." *International Bulletin of Missionary Research* 26:2 (2002): 50–66.

———. "From Missions to Beyond Missions: The Historiography of American Protestant Foreign Missions since World War II." In *New Directions in American Religious History,* ed. Harry S. Stout and D. G. Hart. New York: Oxford University Press, 1997, pp. 362–93.

———, ed. *Gospel Bearers, Gender Barriers: Missionary Women in the Twentieth Century.* Maryknoll, NY: Orbis Books, 2002.

———. *Occupy Until I Come: A. T. Pierson and the Evangelization of the World.* Grand Rapids, MI: William B. Eerdmans, 2003.

———. "The Origin of the Student Volunteer Watchword: 'The Evangelization of the World in This Generation.'" *International Bulletin of Missionary Research* 10:4 (1986): 146–49.

Roberts, A. D., ed. *The Colonial Moment in Africa*. Cambridge: Cambridge University Press, 1990.

Robinson, Marilynne. *Gilead*. New York: Farrar, Straus and Giroux, 2004.

Robinson, Ronald, and John Gallagher. *Africa and the Victorians: The Climax of Imperialism*. New York: Anchor Books, 1968.

Rodgers, Daniel T. *Atlantic Crossings: Social Politics in a Progressive Age*. Cambridge, MA: Harvard University Press, 1998.

Roe, James Moulton. *A History of the British and Foreign Bible Society, 1905–1954*. London: British and Foreign Bible Society, 1965.

Rogan, Eugene. *Frontiers of the State in the Late Ottoman Empire: Transjordan, 1850–1921*. Cambridge: Cambridge University Press, 1999.

Rufayla, Ya'qub Nakhla. *Tarikh al-Umma al-Qibtiyya*. 2nd ed. Cairo: Matba'at Metropole, 2000.

Russell, Mona L. *Creating the New Egyptian Woman: Consumerism, Education, and National Identity, 1863–1922*. New York: Palgrave Macmillan, 2004.

Ryad, Umar. "Muslim Responses to Missionary Activities in Egypt: With a Special Reference to the Al-Azhar High Corps of 'Ulamâ (1925–1935)." In *New Faith in Ancient Lands*, ed. Murre-van den Berg, pp. 281–307.

———. "Rashid Rida and a Danish Missionary: Alfred Nielsen and Three *Fatwas* from *Al-Manar*." *IslamoChristiana* (Rome) 28 (2002): 97–107.

Saeed, Abdullah, and Hassan Saeed. *Freedom of Religion, Apostasy, and Islam*. London: Ashgate, 2004.

Said, Edward W. *Orientalism*. New York: Vintage Books, 1979.

Salama, Adib Najib. *Al-Injiliyyun wa-al-'amal al-qawmi: Dirasa tawthiqiyya*. Cairo: Dar al-Thaqafa, 1993.

Salama, Jirjis. *Tarikh al-ta'lim al-ajnabi fi Misr fi al-qarn al-tasi' 'ashara wa-al-'ishrin*. Cairo: Al-Majlis al-'ala li-ri'ayat al-funun wa-al-adab wa-al-'ulum al-ijtima'iyya, 1963.

Sanneh, Lamin O. *Whose Religion Is Christianity?* Grand Rapids, MI: William B. Eerdmans, 2003.

Sanneh, Lamin, and Joel A. Carpenter, eds. *The Changing Face of Christianity: Africa, the West, and the World*. Oxford: Oxford University Press, 2005.

Scopes, John Thomas. *The World's Most Famous Court Trial: Tennessee Evolution Case*. 3rd ed. Cincinnati: National Book Company, 1925.

Scouller, James B. *A History of the United Presbyterian Church*. Vol. 11. The American Church History Series, Philip Schaff et al., gen. eds. New York: Christian Literature Company, 1894.

———. *A Manual of the United Presbyterian Church of North America, 1751–1881*. Harrisburg, PA: Patriot Publishing Company, 1881.

Sedra, Paul D. "Class Cleavages and Ethnic Conflict: Coptic Christian Communities in Modern Egyptian Politics." *Islam and Christian-Muslim Relations* 10:2 (1999): 219–35.

———. "Ecclesiastical Warfare: Patriarch, Presbyterian, and Peasant in Nineteenth-Century Asyut." In *The United States and the Middle East: Cultural Encounters*, ed. Abbas Amanat and Magnus T. Bernhardsson. New Haven: Yale Center for International and Area Studies, 2002, pp. 290–314.

————."John Lieder and His Mission in Egypt: The Evangelical Ethos at Work among Nineteenth-Century Copts." *Journal of Religious History* 28:3 (2004): 219–39.

Shadhili, Mahmud al-. *Al-Wathiqa al-Islam al-khatar!: Nass al-khitab alladhi alqahu W.H.T. Jayirdnir fi mu'tamar Idinburah lil-tabshir (al-tansir) al-dawli al-mun'aqid bil-Qahira 'ashiyat al-sabt 18 Juniyu 1910m.* Cairo: Kitab al-Mukhtar, n.d. [c. 1985].

Shalabi, Abd al-Wudud al-Shalabi al-. *Afiqu ayyuha al-muslimun qabla 'an tadfa'u al-jizya.* Jidda: Dar al-Majma', n.d. [1981].

Shankar, Shobana."A Fifty-Year Muslim Conversion to Christianity: Religious Ambiguities and Colonial Boundaries in Northern Nigeria, c. 1910–1963." In *Muslim-Christian Encounters in Africa,* ed. Benjamin F. Soares. Leiden: Brill, 2006, pp. 89–114.

Sharkey, Heather J. "American Mission, Egyptian Church: The Making of a Coptic Evangelical Presbyterian Community." *Journal of Presbyterian History* 84:2 (2006): 170–80.

————. "American Presbyterian Missionaries and the Egyptian Evangelical Church: The Colonial and Postcolonial History of a Christian Community." *Chronos: Revue d'Histoire de l'Université Balamand* (Lebanon) 15 (2007): 31–63.

————. "Arabic Antimissionary Treatises: Muslim Responses to Christian Evangelism in the Modern Middle East." *International Bulletin of Missionary Research* 28:3 (2004): 112–18.

————. "Christian Missionaries and Colloquial Arabic Printing." *Journal of Semitic Studies,* Supplement 15: *History of Printing and Publishing in the Languages and Countries of the Middle East,* ed. Philip Sadgrove. Oxford: Oxford University Press, 2004, pp. 131–49.

————. "Christians among Muslims: The Church Missionary Society in the Northern Sudan." *Journal of African History* 43 (2002): 51–75.

————. "Empire and Muslim Conversion: Historical Reflections on Christian Missions in Egypt." *Islam and Christian-Muslim Relations* 16:1 (2005): 43–60.

————. *Living with Colonialism: Nationalism and Culture in the Anglo-Egyptian Sudan.* Berkeley: University of California Press, 2003.

————. "Missionary Legacies: Muslim-Christian Encounters in Egypt and Sudan during the Colonial and Postcolonial Periods." In *Muslim-Christian Encounters in Africa,* ed. Benjamin F. Soares. Brill: Leiden, 2006, pp. 57–88.

————. "Muslim Apostasy, Christian Conversion, and Religious Freedom in Egypt: A Study of American Missionaries, Western Imperialism, and Human Rights Agendas." In *Proselytization Revisited: Rights, Free Markets, and Culture Wars,* ed. Rosalind I. J. Hackett. London: Equinox, forthcoming.

————."A New Crusade or an Old One?" *ISIM Newsletter* (Leiden), 12 (2003): 48–49.

————. "Umm Kulthum at the American University in Cairo: A Study in the Clash of Christianities." In *The Nile Valley: Politics, Identities, Cultures,* ed. Israel Gershoni and Meir Hatina. Boulder, CO: Lynne Rienner, forthcoming.

Sheridan, Mark. "Coptic Christianity." In *The Blackwell Dictionary of Eastern Christianity,* ed. Ken Parry et al. Oxford: Blackwell, 1999, pp. 129–35.

Showalter, Nathan D. *The End of a Crusade: The Student Volunteer Movement for Foreign Missions and the Great War*. Lanham, MD: Scarecrow Press, 1998.

Shukri, Ghali. *Al-Aqbat fi watan mutaghayyir*. 3rd ed. Cairo: Dar Sharqiyyat lil-Nashr wa'l-Tawzi', 1996.

Simon, Reeva et al., eds. *The Jews of the Middle East and North Africa in Modern Times*. New York: Columbia University Press, 2003.

Skreslet, Stanley H. "The American Presbyterian Mission in Egypt: Significant Factors in Its Establishment." *American Presbyterians: Journal of Presbyterian History* 64:2 (1986): 83–95.

———. "Presbyterians and the Middle East, 1944–2004." In *Presbyterian Mission History, 1944–2004*, ed. Scott Sunquist, forthcoming.

Smith, Charles D. *Islam and the Search for Social Order in Modern Egypt: A Biography of Muhammad Husayn Haykal*. Albany: State University of New York Press, 1983.

Smith, John Coventry. *From Colonialism to World Community: The Church's Pilgrimage*. Philadelphia: Geneva Press, 1982.

Smylie, James H. *A Brief History of the Presbyterians*. Louisville: Geneva Press, 1996.

Solihin, Sohirin Mohammad. *Copts and Muslims: A Study on Harmony and Hostility*. Leicester, UK: Islamic Foundation, 1991/1411AH.

Sonbol, Amira El-Azhary. *The New Mamluks: Egyptian Society and Modern Feudalism*. Syracuse: Syracuse University Press, 2000.

Stanley, Brian. *The Bible and the Flag: Protestant Missions and British Imperialism in the Nineteenth and Twentieth Centuries*. Leicester: Apollos, 1990.

———. "Church, State, and the Hierarchy of 'Civilization': The Making of the 'Missions and Governments' Report at the World Missionary Conference, Edinburgh 1910." In *The Imperial Horizons of British Protestant Missions*, ed. Porter, 58–84.

———. "Edinburgh 1910 and the Oikoumene." In *Ecumenism and History: Studies in Honor of John H. Y. Briggs*, ed. Anthony R. Cross. Carlisle, UK: Paternoster Press, 2002, pp. 89–119.

Steele, Francis R. *Not in Vain: The Story of the North Africa Mission*. Pasadena, CA: William Carey Library, 1981.

Stock, Eugene. *The History of the Church Missionary Society*. 3 vols. London: Church Missionary Society, 1899.

Sundkler, Bengt, and Christopher Steed. *A History of the Church in Africa*. Cambridge: Cambridge University Press, 2000.

Swan, George. *"Lacked Ye Anything?: A Brief Story of the Egypt General Mission*. Rev. ed. London: Egypt General Mission, 1932.

Tejirian, Eleanor H. "Faith of Our Fathers: Near East Relief and the Near East Foundation—From Mission to NGO." In *Altruism and Imperialism*, ed. Tejirian and Simon, 295–315.

Tejirian, Eleanor H., and Reeva Spector Simon, eds. *Altruism and Imperialism: Western Cultural and Religious Missions in the Middle East*. New York: Columbia University, Middle East Institute, 2002.

Thompson, Anna Y. "Mission Work in Egypt." *Women's Missionary Magazine of the United Presbyterian Church* 5:3 (1891): 68–69.

———. "The Woman Question in Egypt." *The Moslem World* 4:2 (1914): 266–72.

Thompson, E. P. *The Making of the English Working Class.* Oxford: V. Gollancz, 1963.

Thompson, John Alexander. *The Major Arabic Bibles.* New York: American Bible Society, 1956.

Thorne, Susan. *Congregational Missions and the Making of an Imperial Culture in Nineteenth-Century England.* Stanford: Stanford University Press, 1999.

Thornton, D. M. "Work among Educated Moslems in Cairo: The Eastern or Azhar University Men." In *Methods of Mission Work among Moslems,* ed. Wherry, 70–78.

Tibawi, A. L. *American Interests in Syria, 1800–1901: A Study of Educational, Literary and Religious Work.* Oxford: Clarendon Press, 1966.

Tignor, Robert L. *Capitalism and Nationalism at the End of Empire: State and Business in Decolonizing Egypt, Nigeria, and Kenya, 1945–1963.* Princeton: Princeton University Press, 1998.

———. *State, Private Enterprise, and Economic Change in Egypt, 1918–1952.* Princeton: Princeton University Press, 1984.

Tisdall, W. St. Clair. *The Religion of the Crescent, or Islam: Its Strength, Its Weakness, Its Origin, Its Influence.* London: Society for Promoting Christian Knowledge, 1895.

Toledano, Ehud R. *State and Society in Mid-Nineteenth-Century Egypt.* Cambridge: Cambridge University Press, 1990.

Tritton, A. S. *The Caliphs and Their Non-Muslim Subjects: A Critical Study of the Covenant of 'Umar.* London: Frank Cass, 1970.

United Nations General Assembly. "Universal Declaration of Human Rights" (Adopted and proclaimed by General Assembly resolution 217 A (III) of 10 December 1948). http://www.un.org/Overview/rights.html (accessed September 29, 2006).

United Presbyterian Church of North America. *Foreign Missionary Jubilee Convention of the United Presbyterian Church of N.A., celebrating the Fiftieth Anniversary of the Founding of Missions in Egypt and India.* Philadelphia: Board of Foreign Missions of the UPCNA, 1905.

———. *Report of Commissioners Appointed by the Board of Foreign Missions of the United Presbyterian Church of North America, to Visit the Missions in India & Egypt.* Philadelphia: Edward Patteson, Printer, 1881.

United Presbyterian Church of North America, Board of Foreign Missions. *Rules and Recommendations for Foreign Missionaries and Candidates of the United Presbyterian Church.* Philadelphia: Wm. S. Young, Printer, 1861.

Upson, Arthur T. *See* Abdul-Fady.

Vander Werff, Lyle L. *Christian Mission to Muslims: The Record (Anglican and Reformed Approaches in India and the Near East, 1800–1938).* South Pasadena, CA: William Carey Library, 1977.

Virtue, David W. *A Vision of Hope: The Story of Samuel Habib.* Oxford: Regnum, 1996.

Viswanathan, Gauri. *Outside the Fold: Conversion, Modernity, and Belief.* Princeton: Princeton University Press, 1998.

Vitalis, Robert. "The 'New Deal' in Egypt: The Rise of Anglo-American Commercial Competition in World War II and the Fall of Neocolonialism." *Diplomatic History* 20:2 (1996): 211–39.

———. *When Capitalists Collide: Business Conflict and the End of Empire in Egypt.* Berkeley: University of California Press, 1995.

Voile, Brigitte. *Les coptes d'Egypte sous Nasser: Sainteté, miracles, apparitions.* Paris: CNRS Éditions, 2004.

Waardenburg, Jacques. "The Contemporary Period, 1950–1995." In *Muslim Perceptions of Other Religions: A Historical Survey*, ed. Jacques Waardenburg. New York: Oxford University Press, 1999, pp. 85–101.

Wacker, Grant. "The Waning of the Missionary Impulse: The Case of Pearl S. Buck." In *The Foreign Missionary Enterprise at Home*, ed. Bays and Wacker, pp. 191–205.

Wakin, Edward. *A Lonely Minority: The Modern Story of Egypt's Copts.* New York: William Morrow, 1963.

Walls, Andrew F. "The American Dimension in the History of the Missionary Movement." In *Earthen Vessels*, ed. Carpenter and Shenk, 1–25.

———. "Islam and the Sword: Some Western Perceptions, 1840–1918." *Scottish Journal of Religious Studies* 5:2 (1984): 89–105.

Warburg, Gabriel. *Islam, Sectarianism, and Politics in Sudan since the Mahdiyya.* London: Hurst and Company, 2003.

Watson, Andrew. *The American Mission in Egypt, 1854 to 1896.* 2nd ed. Pittsburgh: United Presbyterian Board of Publication, 1904.

———. "Islam in Egypt." In *The Mohammedan World of To-Day*, ed. Zwemer, Wherry, and Barton, 23–39.

Watson, Mrs. Andrew [Margaret McVickar Watson]. "The Story of Bamba." Pittsburgh: Women's General Missionary Society of the United Presbyterian Church of North America, 1931.

Watson, Charles R. *The Big Idea.* Cairo: American University at Cairo, n.d. [c. 1942].

———. "The Challenge of the Present Crisis." *Missionary Review of the World* 57 (1934): 123–29.

———. *Do New World Conditions Challenge Changes in Missionary Method and Policy?* New York: Foreign Missions Conference of North America, 1934.

———. "Egypt—What Price Progress?" *Missionary Review of the World* 57 (1934): 71–75.

———. *Egypt and the Christian Crusade.* New York: Young People's Missionary Movement, 1907.

———. "Fifty Years of Foreign Missions in Egypt." In *Foreign Missionary Jubilee Convention of the United Presbyterian Church of N.A.* Philadelphia: Board of Foreign Missions of the UPCNA, 1905, pp. 76–99.

———. "Our Religious Policies: What Are They?" Philadelphia: American University at Cairo, n.d. [mid-1930s].

———. "The Partition of Palestine." *United Presbyterian*, February 16, 1948.

———. "Rethinking Missions." *International Review of Missions* (January 1932): 106–18.

———. *The Sorrow and Hope of the Egyptian Sudan.* Philadelphia: Board of Foreign Missions of the United Presbyterian Church of North America, 1913.

———. *In the Valley of the Nile: A Survey of the Missionary Movement in Egypt.* 2nd ed. New York: Fleming H. Revell Company, 1908.

———. *What Is This Moslem World?* New York: Friendship Press, 1937.

Watson, Charles R., et al. *The Presentation of Christianity to Moslems: The Report of a Committee Appointed by the Board of Missionary Preparation.* New York: Board of Missionary Preparation, 1917.

Weigley, Russell F., ed. *Philadelphia: A 300-Year History.* New York: W. W. Norton, 1982.

Weitbrecht, H. U. "The Lucknow Conference." *The Moslem World* 1:1 (1911): 164–75.

Werner, Roland, William Anderson, and Andrew Wheeler. *Day of Devastation, Day of Contentment: The History of the Sudanese Church across 2000 Years.* Nairobi: Paulines Publications Africa, 2000.

Weston, William J. *Presbyterian Pluralism: Competition in a Protestant House.* Knoxville: University of Tennessee Press, 1997.

Whately, E. J. *The Life and Work of Mary Louisa Whately.* London: Religious Tract Society, 1890.

Wherry, E. M., ed. *Methods of Mission Work among Moslems: Being those papers read at the First Missionary Conference on behalf of the Mohammedan World held at Cairo April 4th–9th, 1906.* New York: Fleming H. Revell Company, 1906.

Wherry, E. M., C. G. Mylrea, and S. M. Zwemer, eds. *Lucknow, 1911: Being papers read and discussions on the training of Missionaries, and literature for Muslims at the General Conference on Missions to Muslims held at Lucknow, Jan. 23–28, 1911.* London: Christian Literature Society for India, 1911.

White, Mrs. J. P. "Women's Work for Women: Its Present." In *Foreign Missionary Jubilee Convention of the United Presbyterian Church of N.A.* Philadelphia: Board of Foreign Missions of the UPCNA, 1905, pp. 170–82.

Wilson, J. Christy. *Apostle to Islam: A Biography of Samuel M. Zwemer.* Grand Rapids, MI: Baker Book House, 1952.

Wilson, J. Christy, Jr. "The Legacy of Samuel Zwemer." *International Bulletin of Missionary Research* 10:3 (1986): 117–21.

Wissa, Hanna F. *Assiout: The Saga of an Egyptian Family.* Rev. ed. Sussex, UK: Book Guild, 2000.

Woodward, Peter. *Nasser.* London: Longman, 1992.

World Missionary Conference, 1910. *Report of Commission III: Education in Relation to the Christianisation of National Life.* Edinburgh: Oliphant, Anderson, and Ferrier, 1910.

———. *Report of Commission IV: The Missionary Message in Relation to Non-Christian Religions.* Edinburgh: Oliphant, Anderson and Ferrier, 1910.

Wuthnow, Robert. *The Restructuring of American Religion: Society and Faith since World War II.* Princeton: Princeton University Press, 1988.

Yates, Timothy. *Christian Mission in the Twentieth Century.* Cambridge: Cambridge University Press, 1994.

Zebiri, Kate. *Muslims and Christians Face to Face*. Oxford: Oneworld, 1997.

Zwemer, Samuel M. *Across the World of Islam*. New York: Fleming H. Revell Company, 1929.

———. *The Disintegration of Islam*. Students' Lectures on Islam, Princeton Theological Seminary. New York: Fleming H. Revell Company, 1916.

———. "Editorial." *The Moslem World* 1:1 (1911): 1–4.

———. *Islam: A Challenge to Faith*. New York: Student Volunteer Movement for Foreign Missions, 1907.

———. *The Law of Apostasy in Islam: Answering the question why there are so few Moslem converts, and giving examples of their moral courage and martyrdom*. London: Marshall Brothers, 1924.

———. *Mohammed or Christ*. New York: Fleming H. Revell Company, 1915.

Zwemer, S. M., E. M. Wherry, and James L. Barton, eds. *The Mohammedan World of To-Day: Papers from the First Missionary Conference on Behalf of the Mohammedan World held at Cairo April 4th–9th, 1906*. New York: F. H. Revell, 1906.

Index

Made in the USA
Columbia, SC
02 December 2019